DREAMWORLD AND CATASTROPHE

DREAMWORLD AND CATASTROPHE

THE PASSING OF MASS UTOPIA
IN EAST AND WEST

SUSAN BUCK-MORSS

THE MIT PRESS
CAMBRIDGE, MASSACHUSETTS
LONDON, ENGLAND

This book was set in Bembo and Didot by Graphic Composition, Inc.
and was printed and bound in the United States of America.

Library of Congress Cataloging-in-Publication Data

Buck-Morss, Susan.
Dreamworld and catastrophe : the passing of mass utopia in East and West / Susan Buck-Morss.
p. cm.
Includes bibliographical references and index.
ISBN 0-262-02464-0
1. History, Modern—20th century—Historiography.   2. History, Modern—20th century—
Philosophy.   3. Popular culture—History—20th century.   I. Title.
D413.5 .B83 2000
909.82 21—dc21

99-045165

Cover image: Aleksandr Kosolapov, *The Manifesto,* 1983.

FOR ELENA, MISHA, AND VALERII

TABLE OF CONTENTS

III

DREAMWORLDS OF
MASS CULTURE

IV

AFTERWARD

PREFACE

THE CONSTRUCTION of mass utopia was the dream of the twentieth century. It was the driving ideological force of industrial modernization in both its capitalist and socialist forms. The dream was itself an immense material power that transformed the natural world, investing industrially produced objects and built environments with collective, political desire. Whereas the night dreams of individuals express desires thwarted by the social order and pushed backward into regressive childhood forms, this collective dream dared to imagine a social world in alliance with personal happiness, and promised to adults that its realization would be in harmony with the overcoming of scarcity for all.

As the century closes, the dream is being left behind. Industrial production has not itself abated. Commodities are still produced, marketed, desired, consumed, and thrown away—in more areas of the globe, and in greater quantities than ever. Consumerism, far from on the wane, has penetrated the last socialist bastion of mainland China to become, arguably, the first global ideological form. State legitimacy continues to rest on the ideal of rule by the people put forth by "modern" political theories that are now several centuries old. But the mass-democratic myth of industrial modernity—the belief that the industrial reshaping of the world is capable of bringing about the good society by providing material happiness for the masses—has been profoundly challenged by the disintegration of European socialism, the demands of capitalist restructuring, and the most fundamental ecological constraints. In its place, an appeal to differences that splinter the masses into fragments now structures political rhetoric and marketing strategies alike—while mass manipulation continues much as before. Commodities have not ceased to crowd people's private dreamworlds; they still have a utopian function on a personal level. But the abandonment of the larger social project connects this personal utopianism with political cynicism, because it is no longer thought necessary to guarantee to the collective that which is pursued by the individual. Mass utopia, once considered the logical correlate of personal utopia, is now a rusty idea. It is being discarded by industrial societies along with the earliest factories designed to deliver it.

This book is an attempt to come to terms with mass dreamworlds at the moment of their passing. Its point of departure is the end of the Cold War. It argues that the profound significance of this event was not so much its political effects—the replacement of "really existing" (state) socialism by "really existing" (capitalist) democracy—as the fact that this fundamental shift in the historical map shattered an entire conception of the world, on both sides. In a real sense, it marked the end of the twentieth century. From the present side of this temporal divide, the cultural forms that existed in "East" and "West" (to use the Eurocentric terminology of the Cold War) appear uncannily similar. They may have differed violently in their way of dealing with the problems of modernity, but they shared a faith in the modernizing process developed by the West that for us today has been unalterably shaken. It is with the aim of illuminating the changed nature of our present situation that this book compares their dreamworld forms.

The notion of dreamworld is borrowed from Walter Benjamin, who used it not merely as the poetic description of a collective mental state but as an analytical concept, one that was central to his theory of modernity as the reenchantment of the world. The term acknowledges the inherent transience of modern life, the constantly changing conditions of which imperil traditional culture in a positive sense, because constant change allows hope that the future can be better. Whereas myths in premodern culture enforced tradition by justifying the necessity of social constraints, the dreamworlds of modernity—political, cultural, and economic—are expressions of a utopian desire for social arrangements that transcend existing forms. But dreamworlds become dangerous when their enormous energy is used instrumentally by structures of power, mobilized as an instrument of force that turns against the very masses who were supposed to benefit. If the dreamed-of potential for social transformation remains unrealized, it can teach future generations that history has betrayed them. And in fact, the most inspiring mass-utopian projects—mass sovereignty, mass production, mass culture—have left a history of disasters in their wake. The dream of mass sovereignty has led to world wars of nationalism and to revolutionary terror. The dream of industrial abundance has enabled the construction of global systems that exploit both human labor and natural environments. The dream of culture for the masses has created a panoply of phantasmagoric effects that aestheticize the violence of modernity and anaesthetize its victims.

The essays in this volume deal with both extremes of mass utopia, dreamworld and catastrophe. The idea of comparing their forms in East and West grew out of a period of close collaboration with Moscow philosophers. From 1988 to 1993 I was a frequent visitor at the Institute of Philosophy of the Soviet (later, Russian) Academy of Sciences, and worked together with a new generation of intellectuals who were critically analyzing Soviet culture as a system of power. In the course of this exchange, the Cold War world disintegrated. The imaginary topology of two irreconcilable enemies, ready and able to defend themselves by destroying life on this planet, dissipated with the abruptness of a disappearing dream. The historical rupture felt like sudden sanity. For a time the structures of power seemed to us so far in abeyance, and the burden of past history so light, that personal friendships alone would be strong enough to usher in a new, shared cultural era. But when new constellations of power began to coalesce and we found ourselves moving against the historical current, the limitations of personal agency became painfully apparent.

Our collaboration was part of an intense period of newly allowed exchange between thinkers whose work had been held apart by the Cold War order. The projects we helped initiate were the means through which various aspects of Western thought were introduced to the USSR and its successor states, including the first publication of Walter Benjamin in Russian, the first workshop on deconstruction, the first Heidegger conference, the last Soviet International Film Festival, and the first—and last—course at the Dubrovnik Inter-University Centre to include members of what might be called the Continental School of Soviet philosophy, including its leading figure, Merab Mamardashvili. Jacques Derrida, Jürgen Habermas, Fredric Jameson, Jean-Luc Nancy, Slavoj Žižek, and others all played a role in these exchanges, so that the story becomes part of the intellectual history of our time. But hopes that we had for a transformation of political culture were not realized. Our project of establishing a common *critical* discourse was, and remains, marginal to the dominant intellectual trends of the post-Cold War era. In its place, the hegemonic discourse affirms the moral superiority of those who have been the victors in this century. There is little reflection on how many beliefs they shared with those whom they defeated.

Against the often-repeated story of the West's winning the Cold War and capitalism's historical triumph over socialism, these essays argue that the historical experiment of socialism was so deeply rooted in the Western modernizing tradition that its defeat cannot but place the whole Western narrative into question. If the term postmodern is operative here, it is not as the description of a new historical stage—the underlying structures of modernity have far from disappeared—but as the awareness that there *are* no stages of history in the developmental and optimistic sense that modernity's dreamworlds once believed.

The book is divided into four parts. The first part, "Dreamworlds of Democracy," sees the political forms of East and West as embodying a common contradiction between democracy and sovereignty, one that had its origins in the French Revolution and its nemesis in the Cold War logic of mutual annihilation. The second part, "Dreamworlds of History," examines critically the narrative of revolutionary time by telling the story of Bolshevik cultural politics in its terms, and suggests rethinking revolutionary politics without this temporal armature. The third part, "Dreamworlds of Mass Culture," takes its lead from the artists in the late Soviet period who represented the dreamworld of Soviet culture at the moment of awakening from it, and juxtaposes mass culture images of East and West so that the struggle between these systems becomes visible as a competition to excel in producing the same utopian forms. The fourth part, "Afterward," places the book in the historical context of my collaboration with Moscow philosophers, weaving together personal and political history in an attempt to demystify them both.

The thesis of this book goes against standard wisdom that capitalism is desirable and inevitable, the normal natural arrangement of social life. It rejects the neoliberal argument that the social evils of modernity are distortions caused by political interventions into market outcomes, whereby socialism and recently even the welfare state are lumped together with fascism as unhealthy deviations from the norm. The Cold War discursive binary of totalitarianism versus democracy is challenged at its core. At a time when politics on the left as well as the right seems eager to jettison the whole conception of the masses, it cautions that every political and cultural struggle of the past century that called itself democratic was waged for a mass constituency, and in its name. At the same time, it questions whether democracy can ever be compatible with a concept of sovereignty based on violence, whether perpetrated by a single party in the name of the general will, or by a mass army in defense of the nation-state.

Rather than stressing the unique pasts of particular human groups, this book tells a story of similarities. It interprets cultural developments of the twentieth century within opposed political regimes as variations of a common theme, the utopian dream that industrial modernity could and would provide happiness for the masses. This dream has repeatedly turned into a nightmare, leading to catastrophes of war, exploitation, dictatorship, and technological destruction. To continue the same dream into the future, impervious to the ecological dangers, would be nothing less than suicidal. But these catastrophic effects need to be criticized in the name of the democratic, utopian hope to which the dream gave expression, not as a rejection of it. A world organized by global capital in which industrial production continues to expand, but this time indifferent to the well-being of the masses and unfettered by political constraints, is not a world in which catastrophes will disappear. They will continue to happen, and no one will be accountable.

My special gratitude goes to the MacArthur Foundation, which funded several stages of the Moscow collaboration. I also wish to thank Cornell University, the Institute of Philosophy of the Russian Academy of Sciences, the Guggenheim Foundation, the German Academic Exchange Service (DAAD), the Fulbright Program, the Rockefeller Foundation, and the Soros Foundation for their generous support of various aspects of the project. Without Cornell's magnificent libraries, the research would not have been possible. My thanks to its tolerant librarians, particularly Marie Powers, and to Michael Busch, my administrative lifeline, Joan Sage, my philosophical photographer (who first recognized Lenin's likeness to King Kong), and, for various aspects of production, to Laurie Coon, Lindsay Davis, Jessica Ferrell, and Kimberley Shults. Friends whose critical reading of parts of this manuscript helped to make it a better one include John Borneman, Teresa Brennan, Valerie Bunce, Alla Efimova, Zillah Eisenstein, Matthew Evangelista, Hal Foster, Peter Holquist, Aleksandr Ivanov, Christina Kiaer, John Christopher Kern, Brandon Taylor, and Geoffrey Waite. Special thanks go to Matthew Abbate and Jim McWethy of the MIT Press for their expertise in the book's production.

Notes on Method Although written in fragments, this book is meant to be read as a whole, as the argument cannot be divorced from the experience of its reading. I have relied on other books from multiple branches of knowledge, access to which was dependent upon a traditional research library of the most comprehensive sort. Discovery of the facts and images entailed constant disregard of accepted disciplinary classifications. "Keywords" were too random and "subject" files too rigid to do the work of research against the grain. The organizing strategies of data banks were inappropriate. The idiosyncratic intuitions of the author provided the search engine.

The book can be read on several levels. It is a theoretical argument that stresses the commonalities of the Cold War enemies, suggesting that socialism failed in this century because it mimicked capitalism too faithfully. On another level, the book is a compendium of historical data that with the end of the Cold War are threatened with oblivion. It rescues these data within new constellations that may be useful in thinking critically about the present. The book is also an experiment in methods of visual culture. It attempts to use images *as* philosophy, presenting, literally, a way of seeing the past that challenges common conceptions as to what this century was all about. The purpose of the book is to provide the general reader with a cognitive experience that surprises present understandings, and subverts them. It is a warning that the evaluation of the twentieth century should not be left in the hands of its victors.

Each of the four parts experiments differently with the relationship between theoretical claims and historical fragments. Notes on Method introduce these parts, providing a guide for the reader. Here is the general overview:

Part I (chapter 1): The theoretical argument (laid out in section 1.1) is opened up to historical time by hypertext links to a series of keywords that provide partial narratives along its lines (the entries in 1.2).

Part II (chapter 2): The theoretical argument (laid out in 2.1) protesting against a certain idea of time evokes in critical response a series of *time fragments* constructed out of historical images and text (2.2).

Part III (chapters 3–5): The theoretical argument is fully integrated into the historical material in a series of *constellations*. Each of the constellations (3.1–5.3) is constructed as a rescue mission by the present into the past, foraging across temporal and spatial boundaries in search of data, assembled around images, that have the power to alter conventional narratives of the twentieth century.

Part IV (chapter 6) shifts the focus, making visible the invisible present that surrounds the book's writing. Constructed at the *intersection* between lived time and historical time, it is the author's version of a feminist strategy.

DREAMWORLD AND CATASTROPHE

I

DREAMWORLDS OF

DEMOCRACY

A Note on Method

Section 1.1 is a theoretical argument. It was developed as a series of lectures delivered in Moscow in January 1989, when "East" and "West" still referred to distinct political regimes. On the basis of subsequent research, I have restructured the material as a text with hypertext, highlighting keywords to guide the reader to the fragmentary sites of 1.2. The entries under these keywords assemble historical facts around nodal points of the argument. Through them a vertical axis of reading becomes possible that, while breaking the flow of the theoretical presentation, lends it empirical support. Facts once narrated by the Cold War discourse, but now in danger of being forgotten, are rescued in the keyword entries as partial narratives, suggesting possibilities for how twentieth-century history might be retold.

CHAPTER 1

THE POLITICAL FRAME

1.1

MASS SOVEREIGNTY
AND THE IMAGE OF THE ENEMY

From the perspective of the end of the twentieth century, the paradox seems irrefutable that political regimes claiming to rule in the name of the masses—claiming, that is, to be radically democratic—construct, *legitimately,* a terrain in which the exercise of power is out of control of the masses, veiled from public scrutiny, arbitrary and absolute. Modern sovereignties harbor a blind spot, a zone in which power is above the law and thus, at least potentially, a

---

1.2

HYPERTEXT

ee page 35
EXT

COLD WAR ENEMIES   According to official history, the Cold War did not begin until the enunciation in 1947 of the Truman Doctrine to "contain" communism. Yet the structuring logic of its political imaginary was already in place by the end of World War I.[37] For the Western imaginary, the Bolshevik Revolution of 1917 was an absolute threat from the very beginning. It challenged both SPACE as the determinant of sovereignty, and the SEPARATION BETWEEN THE ECONOMIC AND THE POLITICAL as discursive terrains. The whole notion of national defense became problematic. In the words of a U.S. general at the Paris Peace Conference: "It is true that you can prevent an army of Bolsheviks from coming out of Russia by posting on its borders a sufficiently large military force, but you cannot in this way prevent Bolshevism from coming

out."[38] Precisely because of this, the imaginary effects of Bolshevism within U.S. political discourse were hallucinatory in ways that became the hallmark of the Cold War. As the absolute enemy (because it did not behave as enemies should!), Bolshevism took on the fantastic image of a "fire," a "virus," a "flood" of barbarism, "spreading," "raging," "out of control," a "monster which seeks to devour civilized society" and destroy the "free world."[39]

The Allied intervention in the Russian Civil War that began in the winter of 1918–1919 had a specific meaning in this discursive context. By blockading the coastline and providing the White Russians with military supplies, it was an offensive measure that inscribed Bolshevism symbolically onto a geopolitical terrain, set off by territorial

terrain of terror. This wild zone of power, by its very structure impossible to domesticate, is intrinsic to mass-democratic regimes. It makes no difference whether the model of their legitimacy is the liberal claim of political (formal) democracy based on universal, mass suffrage, or the socialist claim of economic (substantive) democracy based on the egalitarian distribution of social goods. Either way, as regimes of supreme, sovereign power, they are always, already *more* than a democracy—and consequently a good deal less.

The wild zone is of course not the whole of modern power. Mass-democratic, political regimes function on many levels in ways that are fully within the law and subject to institutional and informal checks. This normal and legal authority can be called the "civil state," because it is accountable to civil society, and it is the institution commonly presumed by contemporary political theorists of democracy, from Jürgen Habermas to John Rawls. Yet legality does not exhaust the legitimacy of such states. In-

---

boundaries in an attempt to contain an idea—socialism—that had no respect for such boundaries. When the Red Army launched its own offensive campaign against Poland, it seemed to confirm Bolshevik Russia as a belligerent nation-state, one that was potentially aggressive in a military sense. The territorialization of socialism as a spatial threat, which became a fundamental premise after World War II when the Cold War had its official beginnings, was thus already present as the ur-response of the capitalist nation-states to the success of the Bolshevik Revolution. Viewing opposition to capitalism as aggression by a foreign nation normalized the enemy. It followed from this logic that if communist regimes were willing to act like nations (as was the Soviet Union during the Popular Front era of the 1930s), then one could be at peace with them, and even (as in World War II) act with them in military alliance.

In the United States, the Bolshevik Revolution produced a discourse of internal enemies as well.

Known as the Red Scare, it equated the foreign threat of Bolshevism with all organized challenges to the war effort, of which there were many, whether from workers, socialists, pacifists, women, or African-Americans. The Espionage Act of 1918 made criticizing the armed forces, national flag, or military uniform punishable by twenty years' imprisonment. South European immigrants previously described as "racially unassimilatable" were now forced to kiss the flag to prove their loyalty as "100% American." "Radical aliens" were turned back at Ellis Island and denied immigration. The Postmaster General was given the power to remove both antiwar material and socialist papers from the mail. In 1919, when workers' action in the textile and steel industries set off a chain reaction of 3,600 strikes involving four million workers (the general strike that many heralded—or feared—as the worldwide workers' revolution), immigrant organizers were branded as foreign agents of Bolshevism, and deported. Women's suffrage leaders,

deed, when the question of sovereignty is at issue, there is no such thing as merely legal legitimacy. Modern sovereignties also possess a supralegal or perhaps prelegal form of legitimacy, precisely the wild zone of arbitrary, violent power, and it lies at their very core.

The intimate connection between the state and violence has been recognized generally in this century within Marxist and non-Marxist theory alike. When Max Weber defined the state as "a human institution that (successfully) claims the *monopoly of the legitimate use of physical force* within a given territory,"[1] he was in agreement with Bolshevik theory, and he knew it. Citing Trotsky's statement that "every state is founded on force," Weber comments: "That is indeed correct. Without the use of violence there would be no state."[2] Marx describes how bourgeois ideology gained legitimacy in the modern state by presenting its class-specific interests as the general interest.[3] Weber observes simply that gradually, through institution-

protesting against a war to protect "democracy" which all women were denied at home, were imprisoned as political subversives. When the 200,000 African-Americans who had served in the war returned home to continued segregation, and racial demonstrations in many cities turned violent, this "negro subversion" was attributed to Bolshevik propaganda among the demonstrators.[40] The U.S. Attorney General, A. Mitchell Palmer, ordered agents to infiltrate the ranks of the Left, authorizing a series of raids in which "police burst into homes and meeting places all over the country, loading 'suspicious' aliens onto trucks or marching them handcuffed through the streets. . . . Over three thousand aliens were deported."[41] Palmer's language had all the attributes of Cold War hysteria: "Like a prairie fire, the blaze of revolution is sweeping over every institution of law and order . . . eating its way into the homes of the American workmen . . . licking the altars of the churches. . . ."[42] Political radicals were lumped together with prostitutes and

lunatics as a potential threat, and were vulnerable to the new deportation laws. In short, to criticize *in the name of democracy* the existing economic and political structures of the United States was equated with being "un-American" in the sense of both an alien presence and a moral threat.

The record in the Soviet Union is hardly more heartening, and the domestic body count was incomparably higher.[43] The overt violence of the Civil War (1918–1921) claimed over a million lives. Arguably, this was a defensive war, waged against the "normal," class enemy of White Russians aided by capitalist nations, and for that reason, as Fitzpatrick notes, the Civil War "did not frighten the Bolsheviks and to some degree attracted them since they sensed that only violent confrontation with the class enemy would guarantee a true revolutionary victory."[44] Nevertheless, the destruction was extreme, resulting in famine, industrial chaos, shattered cities, and dislocated populations.[45] (It should be noted that there is nothing about "normal" ene-

alization, the state's monopoly of violence came to be accepted.[4] Lenin refers to Marx's description of the "democratic swindle" whereby the bourgeoisie hoodwinks the people into believing that the state is representing them.[5] Yet the question remains: How does the state legitimate the use of violence? As for Marx's concept of the secret exercise of power (i.e., the class interests that manipulate power behind the scenes), this power cannot be the basis of legitimacy. Indeed, to expose its existence is Marx's tactic for *de*legitimating the bourgeois state.

The answer might at first appear obvious. It is the premise of liberal-democratic philosophy that the monopoly of violence by popular sovereignty is legitimate because, mediated by law, popular will and popular sovereignty are one and the same. But this theoretical grounding, seemingly the most secure, is inherently precarious. The criterion of law that separates the "good" state (embodying popular sovereignty) from the "bad" state

---

mies that makes physical violence against them any less probable. On the contrary, because it is a legitimate, indeed heroic act, you kill normal enemies cheerfully. Against absolute enemies, whose physical disappearance would imperil one's own identity, the most violent attacks may be symbolic. The name "Cold War" refers precisely to the fact that by outlawing the enemy's interpretation of the world, the silencing violence was cultural even more than it was physical.)

Truly dangerous to the legitimacy of Bolshevik Party sovereignty in the early years was resistance within the working class and revolutionary movements themselves.[46] Examples of such resistance were multiple, and the party did not hesitate to put them down by force—thereby exposing the non-identity between party sovereignty and popular-democratic rule. This was the case when in the early years the Workers' Opposition movement threatened to strike against the regime for better conditions, higher pay, and more workers' control.[47] It was

the case when in 1919 Lenin withdrew his support from Nestor Makhno's partisans fighting for Ukrainian independence, denouncing this popular, grass roots guerrilla resistance movement as "petty bourgeois counterrevolution."[48] It was clear in the suppression of a series of uprisings by peasants who, protesting against the compulsory grain requisitions of 1920–1921, adopted as their revolutionary slogan "Soviets without Bolsheviks."[49] And it was perhaps most shockingly the case when, in March 1921, the revolutionary workers and soldiers of the island commune of Kronstadt, which had championed the Bolshevik cause in the October Revolution, rose up against the Communist Party and declared their own radical socialist, "soviet" democracy. The Kronstadt communards were denounced as perpetrators of a "White-Guardist plot" and were brutally suppressed under Trotsky's order to "shoot them down like pheasants."[50] During this time the discourse of class enemies expressly excluded the workers of Europe and the

(which escapes the people's control) implies a circular logic, because the state as law defender is itself the constitutor of the law. As Walter Benjamin argued in the early 1920s, when the police are brought in to put down popular demonstrations such as workers' strikes or antiwar mobilizations, their purpose is to protect, not law, but the monopoly of the right to establish law. By the exercise of violence over those who challenge the existing law, the latter, writes Benjamin, "reaffirms itself. But in this very violence something rotten [*Morsches*] in the law is revealed," not its justice but its monopoly of the (violent, physical) power to determine, in the last analysis, what justice is.[6]

To summarize: The class nature of the state may explain its violence, but not its legitimacy; the democratic nature of the state may explain its legitimacy but not its violence. If one rejects the Marxist critique and attempts to redeem the violent state through liberal-democratic theory, appealing to the legality of popular sovereignty, one faces the problem that,

---

United States.[51] As for Western *states,* as agents of the bourgeois class they were the normal enemy. The more they fought the Bolshevik regime, the more legitimacy the latter could claim. More problematic to Bolshevik foreign policy were threats to its monopoly of the claim to be the agent of revolutionary progress.[52] With the establishment of the Comintern in 1919, Communist parties throughout the world were to take their orders from Moscow—or risk falling into the category of absolute enemy. This centralization of power was proclaimed as indispensable for the international proletarian cause.[53]

Both within the Soviet Union and without, "normal" enemies could be tolerated according to the "ebb and flow" of the revolution's historical course.[54] The New Economic Policy (NEP), initiated in March 1921, allowed nonproletarian elements—certain bourgeois elements, intellectuals, and officials—to coexist within revolutionary society. The period of NEP continued to be described by the party as a time of class struggle, but in a peaceful mode. Because peasants were a historically superseded class, it was possible to make an alliance (*smychka*) with them. Because history was on the side of socialism, competition between public and private sectors of the Soviet economy could be tolerated. By the mid-1920s, Bukharin spoke of the economic transformation as occurring bloodlessly, "without the clanging of metal weapons"; the Soviet Union would "outgrow the market"; the time of the Terror was over; class struggle was "dying out," replaced by competition between "semi-friends" and "semi-enemies."[55]

In the late 1920s, however, the slow tempo of history became intolerable. Declaring TIME itself the enemy, Stalin announced that as Soviet society progressed toward communism there would be "an inevitable intensification of class struggle."[56] The policy of alliance with the peasantry was replaced by "dekulakization," the ruthless destruction of those peasants who had benefited materially from

in the case of the use of violence by popular sovereignty against a mass demonstration of popular will, it becomes questionable whether the law that the sovereign is upholding is itself legitimate.[7] When democratic sovereignty *confronts* the people with all the violence that it monopolizes as the legitimate embodiment *of* the people, it is in fact attesting to its *non*identity with the people. Thus the attempt to resolve the contradiction between popular sovereignty and state violence by recourse to the conception of the law becomes caught in a vicious circle. And the effect of this circularity is to undermine the very possibility of the legal/illegal distinction.[8]

It may be necessary to take a different tack. If we concentrate on the origins of the state in a philosophical sense, then all of these elements, democracy, legitimacy, *and* the "wild zone" of absolute power, come together in a coherent configuration. This configuration creates an emblem under the sign of War—not the hidden war that the state covers up (I am

---

the policies of NEP.[57] In a return to the discourse of the Civil War, force was justified in class terms: "The kulaks will not leave the historical stage without a struggle."[58] Again, internal war was framed within the context of a threat from without. The war scare that began in 1927 made constant allusions to "encirclement" of the Soviet Union by imperialist powers. Internal class enemies charged as economic "wreckers" were accused of conspiring with imperialist powers as "spies."[59] Even the peasants were seen as part of an international conspiracy.[60] Stalin proclaimed in 1927: "We have internal enemies. We have external enemies. This, comrades, must not be forgotten for a single moment."[61]

The intensity of this war scare—the "almost hysterical alarm about immanent military attack by the capitalist powers"[62]—was at the time unjustified.[63] But total threat, domestic and foreign, legitimated total, extralegal power. Reviving the imaginary of class war was a means of consolidating Stalin's own power.[64] By interpreting the struggle to

modernize as itself a war zone, Stalin placed the whole society under siege.[65] The discourse of forced industrialization bristled with military terms: "shock brigades" of workers waged "battles of production"; goals and problems became "fortresses" to be "stormed"; collectivization was described as the "storming of the countryside"; Communists were "fighters," "mobilized" on the "grain front," the "planning front," the "literary front," and even the "philosophy front."[66] In the words of one participant: "In the thirties we felt as if we were at war, at war with the entire world, and we believed that in war you should act like there's a war on."[67]

Paradoxically, in the mid-1930s when terror against the enemy within reached its height, Soviet foreign policy sought an accommodation with the capitalist nation-state order, first, during the period of the Popular Front, as championing the cause against fascism, but then, suddenly, in alliance with fascism by the Nazi-Soviet nonaggression pact of 1939. This alliance was justified within Soviet dis-

referring to Marx's argument), but the war that the state defines explicitly as its purpose, indeed as the very essence of its being. For it is the real possibility of war and the threat of a common enemy that constitute the state not merely as a legal entity but as a sovereign entity, the legitimate embodiment of the collective with the power to wage war in its name. As sovereign of the collective, it has sovereignty over the collective, with the right to order to their death the very citizens in whose name it rules.

The wild zone is thus a war zone. The rightful power of the democratic sovereignty to wage war is the source of its legitimate claim to the monopoly of violence, and to the exercise of terror. This much Carl Schmitt saw clearly. Throughout his life, during the Weimar Republic, during the Third Reich when he was briefly a member of the Nazi Party, and during the Cold War in a divided Germany, this professor of international law, whose writings experienced a renaissance in Europe in the 1980s, argued

---

course by describing Nazi Germany as a normal class enemy—just one among the capitalist nations that were destined historically to destroy each other. But when Hitler broke the pact and invaded the Soviet Union in 1941, World War II became the "great patriotic war," fought not by a class but by the "Soviet people" (led in heroism specifically by the Russians). Never was the Soviet Union more integrated into the Western discourse of nation-states than as a wartime ally against Hitler's military aggression.

The "people's democracies" that were constructed in Eastern Europe after Germany's defeat were described as nation-states, allied through a series of treaties with the Soviet Union rather than incorporated into its federation. This marked a transformation in the conceptual terrain.[68] In the late 1940s, class war was articulated as a war about territory and its defense, an international struggle between the Eastern bloc and the nations of the West that were separated by a physical boundary to

prevent "contagion" or "spillover" into the socialist camp.[69] Soviet discourse became state-centered and defensive, aiming, at least in eastern Europe, at preserving the status quo against "capitalist restoration."[70] It was also anticosmopolitan and anti-Semitic, privileging the Russian people as superior due to their special contribution to Soviet history.[71] But in other, key ways, the discourse had not changed. Soviet interventions into Hungary (1956) and Czechoslovakia (1968) were justified within the same logic of international class solidarity that had existed during the Russo-Polish War of 1920, defended as the necessary fulfillment of the Soviet Union's historic duty to protect socialist gains in these countries. Fascism was interpreted as a capitalist phenomenon in a way that exonerated East German Communists from guilt (while in the West, socialists and fascists were lumped together within a new discourse of "totalitarianism").[72] Now, as earlier, sovereign independence meant independence from capitalism, and Soviet military intervention

that the act of identifying the enemy is *the* act of sovereignty, indeed the political act par excellence. But I want to go a step further than Schmitt, which
is also a step away from him, one that turns his justification of national sovereignty into its radical critique. To define the enemy is, simultaneously, to
define the collective. Indeed: *defining the enemy is the act that brings the collective into being.* Now, when sovereignty claims to be democratic, the collective itself is alleged to act. The interests of the people are said to be
immediately, transparently reflected in the sovereign agent, who therefore
has absolute power. But the logical trick in this argument is that the collective of the "people" that supposedly constitutes the democratic sovereignty
does not exist until that sovereignty is constituted. There *is* no collective until the "democratic" sovereign—precisely in the act of naming the common
enemy—calls that collective into being. Subsequently, any popular challenges to the sovereign's legitimacy can be defined as enemy acts. It follows

---

was justified in terms of the special (monopoly) status of the Communist Party of the Soviet Union as
guardian of the future for the proletarian class.[73]

It should be noted that the discourse of enemies
characteristic of the Cold War was not limited to
the political realm. Striking on both sides is the degree to which these imaginaries were fostered in
the popular imagination through mass culture. Science fiction was a favored form of demonization of
the enemy. In the 1920s, the contrast of "communist heaven" and "capitalist hell" was a generic
theme in Soviet science fiction, projecting onto the
"other" all of the negative aspects of industrial society.[74] After World War II, a whole series of U.S.
catastrophe movies concerning "alien invaders"
connected fear of Communism with these science
fiction fantasies. As late as the 1980s, when an ex-
movie star, U.S. President Ronald Reagan, spoke
of the "evil empire" of Red Communists that ruled
the Soviet Union, he drew on images deeply in-
grained in the collective unconscious.[75]

FRENCH REVOLUTION   The French Revolution was "a society in search of a new collective
identity" based on the democratic principle "that
people are power, or that power is the people," implying a transparency, or identity, between the
government and the governed.[76] But what constellation of power could claim to *be* this impossible
transparency?[77] The struggle for power throughout
the revolutionary period, from 1789 through 1795,
was a "competition of discourses for the appropriation of legitimacy,"[78] as each group tried to demonstrate that *it* represented the general will by defining
the political discourse in a way that allowed it to
seize the site of power from which the legitimation
of sovereignty emanated.[79] The historical effect of
this process was the construction of a new machinery of power which, in the name of democracy,
reestablished the absolutism that it meant to destroy.

This is the argument made by the conservative
historian François Furet, whose influential study
was written on the occasion of the French Revolu-

See page 3
TEXT

that the sovereign's legitimate claim to the monopoly of violence cannot be granted by the people, that this power is not and can never be democratic. The claim to the monopoly of violence is itself the act of legitimation upon which the existence of *the people* depends, not vice versa. Hence the paradox: Democratic sovereignty is able to claim as legitimate the nondemocratic exercise of violent power. We can put the matter more strongly. Given the logical trick in the construction of popular sovereignty, the exercise of violence, including terror, against the "enemy" (which, defined by the sovereign agency, may be within as well as without) paradoxically becomes the only proof of this agency's democratic legitimacy, that is, of its claim to *be* the people, for only "the people" would have the right to use violence in the democratic state. The real consequence of this trick in logic is that actual people find themselves confronting a wild zone of sovereign power

tion's bicentennial, at the close of the Cold War era. His rhetorical strategy was to agree with Marx's criticism of the French Revolution as "the political illusion of democracy." But whereas Marx, writing at a time when revolutionary movements were still on the rise, meant that political revolution is merely the dream form of democracy so long as social and economic inequalities remain unchanged, Furet's purpose was to criticize the whole tradition of radical democratic politics. The belief that the "general will" can substitute for the traditions of civil society, or that through an act of revolutionary will the "people" can achieve a mythical identity with power, is, in his words, "the matrix of totalitarianism."[80]

As with the work of Carl Schmitt, Furet's critique of the democratic nation-state can be refunctioned against his conservative, antidemocratic intent. Crucial to our interests is his understanding of the seizure of the site of power within the imaginary discourse as being one with the construction

of the enemy, the counterrevolutionary "other" that in turn defines the "people." This was true in the early stages of the Revolution, when the Abbé Sieyès excluded the whole order of the nobility from the "people" by arguing that "precisely what the citizens had in common" was "the will to found a nation in opposition to the nobility."[81] It was true in the advanced stages of the Great Terror, when the imagined "aristocratic plot" became the embodiment of the "anti-principle of Revolution."[82] And it was true during the revolutionary wars, when the aristocracy was accused of treason against the revolutionary "patriots" in collusion with foreign powers.[83] In all of these forms, the agents of the aristocratic plot were abstract, vague, and hidden, but, because "crushing the plot became a laudable and purifying act"[84] synonymous with saving the Revolution, it became *the* act of sovereign legitimation—to the point that "the Revolution had no objective limits, only enemies."[85] This logic is the ur-form of the wild zone of democratic sover-

over which they have no sovereignty, but which, as the legitimate defender of "the people," has a claim over their very lives.

■

I would like at this point to introduce the concept of the "political imaginary" (*politicheskoe voobrazhaemoe*) as it has been formulated by the Russian philosopher Valerii Podoroga and explicated in the work of his colleague Elena Petrovskaia.[9] Similar terms abound in contemporary discourse. Laclau and Mouffe write about the "Jacobin imaginary."[10] Castoriades speaks of the "social imaginary."[11] And, of course, the stage of the "imaginary" is a fundamental category of Lacanian psychoanalytic theory. But in the Russian language, the concept takes on a representational concreteness lacking in contemporary Western discussions, where, at least among political theorists, it has come to mean little more than the logic of a discourse, or world

---

eignty, the terrain of absolute power, the license for terror. The French National Convention met in September 1792 to draw up a constitution, which was accepted by popular vote in 1793. But it was suspended by the Conventional Assembly that very year in order to combat the two forms of the aristocratic plot, the internal threat of civil war and the external threat of foreign war.[86] For two years, both these forms existed simultaneously. But although the enemy principle (aristocratic privilege) was the same, the conception of the collective that was being threatened differed in significant ways, as did the form of defense: terror and war.

The revolutionary Terror was launched against the internal "enemy of the people," defined in the Rousseauean sense as the opponent of the general will. The executive agency of the Terror, the Jacobin Committee of Public Safety, declared: "Whereas the French people has manifested its will, everyone who is opposed to it is outside the sovereignty; everyone outside the sovereignty is an enemy. . . ."

Between the people and its enemies, there is nothing in common but the sword."[87] Sovereign legitimacy totally superseded constitutional legality in the Reign of Terror. "Under the fiction of the 'people' Jacobinism substituted itself simultaneously for civil society, and for the state."[88] Moreover, the fact that the leaders themselves fell victim to the rage of the guillotine seemed to provide proof that it was not holding power that legitimated sovereignty, but the sovereign people who legitimated holding power.

Robespierre, idol of the Jacobins, embodied the logic of revolutionary sovereignty.[89] His relation to the Terror was to produce the sovereign unity that "democracy" demanded: "He *was* the people to the *sections,* he was the people to the Jacobin Club, he was the people to the national representative body; it was continually necessary to establish, control and restore the perfect fit between the people and the various assemblies that claimed to speak in its name (above all the Convention), for without that perfect

view. *Obraz* signifies "form" or "shape" as a graphic representation, and is used to mean "icon." *Politicheskoe voobrazhaemoe* is thus a topographical concept in the strict sense, not a political *logic* but a political *landscape,* a concrete, visual field in which political actors are positioned. In terms of our present discussion, it can be said that the three icons of the political imaginary are brought into this field at the same moment: the common enemy, the political collective, and the sovereign agency that wages war in its name.

What is at stake in war is the life or death of the collective itself. This must be understood in the double sense described by Podoroga, who distinguishes the "enemy" both as a term within the political imaginary and, on a metalevel, as a threat *to* the political imaginary. The first could be termed the normal enemy, which has already been positioned in the imaginary terrain. In contrast, the absolute enemy threatens the coherence of the imaginary system as a whole. So long as the enemy really acts like the enemy, it poses

---

HYPERTEXT FRENCH REVOLUTION

fit there could be no legitimate power, and the first duty of power was to maintain it: that was the function of the Terror."[90] The identity between Robespierre and the people, based on the "fiction of pure democracy," was, Furet writes, a "surrealist entity," the reverse side of which was the existence of an "inner circle" of power, "an organisation that prefabricated consensus and had exclusive control over it."[91] Thus, in creating a "new god out of the fictive community of the people,"[92] direct democracy produced a new, all-powerful state machine.

It was Marx who called the Thermidorian reaction that put a halt to this machinery of Terror the "revenge of civil society."[93] Robespierre was convicted of conspiracy against the Revolution, and himself guillotined. But, as Furet reminds us, with the end of the Terror, the problem of sovereign power again became acute. Those who had "toppled Robespierre in the name of liberty" had themselves been part of the Terror, "and often personally conducted brutal purges."[94] In order to keep themselves in power, they had to create a counterdiscourse whereby Terror, far from the culmination of democratic Revolution, was seen (in the words of one participant) as "an unfortunate deviation from it."[95] In order to disassociate themselves from the Terror, argues Furet, they "had to assign . . . the entire responsibility for it to Robespierre and his inner circle. Having once been the Revolution itself, the Terror now became the result of a plot, or the expedient of one man's tyranny."[96] The intended analogy to Khrushchev's de-Stalinization of Soviet discourse is clear.

The end of the Terror meant that revolutionary ideology no longer filled the entire terrain of governmental power. But the Thermidorians reconstituted that power by replacing absolute Terror with absolute war, inaugurating the other wild zone of modern sovereign power, the logic of which covered up a fundamental contradiction in French revolutionary discourse. The Declaration of the Rights of Man that provided the preamble to the constitu-

no threat on this second level. Paradoxically, the threat on the metalevel is that the enemy might disappear. But a threat to what or to whom? Clearly to the legitimacy of the sovereign agent. More than that, however. The disappearance of the enemy threatens to dissolve the collective itself.

So far, the logic of the argument can be applied to both capitalist and socialist models of mass sovereignty, but as soon as the phenomenon is examined substantively, this unity dissipates. The criterion by which these models make the split between enemy and friend breaks the common problem of power into incompatible topologies, noncontiguous political terrains. One is based on a political imaginary of irreconcilably antagonistic, warring classes; the other is based on a political imaginary of mutually exclusive, potentially hostile nation-states. Philosophical descriptions provide the rationale for both models, comprising the political imaginary in the weaker sense of an ideological discourse or world view. (Ever since the con-

---

tion of 1792 was contradicted by the male, property-holding provisions of the constitution itself, a fact on which Furet does not dwell, but of which those who drew up the constitution were well aware.[97] Within the discourse of war against a foreign enemy, however, the image of the collective was free of such embarrassing anomalies. The "French nation" implied a different test of revolutionary loyalty, not to the principle of social equality, but to the principle of equality on the battlefield in the face of death. August 23, 1793, was the first *levée en masse,* the first national mobilization of a state for war. Defense of *la patrie* became the very embodiment of the revolution, as the revolutionary agencies of the Terror were transformed into the wartime executors of the nation-state. With the end of the Terror in 1795, the war against the conservative sovereigns of Europe became "the focus of unity and of an ever-escalating revolutionary rhetoric."[98] It was based on the ideological model of democratic nationalism that covered up the dif-

ferences between peasant, professional, bourgeois, and *sans-culotte*—Frenchmen all, engaged in a defensive war that became an aggressive war, glorified as an ideological crusade by the "*grande nation,* henceforth entrusted with a mission of universal liberation."[99]

Furet cites Marx's "brilliant analysis": "Napoleon [wrote Marx] was the last stand of *revolutionary terror* against *bourgeois society.* . . . Napoleon still regarded *the State as its own end.* . . . He carried *the Terror to its conclusion by replacing the permanent revolution with permanent war.*"[100] The absolute war of the nation's democratic crusade "could only end in total victory or total defeat."[101] Under Napoleon, war became "the last refuge of revolutionary legitimacy."[102] The first *modern* emperor, Napoleon had no divine right to rule. His only legitimacy depended on keeping the war going. (He fought eighty battles.) His fall brought the restoration of monarchy. Furet writes: "In making the extraordinarily early synthesis between the messianic call of

---

ception of divine right lost legitimacy as the basis of sovereignty, these descriptions have been of great practical significance; the rationale of modern sovereignty owes much to the inventive fantasy of philosophers.) In the nation-state model, the discourse of war has been relentlessly dominated by the imagery of the seventeenth-century philosopher Thomas Hobbes, who argued that the original human state, the "state of nature," is a terrain of continuous war of all against all. He thereby placed war at the heart of the problem of sovereignty, and it is no surprise to find that his influence on Carl Schmitt was direct and considerable. In the Hobbesian state of nature, nothing is safe, not life, not liberty, and most especially not property. According to Hobbes, this original state is given up voluntarily by self-interested individuals in order to establish a social contract with the sovereign for their mutual protection. But in light of the perpetual danger of a return of the state of war, the contract invests this sovereign with absolute power. Ab-

---

an ideology and nationalist fervor—a synthesis that was destined to have a great future—the French people . . . were the first to integrate the masses into the state and to form a modern democratic nation."[103] The ur-form of revolutionary Terror by the "people" as sovereign; the ur-form of military aggression by the "democratic" nation-state: that is the double legacy of the French Revolution.

Seen through this historical prism, the great COLD WAR ENEMIES, while having been truly dangerous to each other, appear as in fact close relatives. Their common descent from the French Revolution (which Lenin constantly stressed, but with the understanding that since October 1917 only his own regime was the legitimate heir) means that they shared the paradox inherent in the juxtaposition of those two concepts that, while they are the signature of politics in the modern era, do not rest comfortably next to each other: "democracy," rule by the people, and "sovereignty," supreme power of the governing regime. But by turning a blind eye to

this common heritage—each accepting only part, a different part, as legitimate—East and West declared each other not only illegitimate but evil, and projected the problematic aspects of the democratic tradition onto the other side, refusing to face their own failures as democracies in the process.

Furet reveals how the "phantasm" of absolute power as the "legacy of monarchy" has haunted the history of mass sovereignty.[104] But in another sense, the claim of the Revolution to have ushered in a totally new age of human history was justified. Paradoxically, it was the early, more moderate phase of the French Revolution that made a radical rupture with the past. Moreover, it did so in a language not of discarding the past, but of its restoration. The end of the old regime was perceived in 1789 as the *return* of power to society, a reappropriation by the people of their sovereignty, a recovery of their "natural" rights. Of course, just this notion of power residing equally in all the people rather than in the monarch, just this secular conception of legitimate

solute obedience is the price paid for the security of property and domestic peace, as well as for defense from invasion by a foreign enemy.

Liberal-democratic nation-states today, in the less misanthropic tradition of Enlightenment thinkers like John Locke, have a more sanguine view of the social contract, and a more constrained view of sovereign power.[12] But the natural state of war, eliminated from domestic political life through the social contract, reemerges at the level of international relations. Whereas the late Enlightenment philosopher Immanuel Kant argued in *The Project for Perpetual Peace* that, on the contrary, the international system can and should replicate the domestic model of the social contract (a position that has had strong appeal in this century among advocates of the League of Nations and United Nations),[13] the realist school of international relations, which has been hegemonic in the West since the nineteenth century, still argues the Hobbesian position: States have total liberty to pursue their in-

---

power in opposition to the idea of divine right, *was* utterly new, and it marked a decisive rupture from the political imaginary that had existed until then. To found legitimate power on a popular basis, without recourse to divine explanation or unquestioned obedience to authority—this became the political project of modernity. It is a project we have yet to realize. And if Furet puts the blame on direct democracy for the inadequacies of this unfinished project, we might do better to stress the other side of the phenomenon, the sovereign state, with its monopoly of the (violent) power to decide who counts as "the people" by constructing as their enemy a category of human beings who do not.

See page 19

TEXT

SEPARATION BETWEEN THE ECONOMIC AND THE POLITICAL   Carl Schmitt emphasizes the fact that the imaginary system of nation-states developed in Europe as an exclusively political phenomenon.[105] Political sovereignty was split off from the economy, or, better put, its internal

logic depended on the exclusion of the economy from any visible position within the imaginary political terrain. Within modern Europe, a fundamental distinction came to be made between political possession of territory and economic ownership, so that even the *enemy's* property rights were protected. What this meant in practice was that despite all the exchanges of territory among European sovereign powers in the eighteenth and nineteenth centuries—and this was true also of the French revolutionary wars[106]—the system of property within those territories was not touched. As a private owner of property, you might end up owing taxes, political allegiance, or whatever to a new sovereign. Your land or business or factory might suddenly be French instead of German, or vice versa. But it would still be yours. Thus, in regard to actually existing property relations, the whole imaginary apparatus of political sovereignty went on in some extraterritorial (i.e., merely political) terrain. What Schmitt calls the "fundamental respect for private

15

terests. The threat of war among states with competing interests is seen to replicate the original state of nature. Each nation is the potential enemy of the others. Each sovereign political agency has, as a consequence, a degree of absolute power in the field of foreign policy that would not be sanctioned within the sphere of domestic political life. This is the legitimation of the "national security state," a space in which a person like U.S. Colonel Oliver North was able to carry out illegal acts without detection, because this terrain of power is, legitimately, a secret space, uncontrolled by the democratic institutions of the civil state.

The liberal (Hobbes-Locke) tradition of social contract theory is not sufficient for the construction of the political logic of nation-states. Contracts exist internally, a state of war rages externally. But where is the boundary between internal and external? What separates one collective from another, and why should the world be organized into a system of mutually

---

HYPERTEXT SEPARATION BETWEEN THE ECONOMIC AND THE POLITICAL

property" remained.[107] "In the nineteenth century, a change of territory by interstate law is only this, a change of public-legal imperium, not a change of the economic and property order."[108] By the time of the Cobden Treaty of 1860, liberal economic thought had become so hegemonic that the separation of the public or governmental sphere from a "private" realm of "possession, trade and economy" was considered liberty at its minimum, both within European nations and between them. "That the occupying state could interfere with the economy and incorporate it into its own would have been unheard of in the nineteenth century."[109] It should be noted, however, that this standard of behavior applied by Europeans to each other was lacking in the colonies, where the property rights of indigenous people might be violated with impunity.[110]

The United States accepted the European separation of political and economic discourses, as well as the exclusion of indigenous peoples from those to whom private property rights applied (see SPACE). Its

foreign policy was from the beginning a conscious duality of political isolation and economic interrelation. In his farewell address, George Washington made this position explicit: "The great rule of conduct for us . . . in extending our commercial relations, [is] to have with them as little political connection as possible."[111] In keeping with bourgeois liberal theory, these economic relations were expected to counter state animosities and foster peace. In practice, however, the fostering of economic relations with nations that were not economic equals became a means of political domination.

With regard to trade *within* the United States, the relationship between the economic and the political was similarly conceived, but with qualitatively different effects. While they were still separate discourses, operating with different and not necessarily complementary logics, they could be made to support each other.[112] The degree of political sovereignty retained by the separate states weakened the national state, and interstate trade was called upon

exclusive states? A second Western philosophical tradition speaks to this, that of the German idealists—Hegel, Herder, Fichte, Schelling—for whom the collective is the imagined community of the nation, the ontological unity of the "people" (*Volk*).[14] Philosophies of nationalism are not incompatible with cosmopolitanism in that they envision a plurality of nations, each with its own particular destiny, the realization of which contributes to universal human history. And yet, where collective identity implies ethnic homogeneity, racism is never far from the surface.[15] As a consequence, fascism is not aberrant to the nation-state imaginary, but rather its limit case. Within a political imaginary where ethnic-national distinctions between "we" and "they" set the terms of the possibility of war, the concept and hence the real possibility of genocide remain necessarily a part of the picture. Moreover, it is the sanctity of this nation that justifies the suspension of all constitutional procedures and legal protections. Any threat to it, as a "national emergency," may jus-

---

to compensate, strengthening—and indeed building—the nation-state, rather than operating independently of it. Integrating the states within a "national economy" became a conscious political goal. The role of the federal government was to facilitate "free" trade among the states by supporting the construction of railroads and canals, while protecting nascent domestic industries from foreign (particularly European) competition through federal import tariffs. This is in essence the origin of import substitution policy, a means of nation-building through economic industrialization and protection from foreign competition, in order to produce an economically autarchic political regime. Such thinking was taken up by the German economist Friedrich List and applied effectively as well to the German case as an alternative model to Britain's free-trade policy. There is great irony here. It was the thinking of List, not Marx (List's contemporary and outspoken opponent), that subsequently won out in the Soviet Union.[113] But since

List developed his ideas while living in the United States (where he wrote for a local Pennsylvania newspaper from 1825 to 1832), it was U.S. foreign-trade theory from the nineteenth century that provided the theoretical origin for the trade policy of the Soviet Union in the twentieth century.[114]

The United States entered the club of imperial powers in 1898 after the Spanish American War, annexing outright Puerto Rico, the Philippines, Guam, and Hawaii. But with the Roosevelt Corollary to the Monroe Doctrine (1904), a discourse was established that differed from both European imperialism and earlier U.S. policy.[115] While keeping up the appearance of a separation between the economic and the political, it made a connection between these categories, so that "freedom" took on an economic meaning and political intervention was the way to achieve it.[116] Schmitt calls this the American principle of *Grossraum* (great space), a form of economic expansion that employed state violence without political annexation.[117]

tify the use of dictatorial powers, implying the higher sovereignty of the ethnic nation to that of the social contract that underlies its democratic claims.

It can be noted that this imaginary of nation-states is purely political. The economy is seen to inhabit a different terrain. And although (as Friedrich List argued in the early nineteenth century)[16] building an economy may be an explicit policy of the state and a powerful means of nation-building, the violence caused by economic activity is not perceived as political violence. So long as the law is obeyed, it is not a state concern. Indeed, relations of economic exploitation are considered quasi-natural. The state may intervene, using its force to maintain the law and order of property or to ameliorate the undesirable effects of the "free" economy, but these spheres remain conceptually distinct. This fact has allowed the nation-state system, conceived originally as a territorial sovereignty of European princes and kings, to persist into the twentieth century despite radical changes in

---

HYPERTEXT SEPARATION BETWEEN THE ECONOMIC AND THE POLITICAL

The United States claimed "police" powers (a *domestic* term) over countries within its sphere of influence, as defined by the Monroe Doctrine, who were guilty of "chronic wrongdoing," understood primarily as economic "irresponsibility." Such powers were used to maintain the kind of order demanded by the presence in these countries of private American firms whose economic influence was often tantamount to political control. These actions were pictured as peacekeeping functions within the U.S. sphere of influence—temporary interventions that did not violate the territorial status quo. And, of course, far from violating property rights, the whole purpose was to protect them (or at least those of foreign businesses and domestic elites). Latin American countries assumed a third status, guaranteed by the United States: neither equal nation nor colony, but less-than-equal, "immature" nation. This status justified violation of their sovereign power but not of the territorial status quo.[118] Despite the overarching economic con-

text, the external facade of political borders in most (but not all) cases remained intact. The more bogus the separation between the economic and the political appeared to the Latin American countries themselves, the more adamantly it was defended by the U.S. government.[119] No U.S. president spoke more loftily of constitutional democracy and national sovereignty than Woodrow Wilson; few upheld it less than he, sending "policing" troops into Haiti, the Dominican Republic, Cuba, and Nicaragua (which Wilson, thwarted by Congress, tried to annex outright), and ordering the U.S. Army to invade Mexico. Precisely because he eschewed the language of *Realpolitik,* Wilson became deeply entangled within the real contradiction between national democratic ideals and actual economic control.[120]

As we have seen (COLD WAR ENEMIES), the political imaginary of Bolshevism threatened to collapse the economic and political distinction from the start. Wilson acknowledged after 1917 that revolu-

the economic topology. The economy was left to go its own way: "Over, under and beside the state-political boundaries of what appeared to be a political and purely international law between states, spread a free, i.e., non-state sphere of economy permeating everything: a world economy."[17] Yet in the twentieth century, this SEPARATION BETWEEN THE ECONOMIC AND THE POLITICAL became increasingly difficult to sustain.

See page 15

HYPERTEXT

In theory at least, the socialist model was to provide an alternative to the nation-state model. The philosophy of Marx has been indispensable in providing its political rationale. The description of sovereignty as a "dictatorship of the proletariat" is opposed to the whole conception of the bourgeois state.[18] According to Soviet theory, the socialist state "rests on a firm political sovereignty of working people," of which the party is the legitimate representative.[19] It is the party, not the state, that is the sovereign agency of the working class. Hence, the party, not the state, lays legitimate claim to

---

tions "do not spring up overnight," and that the spread of Bolshevism into Europe was based on genuine mass appeal: "The people will not stand for a restoration of the old system of balance of power which led them to catastrophe and bloodshed. They will not let it happen again and if their governments cannot work out something better, they will destroy their governments."[121] He was aware that this revolutionary movement could not be stopped by a "line of armies," as the soldiers, too, could be "impregnated with the Bolshevism they are charged with combatting. A germ of sympathy exists between the forces which we wish to oppose to each other."[122] But when deliberating a response he expressed confusion: "The only way to act against Bolshevism is to make its causes disappear. This is, however, a formidable enterprise; we do not even know exactly what its causes are."[123] He could accept a national, political conception of revolution of democrats against aristocrats (in this sense he described Bolshevism as a case of "the FRENCH REVO-

LUTION all over again").[124] But he could not accept an economic definition, a revolution against a property order rather than a political order, without his own discursive landscape dissolving into incoherence.[125]

We can see just how much was at stake at the Paris Peace Conference. The Allies' task of reestablishing the rules of legitimacy after World War I was made perilous by Bolshevism, and not only in Europe.[126] The U.S. policy of *Grossraum*, economic expansion through political violence, that stood behind the Roosevelt Corollary was also threatened. In the 1920s, Comintern policy in Latin America was "calculated to avoid trouble in a far removed region" and remained "low keyed," but U.S. reaction did not: blaming "Bolsheviks" for "injecting" a "virus" into Latin America became a common metaphor in the 1920s.[127] Ironically, however, if the language of Bolshevism insisted on the absurdity of the separation of the economic and political as it had been articulated in U.S. foreign policy, it

the wild zone of absolute power and terror, in order to combat "counter-revolutionary" activities. The Communist Party is the representative of workers who produce the wealth of society and who, because they lack partial, private interests of a property-holding class, are understood as representing the universal interests of humanity. The logical connection SOVEREIGN PARTY/SOCIALIST STATE is one of causality rather than identity. Whereas political parties in nation-states compete to gain control of a preexisting apparatus and thereby to *become* the state, the Communist Party *constructs* the socialist state.[20] It creates and uses state institutions to administer party policy; it purges those institutions when it carries out a class war within them. But the distinction between the two remains. Moreover, the state is understood as a temporary expedient that will ultimately "wither away," an anarchist vision to which even Stalin gave lip service and which Khrushchev revived in political rhetoric in 1959.[21]

See page 23
HYPERTEXT

HYPERTEXT SEPARATION BETWEEN THE ECONOMIC AND THE POLITICAL.

also provided the United States with a new justification for continuing its policy direction. Again, the figure of Wilson was central.

"Wilsonianism" became synonymous with anti-Bolshevism, as the principle of "national self-determination" was called upon to function as a counterrevolutionary alternative to the principle of class. Economic conflict was translated into the discourse of territorial politics, so that resistance to capitalism was read as a sign of Soviet national presence.[128] With this mapping of class struggle onto the political terrain of the nation-state system, the idea that any domestic social-revolutionary movement might be truly representative of the people of a particular nation became unthinkable. An important corollary was that U.S. foreign policy now had a new field of action, the internal affairs of other nations, in order to prevent, as the highest priority, a successful socialist revolution in any one of them.

One of the effects of this new policy was the establishment by the United States of a covert intelli-gence agency with the mandate to "stabilize" foreign governments against Communism. This institution—a wild zone of power, pure and simple—had its birth during negotiations at Versailles, and got a new and stronger lease on life under similar conditions after World War II, with the establishment in 1947 of the Central Intelligence Agency. In 1919, under the authority of Herbert Hoover, "agents" in civilian clothes were attached to the humanitarian efforts of emergency assistance relief programs in war-torn countries, and charged with the mission of collecting information on the degree of "Bolshevik threat." Poland was of particular concern, where the new government faced an actual invasion by the Red Army forces in 1920. The deploying of secret agents was an application of the Monroe Doctrine's principle of "police powers" well out of bounds of the space for which it was designed, and it was infinitely more dangerous because clandestine.

This was the origin of the U.S. national security state, the institutional bedrock of the Cold War. In

With the collapse of the Second International in 1914 due to the conflicting loyalties of class and nation, the role of nationalism within Marxism became a volatile, highly disputed point.[22] Lenin's position was to affirm ethnic nations as a transitional and tactical means to the ultimate socialist-communist goal (whereas Stalin's regime privileged the Russian nation as historically the most "advanced"). Ethnic nations were assimilated into Soviet society so that their loyalty to sovereign power would not be in doubt. Ironically, seventy years after the Bolshevik Revolution, Western scholars were pronouncing Lenin's original nationalist policy a success in the Soviet Union just as the breakup of the socialist bloc resulted in a whole new wave of nationalist movements, as well as new instances of the limit case of ethnic cleansing (which might have been expected given the logic of nation-states).[23] But rather than going into any more detail about the differing philosophical rationales of these two models of democratic sovereignty, I want to point out

---

1947 the U.S. National Security Council was established, to which the CIA was responsible. It justified the secret use of violence against threats to national security secretly defined, violating every democratic right in the name of protecting democracy. Although a domestic organization, its field of action was international, paralleling the illegal, underground activities of indigenous Communist parties. In effect, the president of the United States bestowed upon himself the right to engage clandestinely in any warlike operation against any group in any country of the world threatening to overthrow a government friendly to the Western political and capitalist order—without that power being checked either by the elected legislative assembly of the president's own country or by any democratic representative of the country in which intervention occurred. During the Cold War, the United States collaborated with foreign police forces in the task of "containing communism" in their countries. It exported the national security state model to Argentina, Brazil, Chile, Colombia, the Dominican Republic, Honduras, Panama, Paraguay, Peru, Mexico, and Venezuela, ensuring the establishment within nominally constitutional democracies of enormous wild zones of state violence, training "civil police" within these countries in terror and torture techniques to be used against their citizens, and giving both clandestine and diplomatic support to their systematic violation of human rights—all justified as the defense of "national sovereignty" against the threat of "communist" takeovers.[129] As Henry Kissinger stated notoriously in response to the Chilean people's choice of a Marxist, Salvador Allende, as president through free democratic elections: "I don't see why we need stand by and watch a country go communist due to the irresponsibility of its own people."[130]

Given the traditional American formula of economic presence and political absence, the Cold War was vital for the legitimacy of U.S. foreign interventions in the twentieth century. Without it, the

their implications for the field of political vision and the terrain of power, that is, for the political imaginary in the strong sense suggested by Podoroga, as an iconographic, visual representation of the political terrain.

■

The most striking difference between these two modern political visions is the dimension that dominates their visual landscapes, determining the nature and positioning of the enemy and the terrain on which war is waged. For nation-states, that dimension is SPACE; for class warfare, the dimension is TIME. Space has absolute priority in the political imaginary of nation-states. To be a nation is to possess a territory (in contrast to Bolshevik theory, which in 1917 recognized nationalities both with and without territories).[24] Thus, as Hannah Arendt observed, the Israeli state became a necessity in the twentieth century, in a Western world where only nation-

See page 32
See page 35
HYPERTEXT

HYPERTEXT SEPARATION BETWEEN THE ECONOMIC AND THE POLITICAL

degree of political interference in other nations' affairs in order to protect the economic order of property had nothing but the ideologically dubious Roosevelt Corollary on which to stand. But as the protection of freedom (rather than private property) from a political threat (rather than economic irresponsibility), this intervention was perceived as a protection of the whole ideal system of nation-states, which then, entering another imaginary space, participated in the "free" global economy.

By taking away this pretext, the end of the Cold War has taken away the unique formula for legitimating the peculiarly American form of domination. This special kind of imperialism that insists it *is* no imperialism cannot continue to exist if the political enemy ceases to exist. One should not underestimate the seriousness of the implications. While the IMF and the World Bank take on the role of punishing economic "irresponsibility" for the good of the "free" world (as yet without military power), United States sovereignty faces an enormous crisis

of legitimacy—not only internationally as a superpower, where it now throws the weight of its weaponry about in military showdowns, flaunting force as an end in itself, but also domestically, where the collectivity of its citizens remains an abstract conception, in practice rent by class divisions that are complicated by collective identities of ethnicity and race.

We have yet to experience fully the concrete forms of this crisis. The earliest response was the production of a wild zone of power as a militarized "war on drugs." Turning away from symptoms of a new enemy within—domestic terrorism by white male citizens from the country's heartland—the U.S. security state again focused on Latin American nations, giving renewed legitimation to their authoritarian practices. By connecting the war on drugs to international terrorism, the United States expanded the war zone to a global terrain. The resulting imaginary landscape, in which the global migrant labor force could be surveilled as "illegal

states have sovereignty and only national citizens have rights.[25] Thus also, Palestinian nationalism has become synonymous with the sovereign claim to a land-based state. Within the territorial system of nation-states, all politics is *geo*politics. The enemy is situated within a geographical landscape. The dividing line between friend and foe is the national frontier. Transgressing that frontier is the *causus belli*. The conclusion of war brings about a redistribution of territorial sovereignty. On the other hand, the terrain of class warfare is temporal. Class revolution is a historical event understood as an advance in time. What constitutes a victory is described in terms of historical progress rather than territorial gain. As Trotsky said, the revolution "does not come to an end after this or that political conquest"; its "only boundary is a socialist society."[26] The protagonists in class struggle are not spatially delineated. Indeed, the terrain of class war, as civil war, is spatial confusion. To cite Medvedev: "The front passes through every city, every house."[27]

---

aliens" and the targeted drug-enemy inhabited the familiar geographical space of Third World countries and urban ghettoes, was an attempt to manage the post–Cold War crisis by denying what was new about it, preserving a traditionally spatial form of state defense.[131]

In August 1998, U.S. air attacks against a so-called "university of terrorism" in Afghanistan and an alleged weapons-producing pharmaceutical company in Sudan initiated a new stage in the attempt to salvage the legitimacy of the U.S. as a global superpower, its monopoly of the right to possess arsenals of weapons of mass destruction and train paramilitary forces in terrorist techniques. These were offensive attacks secretly planned against an enemy secretly identified. With them the United States declared an "unending" war against terrorism with explicit analogy to the Cold War against communism, justifying a secret (wild) zone of violent power of comparable scope. It needs to be understood that, regardless of the intentions of the

policy-makers, such a definition of war feeds upon itself. By justifying the use of terror to stop terror, it generates what it seeks to destroy. In this war, the "enemy" is defined not as anticapitalist but anti-American (equated with being less than civilized), so that whoever opposes the rationale of the U.S. use of terror becomes vulnerable to the charge of sympathizing with the enemy camp. Potentially such a war has no limits, short of undermining the legitimacy of U.S. superpower sovereignty itself, which is precisely what is presently at stake.

SOVEREIGN PARTY / SOCIALIST STATE See pag TEXT Lenin's proclaimed vision in October 1917 was radically anarchistic. He conceived of the self-governing councils, or "soviets," that had sprung up spontaneously before the Revolution as becoming administrative units of a decentralized, participatory structure, a revolutionary "state of which the Paris Commune [1870–1871] was the prototype."[132] Literally all of the population, he wrote during the first

Civil war is a tragedy for the nation-state, a threat to its very being, whereas for class revolution it is a step toward the desired historical goal.

The historical dimension is quite strikingly absent (or perhaps repressed) in the political imaginary of the nation-state system. Geopolitics favors the status quo. Revolution is viewed as destabilizing and abnormal, to be avoided at all costs. Time is a vacant category waiting to be filled by the political drama of wars and the activities of states. Progress does enter this imaginary as a concept, but it is a spatial one, equated with the "spread of European civilization" (colonialism) or the "expansion of the free world" (neoimperialism). Typical of this geopolitical imaginary is the statement "History is space over time," which has become a cliché within the Western discourse of international relations. Compare this with Lenin's explanation in 1918 of his willingness to sign the Treaty of Brest-Litovsk, which ceded the whole of the Ukraine to the Germans: "I want to concede space . . . in order to win time."[28]

---

revolutionary year, was to be involved in society's governance through the system of factory soviets, soldiers' and sailors' soviets, and cooperatives, which elected their own officials and debated policy goals.[133] By means of direct democracy, civil society was to reabsorb the political powers of the imperial state. Lenin explicitly rejected the bourgeois model of state sovereignty, including the state's monopoly of the legitimate use of armed force. He wrote that democracy would be built "from below, democracy without an officialdom, without a police, without a standing army; voluntary social duty guaranteed by a *militia* formed from a universally armed people."[134]

But the citizen militia, the "armed people" that had been quickly affirmed by the "Declaration of the Rights of the Laboring and Exploited," was in fact the first point of compromise.[135] It was believed that because workers' revolutions in Europe were historically immanent, armed defense of the Bolshevik regime from foreign invasion would be unnecessary. History, however, did not arrive on schedule.[136] In mid-February 1918, the German national army renewed its attack on the Russian front. By spring, still no major foreign power had recognized the new Soviet Republic—the state that did not want to be one—and Allied troops landed in the North and Far East to aid anti-Bolshevik forces in the Civil War. Trotsky's appointment as Commissar of the Army and Navy in mid-March signaled a radical change in military policy, the goal of which was now to create a disciplined, professional fighting force. Its attainment meant rolling back democratic reforms, such as election of officers, that soldiers had gained in the first revolutionary year. The right of all citizens to bear arms under a principle of *voluntary* service was replaced by obligatory military training, and army service (as opposed to working-class status) became central to the definition of citizenship. In response to the crisis of the Civil War, the party backed up its sovereign claims with a new instrument of coercion, the Cheka, the political police of the state.[137]

In class warfare, space is merely tactical, not the political goal, whereas for the nation-state, time is tactical and space is everything. I remember from my schooldays maps of Europe in 1870, 1919, 1945, with each map representing a different configuration of sovereign territories, each sovereign state a different color. But even our time charts were spatial, with the size allotted to each civilization expanding or contracting according to its waxing and waning political importance. This exclusively spatial imaginary leads to absurdities. Consider, in the nation-state model, the terminological distinction between friend and foe as East versus West, with Cuba somehow belonging to the East and Japan secured for the West. But this is perhaps no more bizarre than the practice of the Soviet transport system that placed all of the Soviet Union officially on Moscow *time*.

In both political imaginaries, there is a dialectical relation between nation and class. Within the nation-state model, class differences are not denied,

---

Forced requisitioning of grain for the army's provisioning was organized locally by "committees of the village poor" (*kombednyi*) who acted as agents of (and spies for) the center. In August, Trotsky ordered the court martial and shooting of a commissar for desertion, and despite continued protests from the People's Commissariat of Justice, hundreds of soldiers and officers in subsequent months were tried and executed by the reestablished military tribunals.[138] The Central Committee of the Communist Party stated expressly that a continued "Red Terror" in order to counter the White Terror was crucial and should be applied ruthlessly, not only "against outright traitors and saboteurs, but against all cowards, self-seekers, connivers, and concealers."[139] These latter categories, of course, did not necessarily comprise *class* enemies, and it was a portent of future abuses.[140]

During the Civil War, the Red Army's formal allegiance was to the Communist International (Comintern, established in 1919) rather than to the

Soviet state, signaling that the use of violence was legitimated in defense of class interests, not national ones.[141] The 1918 Fundamental Law that established the state embodied the communal principle of the soviets in whose name power had been seized in October.[142] They were to be the highest authorities in their territories, sending elected representatives to the Congress of Soviets, which as the law-making assembly was the "supreme organ of the state."[143] Although their power remained largely symbolic, the "impeccably sound revolutionary origins" of the soviets meant that they remained ideologically central to the democratic legitimacy of the socialist state.[144] The title, Union of Soviet Socialist Republics (founded by treaty in 1922), implied a new transnational form of societal governance.[145] According to Lenin, the establishment of the Soviet federation was to provide a transitional framework toward the goal of complete unity among the workers of various nations, all of whom would be organized within soviets.[146] This vision was given institutional expres-

but acknowledged as proof that national identity transcends class belonging. Thus, the fact that "rich and poor alike" feel themselves equally as "French" or "Americans" appears to justify nations as the natural form of collective political life. Correspondingly, by maintaining national differences, the Soviet Union's very existence as a supranational sovereignty was meant to imply that class belonging transcends nationality, at the same time that nations were temporalized as a concept, understood as historically transient political forms. Note that both models have denied sovereign autonomy to ethnic minorities within their jurisdiction; but nation-states have done so to suppress threats to their territorial boundaries, whereas the threat of ethnic separatism to the class struggle is as a move backward, slowing down historical time.

If we consider the positioning of sovereign power within the two imaginary landscapes, the differences follow logically from what has been said so far. In the model where legitimate sovereignty is the exclusive preserve of

sion in the Soviet constitution of 1924, which, while legitimating the USSR, was described as a decisive step toward the "union of all countries in the World Soviet Socialist Republic."[147] But even if the separate socialist state was understood as temporary, internal state-building during the era of NEP produced powerful institutions of governance that increased the reach and scope of the Bolshevik regime enormously. At the same time, the conceived separation of the state from the party made it possible for the former to take on a degree of political neutrality that would have been impossible for the Communist Party, the legitimacy of which continued to rest on its vanguard position in the class struggle.[148]

While debates raged within the party as to what constituted proper revolutionary practice, state institutions tackled the basic problems of administering society, allowing for compromise without compromising the party. Repeatedly, Lenin's position in the debates within the party was to opt for what he saw as a depoliticized solution, appealing to science

rather than revolutionary ideology, technical expertise rather than class consciousness.[149] Because the knowledge and expertise of engineers and scientists was considered politically neutral, it was thought possible to borrow modernizing techniques from anywhere.[150] The self-standing economic bureaucracy that managed industry could be seen as exemplifying Marx's statement that under socialism, the governance of people would be replaced by the administration of things. At the same time, the intended neutrality of state institutions, which had the advantage of regularizing procedures and enforcing the law in a less arbitrary manner, encouraged a tendency toward bureaucracy and the ascendancy of a class of bureaucrats that Lenin deplored.[151] The number of persons employed by the state rose from 600,000 in 1917 to four million by 1928, centralizing power and structurally eliminating possibilities for the expression of political opposition.[152]

The degree to which the workers themselves could be relied upon by the party became a divisive

nation-states, nation and state appear as one within the imaginary terrain. This presumed identity is attested by the citizen army, with its sovereign claim over the lives of the citizens. It is within the mass-conscripted, national army that a synthesis between the citizen and the state is subjectively experienced, and the gap between civil society and the state appears to *dis*appear. In nation-states, army comradeship is *the* communal act of political solidarity. To cite one U.S. scholar: "Full-scale war . . . purges society of conflicts and differences and unifies north and south, black and white, capitalists and socialists within national boundaries. This is the reason veterans look back nostalgically to wartime days of camaraderie and mutual trust."[29]

In the contrasting model, the sovereign body with the legitimacy to wage class warfare is the party, situated in time as the vanguard of history. Its legitimacy lies in holding the interests of the proletariat in trust for the future, and it follows that forsaking the party comes to be synonymous with treason. Party

---

issue in the early years. Lenin made the statement at the Eleventh Party Congress (1922) that people coming to the factory as workers were often "not proletarians but all kinds of accidental elements."[153] It led Shliapnikov, leader of the defeated Workers' Opposition, to respond with irony: "Permit me to congratulate you on being the vanguard of a nonexistent class. . . . We need to remember once and for all that we will not have another and 'better' working class, and we have to be satisfied with what we've got."[154] Lenin's position prevailed, however, that working-class control meant party control, and it was to be implemented "*only* at the state level."[155] Local party cadres were not to interfere in the activities of technical experts, factory managers, or local bureaucrats, all of whom, as state employees, were answerable to the party indirectly, through their obedience to officials at the top.

Given the growing state bureaucracy, how was party control to be maintained? Policy decisions were made at the highest state level, that of Sov-

narkom (USSR Council of People's Commissars), which was the coordinating body of the bureaucracy made up of the heads of each of the commissariats. The Central Committee of the Communist Party was represented, as a commissariat, on Sovnarkom, but the party was not an administrative body in other than its own concerns. At the same time, following the model developed by Trotsky in the case of the Red Army, state organizations began to be monitored internally from early on by party "factions" (*fraktsii*) appointed to work alongside the experts and guarantee their loyalty.[156] This practice of dual command led to the drawing up of a list of names of party members (the *nomenklatura*), who were available for appointment to designated key posts not only within the governing bodies under Sovnarkom, but in all socialist "state" institutions, including factories, universities, schools, unions, and soviets. A centralized hierarchy of party "cells" (*iacheiki*) evolved that shadowed these organizations in order to keep

actions become identified with historical progress itself, which suggests an infallibility of the party and a deterministic view of the future. On the other hand, if the party admits that it has not fulfilled its vanguard role, it faces a crisis of legitimacy, so that its own members become the victims of the most extreme forms of sovereign terror. It is noteworthy in this connection that in the last years of *glasnost'*, Gorbachev began to shift the base of his sovereign legitimacy when in 1988 he became President of the Supreme Soviet (the elected USSR legislature), deriving support from this *de jure* (if not *de facto*) democratic body rather than from his role as party chief. And it is no surprise that this shift was accompanied by a growing threat to the very existence of the Soviet Union, as the republics of which it was composed evoked the alternative, nation-state model of legitimacy in order to challenge power at the center.

Given the different terrains within which the deployment of power occurs, there are qualitative differences in the forms of abuses of power. In

---

them politically honest and to systematize the maintaining of party loyalty.[157]

Since the party was political, the state did not have to be.[158] That was the rationale in the 1920s for the extension of state institutions that would be answerable to the party at the top level and monitored by party cells within them. The departments of state, or commissariats, were otherwise free to administer policy according to professional norms, implementing party policies rather than producing them. To a certain extent, "stateness" (*gosudarstvennost'*) defused political dissension by holding its institutions apart from ideological battles. But by the late 1920s, these institutions began to be openly criticized by "class-conscious" workers, soldiers, intellectuals, and others, who found themselves confronted with prerevolutionary personnel in positions of power as state bureaucrats, army officials, factory engineers, and university professors. Stalin took advantage of their discontent by giving it political expression. Whereas Lenin had built state institutions as a neu-

tral zone, Stalin purged them by attacking the experts in the name of renewed class warfare, ensuring his own rise to power in the process.[159]

Yet even Stalin did not eliminate the distinction between the party and the state.[160] The significance of this dual system, whereby party sovereignty was separate from and above state sovereignty, should not be underestimated.[161] Scholars have long recognized its existence, and yet, in the words of the social historian Stephen Kotkin, "the duplication of state and party structures remains a question crying out for historical explanation."[162] Kotkin describes the party-state as a theocracy, wherein the party was the site of doctrinal purity and the state was responsible for its implementation.[163] But in arguing that Communism was "a matter of faith" that prevented the development of a secular state and perpetuated the "redundant" parallel of party organizations, Kotkin does not attend to the question of sovereign legitimation on which the existence of the USSR depended.[164]

the geopolitics of nation-states, war as a military practice involves an enormous and grotesque exaggeration of the development of weapons technology. Physical destruction is the dominant tactic of national wars. It is indiscriminate, taking a frightful toll on the lives of soldiers and civilians alike, catastrophically demolishing the material world—cities, factories, farmlands, jungles, industries, transportation networks—and involving the whole planet in these orgies of annihilation. This particular insanity of power is inherent in the political imaginary of modern nation-states, and in the specific kinds of war machines that they create.

The political imaginary of class warfare has its own horrors. Because class war is civil war, the war zone is superimposed upon the space of the "normal" state, so that, potentially, all of civil society is under siege. For a future utopia, the present is sacrificed. The terrain of power extends limitlessly, threatening to obliterate private space completely. Civil society's associa-

---

Party sovereignty did not have *constitutional* status. But the constitution of this revolutionary state was not the source of legitimation, which was and remained the working class—however problematic it continued to be for the party who represented it to define this class.[165] Today, when so many *soi-disant* "progressive" political groups are putting their faith in "civil society," it is worth noting that the Soviet Union was perhaps the first modern state to be under civil society's sovereign control.[166] The Communist Party was not a state organization but public (*obshchestvennaia*) and voluntary, described in the 1936 constitution as one organization of (civil) society among many. However, defined as the "leading core of all organizations of the working people, both public and state," it had the authority to intervene anywhere within both of these domains.[167]

The USSR was a workers' state. If it gave up this definition, it gave up its right to exist. It was the party as "leading core" of the working class that gave legitimacy to the state, and not vice versa.[168]

The party's operations, legitimately, were secret, taking place within a wild zone of power that was theoretically limitless in scope. Its members were committed, as part of party discipline, to keeping secrets and "observing the conspiracy" (*sobliudat konspiratsiiu*). Moreover, it was above the law.[169] Party members were explicitly outside of the jurisdiction of the laws, which were passed exclusively by the Supreme Soviet (which replaced the Congress of Soviets according to the 1936 constitution). At the same time, the party could issue policy "decrees" (*postanovleniia*), consigned by the party secretary and the head of Sovnarkom, that had the power of law. Sovnarkom as a state organization was in turn, at least on paper, under the power of the Supreme Soviet.[170] But who had power over the legitimate use of violence? Here the situation was complicated. The political police (NKVD) was a *state* organization, but it was used to fight counter-revolutionary activity, and that meant to fight the enemy as the party defined it.[171] To fulfill this pur-

tions and institutions find little space to develop, little air to breathe. The danger is suffocation—of private life, individual motivation, free literary and cultural expression, political debate, and popular initiatives. Moreover, the technological dimension of this society results in its own form of war machine, as socioeconomic transformation is conceived in military terms and a notion of social engineering treats human beings as material to be recast like metal (*pererabotaet'sia*), becoming, as Stalin said affirmatively, "little screws" in the great machine of society.[30]

In the constitution of nation-states, the executive is allowed quasi-dictatorial powers in times of war or "national emergency,"[31] just as the very conception of the party as the "dictatorship of the proletariat" implies such power to act against counterrevolutionary activities. Not all party struggles against opposing classes have been instances of party terror, just as not all national emergency powers could rightly be called state terror. And yet extra-

---

pose, it inherited the party's secrecy and its limitless terrain of action.[172] Its task was to protect the existence of the state *as* a revolutionary, worker's state.[173] This complex power arrangement set the stage for events to come.[174]

Because the Communist Party was the legitimating embodiment of the revolution, it was crucial that it remain above reproach. On the one hand, access to the party's limitless zone of power required limitless party obligation.[175] On the other hand, however, because of their privileged access to jobs, goods, and power, members of the *nomenklatura* became local elites, exposed to superhuman temptations to violate the criteria of their special calling.[176] The party was an ideal of which people always fell short, so that purification was necessary to provide for continued sanctity of party power above the law. There were therefore periodic purges (*chistki*) in order to maintain the "purity" (*chistota*) of the ranks. This process was not in itself terroristic. Being purged meant only expulsion from the party; it was

stipulated explicitly that one should not be dismissed from one's everyday job. What made people fear the purges was not the party, but falling out of the party's immunity and into the jurisdiction of law, as in some instances (not all, since violating party discipline was itself not a legal violation) expulsions were followed by arrest by the "secular authority" of the NKVD.[177]

In 1936, as one more extreme measure in a series of verification procedures, all old party cards were to be exchanged for new ones. It provided an occasion for inquiring into the purity of every member, and a "radical revival of the party's ideological mission."[178] What made this purge different from previous ones was the context. On August 19, 1936, sixteen high party officials were tried in Moscow for acts of terrorism. This "Trotskyite-Zinovievite Bloc" confessed to their crimes, and on August 24 they were shot. It was the first time the death penalty had been used against communists expelled from the party.[179] Prior to this, only "bour-

ordinary war powers can be invoked at any time, and, even when this requires procedures of debate and consent (democratic centralism within the party; the declaration of war or the voting of war credits by parliaments), once the state of war exists, the wild zone of power that it creates is a space in which the absolute obedience of the collective is demanded.

There is a special irony in the fact that both models of mass democracy, nation-state and revolutionary class, had their origins—what Walter Benjamin would have termed their ur-form—in the same historical event, the FRENCH REVOLUTION. Unlike Hegelian or Marxist philosophies of history, the conception of the ur-form presumes no continuum of historical development and no deterministic necessity as to the outcome. In our case, it means simply that the paradoxical logic of democratic sovereignty in the two models considered here can be discovered in the French Revolution in early, embryonic form. As "the first experiment with democracy," to cite

See page 9
HYPERTEXT

---

geois" class elements ("normal" enemies!) had been the victims of state terror. Now, every member was potentially at risk of being "unmasked" as a Trotskyite or wrecker, and with so much at stake the universal purging of party members that was under way, with every member of the party coming in with his or her card for questioning, took on a different intensity. At Novosibirsk in November 1936 a "subversive Trotskyite conspiracy" was unmasked of "Soviet-era" personnel in collusion with foreign industrialists and the Gestapo, and six of the defendants were shot, convicted of industrial "wrecking" in a manner vague enough to bring all unfortunate industrial occurrences under suspicion.[180] Industrial mishaps, previously described as "economic crimes," were now reinterpreted as intentional wrecking, a political crime of the utmost seriousness, a violation of article 58 of the criminal code that brought the charge of "counterrevolution."[181] Such a charge could not be forgiven. The enemy—the absolute enemy—was within the party itself,

hence party purges were no longer a merely internal concern. Only the greatest internal "vigilance" of unmasking could save the party; only the maximum quantity of arrests could save the revolutionary state.[182] At the top level, the party (Stalin himself as party secretary)[183] still had power over the NKVD (headed by Nikolai Ezhov since August 1936); but at the lower levels, the legitimate exercise of violence by the NKVD against "counterrevolutionaries" within the party put the latter under pressure to accuse its own members—or risk being unmasked by the NKVD itself.[184] Hence the dynamics of this terror which fed on itself, as any attempt by party members to halt it could be interpreted as an attempt to protect the enemy within by means of the party's extralegal status (the wreckers and spies *were* the party members who suppressed the internal attacks that led to unmasking),[185] and was thus grounds for the NKVD to take the matter in its own hands. Ironically, according to its internal logic, only Stalin could *stop* the terror. This he did,

François Furet, the French Revolution "invented a type of political discourse and practice by which we have been living ever since."[32] It was a utopian discourse of equality, and of the "people" as sovereign. But it also produced, as the two catastrophic forms of modern political life, revolutionary terror and mass-conscripted, nationalist war.

■

According to Hegel, the enemy is: "ethical difference [*die sittliche Differenz*] as an alien being that is to be negated [*als ein zu negierendes Fremdes*] in its living totality [*in seiner lebendigen Totalität*]." Hegel describes the "nothingness of the enemy [*das Nichts des Feindes*]" as the "opposite of the being of oppositions [*Gegenteil des Seins der Gegensätze*]," which implies the absolute character of the enemy. Carl Schmitt cites this passage from Hegel.[33] But his own definition is not so close to Hegel's as he would have us assume. Schmitt

---

abruptly, in late 1938, using Ezhov as the scapegoat and removing him from his post as People's Commissar of Internal Affairs, head of the NKVD. Ezhov was arrested and shot.

See page 22
TEXT **SPACE**   The conception of a world divided spatially seems to have been a distinctly European invention.[186] Beginning as far back as 1492 with the edict of Pope Alexander VI, lines were drawn, literally, to delineate which part of the globe "belonged" to which European sovereign power. This "jus publicum Europaeum" was the beginning of what Carl Schmitt calls "global linear thinking," the first *planetary* political imaginary. The New World of the Americas, along with Africa and Asia, entered into this spatial order in accord with their relationship to the European center. All lands either belonged to a European state or were declared, with extraordinary arrogance, "open spaces," "free to be occupied."[187] The real-world consequences of this declaration marked the history of humankind for half a millen-

nium. It is difficult to take solace in the fact that Eurocentrism, a global imaginary of unsurpassed brutality, needed ideological justification, the legitimating lie that Europe's violent exploitation was a civilizing process imposed on an uncivilized world—the assertion that this spatial domination was itself temporality, the relentless forward march of historical progress. European imperialism increased the wild zone of sovereign power so massively as to affect the entire non-European world.

The United States challenged Eurocentrism by adopting Europe's spatial principle as its own. Two aspects of the U.S. political imaginary were "urforms" in the sense that they anticipated later forms more generally. One was its systematic push westward in order to spread the progress it believed itself to embody by annexing what was referred to as "empty territory."[188] This was done in repeated violation of treaties with Indian tribes, the consequence of which was the near-genocide of these native people.[189] It prefigured in certain (if not all)

stresses the collective nature of the enemy, pointing out the difference between the two terms for enemy, *exthros* cf. *polemos* in ancient Greek, or *ini-
micus* cf. *hostis* in Latin.[34] Whereas the former terms refer to individual persons,
the latter (*polemos* and *hostis*) delineate the political enemy, the public enemy—which, as a collective term, is always an abstraction. You have nothing
against this enemy personally. It is a category within the logic of sovereign
power. Or, to use a different terminology, the enemy occupies the position
of the "other" within the imaginary political terrain. But in occupying this
position—and this is something Schmitt does not see—the enemy loses the
absolute character implied by Hegel's definition. We need to remind ourselves of Podoroga's important point that so long as the enemy stays in its
place, keeping the position allotted to it within the political imaginary, so
long, in short, as the enemy behaves like the enemy, it is not a threat in the
absolute sense. We need to go beyond Schmitt and develop a distinction be-

---

respects Hitler's push to the east to acquire *Lebens-raum* at the expense of an allegedly inferior "race."[190] The second was that by refusing to enter into European conflicts and by claiming that the Americas were not within the European terrain of politics, the United States's conception of the world challenged the Eurocentric spatial order funda-mentally. Because there could not be two planetary centers, this challenge resulted, in Schmitt's terms, in "spatial chaos,"[191] destroying the Eurocentric pic-ture without establishing any "coherent alterna-tive."[192] An alternative planetary imaginary was precisely what the Cold War ultimately provided—a decentered, global space, crossed by multiple boundaries of "containment"—although, given its logics of planetary destruction, the coherence of this new picture was dubious at best.

The United States brought a new abstraction to the political imaginary of global-linear thinking. The Monroe Doctrine of 1823 that proclaimed sovereignty over a "safety zone" 300 nautical miles

off both of its coasts was a line drawn in the open seas, an empty, mathematical space that, according to Schmitt, dissolved political strategy "into geom-etry."[193] This line was self-isolating, intended as a quarantine barrier against the illnesses of old Eu-rope (just as, later, imaginary lines were drawn against the virus of Bolshevism). Abstract lines grew to be so frequent a phenomenon in American po-litical life as to become obsessional. The presiden-tial campaign of 1844 was won by Polk on the basis of the slogan "Fifty-Four Forty or Fight!"—refer-ring to the latitude claimed by the United States (54° 40′) as the Oregon Territory's northern limit; Polk later settled with England on the 49th parallel, a straight-line extension of the Canada-America boundary to the western coast. The Mason-Dixon Line was to resolve the slavery issue by drawing a boundary at the latitude of 36° 30′ between the slave-holding South and the slave-free North. The 38th parallel became the purely geometric goal of United States policy in the Korean War.

tween two types of *political* enemy, allowing for the category of Hegel's "opposite of the being of oppositions," whose threat to the collective is on the metalevel, and who, by not behaving like the enemy, is truly dangerous, because it threatens the legitimating imaginary system *tout court*. There are then two levels, the normal, safe enemy who acts like the enemy as defined within one's own imaginary terrain, and the absolute enemy on the far side of the great political divide between the imaginary systems themselves. It is the absolute political enemy that threatens the existence of the collective not only (and perhaps not mainly) in a physical sense but, rather, in an ontological sense, because it challenges the very notion by which the identity of the collective has been formed. The absolute enemy becomes symbolic of absolute evil, against which no mercy is possible. To give an example from earlier European history, in the logic of medieval Christendom sinners are normal, safe enemies, whereas heretics who challenge the legitimacy of Christian dogma

---

HYPERTEXT SPACE

Such lines were not borders of mutual recognition between nations in the European continental sense. Rather, like the European colonial boundaries that were often drawn with only a vague notion of who lived inside them, they became the *creator* of difference, anticipating territorial sovereignty.[194] This uniquely abstract conception of the nation prevailed under Wilson's influence at the Paris Peace Conference, when representatives of the Allied Powers, sitting in 1919 in a room at Versailles (or later at Neuilly, St.-Germain, Trianon, and Sèvres), used maps and pencils to create "nations" from the complex ethnic regions of central Europe, altering profoundly the borders of Poland, Denmark, Belgium, Romania, Hungary, Yugoslavia, Czechoslovakia, Italy, Austria, Greece, and the former Ottoman Empire—as well as Germany and France.

If nineteenth-century European nationalists had argued that nations had the right to create states, in the American model states had the right to create nations. Because the United States was nei-

ther ethnically nor linguistically united at its founding, the collective became a nation ex post facto, by entering the territorial space in which the social contract applied. Assimilation of immigrants became a dominant theme of U.S. nation-building, producing a multiethnic, international proletariat *within* domestic borders. But class solidarity was not necessarily the result. In the early twentieth century racist and xenophobic rhetoric appealed to U.S. workers threatened by new immigrants, and national borders became their line of job defense. In the 1980s, such nationalism became common in capitalist countries, as the restructuring of the global economy threatened to undermine the welfare gains that workers had achieved. During the Cold War, the working classes within Western nations benefited economically from Western fears of Communism, winning political concessions at the level of nation-states. But global restructuring has caused these states to lose control over the economic system.[195] The new economic blocs—the

itself are the absolute enemy and cannot be tolerated even if they are peaceful, because heretics, by definition, cannot be peaceful.[35]

The analogy to the twentieth-century world is clear. For most of its duration, the models of mass-democratic sovereignty in East and West confronted each other as absolute enemies, because each political imaginary excluded the other's fundamental claim to legitimacy. The COLD WAR ENEMIES were deployed on an ontological divide, and what Churchill named the Iron Curtain became its geophysical manifestation. This boundary was defensive not only in a military sense, but in the conceptual sense that it prevented contamination from the imaginary perceptions held by the absolute "other." The boundary had a different meaning for each side, as we would expect. For the political imaginary of nation-states, it cordoned off socialism, which was perceived spatially by isolating it spatially, in order to prevent its spread to the "free world." For the political imaginary of class warfare, the

See page 2
HYPERTEXT

EEC, Japan-dominated Asia, United-States-dominated NAFTA—represent developments in spatial ordering motivated by interests often at odds with political and social democracy at the national level, challenging the traditional political imaginary in fundamental ways.

The future of the nation-state is by no means secure. If the United States and other governments become increasingly unwilling (or unable) to continue to honor the principles of the welfare state compromise between capitalists and workers, how will the "people" react? Moreover, who *are* the people in the new, globally oriented nation-state? If immigrant groups using the rhetoric of multiculturalism resist the traditional goal of assimilation, will the consequence be universal toleration regardless of nation-state boundaries, or renewed calls for ethnic purity within them? Will the spatial model of nation-state sovereignty survive not only the globalizing tendencies of our time but also domestic struggles against these tendencies? Is the

Balkanization created by ethnic hatred an atavistic return to an earlier era, or a portent of the century to come? The answers to these questions will determine what it means ultimately to have "won" the Cold War.

TIME   Zinoviev as head of the Comintern justified the Red Army's offensive against Poland in 1920 by arguing confidently that "old Europe was hurtling towards the proletarian revolution," and he asserted a fundamental distinction between "revolutionary" and "reactionary" interventions into the space of other nations in terms of time.[196] Likewise, Soviet jurists in the 1920s defended the invasion of Poland as one of the forms of class struggle that would give history a push, whereas the Allied intervention into Russia was an attempt to "stop the wheel of history."[197] Of course, the civil war that followed the Bolshevik Revolution was a spatial struggle, a "defense of the Socialist fatherland."[198] Under Trotsky's leadership, there was a militarization of

See page 22
TEXT

physical boundary was understood as providing a temporal bulwark, protecting the nascent socialist societies so that they could develop in history uncontaminated by the economic and social distortions of capitalism. Isolation was seen as a means whereby socialist regimes could remain autarchic and hence masters of their fate, providing TIME to catch up with the capitalist West in terms of production, while not falling back from the historical level that the political revolution had achieved. But in fact, the great divide served as well the unstated purpose of isolating the political imaginaries themselves, protecting each from being undermined by the logic of the other.

Now, it can be protested that all this is ideology. Indeed, it was a favorite claim of each side during the Cold War that the enemy which seemed to be operating in a radically different terrain was really acting within one's own terrain of the political imaginary. This was soothing and reassuring, because it normalized the enemy. Thus within the landscape of class war, the nationalist

---

HYPERTEXT TIME

that space. But when the anticipation of a European revolution was replaced by the "weakest link" theory (the argument that the proletariat in the underdeveloped countries was most strategically situated to break the imperialist system), and when "socialism in one country" was proclaimed to be economically feasible as well as a political reality, *time* became the overriding concern.

In his report to the Congress of Soviets in 1921, Lenin admitted: "We imagined . . . that future developments would take a more simple, more direct form," but instead, "a strange situation" had developed, whereby the Revolution occurred and was possible to sustain in Russia, "one of the most backward and very weak states."[199] Lenin's response to this anomaly in history was to picture "two worlds" that, while they might temporarily be distinguished geographically, actually referred to two stages of history, "the old world of capitalism that is in a state of confusion . . . and the rising new world, which is still very weak, but which will grow, for it is invinci-

ble."[200] Here already is the origin of the discourse of "peaceful coexistence," never justified as a territorial division between the capitalist and socialist world, but always as a temporary, transitional situation—to use Lenin's words, a "certain unstable equilibrium."[201] Faced with this gap between the political vanguard and historically "backward" economic conditions, Lenin's New Economic Policy (NEP) was one of compromise with peasants and entrepreneurs during an "epoch" (not a *space*) of retreat, justified precisely because Communists could claim that "time is working on our side."[202] Lenin's position on economic development, as well as on the nationalities question, was to tolerate the gap between politics and socioeconomic conditions, encouraging a "breathing space" in which political culture might be articulated and the institutions of civil society might have time to develop. Stalin's policy, in contrast, was to force a closing of this gap. His policy for economic development was itself a declaration of war (see COLD WAR ENEMIES).

conception of states was seen as an ideological displacement that concealed the true locus of power, i.e., the international capitalist class. "Imperialist" nation-states were so called because they acted in the interest of this class. Correspondingly, the other side, the side of nation-states, gladly viewed the USSR as a nation, indeed as a Russian, imperialist nation, acting in its own self-interest.

Regardless of what truth there is in these claims—that the state has acted in class, not national interests, or that the party has acted in national, not class interests—(and there is no doubt a good deal of truth in both of them), what I have been arguing here is that they cannot provide the basis for legitimate sovereign action; and legitimacy is fundamental to any modern, mass-democratic regime. Thus Brezhnev could no more have justified the invasion of Czechoslovakia in 1968 in terms of Soviet (much less Russian) national interest than Johnson could have justified the war in Vietnam in terms of protecting the property interests of the capitalist class. Moreover,

---

There is no doubt that Civil War imagery was resurrected by Stalin during the First Five Year Plan, and that, as Fitzpatrick argues, "War Communism was the point of reference if not the model for many of the policies associated with the industrialization drive and collectivization."[203] But what needs to be noted is that by transposing the discourse of civil war—a political zone—onto the terrain of economic development, Stalin was doing something decidedly different (if not altogether new).[204] He militarized the space of historical transition and turned the terrain of economic development and peasant collectivization itself into a war zone—a "wild zone" for the deployment of the machinery of absolute power. It was not a question, as in war communism, of mobilizing the economy for war, but of mobilizing the economy *as* war. Moreover, it was a war against time.

The rapid industrialization of the First Five Year Plan was conceived as historical "acceleration" (*uskorenie*). Lewin writes: "The pace and violence of

the changes were breathtaking," as no one was positioned in society in 1938 where they had been in 1928; at the same time, "the sense of urgency in the whole upheaval is baffling: the pace imposed suggests a race against time, as if those responsible for the country's destinies felt they were running out of history."[205] Under Stalin, "speeding up by force became the cure-all."[206] Any proposal for "slowing the tempo" (*gromozhenie*) of economic production became tantamount to counterrevolution.[207] The present was an obstacle to be overcome, a continual sacrifice for the sake of the communist future. Mikhail Heller has described the concept of the Five Year Plan, initiated by Stalin, as the "nationalization of time" whereby the head of state became time's master. Historical progress was forced dictatorially by the Plan. The sovereign agent had absolute power not only over material resources, but also over time.[208]

If Stalin could order time to speed up, he could also slow it down—or stop it completely, once "so-

the discourse of legitimation *generates* power as well as rationalizing it after the fact. The Reagan policy in Nicaragua of arming the counterrevolutionaries in order to prevent the "spread" of communism into "our front yard" was, arguably, based less on class interests than on reproducing the spatial-imaginary terms of the Cold War itself.[36] The fact that he had difficulty winning popular support for this policy was an indication that the reproduction of these terms already faced a crisis. And of course the economic realities in Soviet society that belied the continued talk of being in the vanguard of history demonstrated a parallel crisis of legitimacy within the class model of sovereignty. Note that these crises were not caused by the enemy, but by conditions immanent to each system on its own.

This brings me to my concluding point, and it is a materialist, indeed a Marxist one—so let us allow Marx to have the last word. Both political imaginaries that we have been considering on a theoretical level, as ideal

---

HYPERTEXT TIME

cialism" had been achieved.[209] The discourse of time was a field for the exercise of sovereign power, that was the important point. Thus, in March 1930, Stalin gave a speech calling for a slowdown in the collectivization drive which had caused famine, and which he now blamed on overenthusiastic party members who had moved too quickly and become "dizzy with success." Yet scarcely a year later (February 1931) he stated in a speech to industrial managers: "It is sometimes asked whether it is not possible to slow down the tempo somewhat, to put a check on the movement. No, comrades, it is not possible! . . . To slacken the tempo would mean falling behind. And those who fall behind get beaten. . . . We are fifty or a hundred years behind the advanced countries. We must make good this distance within ten years. Either we do so, or we will be crushed."[210]

Translating the spatial struggle between city and country into the temporal discourse of class struggle justified persecution of the peasants as "people

from the past." All peasant resistance was defined as class resistance that slowed down the course of history, and "in this way, the state 'kulakized' the countryside and could therefore wage war on the *entire* peasantry according to the 'iron laws' of history."[211] The national question, too, was transposed into a discourse of time, as backward cultures and ethnic groups came under attack as vestiges of an earlier era. In the 1920s it was still possible to argue that the indigenous peoples of the north and of Central Asia had elements of classlessness and "primitive communism" that might make their transition to socialism easier.[212] But by the 1930s, their whole culture was seen as hostile to revolution and historical progress. The small "vanguard" of indigenous leaders trained by the party provided only a tenuous hold against the "backwardness" that, like a "swamp," threatened to swallow up everyone.[213] "The advanced peoples are tearing along in the fast locomotive of history. . . . At the same time, the backward people have to 'race like the wind' . . . in

types, when considered on the empirical level, as they have actually developed historically, contained an inherent contradiction, a destabilizing tension, a threat to legitimacy that was not caused by the enemy "other." This tension had its source, rather, in the fact that *each* system of political imaginary was deployed within economic and social conditions that were, at least potentially, in fundamental contradiction to that system. Thus: the Communist Party, the self-proclaimed vanguard of history, attempted to sustain power within an economic system that by its own definition repeatedly fell behind industrial development in the West. Thus: the nation-state system attempted to maintain its hegemony within a capitalist global economy that increasingly threatened to escape the control of nation-state political units. If the era of the Cold War is over, it is perhaps less because one side has "won" than because the legitimation of each political discourse found itself fundamentally challenged by material developments themselves.

---

order to catch up."[214] The logic of this vision was self-evident: "If the whole of the USSR, in the words of Comrade Stalin, needs ten years to run the course of development that took Western Europe fifty to a hundred years, then the small peoples of the north, in order to catch up with the advanced nations of the USSR, must, during the same ten years, cover the road of development that took the Russian people one thousand years to cover."[215] The equation of revolutionary time with economic modernization implied necessarily the obliteration of indigenous cultures, as it did that of the traditional peasant class.[216]

During *glasnost'* a serious challenge to the discourse of "development" came from intellectual and political spokespersons for the indigenous groups, who criticized publicly the economic and ecological disasters caused by attempts at modernization that were totally inappropriate for their cultures.[217] This exposure went together with a call for the "restoration of sovereignty" usurped by the party/state to "the people" (*narod*) as its legitimate source.[218] By questioning the Soviet imaginary of time it weakened the legitimacy of the Soviet Union.

The connection between cultural time and political revolution was central to the Soviet experience. It is dealt with extensively in the next chapter.

2.1 Statue of Danton by Nikolai Andreev, Moscow, 1919. The image is from a propaganda film about Lenin.

II

DREAMWORLDS OF

HISTORY

A Note on Method

Section 2.1 assembles historical facts of Bolshevik cultural politics around the armature of revolutionary time to show how this structuring of the imaginary field caused perceptual distortions within it.

Section 2.2 accepts as given the shattering of that time structure. It rescues the past in fragments, accessible to us in disparate images rather than the total picture, in order to challenge the accepted version of the twentieth century and reopen the case.

CHAPTER 2

ON TIME

2.1

REVOLUTIONARY TIME

A revolution is certainly the most authoritarian thing there is;
it is the act whereby one part of the population imposes its will upon
the other part by means of rifles, bayonets and cannon—
authoritarian means, if such there be at all.
—Friedrich Engels, "On Authority"

In some respects, a revolution is a miracle.
—V. I. Lenin, 1921

Several months after the October Revolution, Anatolii Lunacharskii, newly appointed as head of the People's Commissariat of Enlightenment (Narkompros), reported to a meeting of artists and sculptors: "I have just come from Vladimir Ilich [Lenin]. Once again he has had one of those fortunate and profoundly exciting ideas with which he has so often shocked and delighted us. He intends to decorate Moscow's squares with statues and monuments to revolutionaries and the great fighters for socialism."[1] Lenin had told him that this plan for "monumental propaganda" was for long his cherished idea.[2] It was to be public art that wrote history onto urban space. The masses would *see* history as they moved through the city. The revolution entered the phenomenal world of the everyday.

Innovative in Lenin's idea was the adaptation of a nationalist art form for socialist ends. Whereas in the nineteenth century monument-building became an obsession of nation-states as a means of celebrating (and creating) their own particular pasts, Lenin's monuments evoked an *inter*national heritage. The twenty-one Russians on the list of approved "fighters for socialism" included many assassins or would-be assassins of royalty, not the category usually memorialized by national regimes. There were nineteen Europeans, half of them French, among them a cluster of Revolutionary heroes: Danton, Marat, and Babeuf; later, Robespierre was added. Cultural figures were among the "revolutionaries," including Heinrich Heine and Frédéric Chopin. Paul Cézanne's name was seriously considered.[3]

Material was in short supply.[4] Statues were hastily built out of plaster or cement, replacing monuments from the tsarist era that were just as hastily disassembled.[5] Time mattered. The meaning of history was being constructed. If the Bolshevik victory in Petrograd was to be more than an urban coup, it needed to assume the mantle of sovereign legitimacy presently claimed by the provisional government, established after the February Revolution and abdication of the tsar. The Russian people had already been proclaimed "free citizens" in the Western, bourgeois-democratic sense; the "new era" had allegedly begun.[6] When the Bolsheviks led the crowd that forcefully evicted that government, headed by Kerenskii, from the tsar's Winter Palace, nothing less than world history was called upon to legitimate the act. The October events were to be understood in this sublime context, not merely as a case of catching up with the West but of superseding it, advancing the world-revolutionary tradition to its highest culmination. Without this interpretation, the palace storming was vandalism, and the overthrow of the provisional government was treason.[7]

It is history that legitimates political revolution, at least since Hegel and including Marx.[8] The suturing of history's narrative discourse transforms the violent rupture of the present into a continuity of meaning. One has to imagine the tenuousness of the situation. With the expected workers' revolution in Europe delayed indefinitely, Lenin counted the days for proof that the Bolshevik victory could outlast the revolutionary Paris Commune of 1871. Why, when even fellow Marxists believed a period of bourgeois democracy in Russia was a historical necessity, should the Bolshevik splinter group gain hegemony, not only of the political discourse but of the cultural discourse as well? Mass support existed for the October events, but it was not of a single mind. Millennialists, avant-gardists, and utopian dreamers of every sort were eager to interpret the revolutionary future as their own. Bolshevism needed to speak for all of these people, structuring their desires inside a historical continuum that, at the same time, contained their force. In the process of being inserted into the temporal narrative of revolutionary history, the utopian dimension of a wide variety of discourses was constrained and reduced.

2.2 *Memorial Obelisk for the Great Socialist Thinkers and Revolutionaries,* Alexander Garden, outside the Kremlin Wall, Moscow.

The obelisk was first erected in 1913 to commemorate the sixth jubilee of the Romanov dynasty. It was transformed into a Bolshevik monument by engraving on it these names: Marx, Engels, Liebknecht, Lasalle, Bebel, Campanella, Meslier, Winstanley, Thomas More, Saint-Simon, Vaillant, Fourier, Jaurès, Proudhon, Bakunin, Chernyshevskii, Lavrov, Mikhailovskii, Plekhanov.

2.3 Konstantin Iuon, *The New Planet,* 1921. (color plate 2)

*We people are the children of the sun, the bright
source of life; we are born of the sun and will van-
quish the murky fear of death.*
—Maxim Gorky, *Children of the Sun* (1905)[9]

Lenin told the British science fiction writer H. G. Wells, who interviewed him in the Kremlin in 1920, that if life were discovered on other
planets, revolutionary violence would no longer be necessary: "Human
ideas—he told Wells—are based on the scale of the planet we live in.
They are based on the assumption that the technical potentialities, as
they develop, will never overstep 'the earthly limit.' If we succeed in
making contact with the other planets, all our philosophical, social and
moral ideas will have to be revised, and in this event these potentialities will become limitless and will put an end to violence as a necessary means of progress."[10]

Utopian discourses abounded in Russia (and among Russians in exile) in the decade before the Revolution. It was, then as now, the turn of a century, and the pulse of culture was an alternating current of imagined endings and new beginnings. In a country still inadequately connected by rail, flying machines real and imagined were invested with transformative social meaning. The country's World War I bomber was named after Ilia Moromets, the Russian fairy-tale giant who awoke after forty years in possession of colossal strength.[11] With the sudden popularity of science fiction translated from the West (works by Edward Bellamy, Jules Verne, H. G. Wells), leading Russian writers began to create their own other-planetary worlds, as the first successes of airborne flight propelled imagination into outer space. Interplanetary travel was a preferred form of social utopian expression. Aleksandr Bogdanov's two-volume epic, *Red Star* (1908) and *Engineer Menni* (1913), anticipated history by describing a Marxist-communist society existing on Mars.[12] Maxim Gorky developed a theory of god-building (*bogostroitel'stvo*) whereby the masses would become God, creators of miracles and immortal.[13] The prewar generation discovered and made famous the writings of Nikolai Fedorov, a nineteenth-century librarian whose cosmological speculations predicted an immortal humankind comprised of the technologically resurrected bodies of the dead, inhabiting a socially harmonious interplanetary space.[14] Fedorov envisioned a moral universe transformed through social-utopian applications of science (cloud-seeding, solar heat, travel by electromagnetic energy). Among his supporters were a number of intellectuals, including Konstantin Tsiolkovskii, who became the founding scientist of Soviet rocketry.[15]

All kinds of social fantasies were sparked by the new industrial technologies. The futurist poetry of Aleksei Gastev, a metal worker and political agitator before the war, described with passionate enthusiasm the new industrial machines as an animate force with human beings their collectivized extension.[16] Vasilii Kamenskii, who was himself an aerobatics pilot, composed "ferro-concrete poems" out of words suspended like airplanes in space that influenced Kazimir Malevich's suprematist paintings of geometric forms suspended in space.[17] Artists of the avant-garde gave expression to the changed anthropology of modern life in forms and rhythms that left the perceptual apparatus of the old world triumphantly behind. The Bolshevik Revolution appropriated these utopian impulses by affirming them and channeling their energy into the political project. Liberating visions became legitimating ones, as fantasies of movement through space were translated into temporal movement, reinscribed onto the historical trajectory of revolutionary time.

The case of the artistic avant-garde is particularly illuminating, because it was here that the political and cultural definitions of revolution became most visibly, if problematically, intertwined.[18] As a movement, Russian avant-garde art predated the Revolution, which ended its bohemian status by granting it official recognition. These artists heralded

2.4 Vasilii Kamenskii, *Shchukin's Palace: Ferro-Concrete Poem*, 1914 (first published in V. Burliuk and D. Burliuk, *Tango with Cows* [Moscow, 1914]). In the center: "Picture palace S. I. Shchukin." Then, eight sections of autonomous words and phrases, including: "Matisse / Luxemburg Gardens / Pikas [Picasso] / peace / air words / light music / youths side by side / fragrant days / staircase / Arabian cafe / Cézanne," etc.

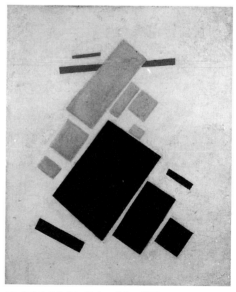

2.5 Kazimir Malevich, *Airplane Flying*, 1915.

2.6 Vladimir Tatlin, *Counter-Relief,* 1914–1915.

2.7 Kazimir Malevich, paintings hung in "The Last Futurist Exhibition, 0.10," Petrograd, 1915–1916. *Black Square* is at the top of the room corner (in the position normally reserved for a religious icon in Russian homes). *Airplane Flying* is in the bottom row, right.

the "new." But their conceptions of time were not limited to "history" in Lenin's sense. The often-cited 1913 "Manifesto of Russian Futurists and Rayonists [Rayists]" praised the greatness of the present epoch, "one that has known no equal in the entire history of the world," in terms of "the whole brilliant style of modern times—our trousers, jackets, shoes, trolleys, cars, airplanes, railways, grandiose steamships,"[19] objects in motion that "embody a mass of moments in time" (in Malevich's words),[20] rather than political actions that progress *through* time. When the avant-garde proclaimed "The future is our only goal,"[21] they were expressing a desire to break radically from past art in its traditional forms, but what was to come remained an open category. Indeed, the artworks were themselves openings in both a temporal and a spatial sense. Vladimir Tatlin's prerevolutionary "counterreliefs" were objects composed of metal and wood hung unframed as "real materials in real space" in order to eliminate the separation of art from life and destroy the "perfect, private . . . and eternal world of the painting."[22] If Tatlin celebrated the forms and materials of modern objects for their own sake, Malevich sought to express what was eternal within them. The latter boasted of having transcended space, advancing toward eternity rather than toward any temporally located goal. "Hurry up and shed the hardened skin of centuries, so that you can catch up with us more easily,"[23] he wrote in 1915, the year his pathbreaking geometrical painting *Black Square* was exhibited in the "Last Futurist Exhibition, 0.10."[24] But it was not along a linear course of history that he was racing. Rather, it was into a realm of metaphysical essences intuited out of the new technologies and urban perceptions, and consisting of pure forms and color masses situated within mystico-utopian geometries of space. Malevich's support for the Bolshevik Revolution did not alter his commitment to the "freedom" of "non-objectivism," which he called suprematism, as his paintings of squares developed systematically from black, to red, to the extreme-minimalist *White Square on White Background* of 1918.[25] He understood these artistic forms as going beyond "our endless progress" into an extraterritorial realm.[26] As he claimed in 1919: "I have torn through the blue lampshade of color limitation and come out into the white. After me comrade aviators sail into the chasm—I have set up the semaphores of suprematism. . . . Infinity is before you."[27]

The "time" of the cultural avant-garde is not the same as that of the vanguard party.[28] These artists' practices interrupted the continuity of perceptions and estranged the familiar, severing historical tradition through the force of their fantasy. Progress for the early Russian modernists meant stepping out of the frame of the existing order—whether toward the "beautiful East," back to the "primitive," or through to the "eternal," no matter.[29] The effect was to rupture the continuity of time, opening it up to new cognitive and sensory experiences. In contrast, the party submitted to a historical cosmology that provided no such freedom of movement. Bolshevism's claim to know the course of history in its totality presumed a "science" of the future that encouraged revolutionary politics to dictate to art. Culture was to be operationalized. Its products would serve "progress" as the latter's visual representation. Once a certain cosmology of history was lodged in the imagination, even artists came to feel that it could not be otherwise. Artistic revolution came to be distinguished from political revolution, of which it was merely symptomatic. Constrained by the historical goal, revolutionary culture became sedate, conserving a past that appeared to lead meaningfully into the present, eschewing new primitivisms that blurred the line of progress, appealing to the masses by means of conventional art forms in order to mobilize them for movement "forward" in time.

The story, of course, is far more complicated than this condensed account implies. It was more than a decade before conventional art triumphed in the Soviet Union. Even then, at the height of Stalin's power, there was never a monolithic art or architectural style.[30] But the special position of the party as the vanguard of history meant that the possibilities, through an open temporality, of an *ungoverned* cultural revolution as the path to

2.8 Boris Korolev, maquette for a statue of Karl Marx, 1919 (left), to be compared with the statue of Marx by Aleksandr Matveev (right), erected in Petrograd, 1918.

Korolev's statue was never executed, although there were no regulations of style for the monuments built under Lenin's proposal. Korolev was a codirector of the Moscow Union of Sculptors to which Tatlin, as head of Moscow's Narkompros, assigned the task of awarding commissions for the monuments, so that his proposal had authority behind it. The stylistic radicality of his futuro-cubist design cannot be denied, but its very strength gives palpable evidence of the nonidentity between the two movements, cultural avant-garde and political vanguard. Historical progress toward socialism could not be read easily into this statue, and the fact that its subject was Karl Marx hardly made the politics of the situation less problematic.[31]

a new society became one of the dead ends of history. Like so many of history's failures, it merits serious consideration, as it is not always the most progressive social practices that succeed in time, but rather those that impose themselves most violently.

■

There are countless possible stories about Bolshevik revolutionary culture, and many have been told. While heroes and villains abound in these narrations, few have engaged this site of the temporary convergence of political and cultural avant-gardes in order to rethink both art and politics in a revolutionary mode. Here the concept of time may be useful, providing a key to unlock the antagonistic embrace of art and politics in this century—the repeating scenarios of art succumbing to politics or, alternatively, politics aestheticized as art—freeing both to relate differently to one another. Let us look at the historical events in more detail.

The early Soviet state supported a variety of artistic tendencies resulting, indeed, in an "ambiguous pluralization" of intellectual life.[32] Proletarian cultural organizations—theater workshops, art studios, and literary circles—had been founded along with militias and workers' councils at the factory and local levels before the Revolution. In 1917 these groups were centralized as Proletkult under the Marxist intellectual leadership of Bogdanov, but this organization was and remained separate from both the party and the state.[33] Funding was provided for a variety of individual artists. The mystico-primitivist Marc Chagall was appointed director of the Vitebsk art school despite the apolitical nature of his paintings, which depicted Judaic and folkloric themes.[34] The painter and musician Mikhail Matiushin received state funding while continuing to paint nature-inspired, abstract canvases emphasizing color and structural clarity that were, he claimed, a form of optical science.[35] Pavel Filonov founded his own school, "analytical painting," depicting forms of the material world and its organic processes in an effort to make visible what was in principle invisible, while affirming his loyalty to the Bolshevik regime due to his sincere belief in the "democratization of the arts" that Marxists proclaimed—although what this meant was far from clear.[36]

Fitzpatrick has written: "All Marxist intellectuals agreed, without even thinking about it, that proletarian culture had little or nothing to do with observable popular lower-class habits and cultural tastes."[37] But that fact did not translate into consensus concerning a positive program. Although there was a self-conscious search for proletarian recruits, the artists remained a separate group, or better, separate groups, endorsing the criterion of "social usefulness" (which distinguished their work from the bourgeois program of *l'art pour l'art*) without toeing any common artistic line. Among those vying for cultural hegemony (and state funding), there were key differences in

2.9 Marc Chagall, *Above the Village,* 1917–1918.

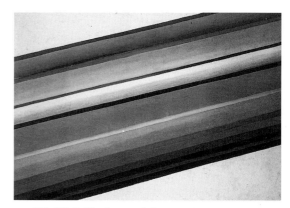

2.10 Mikhail Matiushin, *Movement in Space,* 1918.

2.11 Boris Iakovlev, *Transport Is Being Laid,* 1923.

2.12 Nikolai Nikonov, *Entry of the Red Army in 1920 into Krasnoiarsk*, 1923. "Our civic duty before mankind is to set down, artistically and documentarily, the revolutionary impulse of this great moment in history. We will depict the present day: the life of the Red Army, the workers, the peasants, the revolutionaries, and the heroes of labor." Declaration of AKhRR, 1922.

2.13 Pavel Filonov, *The Formula of the Petrograd Soviet*, 1920–21. "Phenomena such as AKhRR or the Proletkult campaigns are nothing more than amateur arts and crafts or swoops by partisan cavalry. You have to operate with art, to conceive its organization in the same way as with heavy industry or the Red Army, and you should operate with it according to an integrated state plan." Pavel Filonov, ca. 1922.

intellectual position and hence in artistic practice. The AKhRR (Association of Artists of Revolutionary Russia) was a large umbrella organization of easel painters founded in 1922 in opposition to the avant-garde's rejection of representational art. Its expressed goal was to document the "revolutionary impulse of this great moment of history" by depicting themes of industrialization, the October Revolution, and the Civil War.[38] Connecting to the nineteenth-century populist tradition of the *Peredvizhniki* (itinerants), these artists adhered from the beginning to a "realist" style of easel painting, defended in the postrevolutionary era for its accessibility to the masses (*massovost'*) and providing a line of continuity between the prerevolutionary past and the socialist realism of the 1930s.[39] But even AKhRR art differed widely in style, from Boris Iakovlev's quasi-impressionist depiction of trains and tracks in the greatly acclaimed 1923 painting *Transport Is Being Laid,* to the propagandistic depiction by Nikolai Nikonov that same year of the *Entry of the Red Army in 1920 into Krasnoiarsk.*[40]

As for the artists of the original avant-garde, the very liveliness of their intellectual debates after the Revolution, publicized in manifestos that circulated in journals like *Iskusstvo kommuny* (Art of the Commune) and *Lef* (Left Front of the Arts), led to shifting positions and multiple approaches.[41] The rivalry between Malevich and Tatlin that dated back to the prerevolutionary period was not merely personal but based on different ideas of artistic truth.[42] Just what constituted "communist" artistic practice was an issue fiercely debated among the master artists of the avant-garde and their students. They formed schools that included the suprematist-oriented UNOVIS group (Affirmers of the New Art) founded by Malevich and Lissitzky in Vitebsk in 1920;[43] the constructivist group founded in 1921 by Aleksandr Rodchenko and Varvara Stepanova at INKhUK (Institute of Artistic Culture) in Moscow;[44] various groups in the architecture, ceramics, metalwork, and textile faculties at Moscow's VKhUTEMAS (Higher Artistic-Technical Workshops, which replaced the State Free Art Studios in 1920); artists at Petrograd's GINKhUK (State Institute of Artistic Culture) directed by Nikolai Punin and later Malevich (where Tatlin and Filonov also taught); and the antihierarchical, masterless OBMOKhU (Society for Young Artists) at Moscow's First Free State Art Studios, whose members specialized in posters and agitational design, working as a group "without a supervisor" in order, in their words, "to combat the artists in authority who exploit young talents."[45]

Debates among the "futurists," as Lenin called all of these experimental groups, were waged on numerous issues, but they shared a general tendency in their move away from art—particularly away from oil painting—and into "life," the lived experience of the everyday. They understood their work not as documenting the revolution but as realizing it, serving (and also leading) the proletariat in the active building of a new society. Constructivists, suprematists, and others of the avant-garde turned to "production art," applying their earlier formal and technical innovations to the design of everyday objects and architectural spaces that the masses would produce and use.[46] Although production art was variously practiced, it provided the sense of a shared political task.[47] "The proletariat will create new houses, new streets, new objects of everyday life," wrote Nikolai Punin as early as 1918: "Art of the proletariat is not a holy shrine where things are lazily regarded, but work, a factory which produces new artistic things."[48] Vladimir Maiakovskii spoke of making "the streets . . . our brushes and the squares our palettes."[49]

The avant-garde turned to commercial and useful forms such as fabric design, children's books, journal covers, advertisements, theater sets, porcelain design, photo- and cine-montage. The UNOVIS group, which described themselves as collective creators of a "new utilitarian world of things," was commissioned by the city of Vitebsk to apply suprematist design to signboards, street decorations, buildings, interior decors, trams, and even ration cards.[50] Lissitzky recruited the suprematist square as protagonist in a children's book. Popova applied it to costume design. Tatlin designed and produced workers' clothing (a coat and a suit) in five variants and an economical oven, establishing contacts with the Novyi Lessner factory in Petrograd to develop his idea of the "artist-constructor."[51] The constructivists' program of 1921 stated explicitly that artists should enter the factory. Rodchenko wrote: "All new approaches to art arise from technology and engineering and move toward organization and construction"; "real construction is utilitarian necessity."[52]

In the process of championing the revolution, the avant-garde artists were redefining it as their own accomplishment. This entailed, significantly, an appropriation of the meaning of revolutionary time. Tatlin claimed that the "events of 1917 in the social field were already brought about in our art in 1914" when "material, volume, and construction" were made its "basis."[53] Lissitzky went so far as to declare that communism, which had "set human labour on the throne," would have to "remain behind," because its reign of labor would be overtaken by those marching under suprematism's "square pennant of creativity."[54] Malevich claimed for his UNOVIS group the status of a "party" in art shadowing the official one, with UNOVIS branches in other art schools both domestic and abroad, and with his own Vitebsk school as the "Central Creative Committee."[55] The slippage in the meaning of words borrowed from the discourse of the political vanguard and applied to that of artistic practice was a strategy for gaining power in terms of the new idiom of cultural hegemony. The avant-garde's revolutionary enthusiasm threatened the political vanguard because it challenged the latter on its own discursive ground.[56] But even the boldest among the artists acquiesced to a chronological perception of revolution that acknowledged that the party had set the terms of the debate.

Working Clothes for Actor No. 7
1921
Gouache, India ink, varnish

2.14 Liubov Popova, *Working Clothes for Actor no. 7*, 1921, for Meierkhold's production of Fernand Crommelynck, *Le Cocu magnifique* (The Magnificent Cuckold), State Institute of Theatrical Art, Moscow, 1922.

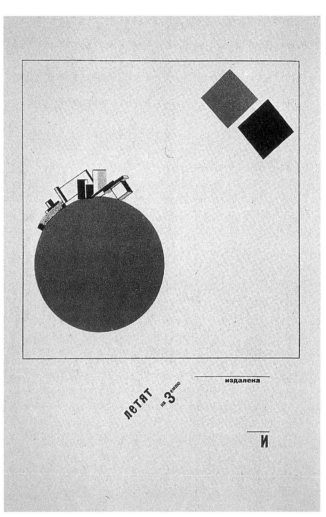

2.15 El Lissitzky, illustration from the children's book *The Story of Two Squares,* 1920: "They fly to earth from far away."

2.16 Vladimir Tatlin, *Everyday Clothes,* one of five variants, from the newspaper *Novyi Byt,* 1923.

2.17 Liubov Popova, textile design with truncated triangles, 1923–1924.

2.18 Aleksandr Rodchenko, advertisement for Trekhgornoe beer, 1923.

2.19 Kazimir Malevich, design for a teapot, 1923 (reproduction early 1970s).

2.20 Aleksei Kadakov, literacy poster, 1920. "An illiterate is a blind man. Everywhere failure and misfortune await him."

In 1920–1921, Lenin campaigned to "quash" independent cultural organizations such as Proletkult (which had become a mass movement of half a million during the Civil War) because it "sought to operate autonomously, beyond the bounds of the party," and he expressed a "growing impatience" with avant-garde movements of "futurist" art which had infiltrated Proletkult groups.[57] I am arguing that Lenin's hostility was not so much a matter of taste as one of time.[58] Lenin shared with the avant-garde artists the elitist conception that a minority would be in "advance" of the rest of the population and hence would need to lead them. And he was a maverick among Marxists in his belief that political movements could speed up the course of history.[59] But this voluntarism only increased his sense of the constraining force of history when it came to cultural matters. In the wake of the devastations of civil war, the logic of Lenin's position was straightforward. The tasks most pressing in culture were mass literacy, technical training, and political education—particularly for the majority, peasant class. In this context, the projects of the avant-garde could indeed appear politically indulgent. As for the Proletkult groups, their impeccably Marxist commitment to the factory workers was to his mind naive, as was their optimism regarding the degree of mass enlightenment. In 1922 Lenin wrote in the margins of an article defending Proletkult: "but the peasants? . . . are the peasants building locomotives?"[60] And regarding the alleged supremacy of "intellectuals, artists and engineers" within the proletariat, he wrote scoffingly, "arch-fiction."[61] But his logic only underscored the temporal paradox that had plagued him from the beginning, the fact that this Marxist revolution, historically the most modern, most vanguard of events, had taken place in what he himself believed was one of the most economically backward countries in Europe. It led the Bolshevik regime to endorse a policy of economic modernization as the very definition of revolution. Only by speeding up this modernizing process could the embarrassing gap between the economic meaning of time and the political meaning of time be obliterated. By the end of the Civil War, after a brief period of social experimentation and despite the temporary concessions of NEP to private enterprise (that of the peasants in particular), industrial modernization *was* the Leninist meaning of "constructing socialism." All other definitions—democratic control (proposed by the Workers' Opposition), popular participation (proposed by the Kronstadt rebels), cultural creativity (proposed by Bogdanov as head of Proletkult), human self-realization (proposed by Lunacharskii as Commissar of Enlightenment)—were dismissed as secondary, criticized as left-wing infantilism, or condemned as downright counterrevolutionary.[62]

With a remarkably even hand, until his resignation from the position of Commissar of Enlightenment in 1929, Lunacharskii negotiated between the party and the various artistic groups, ensuring for the artists a continued space of creative freedom. The state organizations of Narkompros controlled all aspects of artistic culture, including art education (through admissions policies and teaching appointments); museum purchases (through the Museum Office of Narkompros);[63] galleries and exhibitions (within the Soviet Union and abroad);[64] art journals (through the state publishing house Gosizdat);[65] and commissions for every kind of specific project, from monumental statues to literacy posters, street decorations, and interior decors. And yet despite this enormous state control, diversity flourished among contentious and independent-minded artistic groups, creating, de facto, a cultural pluralism that went against the epistemology of the party. Taylor describes this as the "central dilemma of art and literature under Bolshevism": "Very many aesthetic programmes claimed correspondence to the Bolshevik world-view; and yet there was nothing in Bolshevik doctrine—nor for that matter in Marx and Engels—that encouraged the simultaneous existence of many 'socialist' styles."[66] The genial if unintended result of Lunacharskii's leadership was that, by making political commitment more important than artistic style, he encouraged every kind of artistic group to compete with the others in demonstrating that *it* was the authentic one, in terms of being politically revolutionary, culturally proletarian, and historically progressive.[67] The result was to ensure that all groups, no matter what kind of *art* they produced, were united in producing cultural legitimation for the Bolshevik regime.

In practice, then, as head of the state institution of Narkompros, Lunacharskii was pluralistic. But in policy statements, speaking as a party member, he took the Leninist position.[68] Art was to provide inspiration for the socialist project of industrial modernization, but was not a replacement for it.[69] In 1920, just when Lissitzky was making the extreme claim that suprematism would surpass communism in world history, Lunacharskii wrote that art would remain "art" in the traditional sense, with the classics of the European past providing the foundation for "creating purely proletarian art forms and institutions."[70] Futurism and suprematism were corralled and brought back into line, specifically "the line of development of European art" that began with impressionism.[71]

In 1921 Lunacharskii addressed the Communist International in terms that already anticipated the socialist realism of the 1930s:

The proletariat will also continue the art of the past, but will begin from some healthy stage, like the Renaissance. . . . If we are talking of the masses, the natural form of their art will be the traditional and classical one, clear to the point of transparency, resting . . . on healthy convincing realism and on eloquent, transparent symbolism in decorative and monumental forms.[72]

What "time" could art have in this understanding? Art might develop within history, it might express eternal aesthetic forms throughout history, it might propagate "history" as propaganda, it might provide visual models for history in the form of the new man or designs for the new society. But artistic practice could no longer attempt to disrupt the continuum of history as defined and led by the party. It could not challenge the temporality of the political revolution which, as the locomotive of history's progress, invested the party with the sovereign power to force mass compliance in history's name.[73] Hence the lost opportunity: the temporal interruption of avant-garde practice *might have continued* to function as a criticism of history's progression *after* the Revolution. It became instead the servant of a political vanguard that had a monopoly over time's meaning, a cosmological understanding of history that legitimated the use of violence against all opposing visions of social transformation.

■

It is not my intent to produce yet another narrative of how Lenin and the party victimized the avant-garde. Rather, it is to argue that conceptions of temporality have political implications,[74] and that blindness to this fact contributed to the historical failure of the artistic avant-garde and the political vanguard alike.[75] It is difficult to see this situation clearly, because the historical actors themselves did not. The terms "avant-garde" and "vanguard," which I am defining against each other, were not held apart with any rigor in the early twentieth century.[76] In Russia at the time of the Revolution they seem to have been used interchangeably, or just as often not used at all.[77] It was only in the 1960s that Western art historians constructed retroactively an international narrative of the artistic "avant-garde," in which the Russian modernists figured as a critically important moment.[78] As for the political "vanguard," Marx himself never used this term.[79] It was Lenin who put forth the notion that the party was in advance of the rest of the working class—but when he developed this theory in *What Is to Be Done?* in 1902, he appropriated the (Russified version of the) French term "avant-garde" (*avangard*) to describe his minority, Marxist party because this was the term used among Russian Marxists in European exile at the time.[80] The situation is further complicated by the fact that the two terms are not differentiated in all European languages.[81] It is only in retrospect that their different *times* can be seen to matter.

We can present the philosophical problem more clearly if we look again at empirical history, this time focusing more broadly on the changing contextual meanings of the terms. Both words, "avant-garde" and "vanguard," originated in the West as spatial concepts within the military, where they referred to the leading edge of the army, a small force sent out in front to surprise the enemy. The terms came to be used metaphorically when they were transcribed onto the dimension of historical time. *Avant-garde* came into general use in France in the mid-nineteenth century, when it was applied to both cultural and political radicalism as both endorsed, in the spirit of Saint-Simonianism, the idea of history as progress.[82] At the end of the century, in the climate of artistic modernism that was concentrated in bourgeois Paris and other Western European cities (where many Russian avant-garde artists and vanguard politicians, including Lenin, lived before the Revolution), the "avant-garde" took on a more specifically cultural meaning. Although most of the members of the cultural avant-garde would have described themselves as politically on the "Left" and aligned with history's "progressive" social forces, the term did not necessarily imply a political allegiance. It meant being alienated from established bourgeois culture (as a bohemian) or on the cutting edge of cultural history (as a radical), but it did not seem necessary to conflate these positions with an endorsement of any particular political party. It became an issue, however, at least for the Russian avant-garde, with the Bolshevik success in October 1917. As we have seen, Lenin immediately articulated this revolutionary event in terms of a cosmological temporality, situating the October Revolution within world history, and in his Plan for Monumental Propaganda he sought to secure this vision of a particular historical trajectory with the help of art. At the outset the Bolsheviks made a point of trying to engage the avant-garde in their cultural programs. And although the artists' response was generally to support the October Revolution, their situation was both intellectually and existentially ambiguous. Many of the leading avant-garde artists were explicitly anarchist in their political statements. This was particularly true in the spring of 1918, when, under pressure of the renewed war with Germany, the Leninist leadership was cracking down on anarchism.[83] There was considerable unease among radical artists, including Malevich, Tatlin, and Maiakovskii, about the costs for creative freedom of collaborating too closely with *any* state organizations, including the new ones. It is here that the politics of conflicting temporalities becomes important.

Precisely the intellectual prejudice of history-as-progress led both artists and party leaders to assume that political revolution and cultural revolution must be two sides of the same coin. But when the October Revolution brought to history its scenario of proletarian class rule, the logic of what constituted "progressive" art became intellectually confused and politically controversial. The avant-garde artists—suprematists, rayists and futurists—were clearly the most "revolutionary" in terms of their break with traditional artistic practice. But did this prove their clairvoyance as anticipatory of the proletarian culture, or was it, on the contrary, a sign of historical decadence, connecting them fatally to late bourgeois, European modernism, which it was now clear was *not* the harbinger of socialist revolution? In winning *this* battle, defining its rightful place within the historical continuum of art, avant-gardism lost its credibility as a revolutionary strategy in its own right and was reduced in the Soviet story to a historical moment within "art's" development.[84] The avant-garde's claim of being the historical destination of art might indeed be accommodated within the cosmological temporality of the party, but by this same gesture its "truth" was historicized. Already by the mid-1920s, the avant-garde of suprematism and futurism was spoken of in Russia as passé. All art that was not going in the direction of the party was historically "backward," bourgeois rather than proletarian, and hence ultimately counterrevolutionary. Once artists accepted the cosmological time of the political vanguard, it followed that to continue to be revolutionary in a cultural sense meant glorifying the successes of the party and covering over its failures. And this entailed a complete reversal of art's experiential effect; art was no longer to inspire imagination in a way that set reality into question but, rather, to stage affirmative representations of reality that encouraged an uncritical acceptance of the party's monopolistic right to control the direction of social transformation.

■

It could be argued that despite the constructivist call for art's entry into social life, the Bolshevik avant-garde was compromised precisely by attempting to hold onto "art" too tenaciously, that is, to hold onto a historical continuum of art that ran parallel (and was ultimately made subservient) to the cosmological continuum of historical progress.[85] After the October Revolution, the mere gesture of refusal which marked the bourgeois avant-garde was no longer considered sufficient. Artists made the fateful decision, in facing forward rather than backward, to move triumphantly into the future alongside political power. The only argument was at what relative speed, whether, as Tatlin and Lissitzky claimed, artistic practice was chronologically in the lead of the Communist Party, or whether, as Trotsky wrote in 1923, art would generally find itself "in the baggage train of the movement of history."[86]

In acquiescing to the vanguard's cosmological conception of revolutionary time, the avant-garde abandoned the *lived* temporality of interruption, estrangement, arrest—that is, they abandoned the *phenomenological experience of avant-garde practice*.[87] It is politically important to make this philosophical distinction in regard to avant-garde time and vanguard time, even if the avant-garde artists themselves did not. The avant-garde philosophically understood, as a temporal structure of experience, is a cognitive category: it is "aesthetics" in the word's original sense of "perception through feeling."[88] From an empirico-historical, descriptive point of view, it is enough for artists to call themselves avant-garde for them to be it (the Western art strategy). But from a philosophical viewpoint, the artwork itself must demonstrate this claim, within (and against) its historical context. Artworks, not artists, are avant-garde,[89] and even here the category is not a constant. It is the *aesthetic experience* of the artwork (or of any other cultural object: literary text, photograph, cinema, theater performance, musical recording, etc.—but also theoretical texts, also this one) that counts in a cognitive sense. The power of any cultural object to arrest the flow of history, and to open up time for alternative visions, varies with history's changing course.[90] Strategies range from critical negativity to utopian representation. No one style, no one medium is invariably successful. Perhaps not the object but its critical interpretation is avant-garde. What counts is that the aesthetic experience teach us something new about our world, that it shock us out of moral complacency and political resignation, and that it take us to task for the overwhelming lack of social imagination that characterizes so much of cultural production in all its forms.

The art of the Russian avant-garde prided itself in being "nonobjective," and was accused by its enemies of being "formalist," but it remained representational in the important sense that it was mimetic of the experience of modernity. Precisely through abstraction, the artworks gave expression to a human sensorium fundamentally altered by the tempos and technologies of factory and urban life.[91] What was utopian in Malevich's art was the belief that the geometric forms laid bare by industrial production could, in their mathematical interrelationships, bring about a reconciliation between modern human beings and their new environment. Geometric harmony was seen as a model for spiritual and hence social harmony. Insofar as his artworks still have the power to evoke this sense in the observer, it is a mark of their political success.

Lunacharskii criticized the constructivists for their pretensions of being engineers: "They play at being engineers . . . but they don't know as much of the essence of machinery as a savage."[92] It is true that "for the most part Constructivist ideas remained on the level of designs only, and substantial industrial links were few."[93] But to dismiss the *cognitive* power of these images for the reason that they remained imaginary is to miss the political point. Much of avant-garde "architecture" consisted of maquettes and drawings rather than blueprints and buildings. Tatlin's world-famous Monument to the Third International was never built. Konstantin Melnikov's most daring architectural proposals remained on the drawing board. Malevich intended his vertical and horizontal "architectons" to provide models for real buildings precisely because they were "outside everything utilitarian."[94] El Lissitzky's "Prouns" captured the transition between the model as a representation of the imagination and the building as an object in the world, arresting this moment rather than providing a blueprint for the building itself. Iakov Chernikov's "machine architecture" consisted of painted drawings that took literally the modernist call for housing as "machines for dwelling," per-

2. Схема дома — квартала.

2.21

2.22

2.23

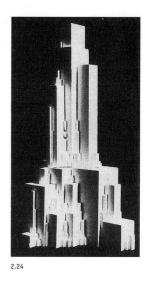

2.24

2.21 Anton Lavinskii, "Sketch of a Housing Block" from *City on Springs,* 1921. In the journal *Lef,* Arvatov discussed Lavinskii's plans for a circular city on springs raised above the earth: Will they work? Probably not, but Lavinskii is "making suggestions," to use Maiakovskii's phrase: "Let the engineers now say what is possible and what is not possible."[95]

2.22 Iakov Chernikov, "Vertical Milling Machine," from the series *Machine Architecture,* 1923.

2.23 Konstantin Melnikov, competition project for the Moscow bureau of Leningrad *Pravda,* 1924, showing each floor opened up to its maximum extension.

2.24 Kazimir Malevich, *Architecton Gota,* 1923. Malevich called these drawings "spatial" suprematism, composed of three-dimensional, "volumetric" forms: "I understand architecture as an activity outside everything utilitarian," and "all the arts as activity free from all economic and practical ideologies."[96]

forming a quasi-magical transformation of tools from instruments used by human beings into habitats that might shelter them. Georgii Krutikov's "City of Areal Paths of Communication" settled for nothing less than the domestication of the planet, while Andrei Burov imagined utopia at the opposite end of the scale: one urban building was to house all of life's activities as a micromodel of the world. Anton Lavinskii's proposal for a "City on Springs" was sheer architectural fantasy, celebrating the audacity of human imagination. These "products" of the avant-garde adhered to a different logic than machine efficiency or industrial engineering. They were dream images, expressing the wish for a transformed relationship between human beings and their environment. Becoming collective property through their multiple reproduction *as* image, they gave sensual representation to the dialectical convergence between revolutionary imagination and material form.[97] This accounts for what Gassner has called the utopian surplus or supplement of production art.[98] The point of this supplement was that it did not lose sight of why in a socialist society humans were making the machines: not to exploit nature but to enhance human existence within it. This goal remained palpable in the works of the revolutionary avant-garde at precisely the time that it was in danger of being forgotten by the political vanguard. The imagination

2.25

2.26

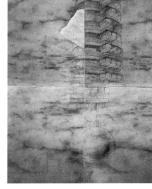

2.27

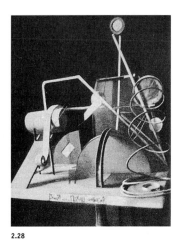

2.28

2.25 Vladimir Tatlin, sketch for a proposed Monument to the Third International, Moscow, 1920.

2.26 El Lissitzky, Proun 1 E, *The Town* (1921). (Proun = Project for the Affirmation of the New.) "The new element of treatment which we have brought to the fore in our painting will be applied to the whole of this still-to-be-built world and will transform the roughness of concrete, the smoothness of metal, and the reflection of glass into the outer membrane of the new life." Lissitzky, "Suprematism in World Reconstruction," 1920.

2.27 Georgii Krutikov, *A City on Areal Paths of Communication,* communal house: perspective. VKhUTEMAS diploma project (workshop of Nikolai Ladovskii), Moscow, 1928.

2.28 Vladimir Liushin, *Station for Interplanetary Communication*, 1922.

of such designs interrupted existing time and space as a non-functional, utopian presence *in* the present. By not closing the gap between dream and reality, the artworks of the avant-garde left both dream and reality free to criticize each other.

The fantastic constructions of the avant-garde could no more be a blueprint for socialist existence than a Five Year Plan can be for how economic activity actually impinges on human lives. Both are utopian representations, the forced actualization of which can have very dystopic effects. The power of art to change life is indirect. But so is (or ought to be) the power of political sovereignty. Once an urban design or building, once a policy or plan enters the interactive world of the everyday, its uses should be allowed and indeed encouraged to transcend the constraints of the creator's intent. Granted, this was not always recognized by the architects and city planners of early Bolshevism. They meant their fantasies to be realized in concrete form, however modified.[99] And if it were not for the shortage of material resources they might more frequently have had their wish. But even in the cases when the projects of the architectural and artistic avant-gardes were realized, their transformation of the environment taught by example, encouraging change mimetically rather than by force. In bringing sensory form to utopian ideas, their "reconstruction of daily life" (*perestroika byta*) anticipated the socialist future *without sacrificing the present.* The manipulative strategy of bringing art into life relied on the mimetic principle of aesthetic analogy rather than instrumental domination or military command. Bodily pleasure and physical comfort were fulfilled, not postponed.

■

It has become fashionable to criticize totalitarian leaders on artistic grounds: Hitler was like a movie director;[100] Stalin attempted to make a "total artwork out of society."[101] But is the lesson that political revolutionaries should not be artists, or is it that they should become better ones? Precisely by refusing "art" as a world of illusion and entering "life," yet true to its own logic that sustains an uncompromised, utopian supplement, the avant-garde may have something to teach the politicians.

What if revolutionary political practice had to justify the imaginaries that it constructs in accordance with the logic of its own ideals? Rather than using society as a stage for illusion-filled action stories, daily melodramas featuring Class War, or Constructing Socialism, or Overtaking the West (while violent power remains hidden behind the scenes), a revolutionary movement would need to see itself as a stage, in full view of society, on which the multiple practices enacted by citizen performers provided visible images of democracy and socialism, which are social processes rather than historically realizable stages, too multifaceted and open-ended ever to be defined or realized completely. Unlike the "show trials" of the Stalin era, such performances would not have as their purpose the staging of the regime's own legitimation but, rather, conducting experiments in democracy or demonstrations of socialism, allowing the citizen audience to draw its own conclusions, becoming experts in the "art" of living with others.

Political power needs to give up the fantasy that by monopolizing the means of violence it has a monopoly over what is real. Sovereignty is as imaginary as art; art is as political as sovereignty.[102] Revolutionary politics needs to take seriously the fact that democratic sovereignty *represents* the masses, and that political actions represent history by giving it sensory, material form. What then does it mean to represent the temporality of revolutionary rupture through armed takeover and protracted civil war? What limitations of social fantasy might be implied by this scenario of violence—or by the project of forced modernization according to the plan of a vanguard party? Both are based on a temporal conception that is theoretically impoverished and practically inaccurate. Social life in fact occupies a plurality of layers of time, from glacier-slow to lightning-fast, from inexorable repetition to ineluctable transiency. Such hybrid rhythms cannot be played out on the diminished space of a linear continuum, however dialectically that continuum may be conceived. The range of temporal connections and disconnections produces a complex force field in which social revolutions in fact take place, rather than lining up obediently behind the leadership of progress. Time must be granted a greater complexity than former revolutionary narratives have allowed.

Consider critically in this context Lenin's commentary in 1902 on a passage by Dmitrii Pisarev, a political radical of the 1860s who was on the list of approved "fighters for socialism" in the Plan for Monumental Propaganda. Lenin cites Pisarev:

The rift between dreams and reality causes no harm if only the person dreaming believes seriously in his dream, if he attentively observes life, compares his observations with his castles in the air, and if, generally speaking, he works conscientiously for the achievement of his fantasies. If there is some connection between dreams and life then all is well.[103]

But all is *not* well with this model. Lenin claimed that this operational approach could be applied to making "history" on a collective level. Utopian visions, "castles in the air," are scientific, Lenin wrote, when they motivate a "new people" to realize a revolutionary plan.[104] Historical actualization thereby becomes the criterion for the acceptability of socialist dreaming. It seems to give proof that the dream was no mere fantasy. But in the process, history itself becomes a dreamworld. The voluntarism of the vanguard party, including the arbitrariness of its revolutionary violence, is rationalized as history striding forward. Using the masses as an instrument for realizing the dreamworld of history, the armed vanguard "submits" to a conception of time that, so long as it remains victorious, legitimates its own rule. If revolution is the "illusion of politics" (Marx), it is the illusion of history that makes the latter seem real.[105] Of course, daydreams are salutary; we could not live without them. But when their logic, in compensating for the disappointments of today, becomes a "plan" that locks in future meaning, time's indeterminacy and openness is colonized, and the utopian dream becomes a reality of oppression.[106]

■

In the last days of the Soviet regime, dissident artists within the Soviet Union represented its past history as a dreamworld, depicting the crumbling of the Soviet era before it occurred in fact. For this generation, the moment of awakening replaced that of revolutionary rupture as the defining phenomenological experience. Exemplary is a 1983 painting of Aleksandr Kosolapov, *The Manifesto,* in which, against a martial, red sky and amidst ruins that include a bust of Lenin, three putti try to decipher a surviving copy of Marx's *Communist Manifesto.* The dreamer who is still inside the dream of history accepts its logic as inexorable. But at the moment of awakening, when the dream's coherence dissipates, all that is left are scattered images. The compelling nature of their connection has been shattered.

It is crucial to recognize that the end of the Soviet era was not limited spatially to the territory of the Soviet Union. The Bolshevik experiment, no matter how many specifically Russian cultural traits it developed, was vitally attached to the Western, modernizing project, from which it cannot be extricated without causing the project itself to fall to pieces—including its cult of historical progress. Those who at this stage of awakening attempt the task of political interpretation are not to compare themselves with revolutionary prophets. They do better to approach the dream fragments like soothsayers who read the entrails of animals before a battle, not to predict which army will win, but to decipher what forces of collective fantasy exist to withstand the violence of any army, aiding those forces by exposing the deceptive representations on which every army depends.

"History" has failed us. No new chronology will erase that fact. History's betrayal is so profound that it cannot be forgiven simply by tacking on a "post-" era to it (postmodernism, post-Marxism). There is real tragedy in the shattering of the dreams of modernity—of social utopia, historical progress, and material plenty for all. But to submit to melancholy at this point would be to confer on the past a wholeness that never did exist, confusing the loss of the dream with the loss of the dream's realization. The alternative of political cynicism is equally problematic, however, because in denying possibilities for change it prevents them; anticipating defeat, it brings defeat into being. Rather than taking a self-ironizing distance from history's failure, we—the "we" who may have nothing more nor less in common than sharing *this* time—would do well to bring the ruins up close and work our way through the rubble in order to rescue the utopian hopes that modernity engendered, because we cannot afford to let them disappear. There is no reason to believe that those utopian hopes caused history to go wrong, and every reason, based on evidence of the abuses of power that propelled history forward, to believe the opposite.

When an era crumbles, "History breaks down into images, not into stories."[107] Without the narration of continuous progress, the images of the past resemble night dreams, the "first mark" of which, Freud tells us, is their emancipation from "the spatial and temporal order of events."[108] Such images, as dream images, are complex webs of memory and desire wherein past experience is rescued and, perhaps, redeemed. Only partial interpretations of these images are possible, and in a critical light. But they may be helpful if they illuminate patches of the past that seem to have a charge of energy about them precisely because the dominant narrative does not connect them seamlessly to the present. The historical particulars might then be free to enter into different constellations of meaning. The juxtaposition of these past fragments with our present concerns might have the power to challenge the complacency of our times, when "history" is said by its victors to have successfully completed its course, and the new global capitalist hegemony claims to have run the competition off the field.

To be engaged in the historical task of surprising rather than explaining the present—more avant-garde than vanguard in its temporality—may prove at the end of the century to be politically worth our while.

2.29 Aleksandr Kosolapov, *The Manifesto,* 1983. (color plate 1)

2.30 Aleksandr Kosolapov, *Egyptian Fresco*, 1983.

2.2

TIME FRAGMENTS

MYTHIC TIME

In time, it was the monumental figure of Lenin himself that, replicated throughout Soviet public space, anchored the revolution. His wife Krupskaia recalled that in the first
weeks of Bolshevik rule "nobody knew Lenin's face. . . . In the evening we would often . . . stroll around the Smolny, and nobody would ever recognize him, because there
were no portraits then."[109] After his death, the predictable inclusion of his icon in the
landscape of everyday life became the cipher of the Revolution. "Lenin corners" in the
home replaced religious representations. Lenin statues decorated urban squares. Lenin

busts adorned public auditoriums, Lenin pins were worn on suit lapels. These reiterations were meant to be material evidence that "Lenin is always with us," effecting the apparent elimination of historical transience by extending the recent past limitlessly into the future. Revolutionary rupture was transformed mythically into a permanent present.

FRAGMENT 1

MYTHIC TIME: A CHRONOLOGY

January 25, 1924—When Lenin died, time stopped.

> *Everything that could make a noise—factory sirens, steamship whistles, train whistles—sounded for three minutes. The noise was deafening. At 4:00 exactly, all radio broadcasts, all telegraph lines, transmitted one message: "Stand up, comrades, Ilich is being lowered into his grave!" Everything stopped everywhere in Russia for five minutes. Trains stopped, ships stopped.*[110]

But the grave remained open. Embalming procedures had been used to extend the life of the body for the biblical length of forty days.[111]

January 26, 1924—Stalin made a speech of mourning at the Second Congress of Soviets, pledging to fulfill Lenin's testament and consolidate the proletarian dictatorship. He began: "We, the Communists, are people of a special make. We are made of special material. The Communist body does not decay."[112] Days later the Funeral Commission chaired by Feliks Dzerzhinskii (head of the Cheka) made the decision to preserve Lenin's body indefinitely. The most modern scientific techniques were to be used to replicate the funeral rites of Egyptian pharaohs. (The four-thousand-year-old mummy of King Tutankhamen had been discovered in Luxor 15 months earlier as the highlight of a slow process of excavating his tomb that received continuous publicity world-wide. In jewelry and design in the West, motifs of ancient Egypt were in fashion.)

January 28, 1924—Stalin recalled being "disappointed" when first meeting Lenin at a Bolshevik conference in Tammerflors, Finland, in 1905. This "most ordinary-looking man, below average height . . . [was] in no way distinguishable from ordinary mortals":

> *It is accepted as customary that a Great Man must arrive late at meetings so that members of the assembly may await his appearance with bated breath, and then, just as the Great Man appears, the people may start whispering, "Ssssh . . . Silence . . . he's com-*

2.31 Lenin on Red Square, May 1, 1919.

ing." This ritual did not seem to me superfluous, for it is overawing and instills respect. How disappointed I was, when I realized that Lenin had arrived at the meeting earlier than the delegates and, ensconced somewhere in the corner, was simply carrying on a most ordinary conversation with the most ordinary delegates of the conference. I will not conceal from you that this to me at the time seemed something of a violation of certain indispensable rules.[113]

January 30, 1924—Lenin's widow Nadezhda Krupskaia protested publicly in *Pravda*:

COMRADES WORKERS AND PEASANTS!
I have a great request to make of you: do not allow your grief for Ilich to express itself in the external veneration of his person. Do not build memorials to him. . . . If you want to honor the name of Vladimir Ilich—build day care centers, kindergartens, homes, schools.[114]

As head of Narkompros, Lunacharskii supervised the design competition for a permanent mausoleum, soliciting ideas from architects, artists, and "every thinking person" in a four-year contest that was itself a propaganda event.[115] Competition entries included designs for a twenty-story-high statue of Lenin, a rostrum in the form of a giant screw and two nuts, and a huge solid block that housed a tractor, locomotive, and flowing brook.[116] In the end, the Immortalization Commission rejected all the entries, and invited Shchusev to recast the existing wooden mausoleum in stone.

> *I don't know how it happened, but the current temporary mausoleum over the grave of Lenin . . . is, in its architectural form, the very image of a similar mausoleum (though in stone) over the grave of King Cyrus near the city of Murgaba in Persia famous four centuries before the start of the Christian era.*
>
> —Kornelii Zelinskii, *Lef*, 1925[117]

2.32 A. V. Shchusev, model of the wooden mausoleum for Lenin, 1924.

2.33 Design variants for Lenin's sarcophagus by Konstantin Melnikov, who won the competition in March 1924.

The design pictured in the center of figure 2.33 was Melnikov's preferred plan, "a four-sided elongated pyramid cut by two internally opposed inclined planes of glass that by their intersection formed a strict horizontal diagonal, thus breaking up the static rectangle of the casket into two lively acute triangles."[118] When the conservative Commission selected a more conventional variant by Melnikov, the latter incorporated the design shown here into the prize-winning Soviet Pavilion for the Exposition Internationale des Arts Décoratifs (figure 2.34). The pavilion, built of wood in Moscow by peasants using the traditional Russian axe, became an icon of constructivism, as did Rodchenko's Workers' Reading Room and Tatlin's Monument to the Third International, which were exhibited inside it.

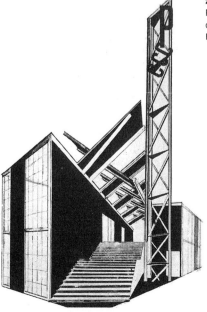

2.34 Konstantin Melnikov, Soviet Pavilion, Exposition Internationale des Arts Décoratifs, Paris, 1925. Final presentation drawing.

February 1924—Leonid Krasin (Commissioner of Foreign Trade) was brought in to supervise the permanent preservation of Lenin's body. He was a proponent Bogdanov's prerevolutionary theory of "god-building" and was influenced by Fedorov's call for the physical resurrection of the dead. He had written in 1921:

I am certain that the time will come when science will become all-powerful, that it will be able to recreate a deceased organism. I am certain that the time will come when one will be able to use the elements of a person's life to recreate the physical person . . . [and] resurrect great historical figures.[119]

March 1924—With the rising temperatures, "time did its work"[120]—Lenin's body began to decay. Krasin set into operation a specially designed refrigeration system to sustain it. A team of scientists reembalmed the corpse using experimental techniques. The Funeral Commission was renamed the Immortalization Commission. Religious tradition merged with science fiction and technical innovation with ancient ritual, conflating temporal difference. Artists of the avant-garde were called upon as mediators between the archaic and the modern in designing the sarcophagus and mausoleum. Malevich had proposed on the day of Lenin's death that his grave be in the shape of a cube:

The cube is no longer a geometric body. It is a new object with which we try to portray eternity, to create a new set of circumstances, with which we can maintain Lenin's eternal life, defeating death.[121]

Tatlin wrote that the mausoleum ought to be a "triumph of engineering," holding huge numbers of visitors and containing an information bureau, radio station, and hundreds of telephones.[122] The architect A. V. Shchusev endorsed Malevich's cube form in a proposal for the mausoleum that pleased the Immortalization Commission. The execution of the design was stylistically remote from suprematism, however, consisting of classical porticos superimposed on a complex of cubes; it was hastily erected that summer as a temporary structure out of wood.[123] Konstantin Melnikov, a protegé of Shchusev, designed the sarcophagus in geometric shapes that could be read alternatively as modernist triangles or ancient pyramidal forms.[124]

August 3, 1924—Lenin's tomb was opened for public viewing. Boris Zbarskii, one of
the scientists involved in the embalming process,

> *told the [foreign] newsmen that the Egyptians had been able to preserve only the bodies of*
> *their leaders and that the features of their faces were unrecognizable. Lenin, on the other*
> *hand, looked simply asleep. Zbarsky added that the entire cost of embalming the body of*
> *Lenin was only $7500, "in striking contrast to the fortunes which the Egyptians spent on*
> *the bodies of their Pharaohs, nobles and high priests." . . . Zbarsky said that, in fact, if the*
> *temperature of the mausoleum were kept constant, "Lenin's body should last forever."*[125]

> *"Lenin" and "Death"—*
>   *These words are enemies.*
> *"Lenin" and "Life"—*
>   *are comrades . . .*
> *Lenin—*
>   *lived.*
> *Lenin—*
>   *lives.*
> *Lenin—*
>   *will live.*
> —Vladimir Maiakovskii, "Komsomolskaia," 1924

> *"Prushevsky! Are the successes of higher science able to resurrect people who have decom-*
> *posed or not?"*
>   *"No," said Prushevsky.*
>   *"You're lying," accused Zachev without opening his eyes. "Marxism can do any-*
> *thing. Why is it then that Lenin lies intact in Moscow? He is waiting for science—he wants*
> *to be resurrected."*
> —Andrei Platonov, *The Foundation Pit*, 1930[126]

2.35 Lenin in his sarcophagus (designed by Melnikov), 1930.

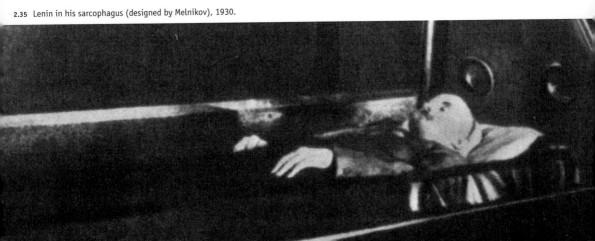

2.36 Courtyard of the Sculpture House in the Vsekokhudozhnik Commune, Moscow (architect: Georgii Golts), for the mass reproduction of Lenin statues, anonymous (unofficial) photograph, 1932–1936.

1930—The permanent mausoleum opened as a monument to the First Five Year Plan. On November 7 Stalin viewed from its top level the Revolutionary celebration in Red Square.[127] It became traditional for Soviet leaders to use the mausoleum as a reviewing platform, just as it became traditional for Soviet citizens to queue up, whatever the weather, to visit the mausoleum, entering its dark depths to view Lenin's mummy under glass and bathed in an eerie light.

This is the very point at which the idea of a political modernization of society terminates in a totalitarian mummified communism. . . . Mummified Lenin is the ultimate ideological sign. . . . It gathers the community together shaping it in two general forms: a mourning line and an exalting parade in front of its dwelling place. . . . The mummy of Lenin is the point at which modernization is terminated and the omnipresence of the Party is imposed.[128]

1941—Germany invaded deep into Russia and the mummy of Lenin was evacuated. It was returned without damage to the mausoleum in 1945.

1949—The Bulgarian Communist leader Georgi Dimitrov "went to Moscow for medical treatment and was sent back mummified through the Soviet method."[129]

1952—The cadaver of Choybalsan, Communist leader of Mongolia, was mummified by the Moscow embalming experts of the Laboratory of the Lenin Mausoleum.

1953—Stalin's mummified body joined Lenin's in the mausoleum.

1961—As a consequence of de-Stalinization, the corpse of Stalin was removed from the mausoleum and buried nearby.

1969—Mummification by the Moscow laboratory team of Ho Chi Minh, Communist leader of Vietnam.

1976—Mao Zedong, Communist leader of China, was mummified by Chinese experts and put on public display.

2.37 Vasilii Elkin, *Long Live the Red Army—the Armed Detachment of the Proletarian Revolution!*, poster, 1932. (color plate 8)

1979—Mummification by the Moscow laboratory team of Agostino Neto, Communist leader of Angola.

1985—Mummification by the Moscow laboratory team of Lindon Forbes Burnham, Communist leader of Guyana.

1991—The Soviet Union ceased to exist. The disgraced monuments of the Soviet period began to be dismantled.[130] The Lenin Museum at Red Square, containing relics of his life, was shut down. The contribution of the state to the budget of the Laboratory of the Lenin Mausoleum was reduced from one hundred percent to twenty percent.[131]

1995—Mummification by the Moscow laboratory team of Kim Il Sung, Communist leader of North Korea, a commission that saved the embalming experts of the Moscow laboratory from bankruptcy. The laboratory team began to take private commissions for "ritual service" from Russian citizens, including murdered mafia members and wealthy "new Russians," who wished to be buried with the dignity of a chief of state.[132]

1997—President Boris Yeltsin called for a national referendum in Russia to determine the fate of Lenin's body, and suggested closing the mausoleum and burying Lenin next to his mother. (The grandson of one former Communist leader offered to take Lenin's corpse on a world tour as a money-making venture.)[133] The Russian legislative assembly (the Duma, then dominated by Communists) voted against any change to Red Square, however minor, and invoked the fact that UNESCO had classified Lenin's mausoleum as part of the "patrimony of humanity."[134]

At the end of the twentieth century, Lenin's mummy is still in place. The mausoleum on Red Square remains open to the viewing public.

2.38 Iurii Shavelnikov and Iurii Fesenko, performance of artists eating cake in the form of Lenin's mummy, 1998.

FRAGMENT 2

REVERSE MOTION

To those who may be unacquainted with the heady delights of the editing-table the sense of control, of repetition, acceleration, deceleration, arrest in freeze-frame, release, and reversal of movement is inseparable from the thrill of power.

—Annette Michelson[135]

When D. W. Griffith's film *Intolerance* (USA, 1916) was chosen to be presented at the first Congress of the Comintern in Petrograd in 1921, "the most glaring problem for the Soviets was the film's insistent theme that history is cyclical. *Intolerance* advances the argument that the same cycles of intolerance and injustice simply recur in different historical dress . . . epoch after epoch."[136] In contrast, Sergei Eisenstein's film version of the Bolshevik Revolution, *October* (1927), uses the technique of reverse motion to represent the impossible desire of political reactionaries to turn time backward. Eisenstein described the opening scene:

The picture begins with semi-symbolic shots of the overthrowing of autocracy, represented by the toppling of the statue of Alexander III. . . . The collapse of the statue was also shot in reverse motion: the throne with the armless and legless torso flew back onto the pedestal. Arms, legs, scepter and orb flew up to join it. The indestructible figure of Alexander III once again sat in state, staring vacantly into space. This scene was shot for the episode of Kornilov's attack on Petrograd in the autumn of 1917 and represented the dreams of all those reactionaries who hoped that the general's success would lead to the restoration of the monarchy. . . . Visually, the scene was a great success.[137]

When the statue of Feliks Dzerzhinskii (head of the Cheka and member of Lenin's Immortalization Commission) was dismantled after the fall of the Soviet Union, the pedestal was preserved for its historical value. Mikhail Iampolskii wrote in 1993: "Of what is the pedestal a monument, if there is no figure on top of it? The answer is, apparently, the stability of time, a stability completely autonomous of any hero or any event, simply stability as such. The pedestal without Dzerzhinskii is unique in that it continues by itself to designate a place of the accumulation of time as pure abstraction."[138] Iampolskii connects this emptying out of time's meaning with the devaluing of paper currency in Russia, and ultimately with the devaluing of the masses themselves:

The disappearance of the stable ruble [he wrote in 1993] is somehow connected with the disappearance of monuments. . . . The special phenomenon of the inflationary crowd has appeared, consisting of masses of depreciated individuals. . . . Its emergence is closely connected with alter-

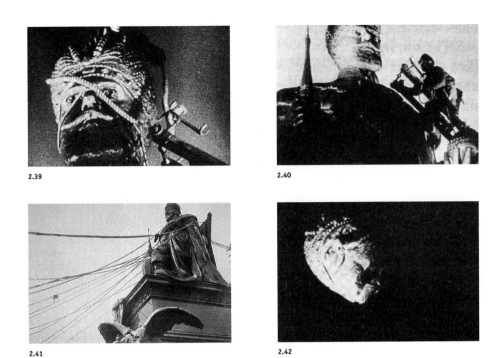

2.39, 2.40, 2.41, 2.42 Toppling by the people of the statue of Tsar Alexander III, stills from Sergei Eisenstein's film *October* (1927). Eisenstein's version of history was factually incorrect; the statue was not destroyed in the 1917 Revolution. In 1918, Maiakovskii could still protest, in a poem called "It's Too Early to Rejoice": "And does Tsar Alexander still stand on Uprising Square? Dynamite it!" The Soviet government finally removed the statue in 1921.[139]

ations in temporality. Such "refuse" appears precisely as a result of the passage of time, which discards certain elements as outdated and anachronistic. It is not hard to observe that, for the first time in all the years of Soviet power, perhaps since the 1920s, an image has entered people's consciousness of a part of the population as being left behind, thrown by the wayside, and doomed. The accumulation of inflationary crowds, of course, is a very dangerous phenomenon, fraught with, among other things, the possibility of fascism.[140]

2.43 Toppled Alexander III, Moscow, 1921.

2.44 Toppled Dzerzhinskii, Moscow, 1991. In December 1998, the Russian parliament voted in favor of putting the toppled statue of Feliks Dzerzhinskii back in its place.

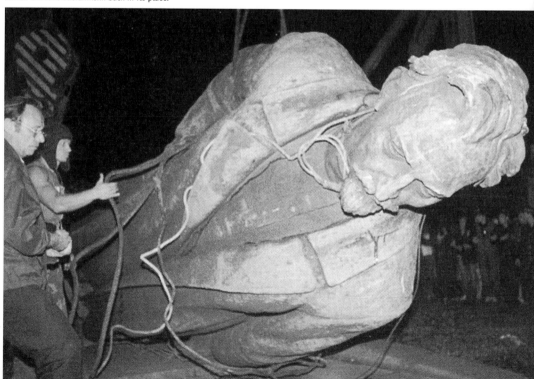

2.45 Mark Lewis, *On the Monument of the Republic* #2, 1990.

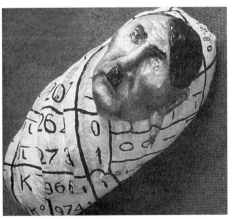

2.46 The Pertsy Group, *Baby Hitler*, Soviet Union, late 1980s.

2.47 Cathedral of Christ the Savior, Moscow, 1883.

In the early 1930s a site was chosen in Moscow for the building of the Palace of the Soviets.[141] The Cathedral of Christ the Savior, built to commemorate the Russian victory over Napoleon (and completed in 1883 under Tsar Alexander III) was dynamited in order to clear the ground. The destruction was filmed. After the Soviet Union collapsed, this short newsreel was shown in Russian theaters and on television "hundreds of times. One could say without exaggeration that this fragment today [1993] is the most shown piece of the Soviet Chronicle. In a significant number of films, the precise moment is shown in slow motion or repeated over and over . . . [as] perpetual . . . immortalized destruction."[142]

Construction of the palace began in 1939. It was interrupted when Germany invaded Russia. After Khrushchev's de-Stalinization speech in 1956, plans for the Palace of the Soviets were abandoned definitively. On the site of "two nonexistent buildings," the cathedral and the palace, a huge public swimming pool was built.[143]

The Moskva open air swimming pool . . . almost in the city centre, open all year, in summer and winter alike, is generally and on first impression considered to be a pioneering move of town planning, not to drive people out of the stone landscape, but to give them more bodily exercise, more nature, sun and air. The pool [is] a gigantic circle. . . . Swimming in winter, in the midst of an icy, snow-covered city, in swathes of steam reaching out to the street, is both fantastic and daring—almost like wanting to pull down the banks in Wall Street to make room for kindergartens.

—Report from 1992[144]

2.48 Moskva open-air swimming pool. Photo from 1992.

2.49 Reconstruction of the cathedral, 1997.

In 1994 the Russian government eliminated the swimming pool and began the restoration on this site of the Cathedral of Christ the Savior, exactly replicating its appearance in 1883. This project, completed in 1998, indeed played the course of history backward, mimicking in reverse the movie of the cathedral's demolition.

One should have more regrets over a screw with a broken thread than over the destruction of the church of Vasilii the Blessed.

—Kazimir Malevich, 1919[145]

2.50 John Goto, *A Marriage Portrait*, 1998. Malevich, his daughter Una, and his third wife Natasha Andreeva Manchenko.

FRAGMENT 3

AGAINST TIME (MALEVICH)

Following a stay in Poland and Germany in 1927, Malevich returned to the geometric, figurative painting of peasant motifs that he had developed before World War I.[146] He dated the new canvases incorrectly, attributing them to the earlier period, which he implied had continued until 1919. The motivation for Malevich's "great break," his move away from abstract suprematism, and for the false dating of his artistic development has puzzled scholars. Their explanations range from the most opportunistic (the prewar peasant paintings had been well received in a Berlin exhibition and he might hope to sell more of them in the West), to the most principled (Malevich, teaching frequently in Kiev in his native Ukraine in 1928–1930, would have seen firsthand the disastrous effects of the famine caused by the dekulakization and collectivization policy, and his peasant paintings express a muted, metaphysical, quasi-religious protest against the regime).[147]

At the very least Malevich was asserting his autonomy by following his own artistic will rather than adhering to a party line.[148] A retrospective exhibition of his work in Moscow in 1929, where the newly painted, falsely dated canvases were first shown, was critically reviewed.[149] Although the official press acknowledged Malevich as an important moment in "the development of our art," so that "familiarity with his work is very useful both for young artists and the new viewer," his work was now seen

as dated and "ideologically foreign to us."[150] In 1930 Malevich was arrested under suspicion of being a German spy and questioned, as he wrote later to Filonov, about the
ideology of modern art: "What kind of Cezannism do you talk about? What kind of
Cubism do you preach? . . . AKhRR wanted to completely destroy me. They said 'do
away with Malevich and all of Formalism will die' but see, they didn't destroy me. I'm
still alive. It's not so easy to get rid of Malevich!"[151] He wrote on the back of one new
canvas, *Complex Premonition (Half Figure in a Yellow Shirt):* "The composition was composed of elements of the sensation of emptiness, loneliness and the impasse of life,"[152]
and dated the painting 1913. But it was a contemporary work executed ca. 1930,
when the revolution, far from at an impasse, was in Stalin's words "dizzy with success."
In returning to peasant portraiture, Malevich was abandoning his own insistence in
1920: "There can be no question of painting in Suprematism; painting was done for
long ago, and the artist himself is a prejudice of the past."[153]

It is possible to read this reversal in style through a temporal index: In knowingly
misdating his paintings Malevich was rejecting, now equally, avant-garde *and* vanguard
temporality. To paint bearded peasants at a time when women were selling their hair
and men their beards to raise money on collective farms,[154] to paint isolated peasants,
sturdy and robust in form, at a time when collectivized peasants were starvingly thin
due to famine, was to criticize the present by refusing to acknowledge it. Some of the

2.51 John Goto, *Monument,* 1998. Malevich (d. 1935) is suspended over the cube that held his ashes
(designed by Suetin), surrounded by artists, writers, Stalin, etc. Included are Gorky, Tolstoy, Matiushin, Eisenstein,
Suetin, Khlebnikov, Meierkhold, Rodchenko, and Tatlin.

peasant paintings can indeed be read as social criticism. But, as critics have observed, their emaciated and "disfigured" bodies suggest the timeless suffering of the peasants by echoing the iconography of the church,[155] rather than connecting their plight to the specifics of modernity. There is nothing recognizably contemporary about Malevich's late peasant paintings (which is why their misdating was possible).[156] Their hermetic symbolism can be read as a critical commentary, not on the times but on time itself. His last paintings (before his death in 1935) include a series of personal portraits of his wife, a friend (the artist Punin), and himself dressed in the anachronistic garb of the European Renaissance.

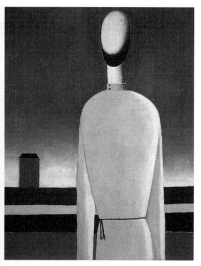

2.52 Kazimir Malevich, *Complex Premonition (Half Figure in a Yellow Shirt)*, 1928–1930.

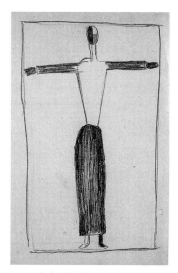

2.53 Kazimir Malevich, *Figure with Arms Stretched Out Making a Cross*, 1933.

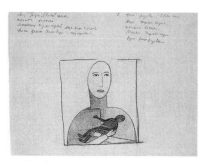

2.54 Kazimir Malevich, *Without Title*, 1931.

2.55 Kazimir Malevich, *Self-Portrait*, 1933

FRAGMENT 4

A Short History of the Square

"Formalist" was perhaps the most damning thing one could say politically about an artist in the Soviet Union in the 1930s.[157] But formalism was precisely the valued criterion for political art in the West, according to the U.S. Marxist art critic Clement Greenberg. His influential article of 1939, "Avant-Garde and Kitsch," argued that painters who followed the laws of art's own intrinsic development were politically more radical than those who agreed to work for instrumental ends, whether political or commercial.[158] Greenberg's cultural radicalism was a protest against the mass-consumed, message-oriented "kitsch" of socialist propaganda and capitalist mass culture alike. This position, which has been called "apolitical politicism," became a weapon in the Cold War, when nonrepresentational art came to be equated with democratic societies as opposed to the representational realism of totalitarian regimes (the latter category did not differentiate between fascism and socialism).[159] The Museum of Modern Art in New York became an institutional embodiment of this Cold War politics.

In this context, it is revealing to trace the fate of the square as its painted form moved through the political landscape of the twentieth century.[160] Always an internationalist, the square was welcomed in the early 1920s at the Bauhaus in Weimar, Germany, and by the modernist movement De Stijl in the Netherlands. In the 1930s, when the Soviet political climate became increasingly unfavorable, the square went into permanent exile. It migrated from Europe across the Atlantic with the aid of Alfred Barr, collector of European modernism, who bought several of Malevich's suprematist works for the permanent exhibition of the Museum of Modern Art, of which he was founding director. Its new home gave it a hero's welcome. As nonrepresentational, geometrical abstraction, the square became the prototype of "pure" and "true" art, which, as experimental and "advanced," could only flourish in a political democracy.[161]

In the second half of the century, the square made so many public appearances in Western art as to lose its revolutionary effectiveness. The original gesture of rupturing the historical continuum became a historical continuum itself.[162] Artists produced a plethora of canvases as variants on the theme, a practice that intensified during the Cold War and reached its climax in the 1960s. The list of monochromatic square-painters (or rectangular variants thereof) reads like a Who's Who of the American school of abstract art: Josef Albers, Ellsworth Kelly, Brice Marden, Agnes Martin, Barnett Newman, Ad Reinhardt, Robert Ryman, Frank Stella. The decade of the sixties witnessed an explosion of artistic imperialism under the banner of "internationalism." As a form of U.S. Cold War cultural hegemony, black squares, yellow squares, red squares, etc., were painted by "avant-garde" artists around the globe.

2.56 Kazimir Malevich, *Black Square,* 1915.

2.57 Josef Albers, *Homage to the Square: Silent Hall,* 1961.

2.58

2.58 Vitaly Komar and Alexander Melamid, from the project *Circle, Square, Triangle,* 1975. The project was addressed "To Prospective Customers": "Take your choice, we can supply you, wholesale and retail, with individual eternal ideas linked a priori to nothing, manufactured from the highest quality of domestic lumber and imported cements and painted by the hands of the virginal maidens employed by the enterprise of Renowned Artists of the Twentieth-Century Seventies, Moscow. A CIRCLE, A SQUARE, A TRIANGLE—for every home, for every family!"

2.59 Visitors contemplate three paintings by Ad Reinhardt, *Abstract Painting,* 1959 (left), *Painting,* 1956–1960 (right), and *Abstract Painting, Black,* 1954 (center), at the retrospective exhibition "American Art in the 20th Century," Martin-Gropius Bau, Berlin, 1993. Photo by Susan Buck-Morss. (color plate 12)

2.59

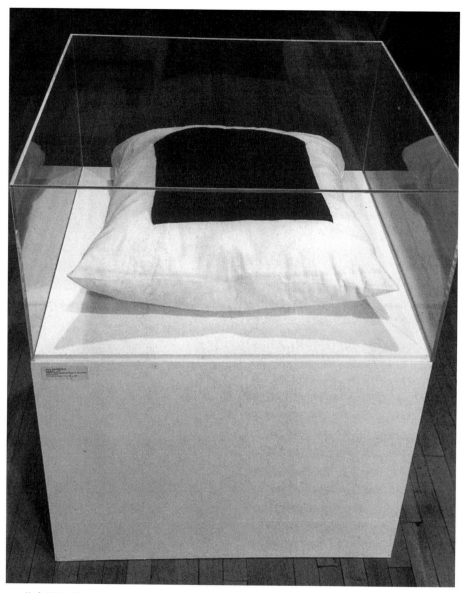

2.60 Maria Konstantinova, *M.K.K.M.* (Maria Konstantinova/Kazimir Malevich), 1990.

The painted subtleties of the square that so fascinate art historians (variations in size, texture, and design features) do not lend themselves to photographic reproduction, the major form of art's contemporary propagation. Overuse has caused the square to lose the mystical power that it had for Malevich in 1915. It has become a cliché, if not itself kitsch, and Robert Rauschenberg's parody hit a sore nerve when he painted his own square with house paint and a paint roller—leading Ad Reinhardt to scream in protest: "Does he think it's easy?"

Cushioned by market recognition and financial success, the square has reached a comfortable old age.[163] Conceived in the revolutionary turmoil of Russia at the beginning of the century, its fate, ironically, is to have become the recognized logo of U.S. "high culture" at the century's end.

Avant-gardes have only one time, and the best thing that can happen to them is, in the full sense of the term, to have had their day. . . . A historical project certainly cannot claim to preserve an eternal youth protected from blows.

—Guy Debord, 1991[164]

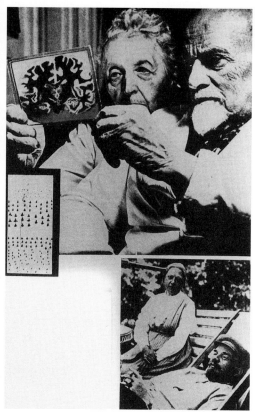

3.1 Brain-scientist couple, Cecile and Oscar Vogt, who made 10,000 cross-section slides of the brain of Lenin, pictured below with his wife Krupskaia after he became ill.

An autopsy was performed on Lenin the same night as his embalming, lasting four hours and forty minutes. "Approximately halfway through the process Lenin's brain was opened, and the direct cause of death was ascertained. . . . When Lenin suffered a stroke on January 21, 1924, a large amount of blood rushed into his brain, much more blood than the sclerotic arteries had been transmitting. This pressure was too great for the brain's damaged vessels, and the walls of those vessels broke down, flooding the brain with blood." An official report of the autopsy was published the day of Lenin's funeral. One reader, a non-party intellectual, criticized it for conveying the message that "Lenin is only *matter,* nothing more than a combination of a cranial hemisphere, intestines, an abdominal cavity, a heart, kidneys, a spleen. . . ."[1]

The weight of Lenin's brain was 1,340 grams.

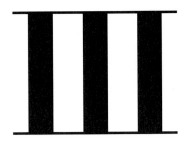

D R E A M W O R L D S   O F

MASS CULTURE

A Note on Method

The next three chapters present a series of constellations constructed out of historical facts, theoretical speculations, and visual images. They provide a series of reflections on Soviet modernism as it connected to Western modernism, crossing boundaries between discursive terrains usually kept apart, trespassing among different academic domains in order to loosen the material from any exclusive possession. Although historically grounded, these constellations are not history in the traditional sense. They are concerned less with how things actually were than with how they appear in retrospect. They reshuffle the usual ordering of facts with the goal of informing present political concerns. Such constellations rescue the past, but not for nostalgic reasons. The goal is to blast holes in established interpretations of the twentieth century, liberating new lines of sight that allow for critical reappropriations of its legacy.

CHAPTER 3

COMMON SENSE

3.1

THE ECOLOGICAL CIRCUIT

The brain, it must be said, yields to philosophical reflection a sense of the uncanny.[2] In our most materialist moments, we would like to take the matter of the brain itself for the mind. (What could be more appropriate than the brain studying the brain?) But there seems to be such an abyss between *us,* alive, as we look out on the world, and that gray-white gelatinous mass with its cauliflower-like convolutions that *is* the brain (the biochemistry of which does not differ qualitatively from that of a sea slug) that, intuitively, we resist naming them as identical. If this "I" who examines the brain were nothing *but* the brain, how is it that I feel so uncomprehendingly alien in its presence?[3]

Hegel thus had intuition on his side in his attacks against the brain watchers. If you want to understand human thought, the German philosopher argued in *The Phenomenology of Mind* (1806), do not place the brain on a dissecting table, or feel the bumps on the head for phrenological information. If you want to know what the mind is, examine what it *does*—thereby turning European philosophy away from natural sci-

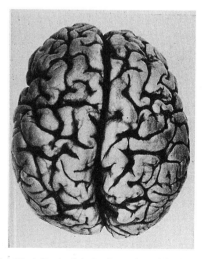

3.2 Brain of Sonia Kovalevskaia, Russian mathematician (1840–1901).

98

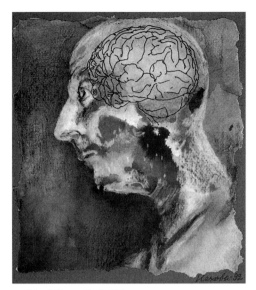

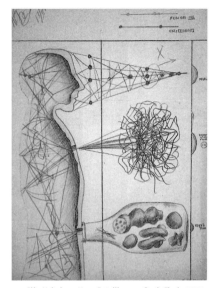

3.3 Irina Nakhova, *Head*, 1992.

3.4 Ilia Kabakov, *Man: Intelligence, Soul, Flesh*, 1961.

ence to the study of human culture and human history. These two discourses henceforth went separate ways: philosophy of the mind and physiology of the brain remained, for the most part, as blind to the activities of one another as the two hemispheres of a split-brain patient are oblivious to the operations of each other—arguably, to the detriment of both.[4]

The brain is the center of the nervous system, composed of hundreds of billions of neurons extending through the spinal cord to the surface of the skin. The nervous system is not contained within the body's limits. The brain is thus not an isolatable anatomical body, but part of a system that connects the individual organism to the environment, passing through the person and her or his (culturally specific, historically transient) world. As the source of stimuli and the arena for motor response, the external world must be included to complete the sensory circuit. (Sensory deprivation causes the system's internal components to degenerate.) The field of the sensory circuit thus corresponds to that of "experience," in the classical philosophical sense of a mediation of subject and object, and yet its very composition makes the so-called split between subject and object, which was the constant plague of classical philosophy, simply irrelevant.[5] There is an ecology to this circuit of cognition. It is a historically specific organization of the human sensorium that must be studied in situ, taking the socio-historical environment into account.

3.5 Sergei Luchishkin, *Hunger in the Volga Region,* ca. 1927 (destroyed).

Lunacharskii refused to allow Luchishkin's picture, which depicted the desperate conditions of the Civil War period, to be hung at the "Art Exhibition on the Tenth Anniversary of the October Revolution," telling the artist: "Famine in the Volga region was a difficult experience . . . but we are celebrating our grand holiday, why cloud it with these memories?" Luchishkin hung it in the next (and last) OST exhibition, but reaction was so negative that he destroyed it.[6] This painting not only recollected the past; it predicted the future. Within two years, Stalin's drastic policies of dekulakization and collectivization of the peasantry led to devastating famines in the agricultural heartland of the Soviet Union outside of Russia, particularly in the Ukraine and the Volga region to the east of the Ukraine. The effects on the non-Russian Soviet peasantry were of genocidal proportions. In terms of political temporality, this was the slow time of death by starvation. No report of the long famine was allowed to appear in the press. The very word was banned as counterrevolutionary slander.

3.6 Solomon Nikritin, *Screaming Woman,* 1928, from a series by that name. Nikritin was a member of the OST group of oil painters. The series was not allowed to be exhibited.

■

The critical power of avant-garde experience is fueled by sensory cognition. It does not depend on the medium of expression. Critical cognition may be produced effectively by an oil painting or a theater piece, and it may be totally lacking in a photograph or cinematic representation. Indeed, "factography" (the early Soviet term), as the technological potential of the camera, may make image representations only more convincingly deceptive. Whether camera image or easel painting, whether filmic montage or architectural design, what matters is that the image provide a sensual, cognitive experience that is capable of resisting abusive power's self-justification. Visual "art" becomes political in this way. It makes apparent what the phantasmagorias of power cover up. Such an aesthetics differs in meaning from aesthetics within modern bourgeois culture—and at the same time revives the oldest meaning of the term.

Aisthētikos is the ancient Greek word for that which is "perceptive by feeling." *Aisthēsis* is the sensory experience of perception. The original field of aesthetics is not art but reality—corporeal, material nature. Hence, "Aesthetics is born as a discourse of the body."[7] It is a form of cognition achieved through taste, touch, hearing, seeing, smell—the whole corporeal sensorium. To be alive is to feel—pain as well as pleasure. It is the a priori condition of existence, the precondition for both culture and history.

Let us resist Hegel's abandonment of physiology and follow the neurological inquiry of one of his contemporaries, the Scottish anatomist Sir Charles Bell. Trained in

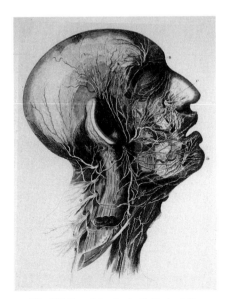

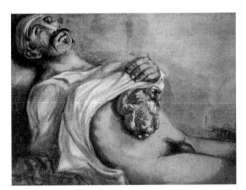

3.8 Watercolor by Sir Charles Bell of a wounded French soldier after the battle of Waterloo. He described the victim's injury: "Peltier, 3rd French Lancers. Belg. Hosp. 2nd July. Belly opened by a sabre. Immediately the bowels protruded. Before he was off the field he had two stools, and none since downwards. When brought into the hospital the third day after the battle, the mass was gangrenous. . . ."[8]

3.7 "The Fifth Nerve," drawing by Sir Charles Bell, from *On the Nerves*, 1821.

painting as well as surgical medicine (as doctors commonly were before the advent of photography), Bell studied the fifth nerve, the "grand nerve of expression," in the belief that "the countenance is the index of the mind."[9] The expressive face is, indeed, a wonder of synthesis, as individual as a fingerprint, yet collectively legible by common sense. Its signs and gestures comprise a mimetic language that—often against conscious intent—gives the truth away. What this language speaks is anything but the concept. Written on the body's surface as a convergence between the impress of the external world and the express of subjective feeling, the language of this cognitive system threatens to betray the language of reason, undermining its philosophical sovereignty.

Hegel developed in cosmological proportions the idea that the movement through space of a victorious army was synonymous with historical progress (Lenin was his legitimate heir). Writing *The Phenomenology of Mind* in his Jena study in 1806, Hegel interpreted the advancing army of Napoleon (whose cannons he could hear roaring in the distance) as the unwitting realization of Reason. Sir Charles Bell, who, as a British field doctor, was physically present a decade later at the battle of Waterloo, had a very different interpretation:

It is a misfortune to have our sentiments at variance with the universal sentiment [among the British who won this battle]. But there must ever be associated with the honours of Waterloo, in my eyes, the shocking signs of woe: to my ears, accents of intensity, outcry from the manly breast, interrupted, forcible expressions from the dying—and noisome smells. I must show you my note book [with sketches of those wounded, friend and foe], for . . . it may convey an excuse for this excess of sentiment.[10]

Bell's "excess of sentiment" did not mean emotionalism. He found his "mind calm amidst such a variety of suffering."[11] And it would be grotesque to interpret "sentiment" in this context as having anything to do with "taste." The excess was one of perceptual acuity, material awareness that ran out of the control of conscious will or intellection. It was not a psychological category of sympathy or compassion, of understanding the other's point of view from the perspective of intentional meaning, but, rather, physiological—a sensory mimesis, a response of the nervous system to external stimuli which was "excessive" because what he apprehended resisted intellectual comprehension. History as the ruin of nature could not be given meaning. The category of rationality could be applied to these physiological perceptions only in the sense of rationalization.[12]

3.9 Iurii Pimenov, *Disabled Veterans*, 1926.

3.10 "Education of the Movements of the Wounded Soldier," from Jules Amar, *The Physiology of Industrial Organization* (1918).

Walter Benjamin on World War I:

"A generation that had gone to school on a horse-drawn streetcar now stood under the open sky in a countryside in which nothing remained unchanged but the clouds, and beneath these clouds, a field of force of destructive torrents and explosions, was the tiny, fragile human body."[13]

"This immense wooing of the cosmos was enacted for the first time on a planetary scale, that is, in the spirit of technology. But because the lust for profit of the ruling class sought satisfaction through it, technology betrayed man and turned the bridal bed into a bloodbath."[14]

Henry Ford on mass production:

The production of the Model T required 7,882 distinct work operations, but, Ford noted [in his 1923 autobiography], only 12% of these tasks—only 949 operations—required "strong, able-bodied, and practically physically perfect men." Of the remainder—and this is clearly what he sees as the major achievement of his method of production— "we found that 670 could be filled by legless men, 2,637 by one-legged men, two by armless men, 715 by one-armed men and ten by blind men."[15]

103

3.2

SHOCK

Walter Benjamin's understanding of modern experience was neurological. It centered on shock. Benjamin wanted to investigate the "fruitfulness" of Freud's hypothesis, that consciousness parries shock by preventing it from penetrating deep enough to leave a permanent trace on memory, by applying it to "situations far removed from those which Freud had in mind."[16] Freud was concerned with war neurosis, the trauma of "shell shock" and catastrophic accident that plagued soldiers in World War I. Benjamin claimed that this battlefield experience of shock had become "the norm" in modern life.[17] Perceptions that once occasioned conscious reflection were now the source of shock impulses which consciousness must parry.

Nowhere was this defensive reflex more apparent than in the factory, where (Benjamin cited Marx) "workers learn to coordinate their own 'movements to the uniform and unceasing motion of an automaton.'"[18] "Independently of the worker's volition, the article being worked on comes within his range of action and moves away from him just as arbitrarily."[19] Exploitation was here to be understood as a cognitive category, not an economic one. The factory system, injuring every one of the human senses, paralyzed the imagination of the worker, whose labor was "sealed off from experience"; memory was replaced by conditioned response, learning by "drill," skill by repetition: "practice counts for nothing."[20]

Under conditions of modern technology, the aesthetic system undergoes a dialectical reversal. The human sensorium changes from a mode of being "in touch" with reality into a means of blocking out reality. Aesthetics—sensory perception—becomes *an*aesthetics, a numbing of the senses' cognitive capacity that destroys the human organism's power to respond politically even when self-preservation is at stake. Someone who is "past experiencing," writes Benjamin, is "no longer capable of telling . . . proven friend . . . from mortal enemy."[21]

■

The sensory experience of modern labor cannot be seen as limited to capitalist production. If the Soviet regime was eager to adopt capitalist industrial production whole-cloth,[22] how could it avoid importing the sensory shock that afflicted workers within it? Lenin thought he could import capitalist forms of labor without their exploitative content.[23] But capitalist form *is* its content. Form is not formalist, as the sensory experience of factory labor clearly demonstrates. Assembly line production does not feel different to the sentient body simply because the worker is socialist. How, then, can one distinguish Soviet modernizing processes from those in the West? In investigating Benjamin's hypothesis of modern shock within the context of "constructing socialism" in the Soviet Union, one is struck by a temporal difference: for the proletariat of the Soviet Union industrialization was still a dreamworld when, for workers in capitalist countries, it was already a lived catastrophe.

The enthusiasm for machine culture in the early Soviet Union has been noted frequently and described at length. But a crucial point often overlooked in these accounts is the degree to which the cult of the machine preceded the machines themselves. Machine culture under Western capitalism was adaptive to an already existing level of industrialization.[24] In the late nineteenth century Frederick Winslow Taylor devised his "scientific management" of labor that broke down the work process into basic motions of optimal effectiveness, treating human beings as machines in order to get the most efficient production out of them.[25] It was the factory owners, not the workers, whose interests were thereby served. The worker's adaptation to the machine was a work requirement, but it was also a mimetic defense. Human robotics functioned as a form of armor. As in nature, where an animal changes its physical attributes to mimic its external environment, the worker who turned her/his body into a machine with deadened senses was protecting against the shock of machine labor itself.

Under the pretechnological conditions that existed in the early Soviet Union, in contrast, the cult of the human-as-machine sustained a utopian meaning.[26] Its ecstatic intensity in the 1920s, at a time when the factory workforce had disintegrated and the country was struggling simply to restore the pre–World War I industrial capacity, anticipated mechanized processes rather than being a defensive response to them.[27] The Central Institute of Labor (Tsentralnyi Institut Truda, or TsIT), founded in 1920 to implement Taylorist work methods imported from the United States, was run by a poet. It was an experimental laboratory in the mechanized rhythmics of labor.[28] In this still preindustrial context, human bodies practicing the rhythm of machines were like shamans practicing magic, mimicking a desired state in order to bring it into existence. Scientifically calculated body movements were the industrial-age equivalent of a rain dance.

The institute's director, Aleksei Gastev, knew firsthand the monotonous tedium of machine labor. During political exile in Paris before the war he had been a metal worker, and he understood capitalist exploitation in its physical, corporeal form. But in his proletarian poetry he developed an ecstatic vision of this still painful process, done now by a global collective of workers, for the purpose of giving birth through their labor to a world of universal harmony and peace. A million hammers striking at the same moment would set the entire world vibrating.[29]

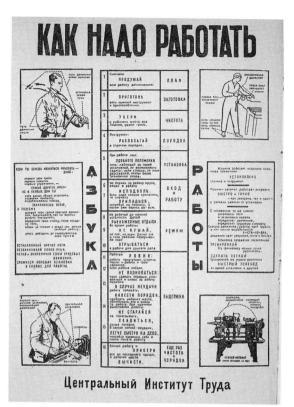

3.11 From Aleksei Gastev (Central Institute of Labor), *Kak nado rabotat'* (How to Work): Rhythms of the day and rhythms of the body (1922). Gastev was proud of the fact that Lenin had this chart hung in his office and personally adapted its methods.

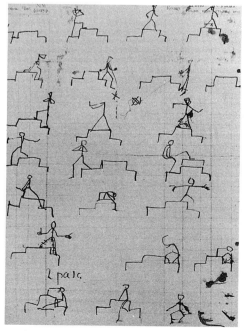

3.12 "Action score" by Lev Kuleshov for a 1921 "film without film."

Gastev acknowledged that only through "powerful inrushes" of foreign capital, amounting to "completely enslaving" Soviet industry to American, English, and German capitalists, could the transformation be achieved. Speed, standardization, and "technical spirit" were necessary.[30] "Catastrophes"—destruction and death—were inevitable.[31] The power of "machinism" would produce a new human sensorium of electric nerves, brain machines, and cinema eyes;[32] and a global, mass body with collective movements, collective feelings, collective goals,

creating one world brain in place of millions of brains. Granted that as yet there is no international language, but there are international gestures, there are international psychological formulae which millions know how to use. . . . In the future this tendency will make individual thought impossible and it will imperceptibly be transformed into the objective psychology of an entire class with its systems of switch-ons, switch-offs, short circuits.[33]

Machine culture, Soviet style, had its origins as the expression of a lack, so that even its brutality could be seen to possess a utopian quality. Only in this dreamlike context could poetry and production techniques converge so irresistibly, attracting dramatists, cinematographers, and choreographers as artists of the human body. Industrial labor became the model of bodily discipline for producing the new man as a creative instrument, fusing work and dance. In contrast, in the United States, mass production was pragmatically motivated, an accommodation with man in his given, imperfect form.

The Soviet ideal in the 1920s was to combine the creativity of art with the exactness of science. There is no doubt that this opened the door for ideological justifications of exploitative technologies, that is, for "aestheticizing" politics in the bourgeois sense of the term.[34] Yet it also promised an overcoming of the bourgeois splitting of mind and body, a return to "aesthetics" in its original cognitive meaning. With no sense of contradiction, Taylorist techniques were brought together in Soviet culture with artistic methods from disparate sources. Exemplary were theories of ballet and mime imported from Europe by Volkonskii and Gardin, who in turn influenced early Soviet cinema directors.[35] The early theory of montage formulated by Lev Kuleshov compared the rhythmic articulation of the actor's body, a series of basic motions as expressive gestures, with film shots: both were segments of movement, the "combination of separate moments of action . . . unfold[ing] in space and last[ing] in time."[36] Montage for Kuleshov was screen rhythm, and the self-conscious, controlled body of the actor was its universal model. As in Taylor's scientific management, each part of the actor's body was treated as an independent module that could be organized with other parts in complex poses. The same process occurred in cinematic construction: segments of film, like segments of bodily gesture, were, as Iampolskii writes, "signs which opposed one another and they make sense in precisely that opposition."[37] Both

3.13 Technical expert teaching a peasant woman the fundamentals of industrial work in the 1930s.

3.14 Photograph (1926) of the construction of the Marx-Engels Institute, Moscow, designed by C. E. Chernyshev. Nonmechanized building methods necessitated wooden ramps to enable wheelbarrows to be pushed to the top of the structure.

3.15 Street vendors selling toy trucks in Moscow, 1920s.

3.16 Moscow, winter 1928.

3.17 Digging the foundations for the shops at
Magnitostroi, the largest construction site in
the country during the First Five Year Plan. A
worker recalled: "It looked queer: digging a
huge circular ditch. We thought it was for containing a wild animal, but it was the foundation for open-hearth ovens."[38]

montage rhythm and body rhythm were taught in the Experimental Cinema Laboratory of the Moscow film school in which Kuleshov took an active part.[39] Theater was affected as well. The dramatist Vsevolod Meierkhold developed a system of "biomechanics," treating the actor as a malleable object of emotional expression. The goal here too was control over the body by eliminating all superfluous and unintended movements. Stop watches and time clocks were used to help acting students pattern their actions. The influence of Gastev and Taylorism was explicit.[40]

In 1923, a theater critic, Platon Kerzhentsev, founded the League of Time, with Gastev and Meierkhold on the board (and Lenin and Trotsky honorary officers), in order to promote temporal efficiency among the general population.[41] The League's journal, *Vremia* (Time), encouraged the grassroots organization of 800 "time cells" within the army, factories, government bodies, and schools. The "Timists" carried "chronocards" in order to monitor incidences of time-wasting due to tardiness, wasted motion, lengthy speeches, etc., and encouraged "spontaneous self-discipline."[42]

Stites observes that there were two cultural receptions of American technology in the Soviet Union, one urban and the other rural.[43] In the case of the peasantry, the motivation was more spiritual than scientific: technology had cosmological significance in that it "promised deliverance from backwardness."[44] It would be wrong to dismiss this fervor among the general population as officially orchestrated.[45] Henry Ford was not only the symbol of the "colossal productivity" of an unskilled, albeit disciplined, workforce; he was also the producer of the consumer item most coveted by the Russian peasantry, the Fordson tractor. By 1926, the Soviet Union had ordered 24,000 Fordsons, "a figure equal to about 85% of the total Soviet production."[46] Ford became, literally, a folk hero:

Peasants called their tractors fordzonishkas. . . . *[They] saw him as a magical persona, asking the journalist Maurice Hindus if he was richer than the tsars and was the most clever American. They longed to gaze upon him personally. . . . Ford's name was better known than those of most communist figures, excepting Lenin and Trotsky. Some peasants named their children after him; others endowed their new 'iron horses' with human characteristics. An American business reporter in 1930 observed that Lenin was the Russian God and Ford his St. Peter.*[47]

Benjamin described Moscow in 1926 as a city still playing "hide and seek" with the village.[48] As late as 1932 an American businessman was "astonished at Moscow pedestrians jaywalking among the vehicles like peasants in country lanes."[49] It needs to be remembered that "constructing socialism" was handwork well into the 1930s. At the building site of the model industrial project of Magnitostroi/Magnitogorsk (the steel plant/town modeled after Gary, Indiana), millions of cubic feet of earth were moved with hand tools. In 1936 two-thirds of all earthmoving work was still being done there without mechanization.[50] This was where unskilled peasants came to become factory workers through the trial by fire of "shock work" (*udarnyi trud*) on the construction brigades.

Shock work, the favored organization form of labor during the First Five Year Plan, was precisely *not* Taylorist. Rather than standardizing rhythms based on scientific calculation of individual body performance, it was executed in rushes, or "storms," by teams of workers. Its origins were said to have been "the very old, rural, rhythm-setting work cry (*vziali*)," the goal of which was higher productivity through extra human effort *without* machines.[51] Whereas Taylorist rhythms set "norms" of labor, the purpose of shock work was to break them.

The choice of words was significant. "Shock" (*udar*) is the Russian word meaning a blow or strike with impacting force in the military sense (of an air attack), in the natural sense (of a thunder clap or musical percussion), and also in the medical sense (of stroke or seizure).[52] The collective thrust of the shock workers *gave* a shock as the agents of historical change, "bringing the time of socialism closer."[53] Their image was superhuman, rather than machinelike and nonhuman. They produced the shock of modernity rather than parrying its effects. At the same time, they bore the brunt of the attack on their own bodies, as shock work entailed physical sacrifice and exhaustion for the sake of the collective goal.

Beginning in 1929, the authorities promoted shock work by means of campaigns for "socialist competition," whereby one factory, shop, or brigade was "challenged" by another in order to accomplish more in less time.[54] Machines, no longer the measure of man, were brutally exploited, "injured" and run into the ground during these norm-breaking attempts.[55] Workers vied with each other like athletic teams in order to set records, often with primitive technology. The winners were nicknamed "airplanes" and "lightning sheets"; the losers were "slackers" and "crocodiles."[56] The "prizes" included media fame, higher wages, and coveted consumer goods like apartments and motorcycles. The bodily pain produced by such physical exertion was dismissed, as was its irrationality from an economic point of view.[57] This was a passionately emotional affair involving team spirit, daily drama, and heroic achievement. Shock workers, whose experience bears a striking resemblance to today's professional athletes, seem to have been genuinely exhilarated by the overexertion—and as exhausted as their machines as a result.

3.18 Left and right: Nikolai Sokolov, VKhUTEMAS project for a resort hotel, 1928.

In 1929 *Pravda* suggested that an ideal socialist community be built outside of Moscow, a proposal that turned into the "Green City" competition.[58] Green City was to be a recreational, collective space not devoted to production. The competition proved embarrassing, however, as some of the best-known architects suggested environments that, as compensatory relief from the strains of production, were so antithetical to the socialist work world as to imply a radical criticism of it.

The constructivist architect Moisei Ginzburg and his student Mikhail Barshch submitted an entry that articulated leisure space in anarcho-individualist terms, stressing privacy, voluntarism, and lack of conformity—the antithesis of the collective values of socialist production. Their entry was a linear city, based on the "ribbon scheme" that "cut a pair of automobile roads through a territory and strung houses along them, with public facilities at appropriate intervals."[59] The buildings were in the international style of the Bauhaus and Le Corbusier; the social outlook was noncompulsory. "In the plan as a whole [Ginzburg] opposed 'natural' order to geometric order; in transportation he favored the individualistic private automobile over the scheduled train or bus; in housing, he designed dwelling units for individual families, placing a sliding door between areas designated for husband and wife, so that 'ties among people, even among man and wife, will be voluntary.'" The goal was not efficiency but "the flowering of human personality."[60]

Konstantin Melnikov's Green City proposal was collectivist enough. He designed a retreat with hotels rather than private homes, combining private entries and living spaces with communal kitchens and large common corridors where people could meet and socialize, reminiscent of the nineteenth-century phalansteries proposed by the French utopian theorist Charles Fourier.[61] But the plan's structuring of leisure space was implicitly critical despite its collectivism. Frederick Starr writes: "Melnikov quite correctly began with the assumption that members of the overworked laborforce were exhausted. The recently lengthened working day, combined with the acute housing shortage and the introduction of rationing in 1929, pushed urban workers to the limit of their physical and psychological endurance."[62] The space was designed to provide "temporary respite for workers brought there on a rotating basis from teeming Moscow. His Green City would offer relief by placing industrial laborers in a direct and intimate relationship with the primary forces of nature. All forests were to be carefully pruned so as to combine sunlight and fresh air in ratios most beneficial for those walking through them. Specially constructed solar pavilions were to be erected in open areas to enable sallow mill-workers to expose their bodies to the concentrated rays of the sun, even in winter."[63] Melnikov's solutions highlighted ecological concerns that were totally absent from the mentality of Stalinist industrialization. "Energy for the city's needs would be drawn exclusively from the wind, and . . . [in an] allusion to Fourier,

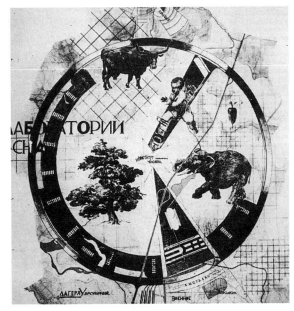

3.19 Konstantin Melnikov, plan for Green City, 1929.

animals would be permitted to roam at will through a large sector of the town, so the weary Muscovite could imagine himself once more a primeval man roaming in God's peaceable kingdom."[64]

This retreat offered a cure—sleep—providing the techno-aesthetics for its facilitation. Melnikov wrote: "Man sleeps one third of his lifetime . . . twenty years of lying down without consciousness, without guidance as one journeys into the sphere of mysterious worlds to touch the unexplored depths of the sources of curative sacraments, and perhaps of miracles."[65] The central hotel of the city was a "Laboratory of Sleep," a total sleep environment wherein all elements of the human sensorium could be effected. "All beds here were to be built-in, like laboratory tables; to obviate the need for pillows, the floors sloped gently to the ends of the structure. The walls were broken with great sheets of glass, for sleep would be encouraged at all times of day and would under some circumstances require sunlight as well as darkness."[66] At either end were control booths, where technicians produced an entire synaesthetic system by using instruments

to regulate the temperature, humidity, and air pressure, as well as to waft salubrious scents and "rarified condensed air" through the halls. Nor would sound be left unorganized. Specialists working "according to scientific facts" would transmit from the control center a range of sounds gauged to intensify the process of slumber. The rustle of leaves, the cooing of nightingales, or the soft murmur of waves would instantly relax the most overwrought veteran of the metropolis. Should these fail, the mechanized beds would then begin gently to rock until consciousness was lost. At this point, the natural sounds might continue or, at the command of trained specialists in the control booths, specially commissioned poems or works of music would be performed so as to obliterate any residual tensions or anxieties from the world of consciousness. Step by step, the worker would relax and his psyche would be rehabilitated by the combined forces of art and technology. Taken together, the building would be a "Sonata of Sleep," or, in Melnikov's pun on son, the Russian word for sleep, a SONnaia SONata.[67]

Melnikov sent a placard to the jury for the competition: "Cure through sleep and thereby alter the character. . . . Anyone thinking otherwise is sick."[68] The much-debated entry received criticism ranging from "romantic" to "anti-socialist," the work of a "wrecker." "How, the jury wondered, could a major architect permit himself to apotheosize sleep at the very time when the nation was gearing up to transform life through work?"

One of the few to express unabashed enthusiasm for Melnikov's proposal to manipulate completely both the physical and psychic environment was New York's ebullient showman "Roxy" Roth, who, accompanied by his architect, Wallace Harrison, and several advisors, visited Moscow in the summer of 1931 as part of a continental tour to gain ideas for the proposed Radio City

3.20 Konstantin Melnikov, "Laboratory of Sleep" for the Green City, 1929.

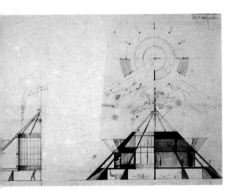

3.21 Konstantin Melnikov, solar pavilion for the Green City, 1929, first variant.

Music Hall. Melnikov recalled meeting with the delegation just as he was completing work on the SONnaia SONata. Roth had been directed to Melnikov because of the many auditoriums the Russian had recently designed for workers' clubs, but it was the SONnaia SONata that immediately caught Roth's imagination. He recognized at once the theatrical potential of Melnikov's fantastic control booths, and resolved to provide his own technicians with similar facilities for controlling the temperature, atmosphere, sounds, and smells in Radio City Music Hall. Within months, Roth's publicity department was bombarding the American public with the Melnikovian claim that "two hours in the washed, ionized, ozoned, ultra-solarized air [of Radio City Music Hall] are worth a month in the country."[69]

This U.S. entrepreneur had no trouble from the authorities in his own country in advertising the compensatory nature of his techno-aesthetic environment. On the contrary. Making up to the consumer what was robbed from his or her life as a productive worker was the norm of capitalist culture. But precisely the rejection of this human cost-accounting was at the basis of socialist legitimacy—as well it should have been. By adopting the capitalist heavy-industry definition of economic modernization, however, Soviet socialism had no alternative but to try to produce a utopia out of the production process itself. In making this choice, the Soviets missed the opportunity to transform the very idea of economic "development," and of the ecological preconditions through which it might be realized.

3.22 Vitaly Komar and Alexander Melamid, Bayonne, New Jersey, *Bayonne Labor,* from the series *Bergen Point Brass Foundry,* **1988.** (color plate 9)

The mastery of nature, so the imperialists teach, is the purpose of all technology. But who would trust a cane wielder who proclaimed the mastery of children by adults to be the purpose of education? Is not education above all the indispensable ordering of the relationship between generations and therefore mastery, if we are to use this term of that relationship and not of children? And likewise technology is not the mastery of nature but of the relation between nature and man.
—Walter Benjamin, 1926[70]

A great business is too big to be human.
—Henry Ford, 1929[71]

3.3

THE NATURE OF MACHINES

Socialism necessitates a totally new relationship to nature. The technology of capitalism will not do to realize its aims. Capitalism organizes the exploitation of nature for private gain. Exploiting labor power is one part of this process, but not the whole. And just as capitalism will not pay for the reproduction of labor power (the social welfare bill) unless compelled to do so by state taxation, it will not by its own volition pay for the reproduction of the forces of nature that it consumes so voraciously.[72] Lenin was wrong to believe that technology is nothing more than the embodiment of objective science, hence value-free. Technology is the material manifestation of human beings' relationships with nature and among themselves.

Nature can be brutal in its effects on the physical body. Hunger, cold, sickness, and death are its manners of assault, holding all of humanity in their power. It is not surprising that the potential of modern technology has prompted the dream of the domination of nature. But as humans are themselves natural bodies, the dream is self-damaging and ultimately self-defeating. Marx knew as much when, in 1844 at the age of 26, he wrote that the overcoming of human alienation would necessitate a reconciliation between humans and nature, "the realized naturalism of man and the realized humanism of nature."[73] Such formulations all but disappeared in his later texts, which are expressed in the language of political economy, the legitimating discourse of his time. The 1844 manuscripts remained unknown and unpublished until the Marx-Engels Institute in Moscow launched an edition of the complete works of Marx in 1927, under the editorship of David Riazanov.[74] A partial Russian translation appeared that year. The first full, German edition of these "Economic and Philosophical Manuscripts" was published in Berlin in 1932, and the timing could not have been less auspicious. Riazanov had been arrested in 1931, victim of the general purge of the Soviet Academy of Sciences.[75] Hitler came to power in 1933 and the German discussion of Marx's writings was quickly repressed.

The fact that the 1844 manuscripts continued to have a strong underground existence in Europe, fundamentally shaping the tradition of (anti-Stalinist) "Western Marxism," is well known.[76] But what of their influence in the Soviet Union? Riazanov belonged to left-intellectual circles in Moscow and no doubt would have spoken with colleagues of his discovery. Georg Lukács recalled having access to the manuscripts through a "stroke of luck" in 1930, when he held a research post at the Marx-Engels Institute.[77] Of course, not all readers of the manuscripts interpreted them similarly, and Lukács remained loyal to Soviet Marxism despite his exposure. One can find in the "Economic and Philosophic Manuscripts" (as in all truly significant texts) evidence for a multiplicity of arguments. Perhaps not until the ecological crisis of the end of the twentieth century does the young Marx's commitment to a reconciliation with nature appear to be not merely an expression of nineteenth-century romanticism or youthful idealism, but an intensely practical political concern.

It is possible to piece together fragments of a different sensitivity existing within Soviet culture, one that might have found nourishment in Marx's early writings. Proving that it did is not the important point. Nor does it matter if historians have failed to find these fragments particularly significant. Even if not representative of their own time, they resonate with ours and, politically, that is what counts.

■

Consider in this context the "utopian surplus" in the machine fantasy of the constructivists, precisely the element that made their designs open to criticism from a practical point of view.[78] The constructivists' attempts to liquidate the distinction between artist and worker, not by the subservience of aesthetic pleasure to industrial instrumentality but by the interpenetration of these activities, provided images suggestive of a reconciliation with nature, wherein sensual (aesthetic) pleasure was understood as the goal, transcending mere physical need. Soviet sensuality was not nearly so closely intertwined with sexual pleasure as it was in the consumerist West.[79] Indeed, there was a strong strain of sexual asceticism among the Soviet avant-garde, from Filonov to Malevich, from Fedorov to Rodchenko, and it was a broadly held Revolutionary sentiment.[80] But a utopics of sensuality did exist as part of Bolshevik discourse, and it retained a strong hold within the culture. In the daily-life context of extreme cold, dark days, epidemics of disease, and wartime suffering in the Soviet Union, all of the attributes of organic "life" (*zhisn*)—light, movement, sun, air, water—had utopian appeal. Alla Efimova has argued on this basis that the sun-drenched canvases typical of socialist realist paintings were effective not because of what they depicted, but how. Their visual style of representing bodily comfort—life over death, health over illness, plenty over want—appealed to the viewer on a somatic level that had little to do with their ideologically contrived content. Efimova cites evidence from the contemporary texts showing that "Realism is understood as making the viewer feel 'real'—alive and sensually responsive. Such goals as to 'stir up' to 'awaken,' to 'touch on the raw' take precedence over purely ideological indoctrination."[81] In this context of utopian desire, it needs to be remembered that socialism did deliver to the general population of the Soviet Union levels of public health, medical care, and leisure facilities that had never before existed, and that their democratic distribution set a model for the world.

3.23 Aleksandr Laktionov, *Letter from the Front*, 1947.

Life over death: Lunacharskii in a particularly passionate moment contrasted the fossilized and morbid romanticism of bourgeois culture to "our" culture, organic and pulsating: "The smell of such 'romanticism' is the smell of death. And not just death. The dead at the cemetery are of no interest to us and even when they are buried by the dead, we say: 'Let the dead bury the dead.' But the dead who sit in the office chairs of publishing houses, god damn them, who write novels or plays as dead as they are . . . these dead spread miasma and poison [to] living life."[82] If the dead past was to be prevented from contaminating socialist life, so too was dead matter.[83] The utopian promise of industrialization was not only in mastering nature, but in releasing its living force. Animation became a value in itself.[84]

Soviet experimental cinema included experts in the genre of animation, wherein microdivisions of montage gave the illusion of life to inanimate forms.[85] When Gastev, Lissitzky, and Vertov celebrated machine-man, it was not as a somnambulant automaton but as the dynamic counterpart to the sounds, rhythms, and vibrancy of the industrial process which they understood as itself a vital force. Striking too were constructivist theories of "socialist" commodities that, as intersubjective partners, were to provide alternatives to objects of consumption in their reified, capitalist form. Hubertus Gassner writes:

In the constructivist universe, objects exist solely as organs of human activity. They adjust to people's actions, expand and die with them, while constantly renewing their own shape and function. The constructivist objects are congruent counterparts of the subject. Therein lies their utopian potential.[86]

Rodchenko called these objects "comrades."[87] Christina Kiaer has rightly emphasized that this conception made inorganic objects a "doubling of the human body"— whereas Marx had criticized the capitalist commodity for having precisely the opposite effect.[88] Writing home from Paris in 1925, where his design for a Workers' Club was on display, Rodchenko expressed disgust at the commodification of pleasure that typified the city's life, the "endless bidets" and "indecent" postcards—even the Brie and Roquefort nauseated him.[89] And he deplored the way Paris's commodity culture

3.24 Aleksandr Rodchenko, Workers' Club interior, 1925. It was displayed in the Soviet Pavilion (designed by Melnikov; see figure 2.34) at the Paris Exposition Internationale des Arts Décoratifs, 1925. French workers who visited the display stroked the furniture and said "this is ours."[90]

3.25 Varvara Stepanova, folding furniture for the theater production *The Death of Tarelkhin* by A. Suchov Kobilyn, 1922. Reconstruction by A. N. Lavrentiev and I. Presnezova, 1981.

turned women into "a thing."[91] In contrast, the constructivist commodities as "comrades" were the height of interactivity. Multifunctionality, mobility, and convertability were their virtues. Use value dominated over display value. Coziness was avoided. Beds metamorphosed into tables or became armchairs.[92] Cooking utensils collapsed into small packages.[93] Unisex clothing celebrated movement. Chairs folded up when not in use. Tatlin launched an attack in "The Problem of the Relationship between Man and Object: Let Us Declare War on Chests of Drawers and Sideboards."[94] Theater sets advertised the new conception of living space. Rodchenko's designs for Anatolii Glebov's play *Inga* (1929) used the performance as "merely a pretext to set up a complex system of furnishings. . . . The concept of transformation governed the whole artistic approach to the play," with the walls opening up into tables and benches and the armchairs opening into a bed.[95] Benjamin, visiting Moscow in 1926–1927, commented on the "astonishing experimentation" that characterized daily life: "Indeed, what distinguishes the Bolshevik, the Russian Communist, from his Western comrade, is this unconditional readiness for mobilization."[96]

The post-Soviet critic Vladimir Papernyi sees this mobility as the key distinction between the culture of the artistic avant-garde, which he calls Culture One, and that of Stalin's time, Culture Two.[97] He cites the artists:

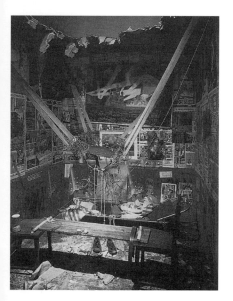

3.26 Ilia Kabakov, *The Man Who Flew into Space from His Apartment,* 1981–1986. From *Ten Characters,* installation, 1988. (color plate 3)

"I have, says Culture One, henceforth freed myself forever from human immobility, I am in constant motion" [Dziga Vertov, 1923]. It is a culture of displacement, changing states, instability and unsteadiness. . . . "An instant of creative tempo, rapid shift in forms; there is no stagnation, there is only turbulent movement" [Kazimir Malevich, 1919].

In this culture architectural constructions must be mobile—only because "the very idea of movement has a great potential for development" [Georgii Krutikov, 1928]. Houses should be "able to turn to the sun" [Kornelii Zelinskii, 1925]. . . . "The cabins of ships, airplanes and train cars become the prototypical dwellings" [Moisei Ginzburg, 1927]. The house turns into "a glass box or a passenger cabin fitted with a door and put on wheels, the inhabitant inside" [Velimir Khlebnikov, 1928–1933].

In fact, "change of residence" in such circumstances is unnecessary. If you want, just "attach the wings and the wheels and take off, the house and all" [Vladimir Maiakovskii].[98]

In contrast, according to Papernyi, Culture Two, the Stalinist culture, abhorred uprootedness. Cosmopolitanism became synonymous with betraying the motherland. The architectural style of Culture Two was monumentally permanent. Huge blocks of buildings pressed their heavy weight into the ground, constructed to embody principles of hierarchy and centralization. Not only buildings but people too were tied down in place. "Beginning in 1932 the internal passport system was gradually implemented. . . . In 1940 the 'voluntary departure of employees from factories and offices' was forbidden once and for all." "The sight of a man lifted off the ground makes Culture Two cringe."[99] Exemplary of Papernyi's argument is the fact that in Culture Two even a monument to space flight appears unrelentingly grounded. No matter how high the pedestal or how soaring its shape, the cosmonaut seems to struggle against gravity in vain.

■

During the famine years of the 1920s Vladimir Tatlin "cracked open the pavement in the yard of the Leningrad Academy of Art and planted potatoes."[100] Anti-urbanism became a movement on the eve of the First Five Year Plan.[101] The architect Moisei Ginzburg suggested solutions for dwelling places that were implicitly critical of the social hierarchy fostered by urban centralization. In Moscow there was an experimental center for the use of windmills as an energy source. A proposal was made for transforming Moscow itself into a Green City. Taylor writes:

Such attempts to "de-centre" the traditional city clearly implied a new type of relationship between city and countryside, hence between proletariat and peasant. These schemes attempted to incorporate principles of planning suggested by "nature," in opposition to the "hard" design principles of orthodox technology and science. They implied a high degree of mobility and a collapse of the conventional symbolic hierarchy in which power is vested in the city and handed out to the provinces. In this sense they were "organicist" as well as "communist," and might well have had far-reaching consequences for Soviet life.[102]

The fact that they did *not* have far-reaching consequences was a lost opportunity not only for Soviet urban development, but for the history of socialism generally. While tons of asphalt were being dumped on the city streets to make them look like those of a Western capitalist metropolis (only bigger), Ginzburg and visionaries like him were nudged to the periphery.

Against the current that glorified heavy industrial development (again, on the Western capitalist model), Tatlin undertook a pointedly individualist project that experimented with low technology, justified in socialist terms. It was necessary, he wrote, to produce "an original object which differs radically from the objects of the West and America," necessary because "our way of life is built on completely different principles . . . on healthy and natural principles. The Western object cannot satisfy us. . . . Therefore I show such a great interest in organic form as a point of departure for the creation of new objects."[103] Working in the Novodevichii monastery on the outskirts of Moscow from 1929 to 1931, Tatlin built such a "new object," a flying machine that worked as an air bicycle, which he called Letatlin.[104] He hoped that this birdlike structure would become a mass item of use and as cheap as a regular bicycle.[105] It would, he claimed, return to humans the power of flight, which they had lost during biological evolution.[106] Moreover, it was environmentally sound: "The air bicycle will relieve the town of transport, of noise, and overcrowding, and will cleanse the air of petrol fumes."[107] "We have been robbed of our feeling of flight by the mechanical flight of the aeroplane," Tatlin wrote. "We cannot feel the movement of our body in the air."[108] His lament resonates with the earliest fantasies evoked by airplane travel, depicting technology as an enhancement of human sensory existence, an aesthetics of everyday life.

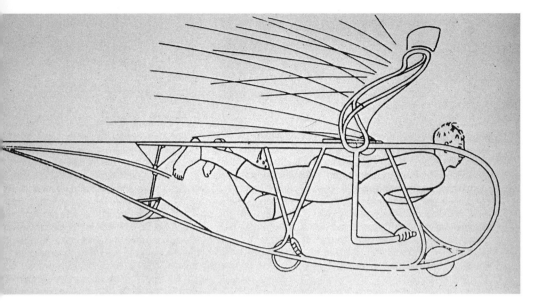

3.27 Vladimir Tatlin, *Letatlin without Skin,* displayed at the Museum of Fine Art, Moscow, 1932.

Nature is more clever than mechanics. —Tatlin[109]

3.28 Vladimir Tatlin, *Letatlin.*

3.29 Cigarette card depicting life in the year 2000 (*en l'an 2000*), part of a series by the French commercial artist Jean Marc Côté, 1899.

■

Outside of the city of Berlin in what used to be the German Democratic Republic, a mechanical construction looms up from the landscape, rising sixty meters high above the village of Niederfinau. Its construction was begun in 1925 under the Weimar republic and completed in 1934, the second year of the Nazi regime. The structure connects the canal systems of the geophysically disjoined Havel and Oder rivers. It functions as an elevator for boats. They enter a tub of water that is raised or lowered 36 meters vertically, and they exit to continue on their route along a system of canals that stretches from the North to the Baltic seas, crossing the entire state of Prussia.

The structure exemplifies the machine utopia of a literate culture in that its appeal is fundamentally intellectual. The principle of its design, while technologically pathbreaking when compared with previous lock systems, is as old as Archimedes: Volumes displace their equal weight in water. Because all boats that enter the elevator

3.30 The ship lift at Niederfinau, Prussia, built 1925–1934.

3.31 Ship lift at Niederfinau, interior.

tub displace a weight of water equal to their own, the weight of the tub remains constant—at 4,250 tons. The mechanism of the lift is regulated according to this principle. It operates by a system of 192 counterweights that balance the tub with the support of 256 wire cables, so that only a very small force (four motors of 75 horsepower each) creates the differential that will raise or lower the whole. Each functioning of the ship lift moves 4,250 tons at 12 centimeters per second, achieving the vertical distance of 36 meters in five minutes' time.

Utopian desire is evoked here in the calm balance between nature's laws and human needs. Human mobility and machine mobility are perfectly synchronized to accomplish a goal with the least amount of effort on both parts. The apparatus, rather than spewing smoke through phallic chimneys, opens up to take you in. Holding you gently in its watertub, it brings you slowly and quietly to a different space, raising or lowering you through montaged layers of air, water, and earth that follow each other like film frames—and lets you go again. This is human intervention into nature by means of its own laws, in order to facilitate human beings connecting with each other. Compared to the massive autobahn system that Hitler implemented in the 1930s, the environmental disruption is minimal. Although officially out-of-date with the arrival of highway technology, it has functioned without interruption since its construction. Canals are still an efficient means for moving people and goods. But highway systems move military units, and they are the state-preferred form of infrastructure.[110] The shiplift at Niederfinau, now a tourist destination, is emblematic of a kind of machine utopia the developmental path of which was cut off abruptly when technology was brutally forced into the production of instruments of war.

3.32 Ship lift at Niederfinau, upper entry to lock.

■

The sculptor Vadim Sidur, interviewed by a German journalist in 1980, recalled that as an eighteen-year-old soldier during World War II his unit arrived at his home town of Dnepropetrovsk in the Ukraine. The house where he had been born had been totally destroyed: "Only the chimney towered upward, like a modern monument of my childhood and youth, and next to it grew the spreading maple that had once been the little tree my father and I planted a few years before the war."[111] Shortly thereafter, Sidur was wounded in battle. "For quite a long time I wavered between life and death, among shellshocked men with jaws missing and torn yellow flaps of skin on their stomachs."[112] The side of his face had been shattered by a dumdum bullet from a German sharpshooter. Sent to the Central Institute for Traumatology and Orthopedics, where all those were treated who had lost their faces during the war (eyes, tongues, noses, chins), Sidur became one of the millions of cyborgs produced from the injured of this war. The side of his face was totally reconstructed. When he studied art in Moscow after the war, he chose to specialize in sculpture, the art that metamorphoses inorganic material into organic forms.

In the intellectual climate of anticosmopolitanism, Sidur's training was traditional: "The name Malevich said nothing to me."[113] He saw himself as the last of the species of artists in a tradition that reached back to the Scythians, Assyrians, and Egyptians, as well as to the archaic Greeks. And yet in his "underground cellar" in Moscow, the basement studio where he worked in increasing isolation from official culture, the thematics of his sculptures were persistently contemporary. A central focus was the transformation of industrially produced objects, salvaged from the refuse, into evocatively anthropomorphic forms. This practice was not original, having become a commonplace with dadaism at the time of the First World War. But Sidur's work was uniquely serious in its fusion of the organic and the inorganic. It criticized social reality rather than the institution of art. One of his sculptures of industrially produced parts was rooted in his studio like a tree, so large that it could only see the light of day if the building itself were destroyed. His work encourages metaphysical reflection on the fact that industrial objects are themselves nature, and that this nature, twisted and bent into weapons, has been turned with fierce destructiveness upon itself.

To produce a mass army as a precision instrument of military attack was a conscious goal of Nazi culture, its own form of machine utopia. It had no counterpart in the Soviet Union.[114] For all the brutality of Stalin's regime, the deliberate creation of an armored, mass army trained for offensive military purposes was not on the agenda. Despite propaganda shows of military preparedness in the 1930s, Stalin's war of industrialization, waged against time, was not a means for expansion in space. On the con-

3.33 Vadim Sidur, *Self-Portrait* (*Father of Coffin Art*), 1982.

3.34 Photograph of Vadim Sidur (d. 1986).

3.35 Civilian women and old men shovel a huge ditch as a tank trap to halt the German panzers advancing on Moscow, fall 1941.

3.36 Stalingrad in February 1943. Photo by Georgii Zelma.

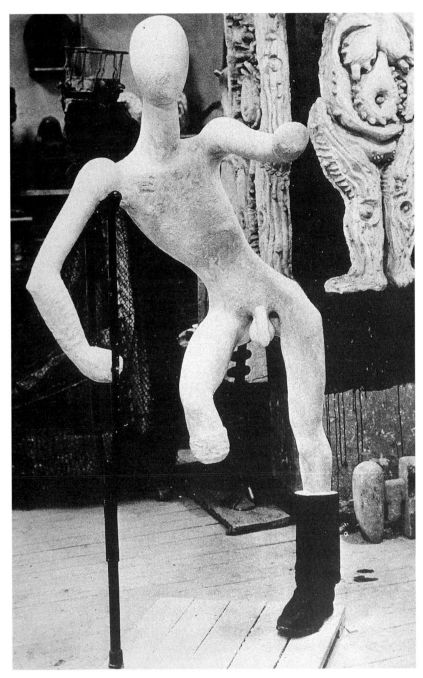

3.37 Vadim Sidur, *The Victor,* 1983.

trary, criticism has been directed at his lack of military preparedness.[115] Preoccupied with building a canal system studded with gigantic statues that glorified himself (and so grandiose that it could not deliver water rationally where it was needed), Stalin had not prepared the country to meet the Nazi onslaught.[116] When it came, the blow was traumatic.[117] The shock affected all aspects of social life.[118] The Soviet death toll in World War II, military and civilian, is estimated at twenty million,[119] brought about by a devil's alliance between the technological brutality of Hitler's heavily armored army and the brutality of natural forces—freezing, sickness, hunger—that became the decisive weapon against the invading army itself.

In April 1941 Hitler brought total destruction to the Yugoslavian capital of Belgrade through a massive air attack; in June he invaded Russia. Vadim Sidur recalled: "It began with Guernica [in the Spanish Civil War]," and after Belgrade "hundreds of cities in my country had to believe it. . . . And then we heard of Coventry, Dresden, Hiroshima, and Nagasaki."[120] No country suffered modern warfare with such intensity as the Soviet Union in the Nazi invasion—until August 1945, when the United States dropped atomic bombs on two Japanese cities. With this act—announced by U.S. President Truman on the radio as the technological triumph of harnessing the nuclear power of the sun—the use of nature's energy to destroy human beings reached a qualitatively new level of barbarism. After the war in the Soviet Union, "catching up with the West" took on the meaning of developing equal weapons of mass destruction.

"Art in the Age of the Balance of Terror" is how Vadim Sidur's work has been described.[121] Not the machine nature of humans but the human nature of machines is brought to life in his sculptures. In one of his last series, the "coffin works," machine parts are assembled into animate, human forms, which he called "technological cadavers." Pressed into too-narrow coffins, they refuse to be contained. The nature in them, still alive, screams out in protest against its treatment by the human species.

3.38 Vadim Sidur, *Coffin Man,* 1972, from the series *Coffin Art.*

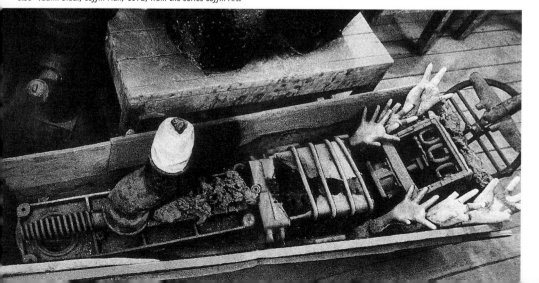

3.39 Vadim Sidur, *Coffin Woman*, 1975, from the series *Coffin Art*.

Bomber planes make us remember what Leonardo Da Vinci expected of the flight of man; he was to have raised himself into the air "in order to look for snow on the mountain summits, and then return to scatter it over city streets shimmering with the heat of summer."
—Pierre-Maxime Schuhl (1938)[122]

CHAPTER 4

CULTURE FOR THE MASSES

4.1

THE MASSES

Who are "the masses"? The word was launched in the modern era as a term of contempt. Its predecessor, the mob, was an unruly crowd occupying public space and threatening to destabilize the public order. The masses, however, unlike the mob, were not just an occasional social formation. With nineteenth-century industrialization and urbanization, processes that drew people together in large aggregates as a matter of course, the masses became a permanent presence in social life. In quotidian rhythms, they flowed through space as a spontaneous accumulation of persons, anonymous, fungible, and rootless. Organized, the masses are a physical force, a lethal weapon, and as such indispensable to sovereign power. In the nineteenth century, nation-states produced mass armies through universal conscription. And yet the explosive force of the masses could always turn against the sovereign agent of the state, which means that absolute obedience in the military was institutionally required.

Mass *society* is a twentieth-century phenomenon. How it differs from mass military institutions is an organizational question. Whereas communication in the latter follows hierarchical lines of command, society as a mass is addressed directly. Modern media technologies are indispensable here, not only for the manipulation of the masses but for mass solidarity in a positive sense. Speed is a decisive factor in media effectiveness. Books are slow organizers, producing mass predispositions but seldom inciting direct action. Newspapers are known generators of mass action, and no modern political party of any importance has been without one. Placards, banners, and posters move the word out into the street, changing its nature. When words become part of a mass spectacle and integrated into the scene, the masses speak through them rather than being addressed by them. Photographs of street demonstrations show words in this changed capacity, as identifying logos rather than logos-in-writing. How the words look matters. Letters take on modern shapes; graphic design gives the masses a revolutionary identity, and identity *is* the new means of mass organization. Mimesis replaces written argument. People become part of the collective by mimicking its look.

Mass cathexis onto one person is a powerful organizer, but it requires at least the trace of physical presence: an image, a voice, clothes worn by, objects touched by, beds

4.1 Vasilii Kuptsov, *May Day,* 1929.

Why did only revolutionary futurism march in step with the October Revolution? Is it just a question of outward revolutionary fervor, just a mutual aversion to the old forms, that joins futurism with the proletariat? . . . We maintain that there is a deeper link between futurism and proletarian creation. . . . Take any work of revolutionary, futurist art. People who are used to seeing a depiction of individual objects or phenomena in a picture are bewildered. You cannot make anything out. And indeed, if you take out any one part from a futurist picture, it then represents an absurdity. Because each part of a futurist picture acquires meaning only through the interaction of all the other parts; only in conjunction with them does it acquire the meaning with which the artist imbued it. A futurist picture lives a collective life: By the same principle on which the proletariat's whole creation is constructed. Try to distinguish an individual face in a proletarian procession. Try to understand it as individual persons—absurd. Only in conjunction do they acquire all their strength, all their meaning.

—Natan Altman, "'Futurism' and Proletarian Art," 1918[1]

4.2 Moscow street demonstration, 1927.

4.3 Club prepares decorations for demonstration, 1929.

occupied by the person in whom the mass's psychic energy is invested. The written word, in contrast, is decorporealized. The materiality of the text acts like a screen, prohibiting the author's physical attributes—gender, age, ethnicity, attractiveness—from being seen. As a consequence, a certain kind of mass cathexis is impossible, and although there have long been best-selling writers and popular political leaders, there were no heroes as media stars before the photograph.

The voice as a means for organizing the masses demanded a new technology. Megaphones magnified sound by directing its focus, but still required the visual presence of the speaker to reach a mass audience at all. Speakers' podiums recognized this fact, and they were a common design of revolutionary artists in the early years of the Bolshevik regime, even after electronic loudspeakers increased the audio range.

Radio towers, working from totally different physical principles than that of the megaphone or loudspeaker, incidentally echoed their form. Radio produced the "universal ear," the "newspaper without paper," Lenin said, "without borders."[2] And although Lenin's speeches were reproduced on gramophone records for mass distribution, it was the live voice, the history-making event of its speech in present time, that carried mass-political charisma.[3] When the voice was transformed into electrical surges transmitted through wire grids rather than the open air, the extension of the aural sense became limitless, as did the visual sense through photographic reproduction. Mass society was synonymous with this infinity of sense perception, achieved through the technological prostheses of the human sensory apparatus.

The electrical grids over which the Soviet radio voice traveled were developed as a centralized infrastructure.[4] In 1920 a plan for the electrification of the entire country was unveiled in an "elaborate show" to "enchanted listeners" at a congress of experts convened to consider it.[5] Again, rather than proposing any real alternative to capitalist energy development, socialist technology copied Western forms. With models like the Niagara Falls project in mind, the plan's emphasis was on hydropower, which was, notes its historian, "an interesting priority for a country with only two small commercial hydroplants."[6] The grid system privileged large-scale high-voltage transmission networks that required an enormous investment and were fully dependent on foreign technology.[7] A decentralized plan for local electrification and village stations was debated and rejected despite its economic rationality for rural areas (where it would have provided service sooner to those peasants whose exported grain was to pay for the foreign equipment). Given the preconception of what constituted progress, more appropriate technologies—better hand tools and more horses, for example, in a country where as much as 70 percent of fuel consumption was provided by vegetable fuels (wood, straw, manure)[8]—could not be seriously considered.[9] Realism in regard to energy policy meant only that "dreams should not proceed faster than the ability to

4.4 Silent-film star Douglas Fairbanks at Wall Street, New York City, promoting the sale of U.S. Government bonds during World War I. His hand-held megaphone was no match for the size of the crowd.

4.6 Loudspeaker. Photo by Aleksandr Rodchenko, 1929.

4.5 Studio of El Lissitzky and the UNOVIS collective, *Lenin Podium*, 1924.

4.7 Shabalovka Radio Tower, Moscow, 1922 (from which Radio Comintern made its first international broadcasts in 1922), designed by Vladimir Shukhov. Photo by Aleksandr Rodchenko, 1929.

Tatlin's model was exhibited at the Eighth All-Russian Electrotechnological Session in Moscow, 1920, as part of the show presenting the GOELRO plan for the country's electrification. The monument was to be built out of iron and glass; its three transparent volumes, rotating at different speeds (one completing its revolution in a year, the second in a month, the third in a day), were to house the various offices of the Comintern, while the tower acted as a transmitting station for revolutionary propaganda. It was a machine for the generation of world revolution, a working monument commemorating the future rather than the past. Maiakovskii called it "the first monument without a beard."

4.8 Vladimir Tatlin in front of his model for the *Monument to the Third International*, 1920.

fulfill them," but the nature of the dream itself was not questioned.[10] Electrification was a political program as well as a technological one, a metaphor for overcoming peasant backwardness: "GOELRO [the state electrification commission] promised that electrification would accelerate economic reconstruction while simultaneously transforming the country from a poor cousin of Western Europe into a modern, cultured society saturated with electric light and radios."[11] The kilowatt-hour was proposed as "an index of culture and progress."[12]

Not only radio receivers but cinema houses too required electricity, and cinema was central to the construction of mass society. Whereas the radio voice allowed mass identification with political leaders, cinema, traveling to towns and villages to meet audiences halfway, represented a moving image of the masses that allowed audiences to recognize *themselves*.[13] Such mirroring can be important in transforming the accidental crowd (the mass-in-itself) into the self-conscious, purposeful crowd (the mass-for-itself), with at least the potential of acting out its own destiny. But technologies that hold a mirror to the masses can also blind them, if their own image obscures the manipulating power behind the scenes.

Consider the differences between several forms of the observing/observed masses: the carnival, the spectacle, the cinema. The theatrical moments of the carnival, indifferent to technologies of mediation, are spontaneous, and the division between actors and audience is fluid. Roles constantly change as individuals are swept up in the rhythms, sounds, and fragmented images of the crowd. Social identities are transformed behind carnival masks and costumes. Social parody and mockery of power are permitted by the comedic logic of carnivals that causes antisocial emotions to lose their conspiratorial power.

"Revolutions are the festivals of the oppressed and the exploited," Lenin wrote in 1905.[14] But the physical violence of revolutions separates them decisively from carnivalistic play. Whereas carnivals are ritual repetitions, revolutions are one-time-only events meant to change permanently the arrangement of social life. Revolutions disregard the carnival's social boundedness and overshoot parodic reversal, spilling out of the spatial and temporal constraints that are meant to contain collective discontent. To be sure, revolutionary actions are full of symbolic meanings, and their icons produce a powerful visual culture. But they lack a full sense of spectatorship because their immediate audience is the very enemy they are attempting, violently, to annihilate. Only later, with events of revolutionary commemoration, does their spectacularity come into its own. In place of firearms there are fireworks; in place of secrecy, there is display. If revolutions break from the past, their celebration returns to it, dramatized with all theatrical effects.

■

On the first anniversary of the October Revolution, production of the celebratory spectacles was assigned to artists. Buildings were decorated with huge panels painted in a myriad (critics complained, a morass) of different styles, from futurist to folklorist. Natan Altman's design for Palace Square in Petrograd superimposed giant modernist forms upon this traditional architectural space. The masses, assembled under identifying banners, paraded through the commemorative displays like a moving exhibition in an enormous public street-gallery that included the latest in contemporary art. Monuments to the "fighters for socialism" were unveiled. Public theater was provided by a group of young, leftists artists, including Altman, Malevich, and Puni, who, employing a mass of extras, staged a reenactment of the revolution.

In 1920, on the third anniversary of October, the festival atmosphere of the celebration was overpowered by the spectacle as a staged event. The *Storming of the Winter Palace,* produced that year in Petrograd, was mass street theater involving ten thousand participants and an audience of ten times that who joined in the action at the climax of storming the palace.[15]

4.9, 4.10 Natan Altman, design drawings for Uritskii (formerly Palace) Square, Petrograd. First anniversary of the October Revolution, 1918.

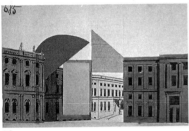

4.9

4.10

I set myself the task of changing the historical image of the square, and transforming it into a place where a revolutionary people would come to celebrate its victory. . . . I decided not to decorate the square. The creations of [the eighteenth-century architects] Rastrelli and Rossi required no decoration. I wished instead to contrast the new beauty of a victorious people with the beauty of imperial Russia. I did not seek harmony with the old, but contrast with it. I placed my constructions not on the buildings but between them, where the streets opened the square. . . . Only three vast paintings, almost the height of the buildings, were placed in front of the facades . . . a worker . . . unfolding a banner . . . "He who was nothing will be everything," . . . a peasant holding a banner . . . "Land to the Working People," . . . a worker . . . bearing the slogan: "Factories to the Working People."

—Natan Altman[16]

4.11

4.12

4.11, 4.12 Staged performance of *Storming of the Winter Palace,* third anniversary of the October Revolution, Petrograd, 1920.
Produced by Nikolai Evreinov, Aleksandr Kugel, and Nikolai Petrov, with designs by Iurii Annenkov, organized by Dmitrii Temkin.

Two weeks before 7 November 1920 there appeared over the gates of the Winter Palace a sign "Headquarters Organiser of October Celebrations." . . . From first thing in the morning a queue of people stood waiting at the entrance to the Headquarters: drama schools, theater studios and clubs en bloc, representatives of military units, detachments of Red soldiers and sailors. This vast horde of manpower was sorted out in a special allocation section and everyone was given work appropriate to his qualifications in the task of staging The Storming of the Winter Palace. . . . *Dozens of producers, writers, stage-designers and technicians worked out an overall scenario for the production, splitting it into five parts: "White," "Red," "Bridge," "Square" and "Palace.". . . The "Bridge" was a real bridge which joined the 64 metre long Red and White platforms, a junction between two worlds, two groups—the Kerenskyites and the Bolsheviks. The "Square" was reserved for the immense battle scene: the assault on the Winter Palace by the people and the insurgent troops who entered through Red Army Arch. . . . The intended scale of the performance ruled out any scenes dealing with individual characters. The entire action was condensed into group movements, animated tableaux and dynamic crowd scenes. The masses were treated as masses. The sole exception was the small figure of Kerensky, which served to emphasise his insignificant role in the events as they were unfolded. . . . It was all combined to produce a single great panoramic review, filled with satire, tragic fervour and historic grandeur. . . .*

A group of young composers wrote the music. . . . Army instructors taught young girls from theater studios marching and rifle drill in order that they could play the Women's Battalion. Hundreds of morning suits, top hats, Generals' uniforms and ball gowns were obtained for the actors on the "White" platform. The Red Army was busy setting up field artillery batteries in Workers' Gardens. The producers, their assistants and everybody else on the production side worked round the clock, living on kasha, tea and frozen apples.

The searchlights installed on the roofs of the buildings surrounding the square lit up the area of action, and one after another, like the episodes in a film, the scenes began to unfold on the Red and White platforms. From the command tower signals were issued by telephone, using a numbered code to refer to the various episodes. Right up to the moment when the troops at the front rebelled and when the masses on the Red platform invaded the White the action developed just as it might have done in the theater. But the moment when the signal rocket sped up from the Square and exploded in the night sky the spectators and the participants too witnessed one of the most astonishing sights imaginable, a sight which burst the narrow confines of the traditional stage, and rose above those earthbound blanks, boldly mixing recent reality with a vivid, audacious, theatricalised interpretation of that reality on a scale hitherto undreamed of.

—K. N. Derzhavin, 1925[17]

The cognitive experience of this spectacle affected the masses in two ways simultaneously. On the one hand, this street theater demanded strict discipline, the subordination of all participants to the will of the director. It was no accident that "the military provided not only the original idea and much of the cast for these productions but also the organizational models: actors were divided into platoons whose leaders were rehearsed by directors according to a detailed score or battle plan and deployed by the use of military signals and field telephones."[18] On the other hand, although this was acting, not reality, and although the rifles were not loaded, the soldiers and sailors were playing themselves. Drawn from the dramatic studios of the Red Army, they were simultaneously involved in the real battles of the Civil War that were raging in the near vicinity of Petrograd, a city under siege and suffering from shortages of food and material goods. It was all the more remarkable, therefore, that they participated in this mock battle with such gusto. A contemporary commented about the general situation: "The quantitative side is staggering. The future historian will record how, throughout one of the bloodiest and most brutal revolutions, all of Russia was acting."[19] And according to the author Viktor Shklovskii, "drama circles are propagating like protozoa . . . all Russia is acting; some kind of elemental process is taking place where the living fabric of life is being transformed into the theatrical."[20]

The reenactment of the Revolution in the precise place of the original events brought the past into the present directly. When the audience-as-mass was drawn mimetically into the performance in a lived repetition of the "act" of revolution, the spontaneity of this street euphoria threatened a breakdown of control that understandably made the authorities nervous. This mass theater staged not only the revolution, but the *staging* of revolution, with all the ambiguous relations to power that such political theater implies. A mass of citizens, by reenacting the revolutionary overthrow that is the legitimating moment of present power, disrupts the sequence of history and exposes the contradictory logic of democratic sovereignty. Are the masses the source of political sovereignty or its instrument? Does revolutionary sovereignty work in collusion with historicism in relegating the revolution to the "once upon a time" of the past? Is this an attempt to insure that, once the revolutionary event has occurred, it is over in more than a temporal sense? Can revolution have any other time but the present?

The Bolshevik response to mass spontaneity was to assert sovereign control. Lunacharskii stated his approval of mass festivals in the tradition of the French Revolution, but he echoed Lenin's concern for limiting the spontaneity of these celebrations. Discipline from the outside was necessary, he wrote, because the mass of the people "lacked its own peculiar instinctive obedience to a higher order and rhythm; it was impossible to expect more from it than joyous clamor and the colorful surging of festively dressed

4.13 Kliment Redko, *Uprising*, 1924–1925.

people."[21] He described two means by which this ordering "rhythm" might be achieved, military command and cinema direction. Strikingly, he treated these two as one:

> *Those art forms that have arisen only recently as, for example, the cinema or rhythmics, can be used with very great effect. It is ridiculous to enlarge upon the propaganda and agitational strength of the cinema—it is obvious to anyone. And just think what character our festive occasions will take on when, by means of General Military Instruction, we create rhythmically moving masses embracing thousands and tens of thousands of people—and not just a crowd, but a strictly regulated, collective, peaceful army sincerely possessed by one definite idea.*[22]

With cinema in mind, the directors of the 1920 street theater version of *Storming of the Winter Palace* treated the palace as a "gigantic actor," producing ingeniously from its architectural form the rhythmic effect of montage. The idea was to present

145

4.14 Hundreds of dead bodies of workers shot down by the police. Still from Sergei Eisenstein's *Strike* (USSR, 1924).

4.15 Scene of the Odessa steps. Still from Sergei Eisenstein, *Battleship Potemkin* (USSR, 1925). "The immense sweep of the rising Odessa steps fills the screen . . . crowded with civilians rushing down the stairs to escape from the troops above."[23]

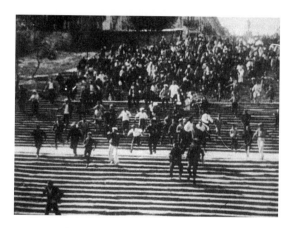

4.16 Police fire on demonstrators during the July Days, 1917. Still from Sergei Eisenstein, *October* (USSR, 1927). "People rushed out of every crevice. . . . Ever new masses poured across the square."[24]

the scenes as sequential "shots" in the palace window frames: "Each one of the fifty windows of the first floor will in turn show a moment of the development of the battle inside. . . . In the form of silhouetted groups, pieces of the immense action will light up and vanish in the darkness."[25]

If the directors of this mass production adapted cinema techniques to the old form of street theater, the next step was for cinema to replace the form of street theater itself. The revolution-as-spectacle was superseded by the virtual reality of the revolution filmed. Sergei Eisenstein was the great director of the crowd and the great controller of its rhythms through montage, showing "the mass" as the heroic protagonist of historical events.

■

It has been argued that "the mass" as a coherent visual phenomenon can only inhabit the simulated, indefinite space of the cinema screen.[26] Cinema creates an imagined space where a mass body exists that can exist nowhere else. "No reality could stand the intensity of the mass shown in cinema," writes the Russian philosopher Valerii Podoroga.[27] He describes Eisenstein's film images of the crowd of people as a composite form, a "protoplasmic being in the process of becoming," a "flow of violence" that fills the screen, with close-ups of faces overwhelmed by shock, extending the human countenance to the "limit of its expressivity."[28] Even more than the civil war newsreels of 1918–1921, Eisenstein's feature films—*Strike* (1924), *Potemkin* (1926), *October* (1927)—gave an experience of the mass that became the reference point for future meaning. At a time when Western directors were filming the crowd as a negative image,[29] Eisenstein glorified the mass as an organic force. In 1927 Walter Benjamin (to whom Podoroga is indebted) described Eisenstein's cinema mass as "architectonic" in character: "No other medium could transmit this turbulent collective."[30]

When later Soviet generations "remembered" the October Revolution, it was Eisenstein's images they had in mind.[31] The particular characteristics of the screen as a cognitive organ enabled audiences to see the materiality not only of this new collective protagonist, but also of other ideal entities: the unity of the revolutionary people, the idea of international solidarity, the idea of the Soviet Union itself. Indeed, it is doubtful whether the Soviet experience would have been possible without cinema, and Lenin turned out to be more right than he could have anticipated when he called cinema, of all the arts, "for us" the most important.[32] Soviet collective identity, like the revolutionary mass, was a phenomenon that needed the cinema world to be perceived. Vertov's *A Sixth of the World* (1926), which synthesized old newsreels and new material, was commissioned by Gorstog (the Government Trade Agency) for international circulation,[33] but its impact was greatest within the Soviet Union, where it gave a simulated immanence to the idea of "socialism in one country" by introducing a pleased public to the myriad of ethnic types as the new Soviet "we."

The Soviet Union as simulacrum! But it was not alone. Precisely in the same period, the United States, laden with new immigrants, was promoting a melting-pot ideology that relied on the silent cinema as it could rely on no other cultural institution. Churches, theaters, schools, holiday rituals, political organizations all embodied specific linguistic and ethnic traditions that worked against this goal. In contrast, Hollywood movies that screened *out* the past became a cultural force for mass assimilation. In John Ford's film *The Iron Horse* (1925) the building of the transcontinental railroad symbolized national unity among the Polish, Chinese, and Italian workers who "can put aside labor conflict for the great opportunities of industrial America."[34] Not only cinema but mass culture generally had a positive meaning in both the United States and the Soviet Union that it lacked in the ethnically constructed imaginaries of Western European nations, where "masses," a visual phenomenon, and "culture," a literary one, tended to be viewed as antithetical extremes. For the USSR, it was being part of the same historical struggle that created the unity of the masses. For the United States, it was being part of the same territorial space. But for both, with increasing technical realism, the cinematic prosthesis shaped political identifications.

Hollywood created a new mass figure, the individualized composite of the "star." It can be argued that, like Eisenstein's protoplasmic mass, this new being could only exist in the super-space of the cinema screen. The star, quintessentially female, was a sublime and simulated corporeality. Close-ups of parts of her body—mouth, eyes, legs, heaving breast—filled the screen in monstrous proportions. She was an awesome aesthetic spectacle, like a huge church icon, surrounded by the symbolic clutter of the objects of conspicuous consumption.[35] The Hollywood star, with a new, nonethnic name, with rhinoplastic surgery on the nose and orthodontic surgery on the teeth, fulfilled her mass function by obliterating the idiosyncratic irregularities of the natural body. The star was a product for mass consumption whose multiplying image guaranteed the infinite reproduction of the same. The deeper the camera penetrated, the more it gave back a universal visage, whose features (like those of Eisenstein's crowd) became surface, ornamental lines and contours on the screen. Of course, a true star had to have a particular, identifiable "look." But this was the opposite of the accidental luminescent quality of the natural face. It was a standardized image, a cliché that, like an advertising logo, was instantly identifiable. This mark of "presence" did not refer to the individual, actual person. Rather, the star's body was itself a sign, and its meaning was erotic sexuality. If the Soviet screen provided a prosthetic experience of collective power, the Hollywood screen provided a prosthetic experience of collective desire.

In Hollywood movies, class movement meant social mobility, the revolution was sexual, the decisive events were marriage and divorce. But the star was as much an indigenous inhabitant of the cinema screen as the revolutionary mass. Both, as simulacric corporealities, were given as an object of cognition only on the surface of the screen, reflecting back to the viewing audience a perception of the mass-as-image which it internalized. The crowd in a movie theater not only experienced the masses; it had a mass experience. The movie audience, more than an assembly of individual viewers, was *one* viewer, infinitely reproduced. The potential power of this mass viewer was enormous, but so was the potential for its manipulation. With cinema as with other media, the means of social control was not organizational but mimetic. In the Soviet Union and in the United States, a certain doubling of the image world occurred as social life rematerialized cinema's virtual forms. Phenomena that at first existed only as images (on the cinema screen, in advertisements, in propaganda posters) began to impinge on reality, a development with important political consequences.

It is enlightening to compare the construction of Hollywood, "Home of the Stars," with the construction of the super-projects of socialism in the time of Stalin. In both cases there was an attempt to create a material environment whose larger-than-life proportions would allow the new super-bodies to move in and take up residence. Hollywood's movie stars and Eisenstein's movie masses begin to leave traces in reality, as signs that these phantasmagoric forms in fact exist: the stars leave their handprints on Hollywood's sidewalk cement; the revolutionary mass haunts the expansive boulevards of Soviet cities. The individual can feel lost in these heroic stage sets. Their larger-than-life proportions make actually lived reality appear impoverished in comparison. The Soviet citizen, like the Western man in the crowd, is exposed to a specifically modern anxiety of the meaninglessness of the individual that leads to enthusiastic endorsing of this process of doubling.

If the collective imaginaries of both capitalism and socialism are virtual worlds, making them real becomes the social project. But the fact that this project is the doubling of a dream image lends to its material construction a phantasmagoric quality. Movie stars had Hollywood homes, but Mr. and Mrs. America too were promised a dream house which, despite its mass production, was studded with superficial luxuries and signs of distinction meant to confer specialness onto its fungible inhabitants. Under Stalin the fantasy of the mass body influenced social projects to the point that enormity of size became the overarching criterion of construction, whether of a factory or a collective farm, a university or a subway system, a hydroelectric project or a canal system. This awesome hugeness was reincorporated within the sublime body of the leader, the gigantically proportioned image of Stalin himself.

"Doubling" duplicated virtual realities as material phantasmagorias that could be really experienced. This gave a special dream character to industrial production in the case of the USSR, and to commodity consumption in the case of the United States. It was when existence was just like the movies, just like the advertising or propaganda image, that one felt truly alive.

4.17 Leonid Sokov, *Stalin and Marilyn Monroe*, 1992.
(color plate 5)

Phantasmagoric doubling: "When Stalin emerged, all we could do was
scream with joy. . . . I lift my hand for the Constitution and Stalin lifts
his hand for it. What happiness there is, comrades. Honestly, I feel like
I am eighteen years old."[36] (Woman worker, delegate to the Congress of
Soviets, December 1936.)

4.18 Mikhail Kaufman, cameraman for *Man with a Movie Camera,*
directed by Dziga Vertov (USSR, 1929).

4.2

Aesthetics of the Surface

In articles written in 1925–1926, Malevich criticized Russian filmmakers for giving
way on the revolutionary artistic goal of leaving representation behind. "Images triumph on the screen," he wrote scoffingly of what he saw as the tendency even among
avant-garde directors of treating camera stills as oil paintings, pictures of something.[37]
The film surface, he argued, should itself be the content of cinema. His foray into filmmaking with Hans Richter in 1927 put this theory into practice.[38] Black forms moved
on a white background, suggesting nothing so much as the movie version of his own
suprematist paintings. In 1929, when Malevich had already made his surprising return
to representational painting, Dziga Vertov produced *Man with a Movie Camera,* a tour-
de-force of cinematic technique. *Man with a Movie Camera* celebrated the productive
process of filmmaking as a form of epistemological experimentation, in ways that still
have power to challenge cognitive conventions in our time. The film demonstrates the
full range of technical possibilities of the camera, which itself plays the leading role,
allowing the audience to learn about moviemaking from the position of expertise of
the cameraman. In contrast, Malevich's interest in an abstract aesthetics of the surface
connects him, surely against his intent, to a very different tradition of films and photographs that treat the mass as geometric pattern of the surface.

Although there was little left to accident in the shooting of Eisenstein movies,
the amorphous flows of his silent-film cinema-masses gave the impression of spontaneity even when they were carefully rehearsed. But in the 1930s, when sound films

152

4.19 "Training." From Aleksei Gastev, *Kak nado rabotat'* (How to Work), 1922.

4.20 Tiller Girls, Berlin, Weimar period (1920s).

used music to provide the organizing rhythms, the masses danced onto the screen surface as an animated, formal design. This choreography of the mass as "ornament," to use Siegfried Kracauer's felicitous phrase, originated in the capitalist West, where it was standard practice on the vaudeville stage. Kracauer believed that the precisely ordered, repetitive moves of the chorus line (his example, in a 1927 article, was the Berlin Tiller Girls) could be deciphered as an image of the epoch: their performance was a mimetic replication—"similarly become flesh"[39]—of the modern assembly line. The Tiller Girls' legs corresponded to the workers' hands in the Taylorist production process.

The mass ornament was politically promiscuous, having no particular party allegiance. In 1933, the right-wing German author Ernst Jünger wrote the introduction to a book of photographs in which the patterns of city streets and tractor-plowed furrows form a surface ornament of abstract orderliness that is the hallmark of instrumental technology. That same year, Busby Berkeley's musical number "Remember My Forgotten Man," choreographed for the Hollywood film *The Gold Diggers of 1933,* used a similarly abstract aesthetics, composed this time of the human body, to lend visual support to a real political event. It was the "Bonus March" of 1932, when a mass of unemployed veterans came to Washington and squatted in a tent village in order to protest against the federal government's inactivity in addressing the hardships for the working class caused by economic depression.[40] In 1936 Leni Riefenstahl captured, in her visually powerful pseudo-documentary *Triumph of the Will,* the aesthetics of the surface of Hitler's mass rally of German fascists in Nuremberg, staged by the Führer as a media event. But this year also saw the release of Grigorii Aleksandrov's *The Circus,* the enormously popular Soviet musical that used a mass-ornamental musical number at the climax of the story of an American circus performer, Marion Dixon, who, persecuted in her own country because she has an interracial child, runs away to join the Russian circus.[41] Here, among the multiethnic audience, she finds acceptance for the baby and herself. It is clear that Aleksandrov, like most Soviet film directors in the 1930s, had Busby Berkeley in mind for this work. And yet the tableau vivant of the mass as ornament had a specifically Bolshevik precursor as well. It had been scripted into the earliest spectacle celebrations of the October Revolution.

Pro-Berkeley commentators have struggled valiantly to separate the mass ornaments composed by this master craftsman of Hollywood musicals from all the rest. Whereas totalitarian variants celebrated the mass as such, Berkeley's musical numbers are said to rescue the individual, who is submerged within the crowd only to appear again.[42] Perhaps more significant in determining the political effect is the fact (it connects him with Vertov) that Berkeley's camera provides a systematic interruption of the dance portrayed. Through the montage of paradoxical points of view and image proportions, as well as the timing of shots, the filmic rhythm supports a counterdance to

4.21 "Remember My Forgotten Man," choreography by Busby Berkeley, from *Gold Diggers of 1933* (USA, 1933).

4.22 Grigorii Aleksandrov, *The Circus* (USSR, 1936).

4.23 "Apotheosis of the Fraternity between Peasants, Workers, and Soldiers," anonymous, 1918.

the one performed, allowing the viewer two experiences of time and space, one representational and one purely cinematic. The latter makes us aware of the process by which the illusions of the former are produced, hence undercutting its phantasmagoric effects. The fact that one can also discover this use of the camera in Aleksandrov's *Circus* is not the point, which is rather that any attempt to make clear distinctions between Soviet, fascist, and Hollywood cinema must close its eyes to the fact, as important as any other at the time, that the "culture" of cinema had a life of its own regardless of political regimes.

■

Cinema was born mute. Its first language was gestural. The propagation of silent film relied on mimetic appropriations, and these occurred remarkably easily across national boundaries. People who made movies shared a passion. People who watched movies shared an experience—including directors who learned internationally from each other, producing what Miriam Hansen has called the first "global vernacular" of modern experience.[43] The world of cinema was a real space as well as a virtual one. Films could be shipped abroad, they could be stopped at borders, but their gestural language defied the barrier of spoken words. American films began to dominate Russian screen even before the Revolution, a trend that continued throughout the period of NEP. The Soviet film pioneer Lev Kuleshov admitted to being infected with "Americanitis," and he was not alone.[44] Hansen describes the increasing "American accent" in Soviet film work generally in the 1920s: faster cutting rate, closer framing, breakdown of diegetic space: "Hyperbolically speaking, one might say that Russian cinema became Soviet cinema by going through a process of Americanization."[45]

"Americanitis" among filmmakers was not limited to technique. Under the influence of Hollywood, Soviet films veered away from "art" as the model and, like their capitalist counterparts, strove to become popular. Iakov Protazanov returned from years of emigration in the West to produce Aleksei Tolstoi's *Aelita* (1924), a science fiction fantasy that combined Western cinematic sensibilities with suprematist costume designs. It tells the story of a Soviet space expedition that incites a revolution against tyrants on Mars and returns to earth via a splashdown in Lake Michigan, complete with a love interest between the Martian princess (Aelita) and a Soviet engineer (who may have been dreaming the fantasy all along).[46]

In the 1920s, the Soviet actress Nina Lee received Soviet acclaim as "the Russian Mary Pickford." Pickford herself visited enthusiastic fans in Moscow in 1926, providing the occasion for the filming of a Soviet domestic production, *The Kiss of Mary Pickford*.[47] She came with Douglas Fairbanks, already famous in the Soviet Union for adventure movies like *Son of Zorro* (1925) and *The Thief of Baghdad* (1924). The latter film filled Moscow's largest (1,000-seat) theater for months, and was ranked in a 1928 survey of Soviet audiences as fifth among their ten all-time favorites.[48]

Up until the First Five Year Plan, foreign films accounted yearly for well over half of total box office grosses in the Soviet Union.[49] It was the Soviet film industry's conscious and successful policy to reverse the logic of import substitution: rather than protecting domestic production from for-

4.24 Poster for 1929 Russian screening of *Son of Zorro* with Douglas Fairbanks (USA, 1925).

157

eign competition, the box office revenues from foreign films were used to build a financial base for an autarchic domestic industry.[50] By the 1930s, foreign films shown in the Soviet Union had dwindled to a very few (all of them previewed personally by Stalin).[51] The need to continue drawing large audiences to keep the industry going financially, however, meant that conscious mimicking of Western moviemaking became if anything more pronounced. The 1934 box office success *Chapaev* (by Vasiliev and Vasiliev), a brilliantly filmed story about fighting the White Russians in the Civil War, was artistically superior to most Hollywood versions of "cowboys and Indians," the U.S. genre of foundational fiction, but it was still an action film about nation-building heroes, in which good triumphs violently over bad.[52] Aleksandr Medvedkin's *Happiness* (1935), often compared with Chaplin's *Modern Times* (1936), was a satirical comedy that pokes fun at the modernizing process including collectivization: the newly collectivized peasant-hero, missing the point, dreams hopefully of owning his own barn and horse.[53]

■

If Hollywood influenced Soviet filmmaking, it was the Soviet avant-garde that had an impact on cinema in the West. Eisenstein's *Potemkin* was shown in Paris at the 1926 International Exposition, where it received more acclaim than it had in his own country, influencing not only the work of French directors Jean Epstein and René Claire but also Hollywood productions.[54] Eisenstein's extended travel in 1929–1932 to Europe, the United States, and Mexico made him the most widely interviewed and cited Soviet director in the West—despite the hostility shown to him by both French and U.S. government authorities.[55] Political suspicion was behind the cancellation of Eisenstein's contract with Paramount to make a film version in Hollywood of Theodore Dreiser's novel *An American Tragedy*.[56] Anti-Communist groups demanded that the U.S. government expel Eisenstein. At the same time, ironically, Stalin notified Upton Sinclair (who was a financial backer of Eisenstein in Hollywood) that he suspected the filmmaker was disloyal to the Soviet regime and intended to defect.[57] The footage shot by Eisenstein on location for *Qué Viva México!* was reclaimed by his Western backers (including Sinclair), so that in the end Eisenstein produced nothing in the West. But the sense of a shared moviemaking community was established nonetheless, a fact that fanned the paranoiac fires of Congressional investigations into Hollywood's "Red plot" in 1947 and the early 1950s—the U.S. version of political purges against cultural subversives.[58]

While Eisenstein resumed work in Moscow in 1932 under a shadow of suspicion, the organizational chief of Soiuzkino (Soviet Cinema), Boris Shumiatskii, was planning

4.25 Charlie Chaplin and Sergei Eisenstein in Hollywood, 1930.

a reconnaissance trip of his own to the West, as head of a commission charged by Stalin with examining the nuts and bolts of the Hollywood entertainment industry. In his book *A Cinema for the Millions* (1935), Shumiatskii criticized the "art films" of the Soviet avant-garde as "typically bourgeois" in their continuation of the "blind alley of pre-revolutionary cinema," and attacked their "overvaluation of montage" for leading to an "isolation of aesthetics from politics."[59] He considered their depiction of the masses as protagonist to be ill-conceived, based on the "petit-bourgeois notion of equality."[60] (In 1937 he intervened to stop the shooting of Eisenstein's *Bezhin Meadow* for indulging in "harmful Formalist exercises.")[61] Shumiatskii considered Hollywood a model far more relevant for socialist realism than the experiments of the avant-garde, praising it for its desire to produce "joyful spectacles" accessible to the masses and its realistic style of conventional narrative, including the *khepi end* (happy ending). He appreciated the preponderance of positive heroes, approved of the star system which depended on professional actors, and praised Hollywood's efficient factory-like production methods and centralized studio organization.[62] In the summer of 1935 Shumiatskii's commission visited Paris, New York, Rochester (the Kodak company headquarters), Hollywood, and (Fascist) Berlin in order to study Western film production. The commission launched a programmatic attempt to revitalize Soviet cinema in the late 1930s, including as the focal point the building of a Soviet Hollywood (*sovetskii Gollivud*) in the Crimea, where the climate was warm enough for outdoor shooting and the scenery resembled that of southern California. Shumiatskii projected production figures of Soviet films in numbers comparable to Hollywood's, with rapid increases from 200 to 800 per year. But in fact production numbers fell in the Soviet Union, and even finished films were discarded as "ideological rejects." In 1935, of 130 films planned 45 were completed; in 1937, of 62 films planned only 24 were released to the public.[63] Shumaiatskii was denounced in the party press for sabotaging the Soviet film industry. In 1938 he was arrested and shot. The construction of a Cine-City in the Crimea never went beyond the planning stage.[64]

4.26 Liubov Orlova, who played Marion Dixon in *The Circus*.

4.27 Mae West in *Belle of the Nineties* (USA, 1935).

Both Hollywood and Soviet cinema in the 1930s were mass entertainment. Politically, both affirmed official culture and denied certain bleak realities of social development. But when one considers the athletic builds of the female mass ornaments in *Circus* (1936), or compares its star Liubov Orlova to her Hollywood counterparts, for example Mae West in *Belle of the Nineties* (1935), it is clear that the erotics of attraction were differently produced.[65] There is nothing seductively languid in the Russian star's representation, which is more about theatricality than sexuality. Orlova's vital energy is productive rather than consuming, suggesting a very different economy of desire. The American public was as hero-needy as the Soviet public in the 1930s, but whereas the personal feats of Soviet heroes—the aviator-explorers who were "Stalin's falcons," for example—were officially sponsored and performed for the glory of the collective, those structuring the imagination of U.S. mass culture were loners—the aviation pioneer Charles Lindbergh, the movie character Superman—figures whose individualized power benefited society from outside of the conforming mass, although they were no more capable of challenging the social order than their Soviet counterparts.[66]

Images circulate within a specific context. They are "framed," first by the photographic or cinematic medium itself, and then by the socio-historical context in which they are shown.[67] The former is fixed; the latter constantly changes. Both are necessarily implicated in the truth of the image, not just (and not primarily) as it existed in the past, but also as it survives in the present. The image is thus subject to a third frame, the narrative structure that connects the past to the present. Typically, the parameters of this structure are policed by the academic disciplines of the humanities, the narrative genres of which cordon off specialized areas of the past (social history, art history, history of technology, etc.) in ways that produce blindness as to their connections with each other. It is this third frame, institutionalized in the universities, that so often obscures the present political significance of the cultural inheritance.

Because framing counts, we need to know that photographs of machine parts by Rodchenko, familiar in our time from gallery shows where they hang like so many abstract designs, were originally published in workers' newspapers where they pictured the site of the readers' daily labor. We need to juxtapose Eisenstein's eroticized, utopian celebration of machine cultivation and peasant collectivization in the cinema classic *Old and New* (1929) with the world into which it was released, when the brutal process of dekulakization was beginning in earnest.[68] And we need to ask what was behind Margaret Bourke-White's caption for the photograph in her book *Eyes on Russia* (1931) that reads: "An American Disc-Harrow."[69] What is a U.S.-made tractor doing as the center of attention in this photojournalist's documentation of the second largest state farm in the Soviet Union?

4.28 May Day celebration, Union Square, New York City, 1936.

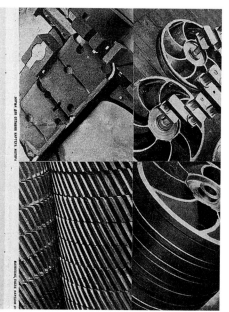

4.29 Aleksandr Rodchenko's photograph in a story on the AMO automobile factory, published in *Daesh'* (Forward), 1929. Rodchenko's photographs are framed by short texts by factory-based "worker-correspondents" (nonprofessional journalists) describing the production process.[70]

4.30 Margaret Bourke-White, *An American Disc-Harrow,* 1930, photo taken at the Verblud State Farm in southern Russia. The 272,000-acre farm was devoted mainly to wheat production and included an experimental station and agricultural school. One of its organizers was George McDowell, an American farmer from Kansas who was the first U.S. citizen to receive the Order of Lenin.

SOVIET INDUSTRY GETS AMERICAN AID

Contracts Involving Millions With Industry Here Are Disclosed.

FORD COOPERATION LAUDED

Details of Soviet contracts with more than fifteen American concerns, involving millions of dollars, were made public yesterday in a joint statement issued by Valery I. Mesh-

52

lauk, vice chairman of the Supreme Economic Council of the Soviet Union, and Saul G. Bron, chairman of the board of the Amtorg Trading Corporation, 261 Fifth Avenue.

Among the outstanding of these contracts is the one with the Ford Motor Company, signed at Dearborn, Mich., last Friday, at which time it was announced that this agreement calls for the purchase of $30,000,000 worth of Ford cars and parts by the Russian interests within the next four years. The other contracts call for designing of plants, technical assistance and exchange of patents.

The statement issued yesterday at the offices of the Amtorg Trading Corporation which was one of the parties to the Ford Motor Company contract, said that "it is significant that American engineering skill is being utilized on many of the principal Soviet industrial projects now under way."

The F
term o
technic:
Ford M
Automo
after th
Nizhni-
to be
years,
nally 1
This pl
than pa

The s
Soviet
cars "a
vanced
large
stateme
that th
quate :
year $
priated
Soviet
Other
with th
Hugh L.
sulting

4.31 From the *New York Times,* June 4, 1929.

4.3

A COSMOPOLITAN PROJECT

At the start of the First Five Year Plan, Soviet engineers came to visit Albert Kahn Co., Inc., of Detroit, the famous industrial architects who had built Henry Ford's River Rouge plant as well as factories for General Motors, Packard, Oldsmobile, Chrysler, and De Soto.

> It was in 1928 . . . [that] the most extraordinary commission ever given an architect came in the door unannounced. In that year a group of engineers from the U.S.S.R. came to the Kahn office with an order for a $40,000,000 tractor plant [at Chelyabinsk], and an outline of a program for an additional two billion dollars' worth of buildings. About a dozen of these factories were done in Detroit; the rest were handled in a special office with 1,500 draftsmen in Moscow.[71]

According to Anthony Sutton, the Cold War historian who documented this case, "The 'outline of a program' presented to the Kahn organization in 1928 was nothing less than the First and Second Five-Year Plans of 'socialist construction'."[72] In authorizing this act of extreme cosmopolitanism, Stalin envisioned a U.S. capitalist firm as designer of Soviet socialist industrialization.[73]

A factory to produce Fordson tractors was prefabricated in Detroit by the Albert Kahn Company and shipped to Stalingrad in 1929, where it was assembled under the direction of American engineers.[74] A contract "under which the Kahn Company became consulting architects to the Soviet Union" was signed in early 1930.[75] "The Kahn group undertook design, architectural, and engineering work for all heavy and light industrial units projected by Gosplan. Kahn's chief engineer in the U.S.S.R., Scrymgoeur, was chairman of the Vesenkha building committee."[76] Scrymgoeur wrote:

> *The Albert Kahn unit was engaged to control, teach and design all light and heavy industry. . . . By the end of the second year we controlled in Moscow, and from Moscow branches in Leningrad, Kharkov, Kiev, Dniepropetrovsk, Odessa, Sverdlovsk and Novo-Sibirsk 3,000 designers and completed the design of buildings costing (these are Soviet figures) 417 million rubles.*[77]

The Soviets seem to have taken advantage of competitive bidding, however, and the Albert Kahn Company did not retain a monopoly. Henry Ford, already a figure of heroic proportions in the Soviet Union, was included in the Soviet plan, given six months to design an assembly line for the Gorky Auto Plant to be built at Nizhni Novgorod.[78] The agreement, signed on May 31, 1929, was for Ford to furnish technical assistance (until 1938) for the plant, which was to be completed by 1933 and which would produce the Model A (called by the Soviets Gaz-A), the Ford light truck (Gaz-AA), and the heavy truck (AMO-3). Soviet engineers were to be provided facilities at the River Rouge factory for the study of Ford production methods.[79] In the economically depressed years of the early 1930s, U.S. firms and personnel were grateful for the Soviet business.[80] "Ford was happy to sell $30 million worth of parts and throw in invaluable technical assistance for nothing. Technical assistance in production of axles, tires, bearings, and other items required payment but, as the marginal cost to American companies was

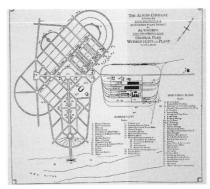

4.32 General plan for Worker's City and plant, Autostroi, Nizhni Novgorod, prepared by the Austin Company under technical assistance contract of August 1929.

4.33 Steel plant at Gary, Indiana (construction begun in 1906 by Freyn and Co.), that provided the model for USSR's Magnitostroi. Photo ca. 1950.

slight, the Soviets reaped a gigantic harvest of technological knowhow for almost no outlay."[81] The Austin Company of Cleveland designed not only the plant at Nizhni Novgorod but the "Worker's City" that surrounded it, complete with community housing, nursery, public bath, Palace of Culture, and crematorium.[82]

> *In mid-1929 the A. J. Brandt Company of Detroit undertook an extensive two-year reorganization and expansion of Amo [the automobile plant in Moscow]. . . . The production equipment was entirely American and German. In late 1929 Amtorg [the Soviet trade organization in New York] placed an order on behalf of Amo with the Toledo Machine and Tool Company for $600,000 of cold-stamping presses. In 1932 an order was placed with Greenless Company of Rockford, Illinois for multi-cylinder lathes. In 1936 a second technical-assistance agreement was concluded for Amo with the Budd Manufacturing Company of Philadelphia and the Hamilton Foundry and Machine Company of Ohio to produce 210,000 chassis and bodies per year for a new ZIS-model automobile.[83]*

4.34 Steel mills at Magnitostroi under construction by Arthur McKee and Co. Photo ca. 1930.

The technology transfer included trained personnel high up in the Soviet economic administration: "Soyuzstroi [the All-Union Construction Trust] had responsibility for about one-quarter of new construction [in the Soviet Union] until 1933 when it was broken into smaller units attached to individual combinats. The Director of Soyuzstroi was Sergei Nemets, formerly an engineer with the Philadelphia construction company of Stone and Webster, Inc. The Chief Engineer of Soyuzstroi was Zara Witkin, whose early projects included the Hollywood Bowl and several large Los Angeles hotels."[84]

Even the Soviet "Dream City" of Magnitogorsk was built according to design specifications created in the United States and supervised by a team of American engineers.[85] In March 1930, Arthur McKee and Co. of Cleveland won the foreign bid to turn the building site at Magnitogorsk, an iron lode in the middle of an empty steppe in southern Russia, into the largest mining-energy-chemical-metallurgical complex in the world. It was to be modeled after the U.S. Steel Company's plant in Gary, Indiana, an integrated design that provided a linear flow from raw materials to finished products.[86]

> McKee undertook to design the entire steel plant, including all auxiliary shops and the iron-ore mine . . . [and to be] responsible for directing work on the site until the factory and mine were put into operation, for consulting on equipment orders, for building an electric power station and a dam, and for training Soviet engineers both at the site and in the United States. The Soviet government agreed to pay McKee 2.5 million gold rubles.[87]

The fact that the United States had no diplomatic relations with the USSR was an obstacle to doing business. Germany, which had recognized the Soviet Union and established trade relations with the Rapallo Treaty in 1922, continued to provide serious competition until Hitler came to power in 1933—not coincidentally the year that the United States finally granted recognition to the Soviet regime.[88]

*Although design and layout during this period [1929–1932] was American, prob-
ably one-half of the equipment installed was German. Of this, a large amount was
manufactured in Germany to American design on Soviet account. In quantity,
American-built equipment was probably second and British third. . . . Cement
mills were largely from one firm in Denmark, ball bearings from one firm in Italy
and another in Sweden, small ships from Italy, and aluminum technology from a
French company.*[89]

Sutton concludes that "for the period from 1930 to 1945" Soviet technology *was* Western technology "converted to the metric system."[90] The fact that Stalin's First and Second Five Year Plans amounted to the largest technological transfer in Western capitalist
history was not something that either side advertised, nor did they care to remember
this collaboration during the Cold War years. Although part of the public record, it remained an embarrassment for both the United States and the Soviet Union as superpower enemies.

And there is more to the story.

■

Payment for the technology transfer demanded hard currency. Soviet grain exports fell
precipitously during the early 1930s, due to the intense famines caused by forced collectivization. The Soviet government found an alternative commodity in the European oil paintings and "household goods" of the aristocracy that had been confiscated
after the October Revolution. In 1928 the Soviet government embarked on a major
effort to sell Russian art abroad in order to gain hard currency to pay for the imports
of the First Five Year Plan. The story of this extravagant international exchange was not
documented until 1980. In the words of its historian, Robert Williams, "American
buyers have been as reluctant to discuss their purchases as the Soviet government has
been to discuss (or even admit) their sales."[91] Yet the Soviet decision was clearly made
at the top: "Tractors were needed more than Titians, Fords more than Fabergé."[92] Millions of dollars' worth of masterpieces of art and thousands of tons of antiques—jewelry, icons, porcelain, rare book manuscripts, Easter eggs, silver, brocades—were sold
abroad, and the largest buyers were U.S. citizens.[93]

In the twelve months between April 1930 and April 1931 alone, Andrew W. Mellon, Secretary of the Treasury of the United States, bought close to seven million dollars' worth of Hermitage paintings from the Soviet government, a figure that equals half
of what the Soviet Union paid in hard currency for imports during that year and
"roughly one third of the official total of Soviet exports to the United States in 1930."[94]

Included were two Renaissance masterpieces of Jan van Eyck, five Rembrandts, four Van Dycks, two Halses, as well as paintings by Botticelli, Chardin, Perugino, Poussin, Rubens, Titian, Velásquez, and, the most expensive purchase, Raphael's *Alba Madonna,* for which Mellon paid almost 1.7 million dollars, at the time the highest price ever paid for a single painting.[95] These purchases were kept secret, laundered through a complex web of American entrepreneurs and Soviet officials, at the heart of which were M. Knoedler & Company (art gallery and dealer) and Amtorg (the Soviet trade representative), both based in New York City.[96] Knoedler was owned by the entrepreneur Armand Hammer, whose pencil and asbestos factories in the Soviet Union were nationalized in 1930 but who, with his special Soviet connections, turned to selling Russian art objects through department stores in the United States, including, in January 1933, Lord and Taylor.[97]

Because the Soviet Union lacked diplomatic recognition in the United States, Amtorg, the delegation for the Commissariat of Foreign Trade, had to maintain the legal fiction of being a private corporation of the state of New York, where it was based.[98] As for the Secretary of the Treasury's part in the major deal, "for five long years there were only rumors of such a purchase and denials by Mellon."[99] According to his lawyer, "Mr. Mellon wanted to keep the thing a surprise until the right moment. It probably would not have been good politics for the Secretary of the Treasury to spend millions for rare paintings at a time when the government was swamped with unemployment, bank failures, and general distress."[100] The "right moment" was forced upon Mellon in 1935 when, for years suspected of a conflict of interest, he was charged by the Internal Revenue Service for failing to pay over three million dollars in taxes in 1931.[101] "At issue was the taxable status of Andrew Mellon's paintings [donated to his own charitable trust] which he claimed as a deduction on his 1931 income tax return."[102] Only after Mellon had written to President Roosevelt that he planned to bequeath his paintings to the government and offered to build a museum for them did the Board of Tax Appeals dismiss charges of tax fraud.[103] "In March 1937, five months before Andrew Mellon's death, President Roosevelt accepted his donation of this entire art collection and a National Gallery of Art in which to house it in the name of the American people."[104] With the opening of the National Gallery in Washington, the Hermitage paintings were once again on public display as "nationalized" property—this time on the other side, and in the capitalist manner.

The British art dealer Joseph Duveen, testifying at Mellon's trial, criticized the Soviet government for its policy, as a result of which "the Hermitage is no more the greatest collection in the world, it has gone to pieces. I do not see how a nation could sell their great pictures of that kind. . . . [Art objects] are not a commodity. You cannot buy a picture like you buy a load of copper or a tin mine."[105] From the Soviet side the

4.35 Margaret Bourke-White, *Magnitogorsk,* 1931.

4.36 Raphael, *Alba Madonna,* at the National Gallery,
Washington, D.C.

The General Form of Value: Relative Design Costs
1 Raphael painting = $\frac{1}{2}$ Magnitogorsk[106]

argument was not convincing. A Soviet museum curator was quoted as saying that such sales were a perfectly acceptable socialist method to "turn diamonds into tractors."[107] There was a strange poetic justice in this economic circuit. Mellon, who made an early fortune from steel mills in Pittsburgh, spent it on oil paintings the sale of which enabled construction of the steel mills at Magnitogorsk.[108] Thus the profits of capitalism (surplus value withheld from the wages of American workers) moved (via the Mellon family fortune) to finance (via the capitalist firm of McKee Construction Company) the building of technologically advanced socialist factories, an increase in what Marx called "constant capital" that in turn increased the value of Soviet labor. Meanwhile, in the counterdirection, cultural "treasures" that had been owned by the Russian aristocracy and nationalized by the Bolsheviks became (via Mellon's "philanthropic" cover-up of tax evasion) the property of the United States government—and the American public received socialized culture in the form of a national museum. How should this strange merging of supposedly antithetical systems be reckoned? What is the proper accounting, when the sale of one Raphael (at 1.7 million gold dollars)[109] buys more than half of the design of one Magnitogorsk (at 2.5 million gold rubles),[110] which translates into jobs for tens of thousands of Soviet workers, and the production (by 1938) of millions of tons of finished metal?[111] How does one make political sense out of an economic exchange whereby the U.S. Secretary of the Treasury uses his private millions to "build socialism" in Stalin's Russia—at the same time as the output of steel mills in the United States is falling precipitously due to a Great Depression that, to Stalin's delight, affects capitalism alone?[112] How does one square with ideological rhetoric the irony of the fact that pre-1929 production levels in the United States were not recovered until World War II when, to Stalin's surprise and against the intent of the Nazi-Soviet nonaggression pact, the steel mills of Magnitogorsk and Pittsburgh, again at full throttle, found themselves producing weapon materials for the same warring side?

CHAPTER 5

DREAM AND AWAKENING

5.1

KING KONG AND THE PALACE OF THE SOVIETS

The movie *King Kong* opened in New York theaters on March 2, 1933. Two months later on May 5, Moscow announced the winner of the architectural design competition for the Palace of the Soviets. If one compares the drawing of the final variant of the Palace, which incorporated Stalin's significant modifications, with a widely distributed publicity poster for *King Kong* (not a still, incidentally, from the film), there is no denying it: in both form and content, the images are strikingly similar.

The original version of the winning Soviet design was a rounded skyscraper topped by a statue of the "liberated proletarian." The architect, Boris M. Iofan, planned the height of the palace as 220 meters, not much more than half that of the newly constructed Empire State Building (401 meters), at the time the highest building in the world. Five days after the prize was awarded, however, the Palace Construction Council met to consider and approve Stalin's suggestion that Iofan's building be larger, and that his "liberated proletarian" be replaced by a gigantic statue of Lenin. The final, revised project of January 1, 1934, was almost double the original size, 420 meters, with a changed shape far closer to that of the Empire State Building and with Lenin's statue towering 70 meters into the clouds, which would make it the tallest building among modern structures.[1]

What can be interpreted from the juxtaposition of these images? What does the gigantic statue of Lenin on top of the Palace of the Soviets have to do with the gigantic King Kong, pictured here in his final scene, fending off the bombers that will kill him? *King Kong* was mass movie entertainment about a captured beast, "a king and god in his own world," who fought against urban-industrial civilization and lost. The planned Palace of the Soviets was the proud symbol of proletarian architecture, its image circulating widely and internationally in the thirties—while actual construction was delayed and ultimately never took place.[2] *King Kong,* directed by Ernest Schoedsak and Merian Cooper with David Selznick as producer, became the first monster screen classic, a "mastodonic miracle of the movies," as the studio publicity said, "the strangest adventure drama that this thrill-mad world has ever seen."[3] The Palace of the Soviets was, for its part, a monster building, with seating capacity in the great congress

5.1 Boris M. Iofan, competition project for the Palace of the Soviets, Moscow, reworked by Vladimir Shchuko and Vladimir Gelfreikh, 1933.

5.2 Poster for the movie *King Kong* (USA, 1933), Ernest B. Schoedsak and Merian C. Cooper, directors.

hall planned at 21,000, and the goliath-sized Lenin statue described as an "assault of the skies."[4]

There are faint possibilities of actual connection: the fact that the Palace competition had been going on since 1931 and received continuous publicity outside the Soviet Union;[5] the fact that the Empire State Building, completed in 1931 and quickly a symbol of New York City, was also internationally known;[6] the fact that Stalin previewed many Western films while preventing their circulation in his country and could well have seen *King Kong;*[7] the fact that one of the (uninvited) entrants to the Palace competition was Hector Hamilton, a New York architect who had visited the Soviet Union as part of a team that, according to a Soviet newspaper report, was building "a radio-city in New York" (where *King Kong* would have its premier), and saw the preliminary Palace projects, admiring their amazing scale.[8] But even if the U.S. filmmakers knew about the Palace competition, the movie predated the announcement of the winner. And if Stalin *had* seen the movie, he would have had little motivation to place Lenin in the compromising position of the defeated beast King Kong. It is likely that both the Palace designers and the moviemakers were influenced by another source, for which there were several possibilities. The idea of integrating monumental human figures into modern architectural forms was characteristic of several entries to the Palace competition.[9] Consider, as well, Malevich's architectons, which were on display in 1932 at the

5.3 Boris M. Iofan, competition project, winning variant, 1932, selected (in 1933) as basis of the final scheme for the Palace of the Soviets, Moscow.

Leningrad exhibition "Artists of the RSFSR During Fifteen Years of Soviet Rule."[10] The center model, tallest in size, is topped by a statue presumably of Lenin.[11]

However obscure the prehistory of these images, their afterhistory has been assured. The Palace of the Soviets has become the quintessential example of Stalinist monumentality, an icon of the architecture of dictatorship, while *King Kong* is the campy ur-form of a whole genre of science fiction films, from *Godzilla* to *Jurassic Park*. Can they, as dream images, be made to speak to each other, circumscribing two complementary economies of desire? Lenin has in common with King Kong the fact that both are symbols *of* the masses, displayed as spectacles *for* the masses. Like all dream images their meaning is ambivalent, vacillating between a desire that is expressed and a fear that holds it in check. This is what gives them their power to thrill. It is through seduction that they exert control.

King Kong is a movie about making a movie. A New York director has a map of an uncharted island and wants to sail there to film its mystery, which turns out to be the monster, Kong. He finds a girl, Ann, on the New York streets stealing apples—it is the time of the Great Depression—and promises to make her a star. When the hero, who will later fall in love with Ann, asks: "Why take a girl along?" the director responds: "Because the public, bless 'em, has to have a pretty face to look at . . . and this time I'm going to give 'em what they want." Of course, the public is not alone. The movie opens with an "old Arabic proverb": "And lo, the beast looked upon the face of beauty." It proves his undoing, at least according to the director, who proclaims over Kong's fallen, furry body lying dead at the base of the Empire State Building: "It was beauty that killed the beast." Because Kong, too, falls in love with Ann, he is identified with the public that "loves a pretty face," precisely the mass audiences whom the di-

5.4 Kazimir Malevich, architectons displayed in the exhibition "Artists of the RSFSR during Fifteen Years of Soviet Rule," Leningrad, 1932–1933.

rector *in* the film and the directors *of* the film hope to attract.[12] Descriptions of the masses as a giant animal, an instinctual, primitive force, were common at the time,[13] an association in the film that intensifies when the director and his movie crew reach the mysterious Skull Island. King Kong is held back behind a giant gate from natives who have forgotten the more advanced civilization that built it. The native "primitives" worship Kong, providing for him the obligatory sacrifice of virgin girls. There is much in the movie that is racist. The dark-skinned villagers are as far removed from civilization as Kong himself.[14] But the film's depiction of the "barbaric" and "primitive" have an antidemocratic association as well. When the natives, planning to kidnap the blond heroine as a sacrifice for Kong, carry torches through the village and sing primitive chants, the director quips, watching from the ship, "It looks like the night before election." The jungle into which Kong abducts Ann is a surreal space where prehistory, populated by dinosaurs, has all of the dreamlike quality of unconscious forces. We are clearly in the realm of sexual fantasy; the prehistoric beasts are raw, virile power, and Ann's abduction by Kong is a seduction as well.[15] Yet the connection between beasts and dangerously powerful masses (the working class during the depression) is sustained in the staging of a boxing match between Kong and a dinosaur that mirrors the cuts and jabs of this quintessentially working-class sport.[16]

Kong is massive, "as big as a house." When he is brought back captive to "civilized" New York, this colossal, bestial force rebels, tearing apart his chains like some revolutionary proletariat that has just read the *Communist Manifesto,* and terrifying the well-dressed audience whom he has been placed on the stage to entertain. Loose on New York's streets, Kong destroys an elevated train like a mob on the rampage. ("It's a kind of Gorilla!" someone says. "Gee, ain't we got enough of them in New York?") Enraged at "civilization," Kong has the brute strength to threaten structures of power. But lured by the spectacle of a pretty face, his subjectivity changes from threatening to loving in a prototypical example of the "metamorphosis of consumption."[17] Diverted by the display of fashionable female beauty, he succumbs, not only to love but to the bourgeois proprietary impulse, the desire for possession. Holding Ann tenderly in his paw like a child's toy, Kong plucks off pieces of her pretty dress like petals. Or he grabs her out of a skyscraper window, as if out of a shop window, and carries her off. The director, making a direct analogy to Kong, observes that even "tough guys," go "soft and sappy" if "beauty gets to" them, suggesting a vitiation of virility connected with consumption and implying a "feminine" side to the masses symbolized by Kong. But it is a dangerous femininity, irrational, primitive, and out of control. King Kong is no Frankenstein produced by the latest in technology but rather an atavistic residue from a past era, a return of the repressed. The audience in the film is terrified by the unleashed monster. The audiences watching the film (we ourselves) feel not only terror

but empathy as well. He embodies the force of our own desire to find in a romantic dreamworld solace for the industrial civilization that brutalizes the physical animals all of us remain.

King Kong was escapist entertainment for a public in the throes of the Great Depression, channeling antisocial forces into romance and adventure while showing the animal symbol of the crowd as defeated definitively. The circuit of desire, like that of the commodity, is acted out in the space between the cultural object (the film) and collective imagination, a space of leisure cordoned off from the production process. And it is important that, although the audience of King Kong sees the story of the movie's movie in the making, they do not see how the real movie was fabricated. Of course, Kong's prehistoric world was a modern technological accomplishment. But to this day, how some of the film's special effects were achieved remains a mystery. In the movie, the director says to the crowd of well-heeled people who have paid twenty dollars to be entertained by Kong: "Seeing is believing." But what cannot be seen remains misunderstood. The fact that the means of production of a cultural commodity is invisible is the trademark of capitalist spectacles. They are phantasmagorias that seduce the senses, a shadowland of the fulfillment of desire.

One last point, a bizarre detail. The directors of King Kong—the real directors, Cooper and Schoedsack—make a brief appearance within the film. They are the fighter team in one of the U.S. Air Force planes that shoot down Kong. (It is, indeed, not beauty that kills the beast, but the technologically armed power of the state.) Cooper is reported to have had the idea of this cameo appearance: "We should kill the sonofabitch ourselves." He had learned to fly in World War I. After the war he stayed in Europe as a mercenary pilot, hired in 1920 to fight on the side of Poland in the war against the Bolsheviks.[18]

■

A maquette of what was renamed (after 1936) the Palace of the Supreme Soviet was exhibited at the Paris world's fair in 1937. Although the site had been cleared as early as 1931, the construction of the actual building was continuously postponed.[19] The Soviet press in the thirties repeatedly discussed its future grandeur, which was to include "17,500 square meters of oil painting, 12,000 frescoes, 4,000 mosaics, 20,000 bas-reliefs, 12 group sculptures up to 12 meters high, 170 sculptures up to six meters high."[20] Size was the most awesome quality of all the elements of the Palace. It was an example of the Soviet sublime, which had a very particular logic. In Kant's classical Western analysis of the sublime, the individual who observes a natural phenomenon of overwhelming magnitude proves the autonomy of the human mind, hence its superiority over nature, by rising above the uncomprehending limits of sensory imagination to understand even the infinite as one of "reason's ideas." But the Soviet sublime works differently. The maquette of the Palace of the Supreme Soviet is a fantasy object that must be imagined into existence on gigantic scale. The idea of the sublime that it suggests is one of overcoming the physical limits of the collective workers who will build it. The latter are required to sacrifice themselves, as sensory beings, in order to build a new world for the proletarian masses. In proportion as their own physical selves are diminished, the collective is enhanced in symbolic form.

"There's a labor of lust and it's in our blood." This statement by the poet Osip Mandelshtam captures the essence of *Homo sovieticus,* or so argued the contemporary critic Mikhail Epstein at the end of the Soviet era.[21] Epstein describes the "frenzied erotics" of Soviet labor: "This love is general, public, and belongs to no one, which is why, in the feverish passion of labor, something hopeless and depraved suddenly washes up: you pour your seed together with everyone else's onto the same eggs ('collective ownership of the means of production'). In this atmosphere, even a truly industrious person feels like a fornicator." This is, says Epstein, a special variant of "aesthetics"—not the "disinterested interest" which Kant described and for which the model of aesthetics is play, but "disinterested labor," gigantic quantities of which are expended for its own sake, indifferent to the results: "All that matters is the bitter satisfaction and oblivion that labor itself provides."[22]

This perverse ecstasy of labor is captured in the novel of 1930 that remained unpublished in the Soviet Union until 1987, Andrei Platonov's *The Foundation Pit* (*Kotlovan*). In it, workers are heroically digging the foundation for an enormous building to provide housing for the proletariat of the world—it might as well be the foundation for the Palace of the Soviets. The workers' zeal is invincible, they have to be made to stop digging.

> *"What do you mean stop work?" asked Chiklin. "We can still get out a cubic meter or a cubic meter and a half more and there's no point in stopping work earlier."*
>
> *"But you must stop work," the superintendent objected. "You have already been working more than six hours [on a Saturday] and the law is the law."*
>
> *"That law is only for tired elements," interjected Chiklin, "and I have a bit of strength left before sleep. Who agrees with me?" he asked all of them.*
>
> *"It's a long time till night," Safronov reported. "Why should we waste our lives. We would do better to do a job. After all we are not animals, we can live for the sake of enthusiasm."[23]*

The Russian philosopher Valerii Podoroga, observing that Soviet Man "lacked several important details," notes: "The head was missing."[24] The problem with Voshchev, the hero of Platonov's *Foundation Pit,* is that he has one:

> *"Do not people lose in their feeling for their own life when construction projects gain?" Voshchev hesitated to believe. "A human being puts together a building— and comes apart himself. And who is going to exist?"*[25]

Voshchev is a Soviet antihero, dismissed from his job due to "a growth in the strength of his weakness," which is to think "about the plan of life as a whole," causing too much "pensiveness in the midst of the general tempo of labor."[26] In Platonov's novel, the cosmocratic language of Stalinist utopia animates the action, and shows how drained of life human beings must become in order for this to be the case. In Podoroga's words, the "extraordinary linguistic power" of this "cosmocratic" utopia "takes reality away and moves the world toward emptiness. . . . [This language's] aim is always one and the same: to dispose of individual bodies capable of committing spontaneous, chance actions—bodies that are difficult to integrate into the nomenclature of the cosmocratic language. . . . To the extent that we ourselves belong to this great cosmocratic body . . . we are 'alive' only by being dead."[27]

The potency of the masses channeled into the cosmocratic body creates an endless productivity of more and larger. There is no limit to this escalation. It is the logic of Stakhanovism, which replaced Taylorism as the model of Soviet labor in the 1930s.[28] The Stakhanovite body is not a machine; it feels pain. The physical suffering that hollows out the individual for the sake of the collective is the ecstasy of the Soviet sublime. The triumph of the body is its destruction as well.

5.6 Aleksei Stakhanov at the head of a group of "Stakhanovites," shock troops of the industrialization drive. Publicity photograph (n.d.).

Aleksei Stakhanov was a Donbass coal miner who in 1934 overshot the scientifically established work pace by hewing 102 tons in a single shift—fourteen times the quota—breaking all established records and Taylorist norms and becoming the symbol of the shock brigades of Stalin's Five Year Plans.[29] Eventually, half the workforce became "Stakhanovites," women as well as men.[30] While practical benefits for these heroes of labor included access to an apartment, consumer goods, and tickets to the Bolshoi, the highest honor was to meet Stalin in person, and conferences were held periodically for this purpose. An exchange of joyous smiles and a handshake with Stalin expanded the size of the labor hero, until his own image mirrored the monumentality of the great leader himself.

5.7 Sergei Eisenstein in Mexico, 1931.

Sergei Eisenstein sent a snapshot of himself straddling a cactus in Mexico to his friend Ivor Montagu in the early thirties. He inscribed it: "Speaks for itself and makes people jealous!"[31] When work drains a human being of potency and bestows it on collective forms, their colossal size, overwhelming actual humans, engenders a sexual economy of sadomasochism. Of course there is humor in Eisenstein's image. The film director was remarkably capable of sublimating desire into artistic creativity. But his own homoeroticism, for which Soviet society had no place, took the form of sadomasochism, thus paralleling the erotics of domination and submission generated by the power of Stalin's regime. The underside of the monumentality of Stalinist style was the bodily punishment of individual workers, their ecstatic smiles expressing pleasure at physical pain.

5.8 Boris Kustodiev, *The Bolshevik,* 1920.

From the earliest years of the Bolshevik regime, the power of the revolutionary masses was represented by gigantic human proportions. Aleksei Gastev, who became director of the Central Institute of Labor, expressed this sensibility in a 1918 poem, "Mbi rastyom iz zheleza" (We Grow Out of Iron), from the cycle "Poetry of the Factory Floor." It describes a worker—symbolizing all workers—who absorbs strength from the metal of the industrial machines that surround him until he grows as tall as a giant: "My shoulders are forcing the rafters, the upper beams, the roof," and shouts from the sky: "Victory shall be ours!"[32] The Soviet sublime reached its apogee with the cult of Stalin. Its ritual expression was the organized demonstration in Red Square, the mass parade of people and weapons filing past Stalin and the high party officials as they used Lenin's mausoleum as a viewing platform. In 1938, on the anniversary of the October Revolution, 360 fighters and bombers flew overhead, forming the giant letters "LENIN" in the sky. Workers bore portraits of Lenin and Stalin and cheered: "Hurrah for our Stalin who has given us a happy life." One and a half million people marched by Stalin, a gigantic receiving line, reflecting the colossal proportions of party power.[33]

5.9 Vitaly Komar and Alexander Melamid, *Bolsheviks Returning Home after a Demonstration,* 1981.

5.10 Still from *King Kong* (USA, 1933). Special effects in the jungle, as the hero rescues Ann.

With critical humor, a 1981 painting by Komar and Melamid brings us round full circle to the monster world of King Kong. Whereas Kong had a boxing match with a dinosaur, here the massive beast is merely an object of certain interest, and, compared in scale to the superhuman figures who behold it, a proportionately small one at that. The painting is entitled *Bolsheviks Returning Home after a Demonstration*. This image can be read as a rebus of the relationship between the individual and mass society, one that mirrored the U.S. experience in an inverted form. Not the power of pleasure, but the pleasure of power provides the key. If one can speak of a repressed "collective unconscious" in both cases, social authority shaped its contents paradoxically by allowing its expression, providing for it an aesthesiological field of play.

■

Carnival festivals in Moscow's Gorky Park of Culture and Leisure were a frequent summertime event in the era of high Stalinism. (One of the attractions in this "strange and Disneylandish" park was a parachute tower reminiscent in style of Tatlin's Monument to the Third International.)[34] Here is a description from 1937:

> In the night of the 5th to the 6th of August, a hundred thousand participants in costumes and masks were dancing waltz and tango, slow and fast fox-trot, they were enchanted by the torch processions of the carnival heroes, by the Ferris wheels, the fountains which resembled burning asters, by the nightly sky brightened by the play of the projectors, by the fireworks and the rockets. . . .
>
> Forty orchestras played for them, and the visitors to the park enjoyed themselves in fair ground booths, in the circus, the theatre, at concerts . . . they were dreaming in the Garden of Reverie or on the Bridge of Sighs; on the Avenue of Fortune they tried to have a look into the future. . . . The crowd was full of life, they felt free and unrestrained.[35]

That same summer Stalin commenced the trial of the Red Army high command. Tukhachevskii, the head of the Army, was arrested on May 22 and shot several weeks later.[36] In the ensuing months, between 15,000 and 30,000 of the 75,000 Red Army officers were fatalities of the purge, and at least one fourth of the engineers of the aircraft industry lost their jobs.[37] It is this double-edged imaginary of Stalinist culture, the dreamworld of happiness promised to the masses and the nightmare awaiting those who were banished from it, that became the effective instrument of mass control. And it is here that Western capitalism and Soviet socialism need to be thought together as systems of power. Capitalism harms human beings through neglect rather than through terror. Compared to the personal will of a dictator, the structural violence of market "forces" appear benign. Those individuals (or groups) excluded from capitalism's dreamworlds appear themselves to be to blame. The fate of the poor is social ostracism. Their gulag is the ghetto.

5.11 Margaret Bourke-White and Erskine Caldwell, *East Feliciana Parish, Louisiana, USA,* 1937, from *You Have Seen Their Faces.*

5.2

DOMESTIC SPACE

The iconography of the "window-on-the-future" tableau appeared so frequently that it became a cliché in U.S. advertising images in the 1930s. In a typical example, an advertisement for Gulf Refining Company (1934), a business executive/research scientist looks out from his office over an industrial complex, the future of which he creates and controls. It is a surprise to find this genre in socialist translation in an illustration from a Magnitogorsk workers' newspaper of the same era, with the caption "My factory." Both are male fantasies in the sense that these dream images would have been illegible had the figures been female, and both are individual rather than collective, the expression of masculine proprietary pride regardless of which anonymous agency, state or stockholders, actually owns the factories. The U.S. man commands his view of the factory from an office high above the scene, his hand on the telephone which (according to a contemporaneous AT&T advertisement) allows control through "the ability to 'multiply' one's personality and issue commands at a distance."[38] The Soviet man views the industrial panorama which he had a hand in creating from a window the height of which creates a perspective slightly below the factory's level, in shirtsleeves rather than a business suit, and—most significantly—from his home. This domestic space is coded in ways that a decade earlier would have been judged from an avant-garde or constructivist point of view as ideologically incorrect: instead of geometric forms there are live flowers; instead of tractor-patterned fabrics there are lace curtains.[39] *Poshnost',* the Soviet equivalent of kitsch, appears to have triumphed over revolutionary good taste.[40] But the biggest obscenity is an object that to Western eyes appears totally harmless. On the windowsill towers a potted rubber plant, quintessential symbol, Svetlana Boym informs us, of petit-bourgeois degeneracy even among socialist realists who rejected avant-garde aesthetics and would have tolerated the flowers and lace curtains. The unacceptability of this tropical house plant was hardly due to the imperialist connections. Rather, it "was regarded as the last sickly survivor of the imagined bourgeois greenhouses, or a poor relative of the ubiquitous geranium in the windowboxes of middle-class residences; geraniums were purged and physically eradicated in Stalin's time."[41]

We do not know if the illustrator, too, was purged for the domestic bad taste of this image.[42] But its open window leads us into the domestic space where people actually experienced the differences between socialism and capitalism in daily life (*byt*), both as dream and as reality. Again, the codependency of the two Cold War enemies is striking. "Good" was defined as the other of the other (that is, as what the enemy re-

5.12 Advertisement for Gulf Refining Company, USA, 1934.

5.13 Magnitogorsk newspaper illustration captioned "My Factory," USSR, 1930s.

jected), entwining them in a dialectical death embrace that ensured neither side would escape the binaries of the discursive frame that contained them both.

If the bedrock of capitalism was private property, which in domestic life meant the private home, then socialism would need to be "anti-home." That was indeed the policy of early Bolshevism. Domestic coziness was viewed as an enemy. Maiakovskii wrote poems in outrage against the feminized, petit-bourgeois domestic scene with its private fetish objects, canaries and kittens, prompting the newspaper *Komsomolskaia Pravda* to launch a campaign, "Down with Domestic Trash" (1928–1929): "Let us stop the production of tasteless bric-à-bracs! With all these dogs, mermaids, little devils and elephants, invisibly approaches meshchanstvo [the petty-bourgeois]. Clean your room! Summon bric-à-brac to a public trial!"[43] The war against domesticity was not limited to style. Within a new proletarian culture of cooperation and communal space, "the very word family loses its meaning."[44] Day care for children, public canteens and hot meals in the workplace, industrial laundries and ready-made foods were to free women from the "backwardness" of privatized domestic labor. Leisure time, too, would be socialized outside the home in clubs, public baths, cinemas, reading rooms, physical-training halls, and parks and "palaces" of leisure and culture. Sentimental love and domestic bliss, the highest ideals of bourgeois morality, were rejected in favor of a demystified sexuality. If capitalism exploited erotic desire as a means for selling commodities, the radical communist response was to treat desire as a need to be fulfilled as unremarkably, in Aleksandra Kollontai's famous phrase, as thirst is by "drinking a glass of water."[45] While there was no room within Soviet socialism for the U.S. dream of the single-family home in the suburbs with its white picket fence (with the correlative nightmare of urban slums for the poor), the universal right of all Soviet citizens to "housing" was championed as fundamental.[46] Women's liberation was defined in terms of liberation from the domestic realm, so that they would be free to enter the realm of productive labor. Patriarchy was attacked in campaigns to eliminate the veil for Muslim women, or to prohibit the practice of polygamy in cultures of the "north people," or to combat the general "absence of culture" (*bezkulturnost'*) in male behaviors of wife-beating, heavy drinking, card playing, and bawdy humor. Abortions were legalized. Divorce was made simple. Virginity was unnecessary. Multiple partners were condoned.

These well-intentioned policies foundered on basic misapprehensions (which fifty years later Western feminists in critical dialogue with Marxism would expose). Fundamentally problematic was the fact that the whole notion of "equality" was in no way distinguishable from the bourgeois-liberal model.[47] Marriages were still imagined in commercial terms as a "free contract" between a man and woman, obscuring the

5.14 Aleksandr Tyshler, *Inundation*, 1926.

5.15 Aleksei Sotnikov, *Baby Bottles and Tray,* 1930.

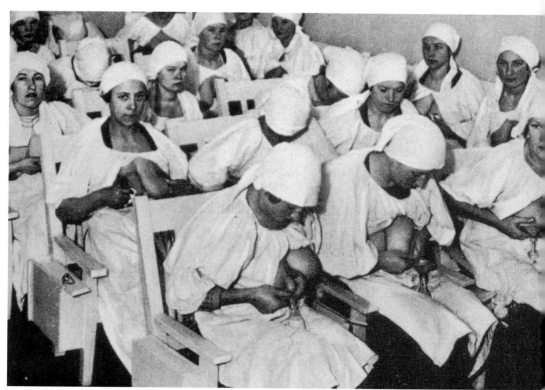

5.16 Working mothers express their milk at a Soviet factory. Photo ca. 1930.

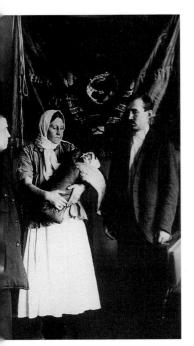

5.17 "Octobering" of a new baby, 1926, Soviet ritual of presenting newborns to society. "Octobered" babies received new names, such as Danton, Marx, Liuksemburg, Kommuna, Avangarda, Barrikada, Elektrifikatsiia.

unfreedom of women within them.[48] The 1918 Family Law treated women as equal to men in ways that devalued their differences.[49] The presumption was naive that the way to eliminate patriarchy was to eliminate families altogether. Although abortions were legalized, no priority was given in the planned economy for developing the technologies of birth control and programs for their dissemination. Although women worked alongside men in almost all occupations, the men did not reciprocate in tasks of childrearing and domestic chores. While the percentage of women rose to impressive levels in the medical and educational professions, these professions, once "feminized," declined in social prestige and pay as a result. Where patriarchal attitudes remained when patriarchal laws were undermined, women continued to suffer from the former while losing the protections that the latter had provided.

It is not surprising that when the Family Law was debated in public forums throughout the Soviet Union prior to its revision in 1926, women expressed great frustration regarding the consequences of the new sexuality.[50] It is understandable that a society organized around the central value of production devalued family life and domestic space, the sites of replenishment and repair. Less to be expected is the degree to which the emotional affect associated with the family was capable of being displaced onto the site of production itself. Workers expressed their "love" for "little Magnitogorsk" (*Magnitka*);[51] they developed a "relationship" with their furnace.[52] Productive labor brought reproductive results: "Life was given" to blast furnace No. 1 when it began to blow on January 31, 1932; workers hugged and kissed and shouted "hurrah"; telegrams were sent off as if announcing a birth.[53] The Soviet factory was the "child of the proletariat" sired ("erected") by the virility of "Soviet power."[54] Moreover, this birthing process was reciprocal, as the creation of the factory was the creation of the Soviet "new man": "What is Magnitostroi? It is a grandiose factory for remaking people. . . . Man himself is being rebuilt."[55] Through the stages of "childhood" (shoveling the foundation), "adolescence" (cementing the structures), and "youth" (working on the steel assembly), the workers grew to become "people of the future."[56]

5.18 Children hailing the start of the AMO factory, Moscow, 1931.

One's "native" factory (*rodnoi*, a word normally applied to one's birthplace) was one's social identity.[57] There was no private realm: "all was 'public,' and public meant the factory": "'Here at Magnitka the whole family takes part and lives the life of our production."[58] Again, there was mutuality in this relationship of familial care, as the factory provided the worker with job security. Reversing the relation of the capitalist factory to the worker, the Soviet factory fostered production for employment's sake.[59] Social security, not industrial efficiency, was the principle of labor practice, and during the 1930s, when workers throughout the capitalist world were experiencing the most basic employment insecurity, the fact that "job rights were taken seriously" by Soviet socialism "was revolutionary."[60]

■

The "Soviet Great Family" was the greater society, described in the 1930s as "the people" (*narod*) rather than the proletarian class.[61] Health, education, and welfare were citizens' rights.[62] But in the context of Soviet power, the term "rights" lacked concomitant autonomy. Citizens showed their devotion not only through their labor, but through their unswerving loyalty and unquestioning affection for the leader. Stalin was the father of them all, and the bestower through his goodness of all bounties. This ideological scenario was repeated relentlessly in the Stalin era, and in the process Soviet citizens were infantilized. That was the heavy price to be paid for the promised dream of social security. A situation that might have empowered people was transformed into a relationship of childlike dependence on state power that ensured the leadership could never be legitimately questioned. Even, indeed especially, the heroes of Soviet society were denied the passage to adulthood that their feats symbolically described. Chkalov, the first aviator to reach the United States by a polar route from Moscow, published shortly thereafter (June 1937) an article entitled "Our Father":

> *He is our father. The aviators of the Soviet Union call Soviet aviation Stalinist aviation. He teaches us, nurtures us, warns us about risks like children who are close to his heart; he puts us on the right path, takes joy in our successes. We Soviet pilots feel his loving, attentive fatherly eyes on us every day. He is our father. Proud par-*

5.19 El Lissitzky, poster for the Russian Exhibition in Zurich, 1929. (color plate 6)

ents find affectionate, heartfelt, encouraging words for each of their sons. Stalin has dubbed his aviators "falcons." He sends his falcons into flight and wherever they wander keeps track of them and when they return he presses them close to his loving heart.[63]

In his parental role, Stalin as father is motherly more than punitive, nurturing rather than disciplinary. The Soviet family drama is pre-Oedipal. It is for *not* loving the mother/leader that the child is punished, which makes the psychic transition to adulthood impossible. Fantasies of pre-Oedipal childhood omnipotence permeate the images of shock work and norm-breaking. In this narcissistic realm of the imaginary, the withdrawal of maternal love threatens the body directly, ranging from the withholding of nourishment to physical disappearance. The corporeal insecurity of famine and terror is the hidden side of Stalin's parenting. The authenticating gaze of the mother merges with the surveilling gaze of the state.

In the mid-1930s, at the height of Stalinism, pro-natalist policies resurrected the family and glorified maternal power. At the same time, actual mothers lost the gains toward adult autonomy that they had made in the revolution. The revised Family Law of June 1936 made abortions illegal except in life-threatening cases, but in all cases "it was up to the doctors to decide and not the woman."[64] The rehabilitation of the family entailed the celebration of fecundity. Earlier iconography of peasant women driving tractors (symbolizing the historical advance of this most "backward" class *and* sex) was challenged by the return of the traditional image of women as mothers: "The theme of rural abundance demanded that women be reconfigured and enlisted as ideological symbols of kolkhoz fecundity."[65]

The woman's fecund body was a productive body; that is what tied the new pro-childbearing imagery to the socialist modernizing project. But this affirmation of biological reproduction on the ideological level did not translate into a transformation of domestic space. If virtuous citizens in fact began to be rewarded with private flats, this concession to the lifestyle of capitalism could not be endorsed as official policy. As

5.20 Soviet workers carrying a model of planned housing. Photo ca. 1930.

5.21 "Something is boiling!" Communal kitchen with separate burners. Detail from Ilia Kabakov, *The Communal Apartment,* installation, 1980s.

for the avant-garde designs for living spaces conceived in the 1920s, such projects were no longer central to the ideological order.[66] In the increasingly crowded metropolises, the domestic reality for millions of citizens was the communal apartment, an idiosyncratic Soviet institution that developed more by default than by design. As a lived-in example of the formula "capitalist in form, socialist in content," it was a microcosm of what was wrong with the Soviet conception. Socialist living was to take place in a differently configured but structurally unchanged bourgeois space.

The communal apartment (*kommunalka*) emerged out of the 1920s as a pragmatic response to housing needs. Whereas all Soviet citizens were to be guaranteed a living space, the question, given the existing prerevolutionary buildings, was how to allot it. The law provided a formal criterion: individuals were to receive a minimum of ten square meters and families a minimum of thirteen.[67] It led to the apportioning of one room—or the partitioned section of a room[68]—in existing bourgeois flats to each individual or family; within these gerrymandered spaces, what remained of private life was lived. People sequestered personal possessions there—saved objects rather than use objects, "repositories of personal memory" salvaged from the catastrophes of class war and World War II.[69] The rest of the communal apartment was common territory: the hallway with its telephone (where conversations could be overheard), the kitchen (where family privacy was impossible and communality did not exist),[70] the "red corner" with its portraits of Stalin and Lenin (where later the television set would be installed), the bathroom (where the intimacy of the body was assigned to common space),[71] and the toilet (where the most basic physical needs had to be collectively negotiated).[72] "The burden of the communal interactions and negotiations rested entirely on women,"[73] who also suffered most from the lack of physical privacy. Surveillance by communal neighbors did not need to lead to reporting to authorities (although it might) in order to exercise control over daily behavior.[74] This hellish arrangement had one advantage, however. The space was deideologized in the sense that the contradictions of the system were experienced there with no covering gloss. In the 1960s, when a counter-collective culture emerged in the Soviet Union based on a new intimacy among freely chosen friends, it became a "kitchen culture," reappropriating this space for citizen resistance.[75] When unofficial art needed a place for exhibition, apartments became galleries for the viewing public.[76]

Well into the twentieth century, indoor plumbing [in the United States] remained a matter of class: the rich had it, the poor did not. . . . By the late 1920s, surveys indicated that indoor plumbing had left the luxury category. . . . Only about 7 percent of the small wage earners studied by the Chicago Department of Public Welfare in 1925 still had to go outside to use the toilet, although many had to leave their apartments to use a shared bathroom. Many of their bathtubs had only a cold-water tap, and frozen pipes rendered all facilities useless for long periods; conditions for these stock-yard, railroad, factory and service workers, 44 percent of whom were black and 17 percent Mexican-born, had improved only slightly over those for workers of the previous decades. Urban-rural differences continued to matter. The President's Conference on Home Building and Home Ownership reported that 71 percent of urban families surveyed and 33 percent of rural ones had bathrooms in the late 1920s.[77]

5.22 Sketch for model bathroom designed by the major U.S. producer of bathroom fixtures, Crane, Inc., ca. 1927. Before the Bolshevik Revolution, Russia had imported much of its plumbing from the West, and the Crane Company, already a leader in the field, gave to the Russian language the word *kran* for faucet.

5.23 Ilia Kabakov, detail from *The Communal Apartment,* installation, 1980s.

The forced intimacy of the communal apartment was a particular kind of terror, affecting the most banal practices of every day. It kept the body in perpetual public exposure and intervened in the ecological circuit of all the senses. Its ideological justification was the utopian claim that public life *was* personal fulfillment. If life had indeed become "better, more cheerful," as Stalin claimed in 1935, then there was no need for a retreat into a private domain. In contrast, capitalist industrialization was grounded on a duality of work life and domestic life. No one claimed that industrial labor would bring personal fulfillment. No one denied the humiliation of factory labor, which brutalized the senses and subjected bodily movement to rigid controls. Utopia was imagined, rather, as compensatory. What was robbed from the worker as producer would be returned to the worker as consumer.[78] Domestic space became the site of this rectification. The ideology of the private home came to bear a tremendous burden, that of legitimating the entire system of industrial capitalism, and nowhere more so than in the United States.

The specific configuration of this domestic utopia underwent several transformations. In the 1920s, while the Soviets were promoting the application of industrial techniques to domestic tasks in order to eliminate domestic space, in the United States the directional tendency was reversed. The home itself was to become industrialized. "Home economics" would make domestic labor scientific. Taylorist techniques would make it efficient. Machines would automate "the business of living" and eliminate the need for a servant class. The consequence of this ideology, which remained an ideal and not a reality for the majority (who had no servants to eliminate in the first place), was to increase the isolation of the nuclear family by making the home even more self-contained, and to intensify the feminization of labor within it. The ideology of the industrialized home privileged specific commodities: sewing machines, refrigerators, vacuum cleaners, electric irons—indeed, electricity itself.[79] The fact that each individual household would need to own these commodities increased the potential market. The fact that Fordist labor policies promised to put higher wages in workers' pockets seemed to ensure the commodity market's continuing growth.

5.24 U.S. Vice President Richard Nixon and Soviet Premier Nikita Khrushchev, "Kitchen Conference," Moscow, August 1959. (Photo by William Safire.) Those in the all-male ranks taking advantage of the photo opportunity include Voroshilov (profile, far left), creator of the Red Army cavalry in the Civil War and People's Commissar of the Army and Navy under Stalin in the 1930s, who helped initiate the arrest of Tukhachevskii; Anastas Mikoyan (with moustache, between Khrushchev and Nixon), Commissar of Foreign Trade under Stalin, who played a crucial role in the international sale of the Hermitage paintings; and Leonid Brezhnev (full face, far right), who had risen within the party ranks during the Terror of the 1930s as Khrushchev's deputy in the Ukraine Communist Party's Central Committee.

The ideological attempt to identify democratic equality with commodity consumption came up against a basic contradiction, the fact that those who have the most need of commodities have the least money to buy them. Nonetheless, U.S. advertisers attempted to make a virtue out of the structural inequality between classes by developing what has been called the "parable of the Democracy of Goods."[80] A 1926 advertisement for Chase and Sanborn Coffee told consumers that although "compared with the riches of the more fortunate, your way of life may seem modest indeed," no "king, prince, statesman, or capitalist" could enjoy a better cup of coffee.[81] Similar claims were made for breakfast cereals, toilet seats, soap bars, and even burial vaults.[82] When the Great Depression cut deep into consumption levels of most people, the appeal of this message of sharing at least something with the wealthy actually increased. In 1932 the Hoover Company launched a "mansion-and-cottage" campaign to sell vacuum cleaners, covering "the whole ground of feminine longing and feminine envy" by constructing around its product the desire to own at least something that "the richest woman in the world can't outdo her in."[83]

The full ideological pressure of commodity culture was not felt in the United States until the 1950s, when it took on new meaning in the context of the Cold War.

5.25 Model kitchen, USA display, Moscow, August 1959. Photo by Elliott Erwin.

5.26 Vitaly Komar and Alexander Melamid, *Double Self-Portraits as Young Pioneers,* 1985–1986. (color plate 7)

Because U.S. production of consumer durables was the only aspect of capitalist industrial culture that had *not* been copied by the Soviet Union, it became the most powerful marker of difference. The United States government joined the capitalist class in its ideological commitment to the expansion of consumption without limits. Similarities of consumer styles came to be viewed as synonymous with social equality, and not merely as a compensation for its lack. Democracy *was* freedom of consumer choice. To suggest otherwise was un-American. The family home and the family car were the fundaments of the American dream, and modern kitchens and multiple bathrooms were its crowning glory. Unlike the arms race and the race to outer space, commodity production was an area in which the Soviet Union was not yet close to catching up.[84] In 1959, as an act of detente, the United States and Soviet Union exchanged cultural exhibitions, and it was no accident that the display sent to Moscow included a model of the American family home. Against the backdrop of its fully modern kitchen, Vice President Nixon engaged Premier Khrushchev in a press-covered "kitchen debate" about the relative merits of the two ways of life.[85] In the Soviet Union, land of the communal apartment, the propaganda effect of this exhibit would have been stunning.[86]

Of course, as Khrushchev himself pointed out, the American dream was not its reality. Those who counted as "consumer citizens" excluded the nation's poor. Class and race mattered. But even among those who were enacting the dream, the ideological burden took its toll. Commodities inserted themselves within every human interaction of U.S. domestic life, mediating all human affect—parenting, loving, caring, nurturing, socializing, and family celebrations. The bearers of this commodity culture, those American housewives who were actually living in the domestic utopia, were far from content. Isolated from adult society, weighted down with household tasks that commodities increased rather than eliminating, infantilized by advertising appeals, and excluded from the public world that counted, women were desolate in ways that challenged the entire hegemonic order. Given the ideological investment in domesticity as the linchpin of the American way of life, their discontent took time to find a name.

It is one of the great ironies of this century that socialism betrayed the interests of women by obliterating domestic space, while capitalism betrayed their interests by idealizing it. Because truly realizing women's interests was not the primary interest of either system, no adequate solution was achieved.[87] With the elimination of the socialist variant of industrial modernization, capitalism alone has become the pivot around which women's dilemmas revolve, still without resolution. In an attempt to free themselves of the "feminine mystique" of domestic life, middle-class U.S. women entered the workforce, but with the result that the two-income family that in the 1970s was an exercise of choice had by the 1990s become for millions a financial necessity. Conversely, women who under socialism might have desired the choice of staying at home were forced to return there because of the structural unemployment that followed socialism's demise.[88] With the end of the Cold War came the dismantling of the welfare state on both sides, undermining the social support that families had relied upon and transforming it into commodified "services" as a growing sector of the capitalist economy.

Industrial modernity in both really existing forms, capitalist and socialist, created a hostile environment for human life, precisely the opposite of the dream of modernity. Within this contradiction, power thrived, inserting itself between the dreamer and the dream's fulfillment, drawing upon the energy of the former and sustaining itself by the perpetual postponement of the latter. In its construction of desire, industrial modernity offers as a substitute for human fulfillment the illusion of omnipotence. Its form under capitalism is the consumer illusion of instant gratification, while long-term needs go unattended and social security is so precarious that unemployment strikes with the fate of a natural catastrophe.[89] Under the Soviet style of socialism, the situation is reversed: the illusion is that the state will provide total security (in return for total dependency), while there is no control over immediate satisfactions. Whether you happen to collide with bread tomorrow is left totally to chance.

5.27 Aleksandr Kosolapov, *Symbols of the Century,* 1982. (color plate 13)

5.28 "Businessmen of the World Unite," advertisement for *Business Week/USSR* in the *New York Times,* 1990.

Existing socialism did not give control to actual individuals over the means of production; that belonged instead to the imaginary masses. Existing capitalism still does not provide for the fulfilment of social needs, profiting instead from the instability of individual desire. The Soviet propaganda of production was as divorced from real production as capitalist advertising was (and is) from the use value of the product. Both infantilized a mass public, whose naivete had limits. By the 1980s, no one in the United States really believed the promises of advertising, just as no one in the Soviet Union really believed the promises of socialist propaganda. Both allowed the dreaming masses to express themselves without giving them their due.

5.3

AWAKENING

Walter Benjamin wrote: "Capitalism was a natural phenomenon with which a new dream sleep fell over Europe, and with it a reactivation of mythic powers."[90] It could be said that the Soviet phantasmagorias of production generated their own "dream sleep," this time falling over the Revolution itself.

In the 1930s Stalin initiated the building of the Moscow metro, a remarkable technological achievement that was also an immense iconography of power. Connecting every neighborhood of this city, cool in the summer and warm in the winter, deep enough in the earth to shelter the entire urban population in case of an air attack, the Moscow metro system was palatial architecture for the working class. Each station was a total environment, combining architecture, mosaics, and sculpture, thematically designed and aesthetically executed to depict a theme: The Ploshchad Revolutsii (Revolutionary Square), with its sculpted reliefs of revolutionary bravery, the grand Prospekt Mira (Prospect of Peace), with its bas-reliefs of agricultural scenes, the "art deco" Stantsiia Maiakovskaia (Maiakovskii Station), with its ceiling mosaics of sky and clouds, flying-machines and flying men, and the sumptuous, tsarlike ornamentation of Stantsiia Komsomolskaia (Komsomol Station), with its mosaics of past national heroes. This was, indeed, interior decoration for the masses. And if in the last years of *glasnost'* you asked the residents of Moscow about their childhood experiences of this extraordinary metro, they would tell you that it was a magical place, comparable to a Disney theme park, except that it cost only a few kopecks to enter, and that its multiple phantasmagorias intervened habitually into their daily life—comparable, also, to a cathedral, except that you traversed it in a distracted state, always moving with, through, or against the crowd, on your way to somewhere else.

Critics have written that the wonderful world of the Moscow metro was all illusion, belying the failure of socialism above the ground. They have criticized its artistic style for abdicating the modernist project and returning to a prerevolutionary aesthetics. They have noted that such architectural forms interpellated a mass subject, dismissing the individual as insignificant. No doubt the critics are right. But precisely because these socialist dreamworlds

5.29 Aleksei Shchusev and others, Stantsiia Komsomolskaia (Komsomol Station), Moscow metro, 1952. (color plate 4)

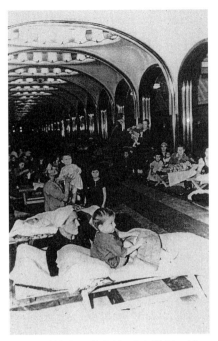

5.30 Air raid in Stantsiia Maiakovskaia (Maiakovskii Station), Moscow metro, during World War II.

entered into the utopian fantasy of child-hood, they acquired a critical power, as memory, in adults. The generation of Gor-bachev and *glasnost'* grew up in Stalin's Rus-sia. Komar and Melamid, enfants terribles of the late-Soviet art world, painted a series of parodic images of Soviet culture sacrile-gious in the extreme,[91] but also ambivalent, as is their painting of a red banner with the slogan "Thank you, Comrade Stalin, for our Happy Childhood." There is nostalgia as well as derision in this message, nostalgia for a world that was *supposed* to be. The gap between the utopian promise believed in by children and the dystopian actuality that they experience as adults can indeed gen-erate a force for collective awakening. This is the moment of disenchantment—of rec-ognizing the dream *as* dream. But a politi-cal awakening demands more. It requires the rescue of the collective desires to which the socialist dream gave expression, before they sink into the unconscious as forgotten. This rescue is the task of the dream's interpretation.

During the Cold War, when East and West were in competition for the loyalty of the masses, there was a political as well as an economic motivation behind the West's promotion of consumerist dreams. Now that the Cold War is over, it is not clear that the working classes in these countries will continue to be wooed by the carrot of com-modity consumerism. Production for export is the blueprint for the success of capi-talist firms, threatening to make obsolete the Fordist principle of putting dollars into the workers' pockets in order to increase domestic demand. Under the new order of global capitalism, workers in the first world are dispensable. And so are the homes and cities in which they dwell.

Benjamin insisted: "We must wake up from the world of our parents."[92] But what can be demanded of a new generation, if its parents never dream at all?

5.31 Aleksandr Rodchenko, poster for Vertov's film *Kino-Glaz* (Cinema-Eye), 1924. (color plate 10)

The "Cinema-Eye" (*Kino-Glaz*) in Rodchenko's famous 1924 poster (the right eye, mirroring our left), advertising the movie of that name, mimics the human eye. Black and white, like the movie that it advertises, it gazes with no clear focus, so that it can be imagined to invert again into the poster, into the two cameras that point downward at the duplicated face of a young boy which, mirrored in reverse, turns upward to return their look.

Rodchenko's mechanically reproduced poster was meant to meet the mass of viewers halfway, moving into their daily life and out again. Its human machine-eye, young and alert, is enthusiastic for the technological future. Prigov's 1991 installation draws on the collective memory-image of this poster, setting up a mimetic loop, into the past. His weeping eye looks backward and remembers.

5.32 Dmitrii Prigov, *For the Poor Cleaning Woman,* installation, 1991. (color plate 11)

The curtains are gray, the image of the eye is black and white. Only the tear is red, a socialist tear, the color of blood. A cleaning woman, a mannequin in khaki coat, kneels before the eye on a suprematist black circle. She bows her head in her hands, sobbing, obediently, "for the Poor Cleaning Woman." Her hand tools, broom and bucket, rest behind her. The parquet floor is swept clean. We observe the scene from behind her, outside the mimetic loop of crying eye and crying woman. Still, it is upon us that the aperture of the eye is focused—the left eye, on our right. That aperture makes it a camera eye. And our own gaze—at the page on which this scene is reproduced *as* photograph—mirrors this eye, obediently, in return: a third mimetic loop.

Paired, these eyes form a face that spans the distance between dream and disillusion—the face of this century.

211

IV

AFTERWARD

A Note on Method

Chapter 6 explains the writing of this book. It tells the story of a small number of intellectuals as they lived through the disintegration of the Cold War world. Some of the characters will be known to the reader, but that is not the point. Rather, it is to demystify the book as knowledge-production by exposing the lived experience behind its pages. This is not a very heroic story. As a friend observed (with Marx's *18th Brumaire of Louis Napoleon* in mind), intellectuals and politicians rush back and forth across the stage while the political and economic structures crumble beneath them. That is not a bad description of what we lived through, and I expect that our experience was typical.

When intellectual history is treated as self-evolving and self-contained, it is impossible to see that its development as a coherent and meaningful story is an ex post facto construction, that events are more a manifestation of historical accident than historical purpose. At the same time, experiences that appear to the actors to be freely willed are structurally defined and limited by history. These are not contradictory statements. History structures human actions even if it lacks a rational purpose; humans choose freely even when they do not control the meaning of their acts. In the story told here, actors seized the chance, but missed their lines.

CHAPTER 6

LIVED TIME / HISTORICAL TIME

6.1

LOSING THE ENEMY

In Moscow in May 1987, even a foreigner could sense that the myths of revolutionary history were lifting like mist. Old political meanings were being challenged under *glasnost',* but what the future held was still anybody's guess. Gorbachev had been General Secretary of the Communist Party since March 1985. Newspapers and television, while in no way governed by market forces, were open to critical reflection and debate. Novelists were publishing manuscripts that had languished in desk drawers for decades. Journals like *Novyi Mir* (New World) functioned as public forums for discussions of the Soviet past, economic reform, Orthodox religion, and political elections. "Unofficial" art that was exhibited openly at Kutsnetskii Most (which was also the black market for books) included the work of Grisha Brushkin, whose painting *Fundamental Lexicon* (1976) sold that summer at a Sotheby's auction for £242,000 ($412,828). Moscow television aired the U.S. television special "The Day After," a post–nuclear war melodrama condemning the futility of Cold War military strategy. A young West German pilot flew, unnoticed, across the nuclear-militarized zone and landed his small plane on Red Square without resistance.

But if gestures of opposition in the public sphere had become frequent in the Soviet Union, the structures of power were still largely intact. Party hierarchies, bureaucratic bottlenecks, networks for the allocation of scarce resources (apartments, consumer goods, vacation accommodations) persisted during *glasnost'* much as before. The urban landscape—strikingly green to the Western eye—was still unchanged, its monumental buildings

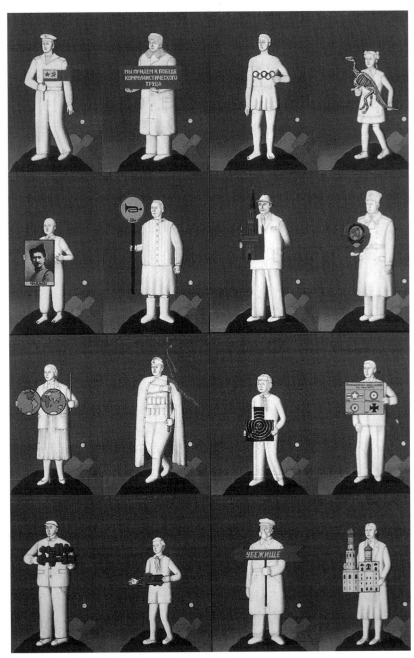

6.1 Grisha Brushkin, *Fundamental Lexicon*, fragment, 1976.

6.2 Igor Makarevich, *"Sotheby's,"* 1988.

surrounded by "empty" spaces that attested to the absence of capitalist urban land values, its streets and stores denuded of advertisements and all but the smallest of signs, so that the noninitiate walked obliviously past shops, restaurants, and leisure centers. State grocery stores were adequately stocked. Tea, coffee, and sugar were not yet in short supply. Street vendors sold fresh vegetables and strawberries. Champagne and Georgian wine could be purchased at state liquor stores, but the drinking of vodka was officially discouraged under Gorbachev. Working people had a surfeit of rubles, which had an official exchange rate of slightly better than parity with the US dollar. They complained that there was nothing new to buy.

It must be said that restricted access and networks of privilege made visiting a pleasure for foreign academics. Few in number, we were housed almost exclusively in the Gostinitsa Akademii Nauk (Hotel of the Academy of Sciences), just off Leninskii Prospekt at the Oktiabrskaia metro station. I was there for the first time, accompanying a U.S. physicist who had been invited by the Landau Institute.[1] Our two-room suite was comfortable enough, complete with humming refrigerator and black-and-white television. It had abundant pseudo-nineteenth-century furniture and patterned drapes and wallpaper, reflecting the fashionable tastes of high Stalinism. There were politically innocuous pictures on the wall, and a remarkable chandelier constructed from what looked like five glass coffee jars, each screwed into a red plastic base. The bathroom had tiles in three colors, randomly arranged. The large windows leaked only somewhat around the edges. Our sole deprivation, as springtime temperatures dipped into the low forties, was that there was neither heat nor hot water—not only in these rooms, not only in this hotel, but in the entire Moscow district during a several-week period of repairs.

Nearby Gorky Park was safe and pleasant. The red brick walls of the Kremlin, failing to measure up to Western photographs, seemed anything but an evil and foreboding fortress. Lenin's mausoleum on Red Square appeared incongruously flanked on one side by the colorful cathedral of St. Basil and on the other by GUM, the three-story, three-hall, iron-and-glass-roofed, late-nineteenth-century, state-owned shopping arcade with commodities sparsely populating the lower floors and noisy birds nesting in the rafters. As I had just finished the manuscript for a book on Walter Benjamin, a visit to Moscow, capital city of twentieth-century socialism which Benjamin had visited sixty years before, seemed entirely appropriate. My status as a tourist was short-lived, however, due to the network of Moscow's intelligentsia. On the second day, through the family connection of a Landau mathematician, I was brought to the Institute of Philosophy on Volkhonka Street and introduced to a small working group surrounding a young but highly regarded philosopher, Valerii Podoroga, senior researcher at the Sector of the Philosophical Problems of Politics. Podoroga had written his dissertation on Theodor W. Adorno, and we had that in common. He had read my book on Adorno, which was available in the library of the Academy of Sciences, a fact that I found surprising—as they did my appearance with neither official invitation nor the standard peace-group affiliation.

Podoroga had been holding a series of increasingly tolerated "underground seminars" at the Institute, in order to consider seriously philosophers and theorists formerly dismissed as "bourgeois": Kierkegaard, Nietzsche, Husserl, Heidegger, Freud, Merleau-Ponty, Barthes, Adorno, Benjamin, Foucault. He was not the only person in Moscow writing on European continental philosophy, nor even the only philosopher writing on Adorno. But he and his close associates were unique in appropriating the methods of Western theorists in order to launch a sustained, critical analysis of Soviet culture. In going beyond a critique of *political* totalitarianism, this group was breaking new ground. Indebted particularly to the theories of the Frankfurt School and of Michel Foucault, their project was to criticize power by philosophizing from cultural phenomena—architectural forms, literary texts, cinematic practices, the modalities of everyday life—and it was here that our interests touched closely. At dinner in Podoroga's home I met Mikhail Ryklin, also a philosopher at the Institute and a friend of Podoroga since student days. He launched into a lecture on Walter Benjamin's *The Origin of German Tragic Drama*—in fluent German. Ryklin was thoroughly acquainted with French poststructuralism as well. I was impressed generally by the European language skills of these intellectuals, long isolated from the West. Numerous Institute members, many of whom had never been abroad, addressed me freely in German, French, or English, while I was only beginning to enter the world of Russian script. The fact that our collective communication reached a level of intellectual rigor, however, was due to the translation skills of Elena Petrovskaia, a young woman working with Podoroga, who as a child had attended the English-speaking United Nations school in New York. Petrovskaia, then writing her dissertation on the image of the Indian as the enemy "Other" in the American intellectual landscape, acted as translator for our official talks and informal conversations. Her American English was flawless, and she transported not only our words but also our souls across the linguistic divide.

There were others whom I came to know during this and subsequent visits—Nellie Matroshilova, head of the Department of the History of Philosophy and an expert in German phenomenology, who would host Jürgen

Habermas's visit to Moscow the following spring; Mikhail Kuznetsov, specialist in contemporary German philosophy who now writes on the philosophy of computer technology and cyberspace; Tatiana Klimenkova, influenced by Foucault and one of the first Russian philosophers to concern herself with feminist issues; Natasha Avtonomova, the Institute's first researcher in the work of Jacques Derrida; Elena Oznovkina, translator of Husserl into Russian; Dmitrii Khanin, aesthetic philosopher and John Dewey expert, who had first escorted me to the Institute and now teaches Russian Literature at Colgate University—and many more. But these three personalities would be the pivot around which our subsequent collaboration turned: Valerii Podoroga, idiosyncratic and brilliant, esoteric in a way considered charismatic by his colleagues, at times blunt and bungling—the very prototype of a Russian philosopher; Mikhail Ryklin, openly communicative, fluent in four languages, and impressive in his knowledge of various theoretical traditions which he delighted in parrying with Nietzschean black humor; Elena Petrovskaia, willfully energetic, able to copy an impressionist painting with the same mimetic skill as translate a text, and raised with a precocious confidence from having been at home on both sides of the Cold War world. Their personalities gave expression to the various objective possibilities that existed at the time. As a specifically Russian philosopher, Podoroga's interest in Western theory was tactical, a means of prying open the past of his own, national culture in its pre- and postrevolutionary forms, whereas Ryklin saw himself more in international terms, affirming the intellectual and aesthetic avant-garde whether it showed itself in Moscow, Paris, Berlin, or New York. Petrovskaia prefigured a new hybridity, choosing to adopt values from both East and West. She loved Moscow, but specifically for its contributions to international culture. Unimpressed with Western materialism, she used the privilege of her family's foreign travel for one purpose, to acquire a collection of recent books that would have made any Western academic envious, and these circulated widely among her Moscow friends.[2]

The fact that I had been schooled in Western Marxism had everything to do with my desire to enter into a collaboration. And yet this Marxist orientation was of little interest to my Moscow counterparts.[3] Granted, at the level of the Academy of Sciences, philosophers had been exposed to a sophistication of Marxist theory lacking in the ideology of Marxist-Leninism. (The general Soviet public did not read Marx himself.) The French Marxist Louis Althusser visited the Institute of Philosophy during the Brezhnev years; the rehabilitation of the Hungarian Georg Lukács had been signaled by a recent translation of his aesthetic theory. But these thinkers spoke to an older generation than the one with whom I was becoming involved. In the Soviet Union, the *shestidesiatniki* or "sixties generation" was that of Petrovskaia's parents—and, indeed, of Gorbachev himself. They were born in Stalin's time, their childhood experiences were of war, they came to maturity during the era of Khrushchev's reforms. As students they discovered the writings of the young, humanist Marx, and many later sympathized with the spirit of the Prague Spring of 1968—the call for "socialism with a human face."[4] There was a time lag between this sixties generation and the one that I had encountered as a student in the United States and Germany at the very end of the decade. Podoroga and Ryklin, my peers, considered themselves already beyond the neo-Marxism of the Gorbachev generation. But if their politics differed from mine, the terms of our critical analyses were close. We understood culture as fundamentally political, operating on the body in a material sense. The machinery of modern power was not so much hidden behind the ideology of mass utopia as it was produced by it. Intrinsic to the politics of modernity was the potential for the abuse of power against the collective, and at the same time in its name. These were problems that neither Western capitalism nor Soviet socialism had managed to resolve.

■

I returned to Cornell and started formal study of Russian, committed to a sustained collaboration—although how such a project would be financed was far from clear. U.S. government funding during the Cold War was geared to area studies, and I was neither a Soviet nor a Russian specialist. Moreover, the critique of problems of power *common* to both systems was hardly a Cold War research priority. The MacArthur Foundation was receptive to less typical projects, however, and we were grateful for its funding on several occasions. The first was for a reciprocal exchange of visitors to take place in early 1988.[5] It necessitated obtaining official permission from the Soviet side, which I had bypassed on my first visit, and access to which meant passing through the red-curtained, bookless offices of the high-placed bureaucrats of the Academy. Their power, it was rumored, was in inverse proportion to their scholarly productivity, and any request that was not their own initiative was met with suspicion. Our exchange was to entail, as the first stage, a January visit to Moscow by a two-woman team, myself and Nancy Ries, a Cornell graduate student of anthropology who specialized in Soviet culture. That two women alone wished to comprise an official delegation was enough to raise eyebrows; that an anthropologist wanted to do field work in civilized Moscow was close to a scandal.[6] The second part of the proposed exchange, to bring younger members of the Institute to Cornell in April, went clearly against protocol, as the list approved for travel to the West generally did not reach below department heads. As one Moscow friend put it: "It is a firm conviction that only chiefs of the tribe are to enter the Wonderland."

Just weeks before our January visit, official invitations for Ries and myself arrived. Podoroga's and Petrovskaia's permission to travel to Cornell was granted, likewise, at the eleventh hour. But the authorities did yield, setting a precedent on which we would rely in the future.[7] I spent the fall of 1988 preparing a series of lectures analyzing problematic aspects of the common, radical democratic heritage of our political systems, and delivered them at the Institute of Philosophy in January-February 1989.[8] In May and June I was back in Moscow to give talks in Podoroga's "underground seminar" and lecture on Walter Benjamin at the Belorussian University in Minsk.[9] Plans

6.3 Jacques Derrida at the Institute of Philosophy, Moscow, April 1990. Photo by Mikhail Ryklin.

were made for a special Benjamin issue of the *Soviet Yearbook of Philosophy* for 1990, published by the Academy of Sciences, that would include the first Russian translations of his works (sections from his "Moscow Diary," among others), and contributions by Podoroga and myself.[10] The group around Podoroga coalesced into a working collective, continuing to develop a political critique of Soviet culture and expanding to attract philosophers from Minsk, the Baltic republics, and Bulgaria, as well as Moscow intellectuals and artists from outside the Institute.

Western visitors became more frequent. I urged Fredric Jameson to contact Podoroga's group when he went to Moscow in October 1988, and he became an integral part of our collaboration.[11] Jürgen Habermas's official visit to the Institute of Philosophy took place in April 1989. A trip to Paris in that month allowed me to make preliminary arrangements with Jacques Derrida for a visit to the Institute the following spring. My trips back and forth (and consequent access to reliable telephone and mail communication) made it possible to help organize two events initiated by members of the Institute that one year earlier would not have taken place.[12] The first was an International Conference on Martin Heidegger, October 17–19, 1989, on the occasion of Heidegger's hundredth birthday.[13] This conference broke old rules by including young philosophers as participants, dispensing with the traditional Marxist-Leninist ideological framing, and having as its stated goal the opening up of channels to Western philosophical debates. Clearly, the younger Russian philosophers saw Heidegger (even more than Habermas)

1 Aleksandr Kosolapov, *The Manifesto*, 1983.

2 Konstantin Iuon, *The New Planet*, 1921.

3 Ilia Kabakov, *The Man Who Flew into Space from His Apartment*, 1981–1986. From *Ten Characters*, installation, 1988.

4 Aleksei Shchusev and others, Stantsiia Komsomolskaia (Komsomol Station), Moscow metro, 1952.

5 Leonid Sokov, *Stalin and Marilyn Monroe,* 1992.

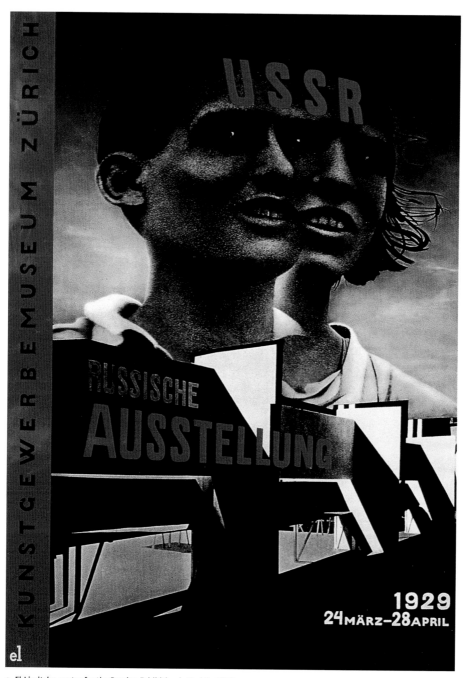

6   El Lissitzky, poster for the Russian Exhibition in Zurich, 1929.

7 Vitaly Komar and Alexander Melamid, *Double Self-Portrait as Young Pioneers,* 1982–1983.

8 Vasilii Elkin, *Long Live the Red Army—the Armed Detachment of the Proletarian Revolution!*, poster, 1932.

9 Vitaly Komar and Alexander Melamid, Bayonne, New Jersey, workers, untitled fragment from the series *Bergen Point Brass Foundry,* 1988.

10   Aleksandr Rodchenko, poster for Vertov's film *Kino-Glaz* (Cinema-Eye), 1924.

11 Dmitrii Prigov, *For the Poor Cleaning Woman,* installation, 1991.

12 Visitors contemplate three paintings by Ad Reinhardt at the retrospective exhibition "American Art in the Twentieth Century," Berlin, 1993. Photo by Susan Buck-Morss.

13 Aleksandr Kosolapov, *Symbols of This Century*, 1982.

as a fundamental departure from the intellectual lineage of Hegel-Marx-Lenin.[14] A debate ensued during the conference among the German participants that rehearsed the "case of Heidegger"—his Nazi connection—to which V. N. Bibichin made the telling reply that the whole issue was not so very significant; Nazi or no, Heidegger was indisputably "bourgeois," and what was truly remarkable in the Moscow context was the fact that he was being discussed seriously at all.

This was the heyday of East-West exchanges. In January 1990, with the official title of "Co-Chairwoman of the International Soviet-French-American Symposium," I was back in Moscow with Jean-Luc Nancy for a workshop of deconstruction.[15] Derrida's ten-day visit took place in April. He was hosted by Podoroga, who in the fast-changing situation had risen to considerable institutional power as head of a newly created institute sector, the name of which marked its experimental nature: the Laboratory for the Study of Post-Classical Philosophy, Literature, and Art. Derrida was accompanied by his wife, a professional psychoanalyst who spoke Russian, having lived as a child in Moscow where her father was assigned as a journalist after World War II. Marguerite Derrida was of great interest to the psychoanalytic community, long suppressed in the Soviet Union but never entirely eliminated. Jacques Derrida drew crowds at the Institute and at Moscow State University, young students who, if they did not understand every philosophical move, knew one thing definitively, that Derrida was a "scandal." His visit took place during the anniversary of Stalin's death—this was perhaps when "specters of Marx" first appeared to him.[16] He has since written about this trip (or rather, written about not writing about it) in an essay entitled "Back from Moscow, in the USSR."[17]

■

The historical constellation changed with each visit. When Ries and I came in January 1989, Gorbachev was at the height of his power. Confirmed as President of the Supreme Soviet the previous October (while maintaining his position as General Secretary of the Communist Party), he called for elections in March of a 2,250-member Congress of People's Deputies, a new institution that was to function as a lower house of the legislature.[18] When I returned to Moscow in May and June, the new Congress was in session. Still largely comprised of party members (85 percent represented the Communist Party, while the rest represented unofficial opposition groups), the deputies were remarkably outspoken and irreverent of party discipline, defining themselves from the beginning as an autonomous political unit. Debates on the floor were televised live from the Kremlin, reaching audiences in Eastern Europe as well. The issues discussed included economic reform, ethnic autonomy, ecological damage, putting an end to one-party rule, and criticisms of the unpopular Afghanistan war which had recently been concluded. These proceedings were followed enthusiastically by an addicted public. Few workplaces lacked a television tuned in constantly to the Congress of People's Deputies. People went strolling in the park with portable radios held to their ears. It was in fact thrilling to witness the construction of a democratic public sphere. Even with access to power still funneled through party membership, there was a wonderful freshness to political life, and a sense of public participation that was direct and unpretentious.[19] I remember standing by the metro entrance at Red Square at the end of the day's session and observing the deputies (multiethnic, mainly young, women as well as men) walking across the square to take the metro home (there were no black limousines in sight). They were buttonholed freely by people waiting to take up with them issues they had just been debating on TV. As a working principle, *glasnost'* had come to mean: "Whatever is not expressly prohibited is allowed." The television show *Vzgliad* (Glance) interviewed disgruntled Afghanistan War veterans, and instructed viewers on how to shop on the black market by discerning the difference between forged Levi Strauss bluejeans and the real thing. In 1989 the hit movie was *Malenkaia Vera* (Little Vera), which depicted alienated youth and featured explicit sex.[20] We had a special viewing of it at the Insti-

6.4 Mikhail Gorbachev, Secretary of the Communist Party, 1985.

tute of Philosophy as part of the latter's newly established Film Club. There was round-table discussion at the Dom Kino (House of Cinema) on the topic: "Umer li Marx?" (Is Marx Dead?) The answer—yes—might, I felt, be considered healthily materialist.

By the summer of 1989, Gorbachev was confronting organized challenges to his leadership from groups claiming that his program of *perestroika* did not go far enough. On July 10, coal miners in Siberia went on strike, protesting against deteriorating working and living conditions. On July 30, approximately three hundred dissident deputies, including Boris Yeltsin[21] and Andrei Sakharov,[22] formed an Inter-Regional Group of People's Deputies that organized the unofficial opposition. On August 18, the fiftieth anniversary of the Nazi-Soviet nonaggression pact (the secret protocols of which had given Stalin the green light to annex the Baltic states), a human chain of a million demonstrators spanned the four hundred miles from Tallinn through Riga to Vilnius in protest against continued Soviet domination. When I arrived in October for the Heidegger Conference, enthusiasm for Gorbachev among the intelligentsia had been tempered, whereas Yeltsin, formerly a figure of derision due to his well-publicized drinking bouts, was just back from a legitimizing trip to the United States and was beginning to be taken seriously. The policies of *perestroika* (market reform within the framework of the socialist economy and democratic reform within a one-party political system) were openly challenged as insufficient. Increasingly, in order to maintain popular support, Gorbachev was forced to undercut the bases of his own power: the Communist Party and, ultimately, the Soviet Union itself. In contrast, Yeltsin's call for "Russian" autonomy in opposition to "Soviet" imperialism was producing a new discourse of political legitimation, one that enabled him to build his own power base on the same ethnic principle that supported the demands of the Baltic states, as well as those of ethnic minorities within Russia. Such a political topology left little space for Gorbachev, the leader of the "imperialist" Soviet Union, a political entity based on neither ethnic identity nor its own territorial domain.[23]

On November 9, 1989, the Berlin Wall was opened. The effect of the subsequent toppling of socialist regimes in Eastern Europe was to undermine Gorbachev's domestic power still further, even as—indeed, precisely because—it made him enormously popular as an international celebrity. His global superstardom was achieved by weakening the Soviet Union's traditional image internationally, thus feeding off of a different economy of power than functioned at home. The political entity of the USSR was nothing if not a superpower, so that if Gorbachev was losing "Russian" support to Yeltsin, those who still identified as "Soviets" were becoming alienated as well. But Yeltsin's populism was also thoroughly problematic. While democratic in form, the principle of ethnic autonomy was seriously deficient in terms of democratic content, as outbreaks of resentment in the Baltic states against the indigenous Russian population were already making clear. In this situation, even the most progressive intellectuals at the Institute of Philosophy followed a time-honored tradition of keeping their distance from politics, of whatever stance. They were willing to accept responsibility as the conscience of the country, and to speak out, like Sakharov, as "god's fool" in opposition to established power. But political organizing of even grassroots movements was an altogether foreign idea. This refusal to act politically, which stemmed from deep-seated distrust, indeed cynicism, regarding every aspect of public power and every form of utopian politics, became a contested point between us.

■

The fall of the Berlin Wall affected the nature of our intellectual relationship. Surprisingly, it made collaboration more difficult. Our interest had been in criticizing the past of our respective cultures, using the same theoretical tools to analyze those structures of modern power that had done violence to humanity on both sides of the great divide. Ironically, in ways that gradually became apparent, the commonality of that project seemed to depend on the very divide that it sought to transcend.

In June 1989, the Communist Party was defeated resoundingly in Poland's elections. Hungary's Roundtable met throughout the summer to negotiate a peaceful transition to a multiparty system. East Germany began to topple in September, Czechoslovakia in October, Bulgaria in November, Romania in December.[24] The League of Yugoslav Communists disintegrated in early 1990. German reunification occurred in spring 1990. These events caused a collapse of structures of signification that had profound effects worldwide. And yet they were not revolutions. The images of dazed and drinking Germans on top of the Berlin Wall gave the world a rush of freedom, but provided little vision of the content of what was to come. The photograph released of Ceausescu's bloody corpse functioned as a sign almost in the commercial sense, advertising the perpetrators as revolutionaries, rather than marking true social change. Satellite television played an unprecedented role as witness, attesting to the reality of change, a situation that encouraged the staging of "revolutionary" events, as if massive social transformation were a matter of gaining access to airtime. It is remarkable how strategically significant television stations became. Their takeover was the contemporary version of storming the Bastille or the Winter Palace.

To claim that the "bloodless" (or "velvet" or "glorious") revolutions of 1989 were in fact no revolution at all is not simply to disagree with how others have defined the term. I am in no way denying what many have argued, that the self-conscious articulation of a "civil society," in opposition to the authoritarian regimes, created a public space in which the power of citizen protest achieved a momentous wave of reforms, culminating in the overthrow of the old guard of Communist leaders. But these new forms of civil society—Poland's Solidarity union, East Germany's New Forum, Czechoslovakia's Civic Forum, Hungary's Opposition Roundtable, the peace and ecology movements—were produced *within* the old regimes, rather than being the consequence of their defeat.[25] The first free elections were organized by members of the radical wing of the Communist Party itself, although in many cases they were digging their own political graves. The tens of thousands of persons marching in the Leipzig demonstrations of September 25 and October 2 sang the "Internationale" as well as "We Shall Overcome." Alexander Dubček, veteran of the Prague Spring, who on November 20 stood so unforgettably next to Vaclav Havel waving to crowds in Wenceslas Square, had been the author of the doctrine of *socialism* with a human face, not a proponent of socialism's demise. The real surge of critical political energy, including the great dissident literature, belongs to the period before the fall of the Wall. The dissolution of critical thinking began almost immediately thereafter, and it is striking how little original thought subsequently emerged. There was no widespread intellectual renaissance, no cultural rebirth, but rather a recycling of earlier dissident literature, followed by a spate of translations of Western texts. With the collapse of Eastern Europe into the outstretched arms of the West, what was advertised as revolution turned out to be something quite different: economic incorporation—not into the European Community on somewhat equal terms, but into a global capitalist system already in the process of restructuring according to neoliberal rules that marked the end of an era of social democracy. Brazil, not Sweden, was the model of the postsocialist future. But I am getting ahead of my story.

6.2

ONE WORLD

It was during this period of the dismantling of Eastern European regimes
that we planned our longest and largest collaboration, a two-week "course"
to be held in October 1990 at the Inter-University Centre in Dubrovnik.
For several decades the Centre's courses had played a unique role as a meeting place for scholars and students from the West and Eastern Europe, but
up until then no Soviets had participated. That situation changed when Dr.
V. S. Stepin, Director of the Moscow Institute of Philosophy, traveled to Yugoslavia in spring 1989 to negotiate arrangements with the Centre. Coincidentally, I was also at the Dubrovnik Centre attending a course on critical
theory,[26] and we discussed the feasibility of a new course codirected by Valerii Podoroga and myself. A month later when I was back in Moscow, plans
for a Dubrovnik course began in earnest. Two further directors were added:
Luchezar Boiadzhiev, a young Bulgarian at the Institute of Art Studies in
Sofia, whose colleague, Vladislav Todorov, had been with us as a long-term
visitor to Podoroga's Laboratory, and Fredric Jameson, whose intellect and
enthusiasm provided enormous momentum for the project.[27] Invited participants represented a variety of theoretical positions. They included Boris
Groys, who had left the Soviet Union for West Germany in 1981 and whose
book *Gesammtkunstwerk Stalin* (Stalin's Total Artwork) put forward the bold
thesis that Stalin had ironically carried into effect the plans of the very artistic avant-garde whom he had suppressed; Wolfgang Fritz Haug from West
Berlin, Marxist philosopher and editor of the journal *Das Argument,* whose
most recent work was a pro-*perestroika* diary of the Gorbachev year June
1989–May 1990 (*Das Perestroika-Journal*); Helena Kozakiewicz a "Western"
Marxist philosopher from the Institute of Philosophy and Sociology in Warsaw,[28] critic of both the old Communist regime and Solidarity's coalition
government that had replaced it following elections unduly influenced by
the United States; Peter Madsen, literary theorist from the University of

W SAMO POŁUDNIE
4 CZERWCA 1989

6.5 Polish Solidarity Party election poster, 1989, by Jan Andrez Gorny and Pawel Zazac.[29]

Copenhagen, committed, in the tradition of the Frankfurt School, to rescuing critical reason from anti-Enlightenment attacks; Merab Mamardashvili, a renowned Georgian philosopher of the Soviet sixties generation who had courageously gone against the grain of official dogma to develop his own French-influenced, existentialist philosophy, and who had been the inspirational teacher of both Ryklin and Podoroga; and Slavoj Žižek, Slovenian-Lacanian-Hegelian-postmodernist theorist, trained in Paris, who taught in the United States and had recently run—unsuccessfully—for president of Slovenia.

Once the regimes in Eastern Europe began to topple, the original working title for the course, "Dismantling the Cold War Discourse," seemed inadequate. We renamed it "Modern Problems of Power and Culture," under which general rubric we might integrate on a long-term basis the efforts of Eastern and Western scholars to reassess the modern project (it was expected that successful Dubrovnik courses would continue meeting in future years). We still needed a specific title for the first two-week meeting in October 1990. Aware that the act of naming was still an issue of political sensitivity in the Soviet Union, I left the choice up to my Moscow friends. They surprised me with the title, "Philosophical Problems of Postmodern Discourse," clearly implying that it was the *times* that were postmodern, not merely the West's discursive forms. Although the choice no longer seems remarkable, at that time it was a radical intellectual move. Until then, even among its proponents, and certainly among its critics (of whom Jameson was one of the most articulate), postmodernity was understood as a condition specific to (late) capitalism and its consumerist, simulacral cultural forms. Perhaps the inclusion of (late) socialist culture within this term should not have surprised me, as I had been arguing persistently for the commonalities of our roots in Western modernity, and "post-" modernity would seem to follow logically as the next step. But such a logical step was in fact a construction of history, not its description. The gesture of including Soviet experience within the meaning of postmodernism was a moment in the process of ideological formation. It had the effect of universalizing the claims of postmodernism as a theoretical discourse with explanatory power, and gave this term pretensions of general legitimacy. Now it was not just a question of a postmodern school of architecture or art existing among other contending schools, nor, as Jameson argued, of a "dominant cultural logic" of late capitalism, but of all contemporary cultures expressing the same "postmodern" world.[30] In short, postmodernism, up until then a phenomenon *within* the cultural field, was becoming naturalized as the name *of* the cultural field, no longer a particular theoretical positioning but the description of a new historical stage. It is clear to me now, although it was not then, that this moment was part of a hegemonic shift in intellectual discourse that was global in scope.[31] Although the term is now so broadly used to describe our age that it is accepted as second nature, it is important to remember that there was nothing self-evident about this outcome: "postmodernism" was not a historical inevitability. But the temptations to see the world through this conceptual lens were strong ones. From the Soviet side the options of moving toward ethnic traditionalism, or of backing the old Communist Party in the hopes that it would transform itself from within, seemed far more dubious. Moreover, in terms of postmodern culture there were ways one could argue that the Soviet Union was in advance of the rest of the world, having attained this new historical stage *before* the capitalist West. Political cynicism, anti–utopianism, distrust of all totalizing discourses—were not these characteristics of postmodernity already well established in Soviet dissident culture as part of the intellectual legacy of de–Stalinization?

■

"To Dubrovnik!" had been the toast each time we met during the eighteen months of planning for the course. "Dubrovnik" became a floating signifier for multiple and various desires. The postcard image of the city shimmered in our dream consciousness as the goal and a new beginning, although no one quite knew of what. The city, the sea, the air did not disappoint us—we had little foreboding of the precariousness of the old town's tranquillity. But the pleasures of sensory immediacy made the problematic aspects of our

6.6 Dubrovnik, the old city, postcard, 1990.

communication all the more disappointing. There were first of all structural inequalities. The official language of the Centre was English, which, especially for the younger Moscow participants who had never attended an international conference, tipped the intellectual power balance toward the West. Accommodations and rates were lower for Eastern participants, but those on full pension were excluded from dinners in town. Per diem stipends for the Soviets were paid in dollars which many preferred to keep, so that even a sociable coffee or a beer was foregone so as not to squander the hard currency. The Soviets rightly chafed under their second-class economic status (a portent of things to come). I had an uneasy feeling that the list of invited participants was taking on the qualities of a new *nomenklatura*. Some Eastern Europeans felt that the whole conception of the course replicated the superpower dominance which they had hoped was a thing of the past.

But the greatest moments of frustration were within the intellectual exchange itself. The term "postmodernism" was a source of dispute. The young Bulgarian participants, Luchezar Boiadzhiev, Ivailo Dichev, and Vladislav Todorov, whose collaborative contribution was a piece of performance art that featured the mummified founders of the Communist states, were fully comfortable with "postmodernism" as a synonym for their own "post-communist condition." Merab Mamardashvili disliked the term intensely, calling it a form of "cultural stupidity" because its celebration of the failure of reason "gave up the philosophical battle" and denied the right to think. The questions of what to think and what to do, he claimed, were always new because the world changed, but to describe this world as "postmodern" was a choice, and hence ultimately an ethical decision: "You don't have to become postmodern."[32] Helena Kozakiewicz criticized postmodernity from the opposite perspective, that of a critical sociology of knowledge which stressed the social and historical determinants of postmodern discourse as ideology. Peter Madsen warned against the postmodern oversimplification of modernism's extremely varied reactions to the process of

modernization, ranging from rationalism to surrealism. Natasha Avtonomova cautioned us to distinguish in our own work between investigation
and creation, preferring the humbler claims of the former to the arbitrariness of the latter, of which postmodernism could be seen as an example.

My own plea was to seize the term "postmodern" and reappropriate
it for the purposes of a common critical strategy—the project that had been
the original impetus of our own collaboration.[33] But my Moscow colleagues were now resistant. Rather than stressing what was common to the
methods and substance of our critiques of modern power, they seemed
compelled to emphasize the differences—despite the fact that we were considering cultural phenomena that the East and West had shared during the
process of industrial modernization: early cinema, urban architecture, mass
leaders, media manipulation, the mass-utopian myth of industrial "modernization" itself. We had purposely decided to focus at Dubrovnik on ob-

6.7 Stantsiia Beloruskaia, Moscow metro, 1951, designed and constructed by Z. Abramova and I. Taranov.

235

jects of visual culture because these might be more easily accessible to a common analysis across language differences. But shared vision turned out to be as difficult as shared language. Looking at the same images, we did not see the same things. Mikhail Ryklin read the iconography of the Moscow metro—which to any New Yorker must appear glorious—as the epitome of Stalinist terror. Valerii Podoroga interpreted the work of the Bolshevik filmmaker Sergei Eisenstein, idol of the Western avant-garde, as giving cinematic expression to the sadomasochistic body produced by Stalin's machinery of power. Boris Groys condemned the entire aesthetic avant-garde, East and West, as the precursor to the Stalinist "aesthetic" project of creating a new society. Vladislav Todorov found a similar aesthetics in Soviet economic practices, in the sense that factories were organized to produce ideology, not products, fabricating the fabulous "working class" as the party's own missing constituency.[34] Against their absolute rejection of the past, Haug, Jameson, and I were intent on criticizing the dream forms of both capitalism and socialism from within in order to salvage the transcendent moment to which they gave expression. Jameson tried to encourage the reconsideration of our position as intellectuals by means of a new cognitive mapping that would describe the postmodern condition self-critically, from the inside, not only as a cultural style but as an economic system and a life-world (in which "cities are modified, bodies are modified"), in order to articulate a leftist politics adequate to the present.

We had prepared in advance to discuss one literary text in common, a section of Andrei Platonov's novel *The Foundation Pit*. During this discussion, Podoroga began to insist that we simply could not understand the novel without access to both the experience of Stalinism and Platonov's use of the Russian language. His exclusionary hermeneutics were rejected by Western participants unwilling to cede the debate to arguments of national difference. But in our own critiques of capitalism, our neo-Marxist categories remained largely unmodified despite sea-changes in the global political and economic situation. We seemed, generally, to be reviving the official polarization between Eastern and Western discourses but this time with the positions reversed, the "East" using every stereotype of the Cold War to characterize its own totally unique, totally totalitarian past, and the "West" mouthing a standard criticism of capitalist, commodity culture that would have been acceptable in the USSR long before *glasnost'*. Neither side seemed willing to give ground in this carnivalesque performance of Cold War rhetoric. Tempers grew short. An incident in which gender relations collided with power relations brought me to the boiling point.[35] Peter Madsen pleaded with us in Habermasian terms to "be reasonable!" Jameson later described the dynamics this way:

> *Unfortunately Cold War anticommunism has lavishly supplied all possible and imaginable stereotypes . . . so that even experiential truth from the East now looks indistinguishable, not merely from media commonplaces and simulacra but from its most ancient Cold War forms. . . . The more their truths are couched in Orwellian language, the more tedious they become for us; the more our truths demand expression in even the weakest forms of Marxian language—that of simple social democracy say, or even the welfare state or social justice, or equality—the more immediately do the Eastern hearing aids get switched off.*[36]

And further:

> *To put it briefly, the East wishes to talk in terms of power and oppression; the West in terms of culture and commodification. There are really no common denominators in this initial struggle for discursive rules, and what we end up with is the inevitable comedy of each side muttering irrelevant replies in its own favourite language.*[37]

Jameson's suggestion that this incompatibility of languages was simply an extension (and reversal) of the dualisms of the Cold War past is not a sufficient explanation. In the Soviet case, the individuals making these Cold War-like arguments, Podoroga and Ryklin, were experts in precisely those forms of critical theory that had been created as a critique of *Western* modernity, and the very gesture of adopting them to criticize Soviet cultural life was an admission of the commonalities of manipulative, mass-culture forms. Podoroga's description of the "cosmocratic utopia" of Platonov's *Foundation Pit* as a "catastrophical machine of power" (the book, he emphasized, had important similarities to the novels of Kafka and other non-Russian writers) was expressly indebted to the work of Mumford, Deleuze, and Guattari;[38] Ryklin's interpretation of the Moscow metro iconography used Bakhtin's conception of the collective folk-body against the grain of what he knew was accepted interpretation in the West, not positively, as "a hymn to the common man,"[39] but dystopically, as "horror incarnate."[40]

■

Our difficulties in communicating need to be understood within the constellation of political events in which the Dubrovnik meeting took place. Every socialist regime of Eastern Europe had collapsed. We were meeting in a "post-socialist" country on the brink of civil war. Only in the Soviet Union was Communist Party rule still intact, and even here its power was shaken. Our problem was not that we were still living in different worlds. Rather, our worlds were fast becoming one, on terms that made critical thinking precarious for reasons other than political censorship, and theoretical collaboration problematic for reasons other than cultural difference. While we had been working to criticize the dreams of the past, we were living through the disappearance of a dream of the present—specifically (and it was one of the dreamworlds of modernity) the dream that each side had about the other. Dreamworlds are not merely illusions. In insisting that what is is not all there is, they are assertions of the human spirit and invaluable politically. They make the momentous claim that the world we have known since childhood is not the only one imaginable. For critical intellectuals from the East, the existence of a nonsocialist West sustained the dream that there could be "normalcy" in social life. For their counterparts in the West, the existence of the noncapitalist East sustained the dream that the Western capitalist system was not the only possible form of modern production. Of course we each knew that our hopes were not realized in any perfect way by the other side. But the mere fact of the existence of a different system was proof enough to allow us to think the dream possible—something "normal" outside one's own system that allowed one to describe the latter's internal logic as preposterous; some other social organization of human existence that allowed one to think that the given state of things was not natural or inevitable, so that history could still be envisioned as a space of human freedom.

The possibility of difference is the prerequisite for critical thinking, which, distinct from science, is not content to identify what is. It was this possibility that was threatened by the coming together of our worlds. Their merging was not the convergence that Sakharov had predicted in the 1960s, the felicitous scenario of both sides moving toward some democratic-socialist middle ground. Rather, the Second World was disappearing into the First World at the same time that the ideals of socialism were going under even in their Western democratic forms. In this context, the Soviets' insistence on the absolute uniqueness and incomprehensibility for the West of their own modern horrors was an expression of hope. If really existing socialism was merely one variant of modernism, then its collapse into the other variant could only lead to the most pessimistic conclusions. And it was impossible for them to embrace our own Marxist discourse as an alternative without being led in a circle, in terms of the history of their own cultural context, back to the very intellectual constraints that critical thinking had enabled them to escape. The irony, of course, is that Marx, while a rather poor theorist of socialism, had developed one of the most powerful and cogent critiques of that capitalist system which the East was entering, yet it was precisely not as *Marxist* criticism that a protest against incorporation could be raised. Not all texts are legible at all times; censorship can exist even without political constraint.[41] Elena Petrovskaia gives an everyday example:

> *I well remember how at the very start of perestroika random passers-by were inter-*
> *viewed by TV reporters—they were asked to give their opinion of what was going*
> *on around them, be it changing politics or, perhaps, their daily problems. And many*
> *seemed completely at a loss: not because they had nothing to say, but because there*
> *were no words to say it with. The old media-inspired cliches, something like "we fully*
> *approve and support," were sensed as absolutely inappropriate.*[42]

When the structuring topology between words and the world under-goes a seismic shift, it may happen that the truth cannot be said. Certain phrases, certain discourses become inaccessible, while others may suddenly reemerge with new power. To speak of a crisis in language sounds idealist, yet it can be a profoundly concrete historical experience. At Dubrovnik, Slavoj Žižek described such a crisis as central to the events in Eastern Europe, but in this case the critically powerful moment came from arguing for an *identity* between language and reality, reviving the moribund discourse of socialism itself. The attempt by radical groups in Slovenia and elsewhere to close the gap between socialist ideology and socialist reality by taking the old ideology at its word, paradoxically forced the political situation wide open. Žižek described the "inherently *tragical* ethical dimension" of those who "took socialism seriously" and whose role was that of the "vanishing mediator," a term he borrowed from Jameson:[43]

> *[They] were prepared to put everything at stake in order to destroy the compromised*
> *system and replace it with the utopian "third way" beyond capitalism and "really*
> *existing" socialism. Their sincere belief and insistence that they were not working*
> *for the restoration of Western capitalism, of course, proved to be nothing but an in-*
> *substantial illusion; however, we could say that precisely as such (as a thorough il-*
> *lusion without substance) it was stricto sensu nonideological: it didn't "reflect"*
> *in an inverted-ideological form any actual relations of power.*[44]

Žižek spoke of his experience in Slovenia: "We witnessed a kind of open-ing; things were for a moment visible which immediately became invisi-ble."[45] This moment of contingency and choice allowed space for political agency. But the rhetoric of "taking socialism seriously" was not strong enough to prevent the collapse of that space under the weight of a new ruling ideology, a political myth that immediately rendered invisible "the open, undecided process of its own founding"—the myth of the ethnic nation.[46] The ontology of national belonging bypasses the crisis of language because identities, fixed from the start, are not an issue for debate. One's mere being—the accident of birth—determines one's status as friend or foe, so that there is not any need to speak at all.

The outburst of postsocialist nationalism in Yugoslavia and elsewhere, claimed Žižek, was produced out of the logic of Western capitalism, rather than being external to it. It is an attempt to cover over capitalism's basic social antagonisms and "*inherent structural imbalance*"[47] by imposing "community" (actually the old communist theme) upon it. It is in fact "the fascist dream," the "impossible" desire for "capitalism cum *Gemeinschaft*, a desire for capitalism without the 'alienated' civil society, without the formal-external relations between individuals."[48] Žižek concluded: "The only way to prevent the emergence of protofascist nationalist hegemony is to call into question the very standard of 'normality,' the universal framework of liberal-democratic capitalism—as was done, for a brief moment, by the 'vanishing mediators' in the passage from socialism into capitalism."[49]

Once the transition was under way, however, talk of a "third way" appeared futile, a "heroic daydream."[50] The antagonisms again became invisible and the system closed again. Ivailo Dichev's presentation at Dubrovnik described the Bulgarian experience:

> In [the communist] world you could at least take sides, engage in the struggle led by the situations of desire. But what if you start suspecting that both conflicting representations [East and West] are produced by the same author, that is by power? The ambiguity of your position is multiplied by two, you not only do not know which of the conflicting representations to choose but also whether to choose at all, whether the choice is real, or something like Descartes' demon is cheating you.[51]

Dichev's revealing description of the bleakness of the postcommunist situation, as it appeared to someone unwilling to accept the pseudo-community of ethnic nationalism, deserves to be cited at length:

> [Postcommunism] is a sort of postmodern condition not only because the great discourses of liberation are behind . . . but also because there is no more nature left to come back to. Common sense will object that there exists the normal capitalist world, which represents nature; and really you do not find an "author" behind capitalism in the way the revolutionaries of different types are the authors of communist society. But what is the nature of this nature? . . . Capitalism, [Georg Lukács] insists, has to be based on an overcalculating individual behavior and an irrational whole. There cannot be a project of capitalism nor some sense of the whole; its only principle is, rather, the negation of transcendence [of the given situation]. . . .
>
> Looking West for the natural, post-communist countries see nothing. There exists a vast number of means to solve problems of situations but no representation of ends, no idea of the meaning of the whole. . . . Post-communist countries today are haunted by the idea that there was nothing symbolic in the defeat of communism. Tzvetan Todorov wrote that the feeling was like what happened to the woman in Maupassant's story: she borrowed a necklace and lost it, and then worked her whole life to pay its price, only to find out that the pearls were a cheap imitation and that she had ruined her life in vain. Actually it was even worse, as everyone realized the project of communism was but an act of will; on both sides of the Berlin Wall they knew it was not a symbolic reality [in the sense of being] something imposed on men by God or the like—they knew it was a "political decision." The Wall separated neither nations, nor cultures, nor natures of some sort; it was absolutely arbitrary, running between towns, houses, households: it vanished into thin air (except for souvenirs and tourist-guidebooks), as if it had never existed. Thus there is nothing to learn from the fall of communism, no moral to be taken. The enemy left no corpse behind—you have ruined economies, killed people, polluted land, but the transcendence as artefact [communism's "act of will"] is nowhere to be seen; the will to power disappeared in being defeated and one could ask oneself whether one's life had been real at all.[52]

The so-called transition to capitalism that followed the fall of socialism was an impoverished substitute for the ideal of revolutionary transcendence, providing no new meaning for political life. Symptomatic of this lack was the enormous confusion that resulted from attempts to define the new political terrain in terms of the old binaries of radical and conservative, "left" and "right." Where did present-day communists belong on the left-right spectrum? Were ethnic nationalists radical or conservative? Was cultural pluralism an adequate definition of democracy? Was the capitalist market a meaningful definition of political freedom? Boris Kagarlitsky, active in Moscow politics and frequent contributor to London's *New Left Review* (who was with us at a Duke University conference in March 1990),[53] relates a further confusion: "The pledge of 'steady increases in living standards' became the most important element of the official ideology" of the Soviet Communist Party beginning in the period of Khrushchev's reforms, so that by the 1980s, the official party line was to present

> *a picture of communism as a society of consumer abundance. . . . It is not surprising that a generation later many people in our country, raised entirely in the spirit of Communist propaganda, not only see this ideal society in the West, but conclude in all seriousness that "real socialism" has already been built in the United States or Canada.*[54]

To describe this morass of meaning within political discourse as "postmodern," as if naming the "spirit of the times" were enough—as if we could then just lean back and relax, relying on "history" to move us all along through this new, somehow inevitable stage—is to dismiss the responsibility of thinking through the complexities of the present. I suspect Mamardashvili, who devoted his life to the responsibility of thinking, was warning us of this danger when he insisted on the critical, repeated task of philosophical questioning itself, the necessity always to begin again.

If someone had said to us in Dubrovnik in October 1990: "Merab Mamardashvili will die within a month. In half a year this hotel will be in flames. In a year the Soviet Union will disintegrate," could we have done better?

■

Three months later I was again in Moscow—or rather outside of Moscow, as the city was part of the opposition's domain, and I was attending what was to be the last *Soviet* International Film Festival. Guests invited by the Union of Soviet Filmmakers were housed on the outskirts at Otradnoe, which, as a party retreat, was real estate still controlled by Gorbachev. I was there to participate in a symposium organized by Kirill Razlogov, "The Screen: Dialogue of Cultures," occurring in tandem with the festival running in Moscow that featured "Great European Films Unknown in the USSR," highlighting European and American films from the height of the Cold War era as well as a major Fritz Lang retrospective. A fleet of black cars was at our disposal to bring us into the city, and buses brought a few Moscovites to us for the symposium sessions. But the sense of isolation was not overcome. We were on a political island—a "Soviet" enclave within "Russian" territory.

The events of the past year had changed the power balance definitively. Yeltsin resigned from the Communist Party following his spring election as President of the Russian Federation, dramatically divorcing himself from the old form of political legitimation. Having won the election on a platform of "real economic and political sovereignty" for Russia, his popularity forced Gorbachev to negotiate plans for economic and political restructuring. Gorbachev and Yeltsin at first worked cooperatively on the "Shatalin Plan," a 500-day timetable for a transition to a market economy. But the version Gorbachev presented to the Supreme Soviet was modified to exclude the timetable and preserve more central authority over banking, taxation, and currency. It was approved on October 19. Twelve days later, in a challenge to Soviet sovereignty, the Parliament of the Russian Federation (which supplied 80 percent of the Soviet budget) voted for immediate implementation of the original Shatalin Plan that had Yeltsin's support. On the issue of political restructuring, Gorbachev agreed in principle to negotiate a new Union treaty,[55] but his plan for a Soviet federation modeled on the United States stopped far short of the national independence that had already been claimed by Lithuania the previous March.[56] Among those opposing Gorbachev's federal plan, some questioned the legitimacy of the Soviet Union itself. Alarmed pro-Soviet forces put pressure on Gorbachev to resist change. Clearly, the positions had polarized, and Gorbachev was caught in between. On December 20, Eduard Shevardnadze resigned as Soviet Foreign Minister, warning that reactionary forces threatened the Soviet Union with renewed dictatorship.

When I arrived in Moscow on January 12, 1991, tensions resulting from the struggle between Gorbachev and Yeltsin for Russian (and particularly Moscow's) political support were palpable.[57] The thematics of the Film Festival symposium were intended to be conciliatory, with various USSR "nationalities" represented in their own right (one "working group" was devoted to "the influence of the screen culture on the development of national cultures and their interactions"). But the Moldovans, particularly, used the symposium as an oppositional forum, calling for their own independent national cinema. Their politics was fully at odds with the new capitalist realities of global film production and distribution that were described in several of the presentations. Podoroga and Ryklin, participants at the symposium, were saddened by the sudden death of Mamardashvili and embittered by efforts to claim him, posthumously, as a great "Georgian" philosopher by politicians who had made his life so difficult all along.

My contribution to the symposium was an attempt to work within—and against—Podoroga's Dubrovnik presentation on Eisenstein by considering, in comparative and historical context, the connection between cinematic representations of the masses and the perceptual violence of the cinema eye, again insisting on a commonality between Eastern and Western forms of modern mass culture.[58] But commonality was precisely what many of the Soviet participants least wanted to acknowledge. What concerned them was the present, and the increasing influence of "Western mass culture" that threatened to trivialize Soviet cinema, which had striven for greatness as an art form from the historical epics of Eisenstein to the contemporary metaphysical works of Tarkovskii and Sokhurov. The screening at this symposium of a young director's film, *Stalin in Africa*—a spoof about training a Stalin look-alike so that he could make the trip to Africa while the real Stalin stayed home, and ending with the non sequitur of contemporary footage shot from a car riding down New York's Broadway by night—was received with stony silence. I was the only one to speak, supporting the director's effort. He responded, rather, to the silence of his compatriots, and without humor or irony made a self-confession of "hooliganism." It was clear that political differences had worked their way into cultural policy, and that here, too, the situation had become polarized. There was no agreement among those present as to how much influence from the new, globalized cinema was desirable, or how one ought to evaluate the early Soviet film avant-garde given the changing contemporary conditions. Annette Michelson from the United States, who for several decades had done pathbreaking archival work in Moscow on early Soviet cinema, continued to argue for the politically critical power of the Bolshevik avant-garde, but others took the same position as Groys, claiming that the political commitment of early Soviet cinema culminated logically in the cultural politics of Stalinism. The extreme disparity of views among the participants made the sessions politically revealing. But the symposium was entirely overshadowed by historical events. On January 13, KGB elite troops were dispatched to Lithuania and attacked the Vilnius radio and television center, attempting a pro-Soviet putsch on behalf of the so-called "Lithuanian National Salvation Committee." Fourteen persons were killed and 580 wounded in the assault. On January 16, just three days later, President Bush ordered the bombing of Bagdhad and the United States was at war with Iraq.

It was difficult for us not to believe that these events had been coordinated.[59] It appeared at the least that both former Cold War opponents were willing to close an eye to the activities of the other. The simultaneity of the

Lithuanian crackdown and the outbreak of the Gulf War was a devastating experience for us because it demonstrated how quickly and easily, on both sides, the machinery of violent state power could be reassembled despite the absence of Cold War justifications. But these events also revealed how far apart we still were in our instinctive political reactions. My colleagues responded with immediate alarm to the tragedy of the events in Lithuania, whereas I, with my enthusiasm for *glasnost'*, was willing to give Gorbachev the benefit of the doubt regarding the degree of his involvement. Nor could they appreciate how troubling it was for me to witness the reassembly of the patriotic war machine of American power that had been challenged only by so much citizen effort during the Vietnam War.[60] It was the way television mediated these events that made the experience so distressing. The telltale sign to my colleagues of Gorbachev's complicity in the Lithuanian crackdown was the fact that the Moscow evening news program, *Vremia,* reverted almost immediately to the propagandistic rhetoric and visual censorship of the pre-*glasnost'* era. What was most upsetting to me was the complicity of the supposedly independent voice of CNN with U.S. government policy, so that the chauvinistic language of television coverage folded seamlessly into the official government line. In the lounge of the Dom Kino, I watched CNN footage of the bombing of Baghdad, which alternated between groundshots of the exploding bombs as an aesthetic spectacle of fireworks over the city, and the technically depersonalized, video game representations sent back by the "smart bombs" themselves. The chauvinistic good humor of those images of destruction sickened me. Russians in the lounge mistook my sentiments, assuring me that Iraq was armed with Soviet weapons which most definitely would not work. Afterward I sat with my friends in Podoroga's kitchen. We got drunk. Had we spoken out publicly that night against both events, might we have made a difference?

■

January 1991 marked the end of our era of innocence. The relatively unqualified optimism that underlay our exchanges had depended on the fact that we were moving along with the political current. As a department head at the Institute of Philosophy, Podoroga was now an established figure. Ryklin was an internationally published theorist of Russia's literary and artistic avant-garde[61] and had just been awarded a grant by the Maison des Sciences de l'Homme for philosophical research in Paris. Petrovskaia had left behind her student status and was a published philosopher in her own right. Now a full professor, I had become some kind of Phil Donahue of intellectual exchange, building "bridges" (as Donahue called the live, satellite television dialogues he hosted with Vladimir Posner between citizens of New York and Moscow) over which we intellectuals passed with little bureaucratic difficulty and substantial financial support. The mood of political power was changing, however. Gorbachev had been a cosmopolitan figure, but now "cosmopolitanism" (the code word for Jewishness among Russian anti-Semitic groups) was under attack. Political leaders still played on a global stage, but they felt far less constrained by the opprobrium of a general audience. That was the lesson of the Lithuanian crackdown, and it was the lesson of the war in the Gulf as well. Television, the most powerful medium of political life, showed itself to be vulnerable, on both sides, to appropriation by the "wild zone" of sovereign power—the war zone that I had described in my earliest Moscow lectures on the modern, mass-democratic state. Those lectures had discussed a future crisis of sovereign legitimacy within the superpowers as a consequence of the disappearance of the Cold War enemy. In the USSR in 1991, this crisis was in full swing.[62] It culminated in the abortive coup of August 19–21, which sounded the death knell of the Soviet Union as a sovereign form.

Circumstances surrounding the August 1991 coup are still obscure, as the version that has been offered to the public leaves several key questions unanswered.[63] The accepted narrative is that it was planned by reactionary Soviet officials backed by the KGB, who placed Gorbachev under house arrest in the Crimea and on August 19 made the by now predictable first move of taking over the Moscow television station. Vice President Ianaev announced at 6:00 a.m. that Gorbachev was ill, and that he was in charge as head of the "State Committee for the State of Emergency."[64] Hundreds of tanks took up key positions on Moscow streets. Yeltsin forces formed an opposition, taking their stand in the Russian White House and using every technological medium at their disposal to challenge the constitutional legality of the emergency decrees. They did not hesitate to call the coup leaders "criminals" and "traitors"—that is, enemies of the true "state," which by "defending" Yeltsin himself appeared to personify. He telephoned George Bush and John Major, receiving assurances that neither the United States nor Great Britain would grant legitimacy to the coup. He used a ham radio frequency to repeat the charge of criminal illegality to the outside world, and was in contact with journalists from Radio Liberty in Munich, the Voice of America, and the BBC.[65] Most dramatically, Yeltsin attracted the cameras of foreign reporters with a fiery speech atop one of the army tanks surrounding the White House. Seen on television throughout the world, his speech was ostensibly addressed to those unarmed citizens encircling the White House for its protection who had come out in answer to Yeltsin's appeal, and who, representing "the people," were the symbol of his own democratic legitimacy. In this narrative, which dominated the reports of Western commentators, Yeltsin appeared as "the right person at the right time," almost single-handedly putting a stop to the nefarious leaders of the coup.[66]

Kagarlitsky has suggested the plausibility of a different version, however. He speculates not only that Gorbachev was a party to the coup from the start, but that Yeltsin, too, had been informed of the plans, and agreed not to intervene in return for guarantees that he would be allowed to stay in power. According to this version, the coup, staged just one day before the compromise Union treaty was to be signed, was meant to ensure law and order in the period of transition to a new political form of power-sharing between Russia and the Soviet Union, and to protect the ruling center against the centrifugal force of non-Russian "nations" for self-determination. But, Kagarlitsky's speculation continues, Yeltsin suddenly changed the scenario by going back on his agreement to remain neutral and, despite all his rhetoric of constitutional legality, in effect staged a countercoup, demanding that "all the power structures on the territory of the republic should be put under the control of his government," an act which, Kagarlitsky notes, was in violation of the constitutions of both the USSR and Russia.[67] Whatever version of the events is correct, their effect was to destroy Soviet legitimacy definitively, initiating a wave of declarations of independence among the republics. On December 8 the presidents of Russia, Ukraine, and Belarus announced that the Soviet Union had ceased to exist, proclaiming a new "Commonwealth of Independent States." On December 25 Gorbachev resigned, and the Russian flag, replacing the Communist hammer and sickle, was raised over the Kremlin.

It is not unreasonable to suggest that the Gulf War, too, was evidence of a crisis of sovereign legitimacy, this time for the United States as a world superpower.[68] The crisis was handled by projecting onto a new enemy, personalized in the figure of Saddam Hussein, the same morally absolutist discourse of "good versus evil," freedom versus totalitarianism, that had been used against the Soviet "evil empire" during the Cold War—even though it was Hitler with whom Hussein was explicitly compared.[69] In fact, President Bush's saber-rattling rhetoric can perhaps be understood as having more to do with reestablishing the legitimacy of U.S. superpower sovereignty in the post-Cold War era than with any actual Iraqi threat. The whole scenario of "Desert Storm," along with "Desert Shield" during the preceding months, was a televised, double-feature replay of the "political imaginary" peculiar to the United States, including its characteristic form of legitimating the use of violence against its enemies. Specifically, Bush's performance of sovereignty was a mythic, monologic reproduction of the *spa-*

tial terms prototypical of the U.S. political imaginary.[70] What defined the "enemy" was the geopolitical crime of crossing the border into the "sovereign state" of Kuwait.[71] As defender of the boundary principle of national sovereignty, Bush drew a "line in the sand" that would be held at any price.[72] In fact, the line was arbitrary because there *was* no officially ratified delineation between the two nations, and border disputes had been going on for decades.[73] But once Bush drew his line, in his words, there was to be "No concession. No negotiation for one inch of territory."[74] In order to hold that line, a technologically terrifying war machine was deployed that caused the death of hundreds of thousands,[75] devastated the infrastructure of Iraq,[76] and resulted in enormous ecological damage when the oilfields burned in Kuwait.[77] What was new in the case of the Gulf War, however, was the use of television—a cyberspace distinguished precisely by its *lack* of geopolitical boundaries—as an instrument for reconstructing the myth of the spatial system of nation-state sovereignty, and of the United States unshaken as the world's only superpower with the military capacity to sustain it.

■

The collaboration we had created was a creature of *perestroika,* no matter what we might have thought personally of Gorbachev's politics. When the Soviet Union disintegrated, waning power translated into waning interest among certain funders, while others turned, understandably, to more pragmatic projects.[78] War in Yugoslavia made the continuation of our Dubrovnik course impossible. It was almost two years before we met again—time enough to reflect on what we had been living through. Although we experienced these events as intellectuals, hence with only a very narrow and some would say hopelessly distorted point of view, we were bodily engaged, moving through passport controls, struggling with languages, experiencing the changing environment with all of our corporeal senses. I never met the "Russian people," let alone the "working class." I met and knew individuals; and under privileged conditions, in an abundance of different sensory

6.8 The working collective: Mikhail Ryklin, Valerii Podoroga, Elena Petrovskaia.

surroundings, we spent time together: in the great Red Hall of the Institute of Philosophy with its larger-than-life bust of Lenin (which disappeared overnight), in Elena Petrovskaia's living room, with its soft brown couch and special chair for visitors, in a vodka-warmed forest dacha on an icy night, at a swimming hole near the student dorms one summer evening. There were theater performances, artist's studios, and poetry readings. There was being lost, and found again, in the Moscow metro, sliding and falling on icy city pavements, playing Russian-language tennis at the Lenin Stadium, diving into a nighttime sea in Dubrovnik, squeezing around a table at the Black Swan Armenian cooperative in Moscow, and lingering over the *prix fixe* at a Chinese restaurant in Paris. We sat at a "round table" on knowledge and power, and at numerous square ones stocked with cake and tea. There were discussions of "technoculture" in the Lenin Hills, "postmodern economics" on a screen porch in Ithaca, "the body without skin" at Taughannock Falls

Park, and "micropower" in front of Karl Marx's dilapidated green reading chair, preserved under glass at the Marx-Engels Museum on Volkhonka Street.

My friends laughed when I described our collective erotics as socialist. But shared physical presence is a kind of communication, and it is conducive to a different intellectual production than is conceived in isolation and communicated through the written word alone. Although it may be packaged and published in the same way, although it may never mention personal experience, its conviction and claim to truth come from a source in addition to the scholarly argumentation in which it is presented. This is the case with the essay "Aesthetics and Anaesthetics," which I wrote as an academic lecture for presentation at conferences celebrating Walter Benjamin's hundredth birthday in 1992. Everything about the lecture, from its politics to its images, was a response to experiences of the previous five years. Although it was delivered in Detroit, Princeton, New York, Madrid, London, and Hong Kong before being presented in Podoroga's seminar in Moscow, it was a part of the Moscow project, and I have included a section from it above in chapter 3. On the one hand, it is an attempt to counter the extreme anti-utopianism of the position of Groys and others, the argument that Stalinism is a logical culmination of the modernist avant-garde which it suppressed.[79] On the other, it outlines a philosophical anthropology of modernity deeply influenced by discussions during the five years of our exchange.

I am aware as I tell this story of how often television plays a part, from the televising of the debates of the Congress of People's Deputies in 1989 to the televising of the Gulf War; from the storming of TV stations as a revolutionary act in Eastern Europe to their takeover as an act of government suppression in Vilnius and Moscow. Surely, the live imaging of events and their global dissemination, as well as the speed with which edited images can be televisually inserted into live time, are technologies that produce an intensely powerful political field, one in which virtual reality can have the impact of an actual event.[80] But it would be wrong to conclude that the political uses of these technologies have been a radical break from the past. Some critics want to make of the Gulf War a postmodern watershed, the first "cyberwar," to use Der Derian's description: "a technologically generated, televisually linked, and strategically gamed form of violence," no longer performed on "a territory, a referential being or a substance," but rather on a "simulation": "It is the generation by models of a real without origin or reality: a hyperreal."[81] But the crucial factor in the politics of the image during the Gulf War was not high technology. Rather, it was government censorship, as old as mass media itself.[82] It was the same politics that prevailed in the Soviet Union during the Lithuanian crackdown and the August coup[83]—except that George Bush did not need to storm the TV stations to gain their compliance.[84] Similarly, the televised "media war" in early 1991 between Croatia and Serbia, in which both sides showed World War II atrocities perpetrated by the other side, was itself a repetition of the World War II practice of stirring up chauvinism before an invasion.

Der Derian does truth a disservice by describing the Gulf War as a simulation. The suffering in this war, as in any war, was inflicted on actual, not virtual bodies, and their pain continued long after the journalists in the pool packed up their suitcases and flew home. If there *is* a simulation produced by television, it lies on the other side of the apparatus. It is the simulated "whole world" that watches, the virtual collective assembled in cyberspace, of which viewers, sharing the same televisual experience, imagine themselves to be a part. In the case of the Gulf War, the government-controlled media coverage sought to produce a specifically "American" collective identity, patriotic and partisan, confronting an enemy "other" that was less than fully human. But in order to achieve this goal, it was necessary to suppress images of the war—necessary, because uncensored coverage of war produces a very different effect. It does so precisely because of that quality of television so often criticized, its capacity to decontextualize the image. When images are not confined by cultural context, including the propagandistic context that governments want to convey, viewers react to the pure physicality of what they see. They respond not with sympathy to the contextualized meaning of the image, but with empathy to the vulnerable human body, all the more visible because of the paucity of interpretive glosses. Sympathy requires a shared cultural horizon, but empathy is a mimetic, physical response to a sensory perception.[85] The real danger of uncensored television in times of war is not that people will react to seeing *their* soldiers dead or wounded, but that they will find images of the human pain and suffering of the enemy intolerable: napalmed children, war prisoners being executed, and, yes, women sobbing in grief at the bombed Amiriya bunker in Baghdad.[86] Paradoxically, this physical reaction to the sight of human pain, a concrete and immediate individual experience, becomes the basis for imagining the most general form of virtual collectivity: a humanity that transcends cultural difference. When demonstrators being beaten by the police at the 1968 National Convention of the Democratic Party in Chicago first chanted, "the whole world is watching," they were expressing a cyberdream with extreme utopian appeal.[87] The "whole world" is the collective dream of a humanity beyond the boundaries of particular cultures, a humanity capable of protest against culturally authorized suffering wherever it occurs.

Corporeal revolt against culturally sanctioned violence is a common experience in times of war when, despite the ferocity of military training, despite the lifting of cultural sanctions against torture and rape, the body of the soldier refuses to be patriotic. It vomits involuntarily at mass executions, loses eliminatory control during the terror of battle, refuses in dreams to forget scenes of bodily dismemberment, or succumbs to feelings of erotic love for individuals who belong to the category of enemy. There is a somatic moment in cognition, and the mere fact that perception is mediated by television does not necessarily eliminate its effect. What is being seized with the TV station is the capacity to frame the image or delete it, to manipulate its meaning through contextualization or to ensure that it never becomes visible at all. This is mass media in its most politically cynical form. But "live" television coverage is always capable of escaping the context, which means that it can always go out of control. The chance of this happening is what threatens the structures of power, and therefore precisely what a democratic media policy needs to defend.

It is striking how timid the "free world" has become since the end of the Cold War. Everyone is for democracy, but no one trusts its institutions. At a conference I attended in Warsaw in June 1990, at which scholars from the United States advised the Polish parliamentary committee in charge of drafting a new national constitution, a model for voting was suggested based on rational choice theory which, by means of a system of multiple ratings of candidates, weighted the results in such a way as virtually to guarantee that no "extreme" candidate could ever win. It was a least-common-denominator of choice, working to the advantage of the candidate whom the largest majority of the people could tolerate rather than anyone they really wanted, and it was far more likely to produce apathy about the voting process than to provide for democracy's guarantee. Controlled democracy is an oxymoron. Democracy in voting, like democracy in media, is about risk, or it is about nothing. Moreover, these two institutions need each other, for no matter what the images are to which the cybercollective of the "whole world" is exposed, the passivity of media reception limits audience response to the totally inadequate choice of switching the channel. Political institutions provide people with at least some means of active participation. In the present world order these institutions are national. But by seeing past the nation, television audiences perceive the world differently from the view presented to them by state power, and they may become radicalized as citizens as a result.[88] The point is that when such perceptions function as criticism, it is because they interrupt justifying contexts, shocking viewers out of their ideological preconceptions. They are subversive in their concrete materiality, not because they provide another interpretive or cultural point of view.

The critical power of the empathic body is "aesthetic" in the original meaning of the term.[89] The body can *sense* when reasons have become rationalization and culture is a euphemism for oppression. As a "piece of nature" (*Stück Natur,* to use Adorno's term), the body's resistance to cultural domestication sets limits to the validity of arguments honoring cultural difference. It follows that ideology needs to work directly upon the bodily senses in order to contain this rebellious potential. It does so not only through disciplinary techniques (fear of punishment or the internalization of social constraints) but also through sedation and seduction of the body's cognitive power, a set of practices that, as *an*aesthetics, act as a buffer against the violent shocks of modern life.

The philosophical anthropology that underlies this argument is indebted to the work of Petrovskaia, Podoroga, and Ryklin, although there are significant differences even among these three, and although our work together does not add up to a philosophical "school." As with Foucault, the focus is on the question of power, and the flesh of the body figures as the site of both cultural inscription and individual resistance. But unlike Foucault's analysis, here the body is not understood as a biological force perceived by an alienated consciousness. Rather, the sensory circuit of the body, as a critically perceptive agency, *is* consciousness. The world of the corporeal senses is the ground of philosophical experience and the source of metaphysical illumination.[90] Metaphysics here does not mean *above* the physical but *within* it—again, a return to the ancient Greek meaning.[91] This metaphysics is materialist in the sense that the truth which it reveals about human beings includes their world—not "world" in the Heideggerian sense of a shared horizon of cultural meaning, but world as it is encountered directly by the cognizing body, experienced by the entire sensory apparatus against the grain of cultural preconceptions.

There is an existentialist element in this understanding, indebted in my case to Benjamin and Adorno, and in theirs to Mamardashvili as well. Ryklin speaks of the "irreducibility of corporeal phenomena," which forces us

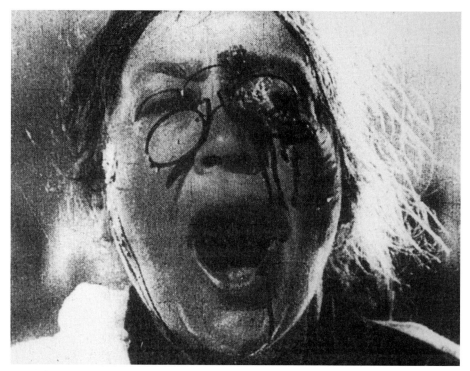

6.9 Still from Sergei Eisenstein, *Battleship Potemkin* (USSR, 1926).

"to think through the skin."[92] Petrovskaia analyzes the techniques of painting that allow Goya and Picasso to reproduce not merely the fact but the
corporeal *experience* of political violence, depicting its horror in a way that
undercuts the justifying discourse of the enemy "other." Ryklin investigates
the opposite cultural phenomenon, the denial of bodily suffering that characterized the style of "High Terrorism" in Soviet art. When he describes
the cheerful scenes of the collective in Stalinist iconography, the "abundant
numbers of rejoicing figures," as the "monstrous ecstatics" of "communal
bodies," he evokes physically the terror we experience when faced not with
state violence, but with the fact that official culture in its most optimistic,
utopian form so easily obliterates the pain of individuals who suffer under
it.[93] Podoroga describes how certain artworks "rediscover, or to be more ex-

6.10 Francis Bacon, *Study after Velásquez's Portrait of Pope Innocent X*, 1953.

act, *invent* the catastrophic spaces and times" that official culture covers over: "The open mouth without sound reaching anyone in the paintings of Bacon, the human being so utterly consumed in the act of producing a sound that it cannot be heard, coincide with the way in which pain engulfs the one [who is] suffering pain, but remains unsensed by anyone else."[94]

The metaphysical problem of evil in the modern world is not only that of intentionally inflicted pain, but of the cultural dismissal of this pain; not only the fact of Auschwitz, but the everydayness of its horror. These realities are reanimated by artworks in which the catastrophes of history are imprinted on the natural body, producing what Podoroga calls "mutant forms": "Figures of Beckett's plays—bodies-cripples, bodies-skeletons, bodies-stutterers—represent our new bodies, those that survived the catastrophe of Auschwitz."[95] Podoroga has in mind his own, post-Soviet situation when he observes in Kafka's texts that "the language of the old empire offices and the language of national minorities are constantly at war":

> *This language is saturated by fear; listen to it—surpassing the threshold of normal hearing, we begin to "see" these sounds-gestures; the words begin to scream, squeak, cry, whisper and mutter, binding us with the invisible threads of mimetic resonance . . . to the inner dimension of catastrophic space. Indeed, these threads of fear transform us as readers into others, into animals, and we become those creatures on the surface of our skin.*[96]

259

6.3

KNOWLEDGE PRODUCTION IN A GLOBAL ECONOMY

When Podoroga came to Cornell in the fall of 1992, his political analysis was bleak: the breakup of the Soviet Union had not eliminated imperial relations but rather multiplied them. Every republic, every nationality was becoming an empire in miniature.[97] Ryklin, following a year in Paris, was at Cornell as a Fellow at the Society for the Humanities, and was discovering firsthand the sense of fragmentation and isolation felt by intellectuals who live the internationalism of their beliefs. When Petrovskaia's parents moved to New York (where her father was working for the Secretary General of the United Nations), she chose to stay in Moscow, newly married to Aleksandr Ivanov, a philosopher originally from Minsk who had joined Podoroga's working group. Petrovskaia and Ivanov came with Podoroga to Cornell to attend a November 6–8 workshop and round table, "Critical Reflections on Modernity and Postmodernity," held on the occasion of the seventy-fifth anniversary of the Bolshevik Revolution—a Western university being one of the few places left in 1992 where such a celebration might take place.[98] And yet the university was ill prepared to handle the new situation. The bafflement began in the planning stage. What word existed to name the foreign participants? If they were no longer "Soviets" and not all "Russians," who were they? And why were *they* being asked to a conference on Modernity and Postmodernity, from which Western Europeans were largely excluded? The panel sessions were devoted to interpretations of Soviet culture within Western theoretical discourses, leading to debates common enough for the participants, but not, institutionally, for Cornell, where during the Cold War all study of "Eastern" cultures had been relegated to departments of Slavic Studies and Russian Literature, whereas we were contesting the issues within a general theoretical field. Given this context, the closing debates were heated, as all sides argued passionately for the centrality of their experience in order to understand what this century had been about.[99]

6.11 Vitaly Komar and Alexander Melamid, *Ithaca's Most Wanted Painting*, 1996, rendered by the artists to accord with the results of a public opinion poll of Ithaca inhabitants.

If new narratives were still in confusion, the old ones had lost conviction. A public screening of *October,* Eisenstein's 1927 film version of the Bolshevik Revolution, introduced the new generation of students to a utopian dreamworld that by their lifetime was well-nigh extinct: the socialist dream of violent, mass revolution seemed indeed a political dinosaur. Nonetheless, celebrate the Revolution we did, with a dancing party featuring rock music from Russia that lasted well into the night.

The discussions generated by the workshop did begin to produce a common discursive ground that might make it possible to transcend the old East/West divisions of the Cold War era. But "common ground" among intellectuals remains a space hovering above very mundane realities. In terms of practical existence, the issues were fundamental: For whom were we writing? Was there a common reading public in the wake of the breakup of the East and West blocs, or was intellectual relevance a matter of remaining within one's own linguistic and cultural tradition? In his essay "Back from Moscow, in the USSR," Derrida reflects with disarming frankness: "I ask myself what I am doing with my life today when I travel between Jerusalem, Moscow, and Los Angeles with my lectures and strange writings in my suit-case."[100] The life of the "global intellectual" is a recent phenomenon, dating back to the early 1970s, when airports and hotels became the habitat of a new breed of professors who began to orbit the world in the wake of global capital. This trend now sets the standard for competitive performance of mental laborers in general. All of us sense (rightly) that our success depends on global name recognition. To achieve the status of a global intellectual, it is not necessary to saturate national markets, not even one's own. No one speaks of writing for the majority, much less for the masses. It is enough to be known among a tiny but mobile transnational elite, who have inordinate power to replicate locally the hegemony of globally transmitted discourses. If one wanted to be dramatically pessimistic, one might describe this phe-nomenon of globalization as a membrane that spans the world like an oil slick, thin but tenacious, and capable of suffocating the voices of anyone speaking beneath it. There are thus good political reasons for resisting the global trend. But are the compromises any less in writing self-consciously for a national constituency? Whose interests, in each case, is one serving? For intellectuals in postsocialist countries, these concerns were magnified enor-mously. At the most basic level, it was a matter of economic survival.

Petrovskaia wrote to me from Moscow in March 1992: "Of course, economically life is simply stupid or ridiculous—the most advanced of us re-ceiving about 20 dollars a month. And if you have children—the strain is too great. There is something humiliating about the fact that the best intellec-tuals can hardly make ends meet." The sudden descent into poverty of Rus-sia's cultural workers was the consequence of "market reform," a euphemism covering over the social turmoil of the economic transition to capitalism that was the stated goal of Russia after the fall of the Soviet Union. In January

1992, Yeltsin lifted government controls on prices, and within days the cost of living soared. This initial hyperinflation was declared beneficial by Western-oriented reformists, who renamed it "repressed inflation," because it eliminated "monetary overhang," that is, the rubles accumulated by working people because there was nothing to buy—leaving them overnight with the opposite problem, that of having nothing to spend.

If there ever was a series of historical events in which, beneath the surface of political struggle, the issues were fundamentally economic, it was those surrounding the demise of "really existing socialism." Ironically, the socialist ideology of economic determinism was discredited just at the point when it could have had compelling explanatory power, whereas, on the level of politics alone, these events must forever appear mysteriously fortuitous. As soon as the Soviet Union disintegrated, economic issues became dominant. The overriding policy concern was not whether incorporation into global capitalism should occur, but how quickly and on what terms. Yeltsin's economic advisor, Egor Gaidar, was a believer in "shock therapy," (Russians used the English term "the big bang") the method of abrupt rupture and sudden transformation promoted by Harvard economist Jeffrey Sachs, advisor to Poland's postsocialist government, who had worked in Yugoslavia and Latin American countries before that. Not since the pseudoscience of biological racial difference, generated in the first decade of this century, has Harvard University produced a knowledge discourse with such far-reaching social implications.[101] Its rise to hegemony was a prototypical case of intellectual globalization, showing both the power and the vulnerability of such knowledge production, and in this sense it is instructive for all intellectuals whose "space" has become global.

■

Told as an economic story, the collapse of Eastern European and Soviet socialism loses its heroic dimensions, becoming yet another chapter in the general narrative of the restructuring of global industrialism that occurred in response to the economic crisis of the 1970s. This crisis was systemic within the Fordist model of industrialization that featured giant firms, centralized production, heavy industrial technologies, and standardized output. The Soviet Union's enthusiastic adoption of the Fordist model in the 1920s and 1930s meant that the crisis, when it came, *was experienced in the East and West alike.* To cite Charles Maier:

> The superiority of the Western economies lay not in their immunity to these systemic challenges, but in their capacity to overcome them. . . . Economic difficulties of the 1970s posed harsh alternatives for both East and West. Beset by social conflict and confusion over policy, the West eventually opted for the discipline of the world market. The East, however, retreated from economic reforms it had begun to institute. In retrospect we can see the [political] collapse of 1989 in that divergence.[102]

In the West, the "discipline of the world market" was inflicted upon the working class. It entailed tolerating levels of unemployment that had formerly been politically unacceptable, in order to "adjust" to changing industrial technologies and to the "comparative advantages" of underdeveloped countries in the global labor market.[103] And it meant curbing spending on social welfare programs in ways that threatened the very existence of the capitalist welfare state. Socialist governments in the 1970s avoided making these painful readjustments—ironically, because loans of overabundant petrodollars from Western banks extended the life of central planning, enabling old-style socialist industrialism to continue in the short run.[104] By the 1980s, servicing this debt with hard currency put socialist economies under enormous strain. Exports were required to generate hard currency, but it was Western imports that were in demand. Although the USSR's foreign debt was less onerous than that of Eastern European countries, Soviet imports of everything from U.S. grain to Japanese technology rose significantly.[105]

What changed for all socialist economies was that they became increasingly entangled—on unfavorable terms—within a global capitalist system that was itself undergoing a major structural transformation.[106] Socialist leaders proved to be remarkably naive in evaluating the political implications of this process. In June 1989 I attended a conference in Moscow organized by the International Herald Tribune on the possibilities for "East–West Economic Cooperation," at which Gorbachev's economic advisor Abel Aganbegyan made a plea for a new U.S. Marshall Plan to restructure the Soviet economy.[107] He was giving expression to a widely shared fantasy, based on a serious misreading of economic realities. In the 1950s, motivated by Cold War fears of the spread of communism, the Marshall Plan financed the rebuilding of Western European countries by loans of dollars to purchase the surplus industrial production of U.S. domestic firms. In the 1980s, the United States, itself in debt as an importer of foreign manufactures, was not capable of being the motor force for its own industrial recovery, much less anyone else's. When U.S. Ambassador Jack F. Matlock, Jr., responded to Aganbegyan by saying that investment would depend on economic, not political, considerations, specifically the existence of a "favorable business climate" (weak or nonexistent unions, low corporate taxes, lack of environmental controls) and a "disciplined" (low-paid, nonstriking) workforce, he was simply stating the facts of the new situation.

The global restructuring of capitalism had fundamentally changed the relationship between the political power of nation-states and the economic power of the world system, clearly to the detriment of state power. Superpower political status no longer translated unambiguously into economic status. This was true on both sides. With the end of the Cold War, the new postsocialist regimes hoping to "return to Europe" found themselves at the mercy of IMF debt-rescheduling guidelines developed for the economic restructuring of countries like Mexico and Brazil. The psychological impact of being considered economically a Third World country was humbling, exacerbated politically by the fact that the terms of integration into the global economy questioned the self-evidence of workers' social rights. The IMF guidelines for economic restructuring signaled the end of Keynesianism, the economic policies of which had been the backbone of the Western welfare state, and the rise to hegemony of what was called, without apology, "IMF orthodoxy," the neoliberal tenets of which were proclaimed to be beyond question. Translated into a program for the transition from a planned to a market economy, these tenets were three: *stabilization* (anti-inflation policies, hard budget constraints, and a convertible currency); *liberalization* (domestic market competition and export-oriented production in order to establish one's competitive advantage, or "market niche," in the global system); *privatization* (denationalization and deregulation of industry, downscaling of government programs with the goal of increasing "market efficiencies").[108] It was by designing reform programs to meet these goals that Jeffrey Sachs rose to global prominence.

The term "shock therapy" refers to the speed of the reforms. The metaphor implies jolting the system into gear through rapid acceleration of the transformation process. Sachs's rhetoric raised a threat of imminent catastrophe if the process was allowed to slow down. In 1991 he enumerated the "enormous risks" of "microeconomic instabilities" that Poland faced, which "could prove deadly to the privatization effort."[109] One year later he wrote: "Russia's post-communist future balances precariously on the knife-edge."[110] He did not hesitate to state the reason for the hurry: Speed of implementation was necessary in order to avoid "parliamentary paralysis," that is, *to prevent political debate about the social desirability of the transformation.*[111] At this point Sachs's argument becomes circular. If speed is necessary to avoid political debate, political debate needs to be avoided because it slows down the speed of implementation. Circularity, hardly fortuitous, is the epistemological essence of his project, as shock therapy produces by its speed precisely those problems which the speed of its implementation is designed to defuse: rising unemployment, declining real wages, cutbacks in social welfare, growing disparities of income, drastic increases of poverty, deteriorating health and education—in short, a massive decline in the standard of living of the majority of a country's citizens.

When Sachs writes, "the entire process could be stalled for political and social reasons for years to come, with dire consequences for the reforming economies of the region," his conception of the transition to capitalism is strangely cut off from the sense of well-being of those people who are living through the process.[112] It is, indeed, the World Bank and other international institutions whom he is addressing, and whose interests in "reform" of the economy are not the same as those of the majority of the country's citizens.[113] Sachs's supporters acknowledged these "unfortunate" side effects of shock therapy, but claimed that certain "politically and socially often inconvenient" actions cannot be avoided: "The simple, even if somewhat unfortunate fact seems to be that there is no method of privatization that would be simultaneously fast, economically efficient, and socially acceptable."[114] In the absence of arguments to convince the public (as opposed to World Bank economic advisors), the proponents of shock therapy turned to the language of market fundamentalism, stating categorically: "free markets will work": "That is why patience is vital. The harsh economic medicine will ultimately have the desired effect."[115] The public was supposed to accept this on faith, no matter how much empirical evidence there was to the contrary.

> If the people of formerly communist Europe can endure the hardship that the policies of stabilization, liberalization, and [private-property-] institution-building inflict, they will emerge at the end of the greatest upheaval that any democratic government has ever brought deliberately upon its own people, at the other end of the valley of tears, into the sunlight of Western freedom and prosperity.[116]

This rhetoric of consolation, the proverbial doctrine that "things get worse before they get better,"[117] would be humorous if it did not translate into such tragedy for so many human beings—humorous because it is a literal repetition of the rhetoric of high Stalinism, when the masses were told during collectivization to make sacrifices in the present for a time yet to come, to look ahead to the "sunlight" of the future, and to work together to "accelerate" the economic transformation. Not only does the word "shock" return in a new context. There is repetition as well in the new proliferation of acronyms, the capitalist IMF, GATT, SPA, and EBRD replacing the earlier Soviet NEP, NOT, NKTP, and VSNKh.[118]

Without blind faith, the "unfortunate" repercussions of radical transition could not be sold to the public.[119] When transition experts spoke among themselves, however, they did not use the rhetoric of market fundamentalism. Rather, they prided themselves on pragmatic flexibility, no more wedded to neoliberal orthodoxy than to any other economic school. The language of Sachs and his Harvard-trained supporters is filled with curious expressions—"the Gaidar gang," "quick and dirty," "soft big-banger" versus "hard gradualist," making "brave choices," "moving vigorously," and starting "the real game, played for keeps"[120]—insiders' jargon that sounds only vaguely familiar to this woman author, reminiscent of rough-and-tumble boys' talk, rebellious yet hip, youthful yet powerful, located in U.S. culture somewhere between *The Hardy Boys* and *Teenage Mutant Ninja Turtles*.[121]

A supporter of shock therapy rightly reminds us that it was a "myth" to believe "the hand of Jeffrey Sachs, the Harvard economist, is directing everything."[122] Yet, in the case of Russia, at the source of this myth were some powerful political realities. When postsocialist government leaders took up the discourse of "shock therapy" and endorsed its principles, they acquired certain practical political benefits. They tapped into the legitimating aura of Western expertise.[123] They spoke the language of private property that garnered sympathy from the IMF, the World Bank, and other international pro-capitalist agencies. They stood to gain from the lobbying effect in foreign countries of the shock therapists' persistent appeal for "massive foreign *governmental* assistance."[124] They could cover over their own helplessness in the face of economic decline by saying they were "letting markets work." They could conveniently vacillate between policies of radical government intervention—the paradoxical planning which shock therapy "perversely" demands[125]—and the extreme neoliberal dictum "The best industrial policy is no policy,"[126] which divorced themselves from all responsibility. But more significant than any of these political conveniences was the fact that shock therapy separated decisively two projects that at first appeared to be inextricably linked: the economic project of free markets, and the political project of democratic rule. In this separation, it was democracy that was considered expendable. The goal of instituting capitalism had clear priority.[127]

The tragedy of this separation was not the destruction of the old socialist economy, but the fact that "Westernizers" in postsocialist governments no longer identified the elimination of socialism with the establishment of principles of democracy.[128] In the case of Russia, it meant that neither side, Yeltsin's Westernizing "reformers" nor the anti-Western "hard-liners"—those nationalists and communists who dominated in his parliament—felt themselves necessarily burdened by the encumbrance of democratic procedures.[129] In December 1992, a fistfight broke out in parliament over the nomination as prime minister of the pro-Sachs "Westerner," Egor Gaidar. In May 1993, over five hundred people were wounded in a Moscow May Day riot. But it was in October that the most serious crisis to democracy occurred. President Yeltsin's opponents—nationalists, monarchists, Communists—occupied the White House, and, in a strange role reversal of the August coup two years earlier, it was they who declared his actions unconstitutional.[130] The October rebels, led by former Vice President Aleksandr Rutskoi, whom Yeltsin had removed from office a month before, refused to accept Yeltsin's decree dissolving parliament, calling it a coup d'etat—just as Yeltsin had called the executive emergency decrees in August 1991—and they voted to depose him, swearing in Rutskoi as new acting president. Yeltsin responded with force, sending tanks to surround the parliament building. When the opposition refused to give up, he ordered the tanks to open fire. When pro-parliament groups attempted to take over Ostankino, the main Moscow television broadcasting center, violence broke out again. In all, 187 people lost their lives, including 76 noncombatants.

Such public slaughter had not been seen on the streets of Moscow in the worst days of Stalin's dictatorship.

■

Of the three members of the Cornell community whom I knew living in Moscow in October 1993, two were shot by stray bullets during the street violence—a statistic sobering enough to induce me to delay my grant to teach as a Fulbright Professor at Moscow's new Russian State University for the Humanities. I arrived in early November. In the six years since my first visit, the city had changed its face. It was not just the blackened facade of the White House that provided a record of events. Throughout public space, the strains of history had left their mark. "For Sale" signs (in English) were hung, replacing party banners, on the crumbling sides of elegant, prerevolutionary buildings. The huge Moscow metro was overburdened by crowds of private citizens using it as a trucking system to transport commodities, large and small, to be sold at improvised street markets, or sequestered within apartments already bulging with new acquisitions. The state stores appeared more dingy and dismal than ever when positioned next to new, private enterprises, gleaming white from floor to ceiling, while workers posted at the entrance performed the Sisyphian task of mopping up the gray-black snow of Moscow streets. As a commodity spectacle, the potatoes and cabbage of the state stores could not begin to compete with the German cheeses, Scotch whiskey, Italian grapes, rippled potato chips, frozen pizzas, and New England lobsters available at these new fairylands—dreamworlds built not for the masses but for an emerging elite whose wealth depended upon foreign connections. Outside their doors, ordinary Moscow women and men stood silently, holding some private possession—baby shoes or an electrical appliance—offered for sale to those with hard currency to exchange. Again and again, the scene was of new extremes of class difference. Chic women in makeup, fur coats, and high-heeled boots shopped at Western department stores and exclusive boutiques, while old women and veterans begged in pedestrian tunnels. The top ten U.S. songs blared out of kiosks selling imported vodka, and men lying drunk on the streets died overnight in the cold. In the metro stations pornography and body-building posters, for sale from itinerant peddlers, vied for visual dominance over the old propagandistic mosaics from Stalin's time. Despite an initial wave of destruction of Soviet monuments, the public iconography of socialism was simply too pervasive to be removed or covered over. It was left, deteriorating, alongside altars to the new gods of consumerism: Marlboros, McDonalds, Pizza Huts, and the omnipresent signs for Snickers bars. On television, the U.S. serial *Santa Barbara* was an evening narcotic addicting even the intelligentsia. An American charlatan on a television talk show peddled laxatives (via call-in number) with the claim that they kept the body young. Black BMWs that screeched around streetcorners were reputed to belong to mafia members from the Caucasus. Pickpockets roamed the city center where tourists were concentrated. Private residences were protected by elaborate electronic devices, telephonically disengaged by uttering a Russian city code name newly memorized each day, taxing my knowledge of Siberian geography enormously. An anti-crime measure, the practice of compulsory registration for foreign residents, renewed Kafkaesque rituals of submission to an incomprehensible bureaucracy. The cavernous Institute of Philosophy where we continued to meet was half-deserted, as researchers took on several jobs to survive. Its loudspeaker, once used for party announcements, now informed philosophers that frozen turkeys (the U.S. Thanksgiving surplus?) could be purchased in the cafeteria, and that Cuban sugar would be available Friday in bulk. A five-minute walk away, a new Italian restaurant catered to customers with credit cards from foreign banks.

Daily, the inhabitants of this capital city of a former superpower endured national humiliation in economic form. In the new private stores, a double cash register system provided exchange in any combination of rubles and dollars, functioning as a constant reminder to customers of the

sinking value of the Russian national currency. The dollar, fixed under socialism at an exchange rate of slightly less than one-to-one with the ruble,
was worth 2,400 rubles by fall 1993.[131] There was no incentive to stop inflation among the new Russian ruling class, whose wealth was stored in foreign banks and hard currency. They had little to gain in the short term from
monetary "stabilization." As for "liberalization," its rejection of import substitution policy (closing one's country temporarily to foreign imports in order to develop domestic production to the point that it can compete
globally) did not have the desired effect. Rather than establishing new industries that could create a global niche for Russian products, "free trade"
encouraged the practice, immediately profitable, of selling raw materials
and other already-existing, nonrenewable values in exchange for manufactured
imports.[132]

Most controversial was the process of "privatization," because through
it a new, capitalist class was being created. The initial issuing of ownership
vouchers to 150 million private citizens in October 1992 was a move with
more ideological than practical success. In fact, to a striking degree, those
who benefited from privatization belonged to the same Soviet elite that
controlled the redistributive machinery under the old system.[133] Many
members of the *nomenklatura* took advantage of their insider status in the
military-industrial complex to translate political power into economic
power, necessarily collaborating with certain groups connected with the
second economy from the Brezhnev days, who "more often than not" had
a criminal past.[134] What was called "mafia-nomenklatura privatization,"
leading to "casino capitalism," eliminated Russia's economic independence,
tying the country irrevocably to the global system, but it did not succeed in
reviving domestic production.

Critics of shock therapy have argued that this should come as no surprise. Whereas its policies can be counted on to cause unemployment to rise
precipitously, "not a single economy has so far proved that shock therapy is
leading to an increase of productive investment."[135] Moreover, no developed

capitalist country has ever adhered to the principles of IMF orthodoxy as purely as shock therapy requires. In the case of Russia, the political effects might have been predicted.[136] In the elections of December 12, 1993, a backlash against the economic catastrophe strengthened the hand of nationalist extremists. The Liberal Democratic Party of the radical nationalist Vladimir Zhirinovskii, whose shockingly anti-Western, pro-Russian imperialist, and anti-Semitic statements appealed to a humiliated population, received 22.79 percent of the votes, and formed, together with the Communist Party's 12.35 percent, the largest political bloc. Russia's Choice, the pro-Yeltsin party led by Gaidar, received only 15.38 percent of the votes. At the same time, the voters approved a new Russian constitution that granted the executive new power to overrule the legislature, weakening the prospects for democracy on an institutional level.[137]

My course in Moscow during this time, entitled "The Political Economy of Desire," was intended to encourage critical reflection on the new ideological orthodoxies of postsocialist Russia, and on the alterations of everyday life that were the consequence of the economic transition. I dealt historically with the eighteenth-century origins of the "economy" as a cultural invention, a sublime notion of limitless growth in production and irrational consumer desire only dimly related to today's vision of capitalist economy as a rational and predictable system. Marx's theory of the commodity as fetish was crucial in this context, and I found myself introducing the famous discussion of commodity fetishism from the opening chapter of Marx's *Capital* to a generation of Russian students to whom the culture of commodities was becoming familiar, but for whom the Marxist critique of this culture was a new intellectual experience. As for criticizing the deleterious social consequences of capitalism, there was no need to dust off Marx's texts. The works of Adam Smith (and the early writings of Hegel) were explicit in describing the economy's reckless indifference to the fates of what Smith called "the majority of the working poor."[138]

The Russian State University for the Humanities (RGGU) where I was teaching was founded in 1991 with a mandate "to overcome the profound crisis in the humanities in Russia, the result of 70 years of purposeful extermination."[139] Housed, ironically, in the sprawling building of the former School of the Communist Party, the university was free of bureaucratic encumbrances and receptive to academic innovations, including feminist theory, psychoanalytic theory, cultural studies, and visual culture.[140] Yet for all its openness and all the good intentions, the general economic situation created formidable obstacles for this new institution. Due to the dismal exchange rate, non-Russian books were prohibitively expensive, not to mention subscriptions to foreign periodicals. Exposure to professors from abroad was possible only if the latter could pay the hard currency for airfare.[141] Student exchanges were similarly blocked by the monetary imbalance. The painful consequence of the economic transition was a new isolation of Russian academic and intellectual life, and it threatened to function even more prohibitively than was the case when politics, not economics, was the censoring force.[142]

■

The structural obstacles produced by economic conditions are not impermeable. There has been much innovative cultural production going on in Russia, about which we in the West are not likely to be informed. Underneath the top layers of economic power, small, entrepreneurial projects are now possible, and individual initiatives have made a virtue of the economic chaos. My friends are involved in a new publishing venture, Ad Marginem, that produces critical theoretical texts—"Philosophy on the Margins"—by Russian authors and Western authors in translation.[143] An English bookstore and cafe called Shakespeare and Company and a second, Russian bookstore close by called Ad Marginem help to support the publishing project, creating a new form of public space for gatherings of Moscow intellectuals. Mikhail Ryklin is a frequent visiting professor in Germany and France, and

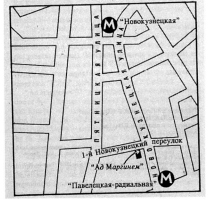

Уважаемые Господа!

Книги издательства "Ad Marginem",
а также литературу других издательств
по философии, филологии, истории
и культурологии Вы можете
приобрести в книжном магазине
"Ад Маргинем"
по адресу: 1-й Новокузнецкий переулок,
д. 5/7 (проезд до станции метро
"Павелецкая-радиальная"
или "Новокузнецкая")

6.12 Map to the Ad Marginem bookstore, central Moscow, appearing on the back cover of the publishing company's books.

is a key figure in the intellectual exchange between Russia and Europe. Valerii Podoroga teaches and writes in Moscow as one of the leading Russian philosophers of his generation. Elena Petrovskaia now speaks French with the same elan as she does English, having worked with Jean-Luc Nancy at the University of Strasbourg in 1995–1996. She and Podoroga teach philosophy at RGGU; she and Ryklin write regular articles on culture for major Moscow daily newspapers and literary journals.[144] Their common home remains the Laboratory for the Study of Post-Classical Studies of Philosophy, Literature, and Art, which continues to hold seminars at the Institute of Philosophy on Volkhonka Street.[145]

One hears frequently in Moscow that despite all the problems of the present, the young will have a better life. And indeed, the new generation in Russia is optimistic about the opportunities that "market freedom" provides. I do not doubt that market freedom exists. But the global power system of "really existing capitalism" is not its habitat.[146] The political fact is that neither nationalist isolation nor global capitalist integration is equal to the real possibilities of the present. Both alternatives, in accepting the given relations of power, sell the future short. A better future is not going to fall into the hands of the next generation without a struggle. This book is intended to encourage reflection on the new dangers caused not by dreamworlds that placate the masses, but by the fact that in the current system of global power, even the idea that the masses need placating is being tossed away as outmoded.

Is there cause to lament the passing of mass dreamworlds? They were compatible with terrifying assemblages of political and economic power: world war machines, machines of mass terror, violent forms of labor extraction. But it was the structures of power, not the democratic, utopian idea, that produced these nightmare forms. As the old dreamworlds dissipate, the power assemblages continue to exist, surviving, indeed thriving, in the new atmosphere of cynicism. Political protest against them today takes bizarre forms. The state is being energetically attacked by those downwardly mobile groups who need its welfare most. Ethnic nationalism is a phantasmagorical political response to a world where the mobility of populations and the mixing of cultures is inescapable. Calls for cultural traditionalism and religious fundamentalism take place incongruously against a backdrop of global communication and globally mediated perceptions that are changing collective fantasy irrevocably. Even notions of cultural hybridity cannot do justice to the contemporary ontological complexities. There is reason for hope, but it may not come from the traditional realm of politics— or from academic intellectuals, for that matter, still tied economically and socially to the old structures of power that we have learned to criticize with such sophistication. Indeed, the whole idea of what constitutes critical cultural practice may need to be rethought.

The dream of mass utopia defined the cultural project of the twentieth century in both the First and Second Worlds. Pronounced a failure in the Second World, it was purposefully abandoned in the First. But the utopian impulse that once animated mass production and mass consumption is capable of new configurations. Perhaps it was a mistake, during the years of our collaboration, to presume that these same superpower sites would take the lead in producing a more adequate cultural project to replace it. There are other worlds, and they too have dreams. While "global intellectuals" orbit above, floating from one international meeting to another, and while "national intellectuals" carry on a rear-line defense of cultural exceptionalism from their home territories below, there are producers of culture working on another level to open up alternative spaces—on the margins, at boundary crossings, at cultural intersections, within electronic landscapes—in subaltern worlds that avoid the homogenizing topology of globalization, while taking advantage of its electronic infrastructures and technological forms.[147] If they succeed in developing alternative intellectual practices where First and Second World intellectuals operating within the old models fell short, it will be at least in part because they are able to develop the political potential of the new means of production—computer information networks, hand-held video cameras, music and voice recording—using them as cultural weapons against the old structures of power that continue to own and contain them.

Oppositional cultural practices, if they are to flourish at all, must work within the present structures. But at the same time they can and do create new cartographies, the contours of which may have little to do with the geopolitical boundaries that confined culture in an earlier epoch. In these changed landscapes, "the masses," abused object of manipulation by both revolutionary propaganda and commodity advertising, are hardly visible. In ways that diffuse their power but also have the potential to multiply it, the masses are being transformed into a variety of publics—including a virtual global humanity, a potential "whole world" that watches, listens, and speaks, capable of evaluating critically both the culture of others and their own.

From the Wall of China to the Berlin Wall, the political principle of geographical isolation belongs to an earlier human epoch. That the new era will be better is in no way guaranteed. It depends on the power structures in which people desire and dream, and on the cultural meanings they give to the changed situation. The end of the Cold War has done more than rearrange the old spatial cartographies of East and West and the old historico-temporal cartographies of advanced and backward. It has also given space for new imaginings to occupy and cultivate the semantic field leveled by the shattering of the Cold War discourse.

As long as the old structures of power remain intact, such imaginings will be dreamworlds, nothing more. They will be capable of producing phantasmagoric deceptions as well as critical illumination. But they are a cause for hope. Their democratic, political promise would appear to be greatest when they do not presume the collectivity that will receive them. Rather than shoring up existing group identities, they need to create new ones, responding directly to a reality that is first and foremost objective— the geographical mixing of people and things, global webs that disseminate meanings, electronic prostheses of the human body, new arrangements of the human sensorium. Such imaginings, freed from the constraints of bounded spaces and from the dictates of unilinear time, might dream of becoming, in Lenin's words, "as radical as reality itself."[148]

Notes

279

Chapter 1
THE POLITICAL FRAME

1. Max Weber, "Politics as a Vocation" (1921), in *From Max Weber: Essays in Sociology,* ed. and trans. H. H. Gerth and C. Wright Mills (New York: Oxford University Press, 1958), p. 78.

2. Ibid.

3. See Karl Marx, chapter 1, section 4, "Social Division of Labour and Its Consequences: Private Property, the State, 'Estrangement' of Social Activity," in Karl Marx and Friedrich Engels, *The German Ideology* (Moscow: Progress Publishers, 1976), p. 43.

4. The history of this process, whereby gradually over the seventeenth and eighteenth centuries private violence was repressed and the state monopolized its uses, has been documented in Charles Tilley, ed., *The Formation of Nation-States in Western Europe* (Princeton: University Press, 1975).

5. V. I. Lenin, *State and Revolution* (New York: International Publishers, 1969), p. 9.

6. Walter Benjamin, "On the Critique of Violence" (1923), in *Reflections,* ed. Peter Demetz, trans. Edmund Jephcott (New York: Harcourt Brace Jovanovich, 1978), p. 279.

7. In such cases, popular referenda that decide by majority may seem to offer a solution, but as de Tocqueville cautioned, democratic freedom has a qualitative sense, one that can be violated by the "tyranny of the majority."

8. The argument here owes a stimulus to Jacques Derrida's seminar in 1988–1989 in Paris, in which I presented a version of this paper. Although his readings of texts by Walter Benjamin and Carl Schmitt are different from my own, I am indebted to his provocations.

9. Elena Petrovskaia, presentation at Cornell University, 1988, based on her Ph.D dissertation, "The Image of the Enemy in American Culture," published as *Chast'Sveta* (Moscow: Ad Marginem, 1995).

10. See Ernesto Laclau and Chantal Mouffe, *Hegemony and Social Strategy: Towards a Radical Democratic Politics* (New York: Verso, 1985).

11. See Cornelius Castoriades, *L'Institution imaginaire de la société* (Paris: Editions du Seuil, 1975).

12. It should be noted that Locke still allowed free reign to the wild zone of power within the colonial territories of European nation-states.

13. Habermas takes this Kantian position as well. So intent has he been on divorcing political theory from the whole tainted tradition of German nationalism that he has theorized about democracy as if it were not always, already *sovereign* democracy. Thus, for example, in his vehement rejection of Carl Schmitt's theory of sovereignty, he intended to dismiss the *problem* of sovereignty as well. Symptomatic of his repression of this problem was the statement he was fond of making during the Cold War that, in the nuclear age, West Germans should have the right to vote for the President of the United States, as the war powers of the latter determined the physical survival of the former. Under the assumptions purely of the contract notion of democracy, he was, of course, totally correct.

14. This term is often not translated in English texts, because it seems to contaminate the "people," a left-populist

term, with the odious historical heritage of the fascist *Volk* with its connotation of ethnic purity; yet no other word in German exists for "the people" in the populist sense. It might be noted here that the term "masses" is also tainted, bearing the connotation of Soviet totalitarianism. While in U.S. discourse in the 1920s and 1930s it was used affirmatively by socialists and communists; in the atmosphere of the McCarthy hearings and the Cold War, it fell into disrepute, surviving more neutrally in adjective form: mass consumption, mass media, etc. I am returning here to the term "masses" as an adequate empirical description of the collective subject of radical democracy, using it interchangeably with "the people" in this sense.

15. For a counter to Derrida's argument that the philosophies of nationalism imply universalism, see Balibar's claim that philosophies of universalism are already a form of racism, or at least that, because a clear line can never be drawn between them, a clear line can never be drawn between "clean" (moderate, purely defensive) nationalism and "unclean" (aggressive, imperialist) nationalism. Etienne Balibar, "Le Racisme: Encore un universalisme," *Mots* 18 (March 1989), pp. 7–19.

16. See Roman Szporluk, *Communism and Nationalism: Karl Marx versus Friedrich List* (New York: Oxford University Press, 1988), and see HYPERTEXT: SEPARATION BETWEEN THE ECONOMIC AND THE POLITICAL.

17. Carl Schmitt, *Der Nomos der Erde im Völkerrecht des Jus Publicum Europaeum,* 2d ed. (Berlin: Duncker & Humblot, 1972), p. 208; trans. in G. L. Ulmen, "American Imperialism and International Law: Carl Schmitt on the US in World Affairs," *Telos* 72 (Summer 1987), p. 53.

18. On Marx's formulation, and Lenin's development of the term, see the entry "Dictatorship of the Proletariat" in Tom Bottomore, ed., *A Dictionary of Marxist Thought* (Cambridge: Harvard University Press, 1983), pp. 129–131.

19. Cited in Robert A. Jones, *The Soviet Concept of "Limited Sovereignty" from Lenin to Gorbachev: The Brezhnev Doctrine* (London: Macmillan, 1990), p. 23. Precisely because Marxism does not accept the legitimacy of the nation-state, the definition of "sovereignty" came to preoccupy Soviet jurists. Jones writes: "In 1930 a Soviet theorist could [still] remind his readers that Marxists marched under the flag of proletarian solidarity rather than sovereignty" (p. 27). But with the Soviet Union's admission to the League of Nations in 1934, the conception of national sovereignty was affirmed. "By the late 1930s, Soviet doctrine on international law had shed most of its 'revolutionary' aspects, and reflected legal positivist thought, in keeping with the Soviet Union's defensive posture towards

the outside world" (pp. 27–28). After World War II, at a time when Western theorists were arguing that, in an age of nuclear war, national sovereignty might be becoming obsolete, there was an attempt in the Soviet Union to "bestow a Marxist pedigree upon the principle of sovereignty," as a major pillar of what came to be called the Brezhnev Doctrine applied to the East European people's democracies (p. 10). An influential postwar textbook of international law argued that "genuine" (i.e., Soviet) sovereignty was manifested in the USSR's "complete political and economic independence from the capitalist world." Jones comments that "if sovereignty in its internal aspect means 'proletarian supremacy,' and in its external aspect means 'independence from capitalism,' then logically only socialist states can be truly sovereign" (p. 24). Any attempted secession from a Soviet state was by definition counterrevolutionary (p. 29). Likewise, any war waged against capitalist nations in defense of the oppressed classes was justified (p. 33).

20. Party sovereignty, according to one Soviet jurist, was "primarily the right of people to build socialism and communism" (F. T. Konstantinov, cited in Jones, *The Soviet Concept of "Limited Sovereignty,"* p. 22).

21. "An International Soviet Republic as a transitional stage in the complete abolition of the state was the primary aim of the Comintern in 1920. . . . Even Stalin . . . could, at the 18th party congress, speak of the 'disappearance of the state' under communism (once capitalist encirclement is liquidated and replaced by socialist encirclement). The prospect of the demise of the state, and with it of international relations, was also to be resurrected by Khrushchev in 1959, who asserted that the triumph of communism on a world scale would lead to the disappearance of state borders." Jones, *The Soviet Concept of "Limited Sovereignty,"* p. 9.

22. I am referring to the debates between Rosa Luxemburg and Lenin, and later among the members of the Bolshevik Party (Trotsky, Bukharin, Galiev, and others). Sultan Galiev of Azerbaijhan developed the idea of "proletarian nations" oppressed by imperialism without a working class, a concept of national liberation movements (and of "backward" countries being more revolutionary because more heavily oppressed) that was strongly rejected by the Bolsheviks in the early 1920s, when Galiev himself was accused of treasonous deviation. See Alexandre A. Benningsen and S. Enders Wimbush, *Muslim National Communism in the Soviet Union: A Revolutionary Strategy for the Colonial World* (Chicago: University of Chicago Press, 1980), pp. 43 and passim.

23. For Western scholars making that optimistic argument before the fall of the Soviet Union, see the anthology edited by Alexander J. Motyl, *Will the Non-Russians Rebel? State, Ethnicity, and Stability in the USSR* (Ithaca: Cornell University Press, 1987).

24. Ethnic "nations" were *entitled* to their own territory, however, as well as their own language, and early Soviet policy did much to strengthen ethnic identities through the creation of "autonomous national districts." But national "sovereignty" in these cases precisely did *not* mean legitimate use of violence in order to defend the nation. Although the right to "secession" was proclaimed as "complete," this was never meant to authorize a challenge to the federation of Soviet socialist republics. National armies were not allowed. Moreover, since ethnic "minorities" and indeed all Soviet "nations" were historically "backward" in comparison with the Russians, the latter group set the standard of cultural development for all. This policy was laid down in 1921 at the Tenth Party Congress, where Stalin asserted that "the essence of the nationality question in the USSR consists in the need to eliminate the backwardness (economic, political, and cultural) that nationalities have inherited from the past, to allow the backward peoples to catch up with Central Russia" (cited in Yuri Slezkine, *Arctic Mirrors: Russia and the Small Peoples of the North* [Ithaca: Cornell University Press, 1994], p. 144). Thus the struggle against "backwardness" became articulated in terms of the war on TIME (see below).

25. Hannah Arendt, *Imperialism: Part Two of The Origins of Totalitarianism* (New York: Harcourt Brace Jovanovich, 1968), p. 155 and passim.

26. Cited in Stephen Cohen, *Bukharin and the Russian Revolution: A Political Biography* (New York: Alfred A. Knopf, 1973), p. 126.

27. Roy Medvedev, *Let History Judge: The Origins and Consequences of Stalinism,* trans. George Schriver (New York: Columbia University Press, 1989), p. 388.

28. Cited in Cohen, *Bukharin,* p. 67.

29. Kenneth Thompson, *Interpreters and Critics of the Cold War* (Baton Rouge: Louisiana State University Press, 1981), p. xi.

30. See Mikhail Heller, *La Machine et les rouages: La formation de l'homme soviétique,* trans. Anne Coldefy-Faucard (Paris: Calmann-Lévy, 1985).

31. Even without declared war, the nation-state is protected from judicial accountability by the legal principle of "sovereign immunity."

32. François Furet, *Interpreting the French Revolution,* trans. Elborg Forster (New York: Cambridge University Press, 1989), pp. 70 and 46.

33. Carl Schmitt, *The Concept of the Political,* trans. George Schwab (New Brunswick: Rutgers University Press, 1976), p. 63. Schwab has modified the citation of Hegel by Schmitt; I have returned to the original, as Schwab suggests to the "critical reader" (ibid.).

34. Ibid., p. 28.

35. As the absolute enemy, heretics must always be fought, but eradicating them completely would carry a danger; should the category of the heretic disappear from the imaginary landscape, there would be no legitimacy for the inquisitional violence of the one true Church. Cf. Ibid., p. 49.

36. On Reagan's merging of Monroe Doctrine mythology and Cold War hyperbole, see Eldon Kenworthy, *America/Américas: Myth in the Making of U.S. Policy toward Latin America* (University Park: Pennsylvania State University Press, 1995), pp. 114–139. Reagan spoke of "freeing" Nicaragua from the "outlaw" Sandinista (Marxist) regime in order to justify Congressional aid to the Contras who opposed it. He stated in 1986: "This is more than a vote, more than an appropriation of money. This is a sign, a declaration, a commitment. We have drawn a line in the sand: this far and no farther [a metaphor George Bush would use five years later to justify war against Iraq]. The Communists and communism must be expunged from the clean, free lands of the Americas. . . . This hemisphere is truly the cradle of democracy. . . . Communism is an unwanted, foreign ideology" (cited in ibid., p. 135).

37. On one level, the debate at the 1919 Peace Conference was between the European principles of old diplomacy (based on the balance of European colonial powers, secularized state relations, and limited war) and the new diplomacy, with its moralistic conception of war and its non-European, decentered spatial conception of the world order (embodied in Wilson's idea of a League of Nations). But behind this intellectual debate stood the historical event of the Bolshevik Revolution. According to one participant, "The effect of the Russian problem on the Paris Conference . . . was profound: Paris cannot be understood without Moscow. Without ever being represented at Paris at all, the Bolsheviki and Bolshevism were powerful elements at every turn." Ray Baker, cited in Arno J. Mayer, *Political Origins of the New Diplomacy, 1917–18* (New Haven: Yale University Press, 1959), p. 29.

38. General Tasker H. Bliss (1919), cited in John M. Thompson, *Russia, Bolshevism, and the Versailles Peace* (Princeton: Princeton University Press, 1966), p. 204.

39. U.S. Secretary of State Robert Lansing wrote from the Paris Conference in a confidential memo: "Bolshevism is the most hideous and monstrous thing that the human mind has ever conceived. It . . . finds its adherents among the criminal, the depraved, and the mentally unfit" (cited in Thompson, *Russia, Bolshevism, and the Versailles Peace,* p. 15; for other examples of the hallucinatory language evoked by Bolshevism, see ibid., pp. 13–20, also Mayer, *Political Origins of the New Diplomacy,* passim).

40. Thomas J. Curran, *Xenophobia and Immigration, 1820–1930* (Boston: Twayne Publishers, 1975), p. 137.

41. Maxine Seller, *To Seek America: A History of Ethnic Life in the United States* (New York: Jerome S. Ozer, 1977), p. 216. Not a few emigrated from the United States and joined the Bolshevik side on their own initiative, as individuals and as collectives.

42. Palmer, cited in Seller, *To Seek America,* p. 216.

43. The proper comparison in terms of deaths caused to the "enemy" would be those human beings killed by U.S. military forces throughout the world in the twentieth century, a figure of an order of magnitude comparable to the deaths to domestic enemies perpetrated by the Soviet regime. See the discussion of the national security state in HYPERTEXT: SEPARATION BETWEEN THE ECONOMIC AND THE POLITICAL.

44. Sheila Fitzpatrick, "The Legacy of the Civil War," in Diane P. Koenker et al., eds., *Party, State, and Society in the Russian Civil War: Explorations in Social History* (Bloomington: Indiana University Press, 1989), p. 388.

45. Moshe Lewin, "The Civil War: Dynamics and Legacy," in ibid., p. 403.

46. It has been pointed out that although "the language of democracy is sanctified in Soviet usage," pluralism is not. "Sovereignty of the people" (*narodovlastie*) meant popular participation in building socialism, not organized popular dissent. See Archie Brown, "Political Power and the Soviet State: Western and Soviet Perspectives," in Neil Harding, ed., *The State in Socialist Society* (Albany: State University of New York Press, 1984), pp. 71–73. The Russian imaginary of society as a collective body, the purity of which could be contaminated by "alien elements" and was thus in need of periodic cleansing—the quasi-surgical removal of contaminating populations—is discussed in Peter Holquist, "State Violence as Technique: The Logic of Violence in Soviet Totalitarianism," in Amir Weiner, ed., *Modernity and Population Management* (Stanford: Stanford University Press, in press).

47. When, for example, workers in the weaving shop of the Red Banner textile factory in 1925 organized sponta-

neously to protest against the speed of production rates, authorities declared "the impermissibility of . . . [the violation of] the correct tempo of factory labor . . . [and] trade union discipline," and denounced the part played by "suspicious characters"in these events. Cited in John B. Hatch, "Labor Conflict in Moscow, 1921–1925," in Sheila Fitzpatrick et al., eds., *Russia in the Era of NEP: Explorations in Soviet Society and Culture* (Bloomington: Indiana University Press, 1991), p. 65. "Lower-skilled female textile workers were also the most strike-prone in the Moscow region during these years" (ibid.). On women's dominant role as workers in the textile industry (and hence in the opposition), see Diane P. Koenker, "Urbanization and Deurbanization in the Russian Revolution and the Civil War," in Koenker et al., eds., *Party, State, and Society in the Russian Civil War,* p. 93.

48. Cited in Michael Palij, *The Anarchism of Nestor Makhno, 1918–1921: An Aspect of the Ukrainian Revolution* (Seattle: University of Washington Press, 1976), pp. 175–176. In February 1920 Trotsky issued a secret order to disarm, disband, and if necessary destroy all partisan units in the Ukraine. Cheka punitive units trailed the partisans and executed Makhno's sympathizers (ibid., p. 44). An estimated 200,000 people were executed or injured in the Ukraine by the Bolsheviks in this period (ibid., p. 213).

49. Fitzpatrick, "The Legacy of the Civil War," p. 408.

50. Israel Getzler, *Kronstadt, 1917–1921: The Fate of a Soviet Democracy* (New York: Cambridge University Press, 1983), p. 256. Fitzpatrick writes of the Kronstadt rebellion: "Despite their firm actions, the Bolsheviks were stunned and appalled by the turn of events. Their own sense of legitimacy depended on the belief that the working class supported them. Moreover, their analysis of politics indicated that a regime without a base of class support must fall. While publicly denying that Kronstadt was a symbol of rejection by the proletariat, the Bolsheviks inwardly feared that it was." Sheila Fitzpatrick, *The Cultural Front: Power and Culture in Revolutionary Russia* (Ithaca: Cornell University Press, 1992), p. 30. "What historical meaning had their revolution if it were not proletarian?" (ibid., p. 34).

51. Western workers never were the enemy. Interestingly, as a strategy of resistance against Stalin's policies, Soviet citizens could claim legitimation by claiming to have their support. During the First Five Year Plan, there was a rumor in the Urals "that the *workers* of America (a frequent subject of discussion in Soviet newspapers) had heard 'the wails of the injured peasantry' and written to Stalin expressing indignation at collectivization and the closing of

churches." Sheila Fitzpatrick, *Stalin's Peasants: Resistance and Survival in the Russian Village after Collectivization* (New York: Oxford University Press, 1994), p. 68.

52. Strictly speaking, the party could have no "foreign" policy. The Comintern, a multinational party organization, was paralleled by the Ministry of Foreign Affairs, a state organization of the USSR, which eventually established diplomatic relations abroad (with Germany in 1922; with the United States in 1934).

53. Communist parties in other nations had to accept the "21 Conditions" for membership in the Comintern, which included secret underground organization and both legal and illegal tactics against one's own government—creating their own wild zone of power by placing party loyalty over national sovereignty. "The Third International was a highly disciplined world organisation with its headquarters in Russia. However . . . Lenin would have repudiated any attempt to elevate Moscow into an immutable 'Vatican' of world socialism. Lenin had affirmed in 1919 that leadership of the international communist movement had passed to Russia only for a 'short time' and elsewhere had alerted other members of the Bolshevik party to the dangers of 'Great Russian Chauvinism.' . . . Zinoviev had predicted that the whole world would become communist within two or three years. . . . However, Lenin's internationalist conception of the international was soon to be replaced by Stalin's Russocentric interpretation of its functions: Bolshevik in organisational form and Russian in goal orientations." Robert A. Jones, *The Soviet Concept of "Limited Sovereignty" from Lenin to Gorbachev: The Brezhnev Doctrine* (London: Macmillan, 1990), p. 84.

54. The language (perhaps surprisingly) was Stalin's during the era of NEP, indicating that his position changed in the late 1920s.

55. Cited in Stephen Cohen, *Bukharin and the Russian Revolution: A Political Biography* (New York: Alfred A. Knopf, 1973), pp. 199–202. Bukharin made this distinction: "Our society has two levels of conflict, internal and external. Externally it stands face to face with the bourgeois world, and there the class war becomes sharper. . . . Inside the country our policy in general does not follow the line of fanning class war but, on the contrary, goes some way to dampen it." Cited in Fitzpatrick, *The Cultural Front,* p. 111.

56. Cited in Cohen, *Bukharin,* p. 100. Recent scholarship emphasizes the fact that the intensification of class warfare and the Terror had multiple origins and was not dictated by Stalin from the top (as earlier historians like Roy Medvedev and Robert Conquest had maintained). "The

victory of the hard line of cultural class war over the soft line of conciliation coincided with Stalin's victory over his opponents in the party leadership. Should we conclude that the policy of class war was Stalin's own? I think not" (Fitzpatrick, *The Cultural Front,* p.113). Millions of Soviet citizens believed in the policies of the First Five Year Plan and benefited from them—at the same time that millions lost their lives. See the works of Fitzpatrick, Getty (who goes so far as to call Stalin a "moderate"), and others; see also HYPERTEXT: SOVEREIGN PARTY/SOCIALIST STATE.

57. Stalin announced the policy of liquidating the kulaks as a class in December 1929. By March 1930, after the most extreme measures had been taken, Stalin called abruptly for a halt to the process of collectivization, claiming that local officials, "dizzy with success," had taken measures against the peasants too far—a betrayal of local Communist cadres who were dumbfounded (Fitzpatrick, *Stalin's Peasants,* pp. 62–63). A year later, Stalin struck out again against the kulaks: "We have put up with these bloodsuckers, spiders, and vampires long enough" (Stalin, April 25 1930, cited in ibid., p. 64).

58. Official statement, 1930, cited in Robert Conquest, *The Harvest of Sorrow: Soviet Collectivization and the Terror-Famine* (New York: Oxford University Press, 1986), p. 118. The party's rationale was summarized in a novel published in Moscow in 1934: "Not one of them was guilty of anything; but they belonged to a class that was guilty of everything" (cited in ibid., p. 143).

59. The Shakhty trial of 1930, which accused "bourgeois experts" of counterrevolutionary "wrecking," was intended, according to an official of the secret police, "to mobilize the masses," "to arouse their wrath against the imperialists," and "to intensify vigilance" against the intelligentsia as a class enemy. Fitzpatrick comments that this mobilization strategy can be seen as "designed to create an atmosphere of crisis and to justify the regime's demands for sacrifice and extraordinary efforts in the cause of industrialization. The trials built on the popular fears aroused by the war scare of 1927, and purported to demonstrate that the 'wreckers and saboteurs' of the bourgeois intelligentsia were potential allies of the encircling capitalist powers in the event of a renewed military intervention. The wreckers also served as scapegoats for economic failures, shortages of consumer goods, and a general decline in living standards as resources were channeled into the priority area of heavy industry." Fitzpatrick, *The Cultural Front,* p. 119.

60. This accusation was not totally chimerical. Beginning in 1929, within the Soviet peasantry there developed a counterdiscourse that challenged Soviet legitimacy by

turning the ideological tables, charging the leaders with continuing the forms of oppression of the old regime. The idea spread that the Soviet regime was allied with the Russian emigrant landowners in promoting collectivization as a "second serfdom," and that if the "war scare" materialized it would be for the better; the invading foreign armies would rescue the peasants. "These rumors were clearly derived from the peasants' reading and reinterpretation of Soviet newspapers" (Fitzpatrick, *Stalin's Peasants,* pp. 46–47 and 67). Collectivization had the effect of dividing the peasantry: "It was not that a genuine class war between kulaks and bedniaks [poor peasants] was bubbling up at the grass roots, as Soviet historians used to claim, but rather that a more or less phony class war espoused by Communists had genuine divisive effects" (ibid., p. 41).

61. Stalin, speech of 1927, cited in Myron Rush, ed., *The International Situation and Soviet Foreign Policy: Key Reports by Soviet Leaders from the Revolution to the Present* (Columbus: Merrill Publishing Co., 1970), p. 61.

62. Fitzpatrick, *Stalin's Peasants,* p. 37.

63. See Sheila Fitzpatrick, "The Foreign Threat during the First Five-Year Plan," *Soviet Union/Union soviétique* 5 (1978), pt. 1.

64. The civil war to which Stalin constantly referred was not the class revolution of October but the *patrie* under attack by foreign invaders, a return to a political imaginary that may have been far more appealing to the cadres of provincial, peasant background that formed the bulk of his popular support. To cite Moshe Lewin: "Institutions and methods which seemed to be entirely new, after deeper insight show the often quite astonishing reemergence of many old traits and forms" (Moshe Lewin, *The Making of the Soviet System: Essays in the Social History of Interwar Russia* [New York: Pantheon Books, 1985], p. 274). Stephen Cohen writes that under Stalin there was a rewriting of Russian history that had the effect of a "neo-nationalistic rehabilitation of Czarism" (Cohen, *Bukharin,* p. 358). The intriguing question is how this reiteration of the political imaginary of an international proletarian revolution under attack, while motivating and legitimating a far-reaching social revolution, managed to touch the roots of anti-Western pan-Slavism, peasant religiosity, and the Czarist relationship between the ruler and his people—how the justification and execution of an enormous social and economic revolution from above occurred within a discursive context that in many ways resurrected the imaginary of the old.

65. In comparison with Stalin's rhetoric, the discourse of Mikhail Gorbachev was striking. While the "course of history" was still described as "irreversible" and there was still need to "speed up" economic growth, the method proposed was antithetical to the warlike rhetoric of Stalin's Five Year Plans, although the word used—acceleration (*uskorenia*)—was the same. Rather than militarizing the economic sphere, Gorbachev *de*militarized it. Indeed, as in foreign policy, his strategy was one of unilateral disarmament. Civil society was no longer seen as a war zone. This transformation of the imaginary was radical and commendable. It faced up to a crisis of legitimacy. But it did not eradicate the roots of that crisis, which has existed ever since Khrushchev undertook the ticklish business of attempting to delegitimate Stalin without delegitimating the Soviet Union. The very sanity of Gorbachev, his willingness to give up the myth of the "enemy," ultimately resulted in the dissolution of Soviet sovereignty.

66. See Edward Hallett Carr, *The Soviet Impact on the Western World* (New York: Macmillan, 1954), p. 25. See also Cohen, *Bukharin,* p. 314; and Sheila Fitzpatrick, *The Russian Revolution* (New York: Oxford University Press, 1982).

67. Cited in Roy Medvedev, *Let History Judge: The Origins and Consequences of Stalinism,* trans. George Schriver, rev. and expanded (New York: Columbia University Press, 1989), p. 420. Even in the bleakest moments, however, the appearance of popular sovereignty was retained. Peasants in the villages went through a process of voting in favor of collectivization before it took place, and the kolkhozes were founded by government charter (Fitzpatrick, *Stalin's Peasants,* p. 117). In the show trials of the thirties, it was considered important that the accused themselves confess. Communists were punished for the idealistic reason of not living up to their obligations to the workers and peasants (which was often the case). The new constitution of 1936 (the first had been passed in January 1924 by the Second Congress of Soviets) was the most democratic in the world at the time, guaranteeing universal social rights as well as political and legal rights. It was debated openly in the press and throughout the country before being ratified (unanimously) by the soviets (ibid., pp. 212–213). Legitimacy mattered (see HYPERTEXT: SOVEREIGN PARTY/SOCIALIST STATE), even if lives were not spared as a result.

68. USSR dominance elicited comparisons between the Brezhnev Doctrine of 1968 regarding Eastern Europe and the Monroe Doctrine and Roosevelt Corollary to it (see Jones, *The Soviet Concept of "Limited Sovereignty,"* pp. 211–229).

69. Jones, *The Soviet Concept of "Limited Sovereignty,"* p. 143. Eugen Varga, Hungarian-born international relations

scholar at the Moscow Institute of World Economics and World Politics, argued that Eastern European regimes would evolve as "people's democracies" from wartime (planned) to socialist economies without coercion from imposed revolutionary political regimes. Stalin suppressed this alternative possibility and in 1947 closed Varga's institute. He imposed social and economic change in Eastern Europe, which was thenceforth linked to foreign and military policy. See William Curti Wohlforth, *The Elusive Balance: Power and Perceptions during the Cold War* (Ithaca: Cornell University Press, 1993).

70. Jones, *The Soviet Concept of "Limited Sovereignty,"* p. 165.

71. Beginning in the 1930s, but decisively in the 1940s during the war, the Russians were spoken of as inherently superior, the most historically "advanced" of the Soviet peoples (see HYPERTEXT: TIME). "The history of the Russian state was the true manifestation of the history of the Russian people and hence the history of universal progress toward socialism" (Yuri Slezkine, *Arctic Mirrors: Russia and the Small Peoples of the North* [Ithaca: Cornell University Press, 1994], p. 305). Their interests "reflected the interests of all progressive people on Earth. Hence anyone who denied the preeminence of Russian ethnography (state, nation) was an enemy of progress, or a 'cosmopolitan' . . . [for example] the 'learned lackeys of Wall Street' who questioned the ontological reality of nations, thereby claiming superiority for the ostensibly nonethnic nationalism of the United States" (ibid., p. 311).

72. The term "totalitarianism" was used positively by Mussolini in the 1920s to describe his own ideal of absolute monopoly of authority by the state (consisting of the executive, its bureaucracy and judicial system, but excluding the legislature and political parties), and to insist that class conflict be subordinated to nation-state power. It was Trotsky who, from exile in Mexico, first equated fascism with Stalin's distortion of the Soviet regime in response to the signing of the Nazi-Soviet non-aggression pact. In 1951 Hannah Arendt (from a very different political position) developed a theory of totalitarianism that might take fascist or Soviet form. Her definition emphasized the role of propaganda and terror in accomplishing the submission of mass populations who experienced the homelessness and rootlessness of modern life. This was its general meaning within Western discourse during the Cold War.

73. Jones, *The Soviet Concept of "Limited Sovereignty,"* pp. 156 and 159.

74. See Richard Stites, *Revolutionary Dreams: Utopian Vision and Experimental Life in the Russian Revolution* (New York: Oxford University Press, 1989), pp. 181–182.

75. These images were powerfully effective. I confess that with my first exposure to a Soviet Communist who came to speak at Vassar College in the 1960s, I was surprised, on a preconscious level, that he looked like any other bureaucrat; there was nothing devilish about him. And during my first descent by air into Moscow in May 1988, I found myself surprised in the same way that the fields around this "red" city were green after all.

76. François Furet, *Interpreting the French Revolution*, trans. Elborg Forster (New York: Cambridge University Press, 1989), pp. 54–55.

77. "The 'people' was not a datum or a concept that reflected existing society. Rather, it was the Revolution's claim to legitimacy, its very definition as it were; for henceforth all power, all political endeavour revolved around that founding principle, which it was nonetheless impossible to embody." Furet, *Interpreting the French Revolution*, p. 51.

78. Ibid., p. 53.

79. Ibid., p. 56.

80. Ibid., p. 180.

81. Ibid., p. 44.

82. Ibid., p. 53. "The struggle against the aristocratic plot began as the discourse on power of revolutionary society as a whole, and became the means of conquering and preserving real power" (ibid.).

83. "For the war unequivocally identified the new [revolutionary] values with the nation that had embodied them and branded as criminals all Frenchmen suspected of not cherishing them" (ibid., p. 69). According to Brissot, a Girondin and an advocate of the war, the Revolution "needed great acts of treason" (cited in ibid., p. 128).

84. Ibid., p. 53.

85. Ibid.

86. "The adoption of the Constitution was solemnly celebrated during the festival of 10 August 1793. On the evening of the festival, the text was, just as solemnly, enclosed in an 'ark of cedar wood' and deposited in the Convention Hall. The Constitution was not put into effect until peacetime." Bronislaw Baczko, *Comment sortir de la Terreur? Thermidor et la Révolution* (Paris: Gallimard, 1989), p. 307.

87. Cited in Schmitt, *Der Begriff des Politischen: Text von 1932 mit einem Vorwort und drei Corollarien* (Berlin: Dunker & Humblot, 1963), p. 47n. This note is omitted from the English translation (see Schmitt, *Concept of the Political,* editorial note on p. 47).

88. Furet, *Interpreting the French Revolution,* p. 180.

89. Robespierre's discourse divided the good from the wicked, giving him tremendous power to decide who was included in "the people" (see ibid., p. 60).

90. Ibid.

91. Ibid., p. 178. Furet refers here to the work of Augustin Cochin, a young, conservative historian who died as a soldier in World War I and whose interpretation has influenced Furet's own.

92. Ibid., p. 177.

93. Cited in ibid., p. 180.

94. Ibid., p. 70.

95. Thibaudeau, cited in ibid., p. 71.

96. Ibid.

97. See the summary of contemporary debates in *Les Déclarations des droits de l'homme de 1789: Textes réunis et présentés par Christine Faure* (Paris: Editions Payot, 1988).

98. Furet, *Interpreting the French Revolution,* p. 126.

99. Ibid., p. 127.

100. Cited in ibid., p. 129. At this point Marx's critique from the left merges with that of Carl Schmitt from the right. Polemically, Furet cites Marx in defense of his own argument, but when he laments that this "first democratic war of the modern era" changed the old notion of European war as "limited conflict over negotiable stakes" (ibid., p. 71), he is in total agreement with Schmitt (whom he does not cite).

101. Ibid., p. 127.

102. Ibid., p. 78.

103. Ibid., pp. 126–127.

104. Ibid., p. 39.

105. Carl Schmitt, *Der Nomos der Erde im Völkerrecht des Jus Publicum Europaeum,* 2d ed. (Berlin: Duncker & Humblot, 1972), p. 173.

106. Ibid., pp. 175–176.

107. Ibid., p. 176. Here Schmitt is criticizing the Allied policies toward Germany after World War I of demanding reparations and occupying the Ruhr industrial area in order to obtain them.

108. Ibid., p. 170.

109. Ibid., p. 182.

110. Schmitt notes (without criticism) that "the land of the New World [was considered by European jurists to be], for European states, free to occupy [*frei okkupierbar*], of course only in the sense that even through colonial occupation it was not identical with the European state territory of the occupying power, but remained always differentiated from it, whether in the form of a trade colony or a settlement colony" (ibid., p. 101).

111. George Washington, cited in ibid., p. 58. The separation of economic and political terrains described here does not contradict the fact that the United States has repeatedly used economic *means* to secure political ends, including outright purchase (of Louisiana in 1803 and of Mexican territory in 1848 and 1853). During the Cold War, anti-communist strategies relied on economic policies: the Marshall Plan for rebuilding Europe after World War II; embargos against Cuba and other communist regimes; foreign aid to deter Third World revolutions; "destabilization" of Chile's domestic economy after the election of a Marxist president, Salvador Allende.

112. "The interests of a nation, and the interests of individuals who are constituent parts of that nation may be, it is true, and often are, in unison. They may be identical, but they are not necessarily so—so far is this from being the case, that they are often directly opposed." Daniel Raymond (1823), one of the U.S. "national school" economists, which included Alexander Hamilton and Matthew Carey; cited in Roman Szporluk, *Communism and Nationalism: Karl Marx versus Friedrich List* (New York: Oxford University Press, 1988), p. 109.

113. This was also Mao's trade policy (based on the revised Marxian interpretation that whereas, in the industrial world, class was the major contradiction, in the Third World the point of struggle was not between classes so much as between overseas dependency and national development), whence it rebounded into debates in Latin America in the 1960s, now combined with the thinking of John Maynard Keynes (who himself read List, and who was translated into Spanish by the Argentinean liberal Prebish), emerging, for example, in Chilean economic policy under Salvador Allende.

114. For the Russian reception of these policy principles already in the late nineteenth century, see Szporluk, *Communism and Nationalism,* pp. 208–216. "This Leninist typology [of economically backward and advanced nations], and Lenin's program as a whole, were obviously Listian, not Marxist. As Meyer points out, Lenin's dialectics of in-

ternational relations were derived from Friedrich List and Alexander Hamilton" (ibid., p. 216).

115. In its original articulation, the Monroe Doctrine (1823) established U.S. foreign policy as part of the abstract imaginary of political SPACE, drawing a line in the ocean to exclude European intervention in the Western Hemisphere. At the beginning of this century, however, the Roosevelt Corollary to the Monroe Doctrine justified U.S. military intervention to protect the freedom of capitalist enterprise in the Western Hemisphere, giving the doctrine the new valence discussed here.

116. Capitalism can, of course, be considered a political system, as a structure of power relations that has resulted in the systematic, social domination of the working class, Third World nations, racial and ethnic minorities, and women treated as a sex class. In terms of the political imaginary, however, capitalism is *not* a political system, i.e., it is not a legitimation of sovereignty. In order, legitimately, to be protected by the state, capitalism has to be transformed into the political idea of "freedom": "free" markets of goods and labor, "free" trade, and the myth that multinationals have the same rights to their "private" property, consisting of the earth's natural resources and society's collective labor, as do individual citizens to a pair of shoes or a refrigerator.

117. Schmitt, *Der Nomos der Erde,* p. 225 and passim. At the turn of the century, U.S. naval strategist Alfred T. Mahan "argued that the nation did not have to emulate European colonialism to enjoy the benefits of empire—markets could be achieved without the burden of governing subject peoples" (Lester D. Langley, *America and the Americas: The United States in the Western Hemisphere* [Athens: University of Georgia Press, 1989], p. 91).

118. "A recurring metaphor for the international relations of the region is a family in which the United States appears as brother [to "sister" republics] while using the voice of father. Researching U.S. editorial cartoons from the end of the nineteenth century to the middle of the twentieth, John Johnson found the larger Latin American nations frequently portrayed as female while the smaller countries were represented as children and, in the pre–Civil Rights era, as racially African." Eldon Kenworthy, *America/Américas: Myth in the Making of U.S. Policy toward Latin America* (University Park: Pennsylvania State University Press, 1995), p. 30.

119. In 1917, the revolutionary government of Mexico (which the U.S. government refused to recognize) challenged the very essence of U.S. Latin American policy by declaring economic alienation of a nation's property to be incompatible with political sovereignty. Article 27 of the new Mexican constitution stated that the government of Mexico controlled subsoil rights to minerals and resources; these rights were not transferable to foreign corporations or governments. See Michael J. Kryzanek, *U.S.-Latin American Relations* (New York: Praeger, 1985), p. 37. The nationalization of foreign property by Latin American governments has been a threat to the United States throughout this century. In the eyes of the latter, predictably, Mexico's position was evidence of a "Bolshevik threat" (Langley, *America and the Americas,* p. 123). At issue is nothing less than the concept of sovereignty. Does it rest on a separation between the economic and the political, or does political sovereignty necessarily imply economic sovereignty, as Article 27 proclaimed?

120. "Wilson was pointedly critical of the stifling of 'legitimate aspirations' of captive peoples, yet he could not bring himself to admit that they might willingly choose a distinctly un-American path to the present." If such a course threatened to become a reality, then the United States would provide "direction and guidance" to assure that it did not. Only "decent government" was acceptable. "Wilson chose to instruct them forcefully 'to elect good men.'" Langley, *America and the Americas,* pp. 111–112.

121. Woodrow Wilson, cited in John M. Thompson, *Russia, Bolshevism and the Versailles Peace* (Princeton: Princeton University Press, 1966), p. 386.

122. Wilson, cited in ibid., p. 204.

123. Wilson, cited ibid.

124. "Part of Wilson's difficulty, both in attempting to reform the world and in dealing with Bolshevism, was the predominantly political orientation of his thought. For him, 'the economic man' did not exist." (Ibid., p. 43.)

125. Wilson's commitment to a new world order of equal nation-states did not include an economic policy—except, of course, the free-trade liberalism that, by definition, existed in an independent, nonpolitical terrain.

126. Arguably, if the Western *ideological* separation of the political and the economic meant that economic *practices* could and did compromise the ideals of political democracy, there were advantages to this separation in a strictly economic sense—advantages not shared by the Soviet Union, where the interpenetration of these spheres was recognized as inevitable. Lenin hoped for a felicitous interaction between economics and politics (hence the NEP policies); under Stalin these spheres became one, with the result that the politicization of the process of economic development fettered the economic with political constraints. As a field of power, the rationale of the Soviet economy ceased to be economic. The most prosperous

peasants, the "bourgeois specialists," and the intellectuals who had been not only tolerated but relied upon by Lenin were liquidated by Stalin, as the war machine of absolute power and terror was deployed on the economic terrain (see HYPERTEXT: COLD WAR ENEMIES and TIME).

127. See Kenworthy, *America/Américas*, p. 35. After World War II, when Communist parties were a significant presence in the political landscape of many Latin American countries, the United States saw world wide communist conspiracy regardless of the facts, giving birth to the most paranoid imaginaries. "When malaria lost its power to frighten U.S. audiences, cancer became the [metaphoric] intruder who passes unnoticed until it is too late" (ibid.). When the threat of a communist takeover was in fact actualized with Castro's rise to power in Cuba, it happened without Russian support: "The Soviets were uninvolved in Castro's victory . . ." (Richard L. Millett, "An Unclear Menace: U.S. Perceptions of Soviet Strategy in Latin America," in Eusebio Mujal-León, ed.) *The USSR and Latin America: A Developing Relationship* [Boston: Unwin Hyman, 1989], esp. pp. 93–95).

128. Inversely, in the Soviet Union, popular protest against the Communist Party was seen as proof of the presence of the economic class enemy.

129. For specifics, see articles in the collection edited by Martha K. Huggins, *Vigilantism and the State in Modern Latin America: Essays on Extralegal Violence* (New York: Praeger, 1991).

130. Cited in Kenworthy, *America/Américas*, p. 36n. Kissinger was referring to the U.S. "destabilization" policy, which he helped orchestrate, that was instrumental in causing the violent downfall of Allende's government. More recently, in the case of the elected communist regime of Nicaragua, "the authoritative interpreter of Nicaragua's choices" was understood to be "neither the Nicaraguan people nor their (by 1986) elected government; rather it is those whom the Sandinistas defeated in 1979 and *their* patrons in Washington" (ibid., p. 136). Kenworthy refers to this U.S. presumptiveness as "the vanguard pretension" (ibid.). "Good Nicaraguans are Americans as we understand Americanness. . . . The flip side is the criminalization of difference. . . . In Reagan's speeches Sandinistas become 'outlaws,' 'at war with God and man,' revolutionaries who 'betray' their revolution" (ibid., p. 137).

131. In January 1986 Reagan proclaimed: "The link between the governments of such Soviet allies as Cuba and Nicaragua and international narcotics trafficking and terrorism is becoming increasingly clear. These twin evils—narcotics trafficking and terrorism—represent the most insidious and dangerous threats to the hemisphere today" (cited in Kenworthy, *America/Américas*, p. 115). Meanwhile in fact the CIA was laundering money through the drug traffic in order secretly to arm the Nicaraguan Contras engaged in their own brand of terrorism (enthusiastically endorsed by the United States). But the substitution of "terrorist" for communist allowed the discourse of enemy threat to the "American way of life" to slide over the rupture caused by the end of the Soviet bloc.

132. V. I. Lenin, cited in Neil Harding, "Socialism, Society and the Organic Labour State," in Neil Harding, ed., *The State in Socialist Society* (Albany: State University of New York Press, 1984), p. 18. "Only the Commune can save us, so let us all perish, let us die, but let us have the Commune" (Lenin, cited in ibid.). It was in this context that the Party's name was changed from Bolshevik to Communist, at Lenin's insistence.

133. The role of the factory and soldiers' councils is well known. The cooperative movement, later regarded by Soviet scholars as petty bourgeois, is much less so, although Lenin made grateful use of it just after the revolution. These prerevolutionary organizations, populist and profoundly anticapitalist, had become a network that reached deep into the peasantry, providing horizontal links to trade unions and municipal organizations. They were meant to be a training ground for democracy and, some hoped, for socialism as well. As leaders of the cooperative movement recalled, "the members were essentially their own shopkeepers acting through their elected representatives. The cooperative store was thus more than a retailing business; it was a school of social and economic responsibilities for the inculcation of self-help, thrift and loyalty to mutual interests." Kayden and Antsiferov, cited in Daniel T. Orlovsky, "State Building in the Civil War Era: The Role of the Lower-Middle Strata," in Diane P. Koenker et al., eds., *Party, State, and Society in the Russian Civil War: Explorations in Social History* (Bloomington: Indiana University Press, 1989), p. 187.

134. Lenin, cited in Harding, "Socialism, Society and the Organic Labour State," p. 18.

135. This Declaration of Rights (January 1918) sanctioned the arming of all laborers and the formation of a socialist Red Army of workers and peasants, in which only people engaged in productive and socially useful labor could play a part. See Mark von Hagen, *Soldiers in the Proletarian Dictatorship: The Red Army and the Soviet Socialist State, 1917–1930* (Ithaca: Cornell University Press, 1990) p. 20. Von Hagen's book provides an excellent and detailed account of the process of compromising the original party program due to military exigencies.

136. Enlightening here in terms of the imaginary of TIME is the debate among Soviet Marxists during the Civil War on the role of modern war in "advancing" the course of history. World War I brought tremendous levels of state intervention in the economy of capitalist states. Certain Marxists interpreted this model of "war communism" as a means of transition to socialism. Others (including Bogdanov) argued on the contrary that the "hodge-podge" of expedient and authoritarian measures of war communism, while speeding up revolutionary conditions, distorted development toward socialism, making the latter more difficult to achieve. While Lenin acknowledged the instrumental (i.e., expedient) nature of war communism, he believed it could be useful during Russia's transition. Once revolutions occurred in western Europe, however, they would take the lead in history; Russia would cease to be a model country and again become "backward" in the Soviet and socialist sense. Lenin, *Left-Wing Communism: An Infantile Disorder* (1920), cited in Zenovia A. Sochor, *Revolution and Culture: The Bogdanov-Lenin Controversy* (Ithaca: Cornell University Press, 1988), p. 92.

137. Cheka stands for "Extraordinary Commission for the Struggle with Counterrevolution and Sabotage." While a state organization, its mandate was political rather than juridical, to use force to prevent counterrevolutionary crimes as defined by the party, rather than crimes against persons as defined by the state. It was the political police force from 1917 to 1922. In 1922 it was replaced by the GPU, the "State Political Administration." In 1934 the GPU was replaced by the NKVD, the "People's Commissariat of Internal Affairs." See von Hagen, *Soldiers in the Proletarian Dictatorship*, pp. xv–xvi and 63–64. This secret, violent police force was itself described as the "vanguard of the party and revolution" and agent of "class self-defense" (cited in J. Arch Getty, *Origins of the Great Purges: The Soviet Communist Party Reconsidered, 1933–1938* [New York: Cambridge University Press, 1985], p. 183).

138. See von Hagen, *Soldiers in the Proletarian Dictatorship*, pp. 303–337. "Members of both the Workers' Opposition and the democratic Centralist group, as well as such prominent party leaders as Nikolai Bukharin, insisted that the military return to more democratic principles—including a renewed political role for soldiers' committees and a corresponding limitation of the powers of the commissar—and that the regime itself thoroughly demilitarize its own institutions." Mark von Hagen, "Soldiers in the Proletarian Dictatorship: From Defending the Revolution to Building Socialism," in Sheila Fitzpatrick et al., eds., *Russia in the Era of NEP: Explorations in Soviet Society and Culture* (Bloomington: Indiana University Press, 1991), p. 161.

139. Central Committee, cited in von Hagen, *Soldiers in the Proletarian Dictatorship*, p. 55.

140. It is a thesis argued by "revisionist" historians in the West (see the works of Stephen Cohen, Sheila Fitzpatrick, Moshe Lewin, Roger Pethybridge) that the Civil War militarized the new society and was thereby the source of distortions in communist development that culminated in Stalin's terror.

141. Robert A. Jones, *The Soviet Concept of "Limited Sovereignty" from Lenin to Gorbachev: The Brezhnev Doctrine* (London: Macmillan, 1990), p. 85. Stalin's "Russo-centric" interpretation of the functions of the Communist International would come later (see ibid., p. 84).

142. Elected delegates to a Constituent Assembly that assembled in January 1918 were composed chiefly of Social Revolutionaries and Mensheviks; the assembly was disbanded by the Bolsheviks. The Fundamental Law implemented in July 1918 provided for a Federation of Soviet National Republics.

143. The transformation of the revolutionary soviets within the socialist state caused a drastic loss of their autonomy. Although the Congress of Soviets, the "supreme organ of the state," was supposed to meet biannually, it met only once between 1929 and 1935. It was replaced by the Supreme Soviet in the constitution of 1936, when soviets were distinguished, as organs of state power, from the organs of state administration (the ministries and local executive committees and departments), while remaining, at least on paper, the most democratic part of the political system. See Ronald J. Hill, "The 'All-People's State' and 'Developed Socialism,'" in Harding, ed., *The State in Socialist Society*, p. 109. The actual power of the soviets was never great: "The soviets, supposedly representative institutions, remained merely symbolic bodies, elected on a restricted franchise that favoured the workers and totally excluded certain other groups . . . ; the deputies selected by the party (rather than by the electorate) were chosen for their loyalty and their hard work" (ibid., p. 113; see also Stephen Kotkin, *Magnetic Mountain: Stalinism as a Civilization* [Berkeley: University of California Press, 1995], p. 542n).

144. The soviets continued to be "a highly evocative symbol that could not easily be dispensed with. A leader who wished to dispose of the soviets might be open to charges from political rivals that he was acting in an un-Leninist manner" (Hill, "The 'All-People's State' and 'Developed Socialism,'" pp. 105–106). The symbolic importance of the soviets was reflected in the architectural competition in the early 1930s for a Palace of the Soviets that was to be the most important building in Moscow, the

hallmark of the Revolution, although construction was continually postponed (discussed below, chapter 5).

145. The idea appealed to the U.S. social critic Thorstein Veblen, who in 1920 (with no Communist Party affiliation) called for "soviets, or governing committees of experts to take the management of the nation's industrial system away from parasitic financiers and inexpert entrepreneurs who were wasting the resources and manpower of the country through their counterproductive greed for profits and their competitive instincts" (Thomas P. Hughes, *American Genesis: A Century of Invention and Technological Enthusiasm, 1870–1970* [New York: Viking, 1989], p. 248).

146. Jones, *The Soviet Concept of "Limited Sovereignty,"* p. 8. "We need a revolutionary *government*. . . . For a certain transitional period we need the *state*. That is what distinguishes us from the anarchists. The difference between revolutionary Marxists and anarchists is not only that the former believe in centralized, Communist production on a large scale and the latter in industrial scatteration. No, the difference vis-à-vis government, vis-à-vis the state, is that we are *for* exploiting the revolutionary forms of the state in the fight for socialism and they are *against* it." Lenin, March 1919, cited in Hubertus Gassner, "The Constructivists: Modernism on the Way to Modernization," in *The Great Utopia: The Russian and Soviet Avant-Garde, 1915–1932* (New York: Guggenheim Museum, 1992), p. 303.

147. Cited in Jones, *The Soviet Concept of "Limited Sovereignty,"* p. 9.

148. See, for example, chapter 2 below, which describes Lunacharskii's role as Commissar of Enlightenment in supporting a variety of cultural positions, not only that of the Communist Party.

149. Although party congresses "remained the forum for vital and animated debate," this was "despite, rather than because of, Lenin's pleadings. He complained bitterly about the 'luxury' of an open party debate on the trade-union question. . . . The Party, he as much as declared, was full of theoretical masturbators." Harding, "Socialism, Society and the Organic Labour State," p. 33. The proclivity of the party members to disagree among themselves caused Lenin to remark: "The Party is down with fever. . . . Personally, I am sick and tired of it" (cited in ibid.).

150. Fordism and Taylorism, means of industrial production developed by and for U.S. capitalist firms, were adopted as industrial policy by the Soviet Union in the 1920s, with the understanding that the socialist content of production would eliminate their exploitative form. What

was not realized then, and has been criticized more recently on both sides, is that the capitalist forms of industrialization produced their own content. The increase in factory size, the vertical and horizontal integration of production, the equation of development with the expansion of firms nationally and continuous growth in output, the corporatist relationship between workers and the state—all of these characteristics of industrialism that were shared by East and West implied a politics as well. State appropriation of surpluses under socialism had disturbing similarities to capitalist appropriation in terms of the lack of popular control. Standardized production and mass consumption produced patterns of social conformity that became endemic to both systems. These themes are discussed in part III, below.

151. On the early bureaucracy, see Orlovsky, "State Building in the Civil War Era." Although Lenin warned against the trend toward bureaucracy, his policies of state institution-building helped to produce it. For legalizing and regularizing procedures, see Neil Weissman, "Policing the NEP Countryside," in Fitzpatrick et al., eds., *Russia in the Era of NEP.* "The new Soviet police would forswear arbitrariness and caprice in favor of firm adherence to the law. By following legal norms precisely and treating the populace with tact and respect, militiamen would be not only enforcers but also legitimizers"—this was Trotsky's meaning when he spoke to the First All-Russian Congress of Militia Workers in 1922 of the need to build a "firm apparatus" that would enforce Soviet law in the countryside, introducing "revolutionary legality" (ibid., p. 177).

152. Harding, "Socialism, Society and the Organic Labour State," p. 37.

153. Sheila Fitzpatrick, *The Cultural Front: Power and Culture in Revolutionary Russia* (Ithaca: Cornell University Press, 1992), p. 32.

154. Cited in ibid., p. 33.

155. Harding, "Socialism, Society and the Organic Labour State," p. 35.

156. Kotkin, *Magnetic Mountain,* p. 292. The principle of "dual command" (*dvoenachalie*) required that all commanders' orders carry the countersignature of a commissar before soldiers were expected to obey them (von Hagen, *Soldiers in the Proletarian Dictatorship,* p. 28).

157. In 1934 these lowest levels of party organization were officially named PPOs (Primary Party Organizations); they "were subordinated to district committees (raikoms), which were in turn subordinated to gorkoms (city committees). City committees came under the supervision of the provincial committees, or obkoms, which

were subordinated to the Central Committee of the USSR in a pyramid. Such centralization of the party was christened 'democratic centralism,' which despite [totalitarian] appearances was not without friction and even open confrontation." Kotkin, *Magnetic Mountain*, p. 296.

158. Of course, the very need for a state was as a political expedient, an instrument of coercion to implement working-class rule, as the term "dictatorship of the proletariat" implied. But except for the army and the internal police, the institutions of the state were not authorized to use force, and their members (unlike party members) were not above the law. The degree of political neutrality expected from state bodies is revealed in this quotation from Lunacharskii, Commissariat of Enlightenment, in 1924: "it would be natural for party journals and newspapers and party critics to come out in defense of their own trends, to subject persons of other views to severe criticism, and in short to conduct a quite specific cultural line. The party would put its own authority, its talent, and its culture behind [this line], *but of course it could not for a moment expect the state power as such to support it.*" Cited in Fitzpatrick, *The Cultural Front*, p. 93 (her italics).

159. Class war against bourgeois experts was launched by the Shakhty trial: "In March 1928 the state prosecutor announced the forthcoming trial of a large group of mining engineers and technicians from the Shakhty area of Donbass on charges of conspiracy and sabotage. The trial, which took place in Moscow in May and June, received maximum publicity and was preceded by highly organized public discussion and condemnation of the accused. This was a turning point in Soviet policy toward bourgeois specialists. From this time on, the technical intelligentsia ceased to be seen as the party's natural ally in industrialization and became potentially traitors whose real allegiance was to the dispossessed capitalists and their foreign supporters." Fitzpatrick, *The Cultural Front*, pp. 116–117.

160. In the 1930s, Stalin held the title of Secretary of the Communist Party and head of the party's Central Committee, but it was Viacheslav Molotov who was head of Sovnarkom, a position equivalent to that of prime minister (and Mikhail Kalinin who was, as head of the soviets, the official head of state—a title Gorbachev acquired in October 1988). Interestingly, Khrushchev assumed the additional title of head of Sovnarkom in 1958, evoking a new "stage" of the Soviet state as the "all-people's state," a definition that had been codified in the 1936 constitution. (See Hill, "The 'All-People's State' and 'Developed Socialism,'" p. 111. Article 1 of the 1936 constitution had defined the USSR as "a socialist state of workers and peasants," signaling the end of the stage of proletarian dic-

tatorship. "It was Khrushchev's contribution to Marxist-Leninist theory of the state to argue that 'the state . . . has in the new, present stage become a state of the whole people, an organ expressing the interests and will of the people as a whole'" [ibid., p. 109].) Sovnarkom was renamed the Council of Ministers (Sovmin) as part of a general trend to mimic the state structures of the West. Khrushchev was criticized internally for pursuing a foreign policy that put unprecedented importance on intergovernmental relations between the two major powers. Cold War weaponry made this an imperative, however. Ballistic missiles were hardly appropriate weapons for the class war waged against TIME.

161. In the spirit of the thesis of a "convergence" between the United States and USSR, the significance of the dual system was played down beginning in the 1960s—on both sides (see Hill, "The 'All-People's State' and 'Developed Socialism,'" pp. 109 and 125n). Throughout the Cold War proper, the language of the "state" in the USSR came increasingly into line with Western discourse. The Soviet Union renamed the commissariats the "ministries" in 1946; the Supreme Soviet was now referred to as the Soviet "parliament." It became common to imagine both sides in the Cold War as states in the traditional sense. Yet the dual system, including the dominance of the party over the state, was reconfirmed in articles 6 and 51 of the constitution of 1977, and it was not redundant. When the state-party system *was* transformed structurally in the last years of *glasnost'*—Gorbachev's election by the Supreme Soviet as President in October 1988, his call for elections of a Congress of People's Deputies of the USSR in 1989, the latter's vote in March 1990 for a constitutional change to institute an office of "President" as a new executive position that would be separate from the Supreme Soviet as legislative institution—the Soviet state did not survive.

162. Kotkin, *Magnetic Mountain*, p. 284. Kotkin's pathbreaking social history of Magnitogorsk examines this new industrial city as a microcosm of the Stalinist "civilization." His post-*glasnost'* access to the archives provided him a wealth of material regarding the daily life of Magnitogorsk, making it possible to apply methods of discourse analysis, indebted to Foucault, that reveal the patterns of reasoning produced by the party-state system.

163. "Whereas the state's role was defined in terms of competent technical and economic administration, the party's was defined in terms of ideological and political guidance. Such a bifurcated political system, with the party analogous to a church, resembled a kind of theocracy." Kotkin, *Magnetic Mountain*, p. 293.

164. The party "was a redundant, theocratic structure" (ibid., p. 353; see also pp. 352 and 361).

165. Hence the (to Western eyes) paradoxical situation that just as the constitution of 1936 was ushering in a new historical stage in which class warfare and therefore the "proletarian dictatorship" was a thing of the past, the terror within the party itself was about to reach its height.

166. Admittedly, it was only a part of civil society, the "most advanced" part; but the goal of communism, still proclaimed in the USSR in the 1970s and 1980s, was, after the withering away of the state, its substitution by mass-democratic participation—"communism" as rule by all of civil society.

167. USSR constitution of 1936, chapter 10, article 126, cited in Kotkin, *Magnetic Mountain,* p. 294. Other parties were not proscribed by law, but the communist conception of TIME made them illogical, as only the Communist Party was the "most advanced" part of the "most advanced" class. In the public debates over the constitution, an official argued: "It would be absurd to grant freedom of assembly, meetings, street processions, for example, to monarchists of any sort; it would be incongruous to have people in our streets bearing Tsarist flags and singing 'God Save our Tsar' in the Soviet land" (cited in ibid., p. 544n).

168. Kotkin points out the contrary, that the legitimacy of the "redundant" party depended on the existence of the state, whose structures it was the party's task to monitor. "If the redundant party machine did not uphold higher ideals or an ideological mission, it was nothing more than a parasitical stratum of apparatchiks [party members released from the duty of holding regular jobs] lording over a rank and file burdened by apparently irrelevant extra responsibilities and resentful of the apparatchiks' 'ruling class' privileges and lifestyles" (ibid., p. 309). In terms of lived experience (rather than legitimating discourse) this is indeed the way things might have looked.

169. "Once admitted, a Communist stood above the law, subject to arrest or criminal investigation only after the party had taken up the matter and rendered a decision" (ibid., p. 295).

170. Ibid., p. 544n. (The Supreme Soviet replaced the Congress of Soviets according to the 1936 Constitution; see above, note 143.)

171. On the NKVD (Cheka), see above, note 137; also Kotkin, *Magnetic Mountain,* p. 547n.

172. As defined by one of its members writing shortly after the October Revolution, "the sphere of the Cheka's work is determined by the activity of counterrevolutionary elements. . . . And since there is no sphere of life that counterrevolutionaries have not penetrated and does not show some evidence of their destructive work, the Cheka must intervene in all areas of life" (cited in Kotkin, *Magnetic Mountain,* p. 547n). The sphere of action of the NKVD stretched to foreign territory. In the Spanish Civil War, for example, while the Comintern organized international brigades to fight on the side of the Republic, the NKVD was secretly and violently eliminating Spanish "Trotskyites" within the Republican forces.

173. The parallel is to domestic armies in national security states, whose paradoxical role is to protect the state (undemocratically) *as* a democracy.

174. Kotkin makes a convincing argument that the dualistic structure of the party-state accounts for the particular dynamics of the Party Terror in 1936–1937. His interpretation challenges that of Cold War historians who blame the terror on the evil figure of one individual, Stalin (although he also rejects the extreme revisionist view that Stalin was a "moderate"). Kotkin is convincing in the case of the Party Terror of 1936–1937, but his argument does not explain the brutal process of collectivization and dekulakization of the early thirties, nor Stalin's elimination of large numbers of the military high command in the mid-thirties, nor his sporadic attacks on "experts" throughout this period.

175. "'Party work' proved to be highly intricate and labor-intensive, consuming enormous energy and resources. In the localities no less than in Moscow, party organizations had to arrange continual public celebrations of their own rule in the form of meetings." Kotkin, *Magnetic Mountain,* p. 294.

176. "Inevitably, with even low-level positions came the spoils of office: not always a motor car with driver, telephone, and secretary, but probably at least the pick of scarce clothing, some extra sausage, and a real apartment" (ibid., p. 298).

177. Ibid., p. 308.

178. Ibid., p. 309.

179. Ibid., pp. 311–312. As late as 1932, a party member, Mikhail Riutin, a former supporter of Bukharin, had circulated a program of "demands" for slowing the economic pace, ending forced collectivization, and increasing democracy within the party, and calling for the removal of Stalin (whom he accused of being "the evil genius of the party and the revolution" and "a provocateur"). Riutin was removed from his post and from the party, but when Stalin demanded the death penalty against him for treason and terrorism, the Central Committee of the Communist Party (Politburo) refused to authorize the execution.

Mikhail Heller and Aleksandr Nekrich, *Utopia in Power: The History of the Soviet Union from 1917 to the Present,* trans. Phyllis B. Carlos (New York: Summit Books, 1985), p. 246.

180. Kotkin, *Magnetic Mountain,* p. 317.

181. "The output of poor quality goods was one of the 'economic crimes' delineated in the 1926 criminal code. In November 1929 a revision of the code (the insertion of article 128a) called for sentences up to five years for 'massive or systematic output from industrial or trade enterprises of poor quality goods.' In December 1933, a further revision singled out managers and specified sentences of 'not less than five years.' The crime of wrecking, however, was covered by article 58. In July 1940, after the terror was over, the penalties for crimes charged under article 128a were stiffened and the output of poor quality goods was called an 'anti-state crime equivalent to wrecking.'" Ibid., p. 564n.

182. "Precisely because the search for enemies was so logical . . . communists could scarcely avoid participating in it" (ibid., p. 315). Party vigilance was conducted "under the banner of 'party revival' and 'democratization,' by a process "far from abstract"; in the case of Magnitogorsk, "throughout April [1937] there were unprecedented secret ballot elections to leadership positions in primary party organizations," and those lower in the party hierarchy were encouraged to criticize their superiors (ibid., p. 327). Likewise, the NKVD's arrests (a "maximum quantity" of which was encouraged by Moscow) were not just actions of brute force: there was a "need for evidence"; defendants were charged under specific articles of the criminal code; much value was placed upon their confessions. In these ways, the "professionalism" of the NKVD and "a certain legality was maintained" (ibid., pp. 334–336). At the same time, the NKVD set up *troikas,* ad hoc boards of three members, who were to expedite judgments for crimes of counterrevolution. These were abolished in November 1939 (ibid., p. 333).

183. Stalin had achieved a personal dictatorship within the party dictatorship beyond the control of its Central Committee (ibid., p. 300).

184. This was the consequence of the ambivalence of "sovereignty" in the Soviet model of the party-state. The NKVD was the site of legitimate violence, the self-described "sword of the revolution"; but as a merely administrative (i.e., state) organization (the "secular arm"), it was under the command of the party, which in turn was under the command of the party leadership. To say that "Stalin" was responsible for the terror is not wrong, but it is misleading to speak of the evil personality of one man

as the sole agency, without taking into account the institutional structures that provided its logical unfolding.

185. Kotkin, *Magnetic Mountain,* p. 332. "Under present conditions: the inalienable quality of every Bolshevik must be the ability to detect the enemy of the party however well he may be masked" (Ezhov, head of the NKVD, in a closed letter to the Central Committee, 29 July 1936, cited in Getty, *Origins of the Great Purges,* p. 113).

186. See here Carl Schmitt, *Der Nomos der Erde im Völkerrecht des Jus Publicum Europaeum,* 2d ed. (Berlin: Duncker & Humblot, 1972. Schmitt describes the European imaginary of nation-states as a specific perception of geopolitical space, which he calls the *nomos.*

187. Ibid., p. 101.

188. Eldon Kenworthy, *America/Américas: Myth in the Making of U.S. Policy toward Latin America* (University Park: Pennsylvania State University Press, 1995), p. 41. Cf. p. 26: "U.S. leaders wanted the land but not the [Latin-Catholic, African, and Indian] people."

189. Schmitt notes that Pufendorf quotes "approvingly" Francis Bacon's comment that "certain peoples [e.g., Indians] are 'proscribed by nature itself' because they eat human flesh. And in fact the Indians of North America were then exterminated." He adds critically, with the reparations demands of the Versailles Treaty in mind: "Maybe one day it will be enough if a people were unable to pay its debts" (Carl Schmitt, *The Concept of the Political,* trans. George Schwab [New Brunswick: Rutgers University Press, 1976], pp. 54n–55n). "While on the one hand the United States treated the tribes as sovereign nations with which treaties could be signed, on the other hand the new federal government claimed ownership of the land on which those tribes had lived for generations as long as that land was not claimed by another 'civilized' (i.e., European) government" (Kenworthy, *America/Américas,* p. 26n). "Convoluted legal arrangements treated tribes as sovereign foreign states for some purposes—obviating the need to make Indians citizens—while reserving to the federal government the right to move tribes from place to place as suited U.S. interests" (ibid.).

190. The difference was the form of ideological legitimation, not the dead bodies. The social inferiority of the Indians was established within a discourse of progress rather than race, while the genocidal effects were the same. Kenworthy finds there is no more adequate word than "vanguard" to describe the United States's conception of itself in this discourse, although this "contentious term" is never spoken by the proponents of the myth (*America/Américas,* pp. 18–19). Such temporal "progress" was understood as extension in space. "The 'West,' Wil-

son noted, was not 'a region,' but, in professor Turner's admirable phrase, a stage of development" (ibid.). As Pocock wrote: "the movement of American history has been spatial rather than dialectical"; "homo faber in this continent is seen as conquering space rather than transforming history, and the American work force has been even less willing than the European to see itself as a true proletariat." J. G. A. Pocock, *The Machiavellian Moment: Florentine Political Thought and the Atlantic Republican Tradition* (Princeton: Princeton University Press, 1975), pp. 543 and 550.

191. Schmitt, *Der Nomos der Erde,* p. 231.

192. Schmitt blames Woodrow Wilson for upsetting the whole "civilized" mode of European international politics, and describes how the negotiations for a League of Nations brought a direct confrontation between the European and American spatial models, disrupting the European order without replacing it on a global scale (ibid., pp. 224–229).

193. Ibid., p. 258.

194. European colonial boundaries had been drawn with a degree of arbitrariness lacking on the continent, and were thus closer to the American model. Schmitt gives as an example of the abstractness of European colonial territorial claims the fact that in 1902, a full 25 years after the establishment of the Belgian Congo, the Belgian government still had only the vaguest idea of the colony's population: the guess was somewhere between 14 and 30 million (ibid., p. 197). Interestingly, when the British government asked the king of Siam shortly before the First World War where the line fell that demarcated his kingdom, he had no answer. Linear thinking did not structure the imaginary of his sovereignty, although he knew full well which villages owed him tribute (some of which were subjected to dual sovereignty). See Thongchai Winichakul, *Siam Mapped: A History of the Geo-Body of a Nation* (Honolulu: University of Hawaii Press, 1994).

195. See Carolyn M. Volger, *The Nation State: The Neglected Dimension of Class* (Hants, England: Gower Publishing Company, 1985).

196. Robert A. Jones, *The Soviet Conception of "Limited Sovereignty" from Lenin to Gorbachev: The Brezhnev Doctrine* (London: Macmillan, 1990), pp. 32–33. Soviet intervention was "a projection of the class struggle across state boundaries: therefore any specific intervention had to be judged by whether it turned the 'wheel of history' forwards or backwards" (ibid., p. 35).

197. Ibid., p. 37.

198. Mark von Hagen, *Soldiers in the Proletarian Dictatorship: The Red Army and the Soviet Socialist State, 1917–1930* (Ithaca: Cornell University Press, 1990), p. 35.

199. V. I. Lenin, cited in Myron Rush, ed., *The International Situation and Soviet Foreign Policy: Key Reports by Soviet Leaders from the Revolution to the Present* (Columbus: Merrill Publishing Co., 1970), p. 29.

200. Lenin, cited in ibid., p. 32.

201. Lenin, cited in ibid.

202. Ibid.

203. Sheila Fitzpatrick, in Abbott Gleason, et al., eds., *Bolshevik Culture: Experiment and Order in the Russian Revolution* (Bloomington: Indiana University Press, 1985), pp. 57–58.

204. Trotsky and others had argued at the end of the Civil War that the soldiers should not be released but turned immediately into a Labor Army. Trotsky defended this "militarization of labor" as the only means to build socialism in a "backward" country—again, it was a question of time (see von Hagen, *Soldiers in the Proletarian Dictatorship,* pp. 117–118).

205. Moshe Lewin, "Society, State, and Ideology during the First Five-Year Plan," in Sheila Fitzpatrick, ed., *Cultural Revolution in Russia, 1928–1931* (Bloomington: Indiana University Press, 1978), p. 59.

206. Moshe Lewin, *The Making of the Soviet System: Essays in the Social History of Interwar Russia* (New York: Pantheon Books, 1985), p. 292.

207. J. Arch Getty, *Origins of the Great Purges: The Soviet Communist Party Reconsidered, 1933–1938* (New York: Cambridge University Press, 1985), p. 13.

208. Mikhail Heller, *La Machine et les rouages: La formation de l'homme soviétique,* trans. Anne Coldefy-Faucard (Paris: Calmann-Lévy, 1985), p. 65.

209. By the mid-1930s, Stalin was declaring that life had become happier, more joyous. This spirit was to inspire socialist realism as a literary program. "Thus the Stalinist novel was supported by a world view that tended to annul time, to write off that unbridgeable distance between its own kind of absolute epic past [the official Heroic Age of Russia's greatness] and the socialist-utopian future." Katerina Clark, *The Soviet Novel: History as Ritual* (Chicago: University of Chicago Press, 1981), p. 40.

210. Stalin, cited in Brandon Taylor, *Art and Literature under the Bolsheviks,* vol. 2: *Authority and Revolution, 1924–1932* (London: Pluto Press, 1992), pp. 91–92.

211. Lynne Viola, *Peasant Rebels under Stalin: Collectivization and the Culture of Peasant Resistance* (New York: Oxford University Press, 1996), p. 99.

212. For the enormous pragmatic difficulties in applying Marxist-Leninist theory to the real conditions of these people, see Yuri Slezkine, *Arctic Mirrors: Russia and the Small Peoples of the North* (Ithaca: Cornell University Press, 1994). Were "national particularities" an ideological defense for private property (p. 199)? Were reindeer herders class exploiters comparable to the kulaks and did reindeer herds need to be collectivized (pp. 193–198)? Could nomadic cultures be defended in the twentieth century (p. 205)? Should certain ethnic differences and "local peculiarities" be respected in the short run "for the sake of future progress" (p. 191)? Or were they "prehistoric survivals," not part of historical time and therefore societies where class analysis was inappropriate (pp. 304–315)? Did being "advanced" culturally mean having domestic possessions (p. 286)? Should women be "emancipated" from loin cloths (in the north) and veils (in central Asia) and were they "the real and most authentic proletarians" (p. 231)?

213. Slezkine, *Arctic Mirrors,* pp. 199 and 220.

214. S. M. Dimanshtein (1930), influential official of the Commissariat of Nationalities, cited in ibid., p. 220.

215. Anatolii Skachko (1930), head of the Minorities Section of the Commissariat of Nationalities, cited in ibid. Their alleged successes in this race with time were visually documented in many articles that appeared in the illustrated propaganda journal *USSR in Construction,* published in Moscow in four languages (Russian, English, French, and German) during the 1930s and 1940s and distributed globally.

216. For an excellent monograph on the Soviet argument that Muslim women had the greatest revolutionary potential as the most socially exploited element of this backward, "tribal-patriarchal" society, and were thus the key to the modernization of these cultures—and for the tragic outcomes of this limited understanding of women's oppression in the terms of class war and the acceleration of historical change (e.g., the dynamics that led from voluntary mass unveilings to forced unveiling of Muslim women by gunpoint)—see Gregory J. Massell, *The Surrogate Proletariat: Moslem Women and Revolutionary Strategies in Soviet Central Asia* (Princeton: University of Princeton Press, 1974).

217. The northern novelist Vladimir Sangi wrote: "It so happened in history that during many centuries Europeans were forced to wage wars, seize something, enslave someone. . . . During the same period, the aboriginal northerners were perfecting their relationship with the environment" (cited in Slezkine, *Arctic Mirrors,* p. 382).

218. Slezkine, *Arctic Mirrors,* p. 377. "Most early properestroika intellectuals agreed that there were at least as many 'Peoples' [*narodnosti*] in the Soviet Union as there were nationalities [*natsiai*]. National (ethnic) governments might be asked to transfer some of their powers elsewhere, but no one seemed to doubt that they should have those powers in the first place" (ibid.).

CHAPTER 2
ON TIME

1. Cited in Christina Lodder, "Lenin's Plan for Monumental Propaganda," in Matthew Cullerne Bown and Brandon Taylor, eds., *Art of the Soviets: Painting, Sculpture and Architecture in a One-Party State, 1917–1992* (Manchester: Manchester University Press, 1993), p. 19. Lunacharskii was in charge of carrying out the plan at Narkompros, the state Ministry of Education and Culture, founded several weeks after the October Revolution.

2. Lodder, "Lenin's Plan," p. 20. Lenin was inspired by an Italian Renaissance example, the plan for educational public art described in Campanella's *The City of the Sun* (1623), a utopian-socialist work first translated into Russian in 1906 and republished by the Petrograd Soviet in 1918 as part of a series of utopian novels.

3. There does not seem to have been any concerted effort to place these figures in a particular sequence, chronological or otherwise; nor were the monuments placed in spatial relation to each other in any particularly meaningful fashion. Rather, these "heroes" were brought into the present as a constellation that suggested a new historical narration, connecting figures of the past across national, occupational, and even political boundaries. The ecumenism of the list was striking. Among the Russians were the anarchist Mikhail Bakunin, whom Marx had criticized repeatedly, and (after his death in May 1919) the Social Revolutionary Georgii Plekhanov, who in 1903 had accused Lenin of "bonapartism," confusing dictatorship *of* the proletariat with dictatorship *over* the proletariat. The Germans included (besides Marx and Engels) the recent Communist martyrs Rosa Luxemburg and Karl Liebknecht. Also named were the Italian nationalist Garibaldi, the English utopian socialist Robert Owen, the French utopian theorists Charles Fourier and Saint-Simon, and a handful of ancient European fighters against tyranny (Spartacus, Gracchus, Brutus). See Richard Stites, *Revolutionary Dreams: Utopian Vision and Experimental Life in the*

Russian Revolution (New York: Oxford University Press, 1989), pp. 89–90. By August 1918 the list of those considered "worthy of sculptural attention" had been extended to 66 (Lodder, "Lenin's Plan," p. 20). The name of the French painter Paul Cézanne appeared on an early list, but was crossed off by government officials "at the top" (Vasilii Rakitin, "The Artisan and the Prophet: Marginal Notes on Two Artistic Careers," in *The Great Utopia: The Russian and Soviet Avant-Garde, 1915–1932* [New York: Guggenheim Museum, 1992], p. 31).

4. This lack of material was to be turned into a democratic advantage, as "the public would be allowed to give their judgement on the merit of the work before some were converted into more permanent materials such as bronze, granite or marble" (Brandon Taylor, *Art and Literature under the Bolsheviks*, vol. 1: *The Crisis of Renewal, 1917–1924* [London: Pluto Press, 1991], p. 59). Lunacharskii wrote that the monuments should be "modest, and let everything be temporary" (cited in Vladimir Tolstoy et al., eds., *Street Art of the Revolution: Festivals and Celebrations in Russia, 1918–33* [New York: Vendome Press, 1990], p. 13).

5. In response to acts of vandalism during the early days of the Revolution, Lunacharskii issued an appeal to "Protect the Property of the People," and appointed artists to a Commission for the Preservation of Monuments that had the power to decide which of the tsarist monuments were to be saved on account of their artistic value. See Hubertus Gassner, "The Constructivists: Modernism on the Way to Modernization," in *The Great Utopia*, p. 301. The issue of monumental propaganda took on increased significance in the context of the Civil War, as Trotsky wrote, "particularly in the outlying areas": "We must say . . . if the bourgeois breaks through the front and comes here, he will sweep away that monument together with the Soviet power and all the achievements we have won" (cited in Taylor, *Art and Literature under the Bolsheviks*, vol. 1, pp. 56–57).

6. Stites, *Revolutionary Dreams*, p. 37. The provisional government adopted as its national anthem the workers' "Marseillaise," "Otrezemsya ot Starovo Mira" (We Renounce the Old World).

7. The provisional government had severely damaged its own legitimacy by resuming the European war, thereby provoking mass street demonstrations in Petrograd on July 4, 1917, which turned violent. Speaking to the demonstrators, Lenin warned them at that time that it was still too early for armed resurrection.

8. Historical progress along a developmental trajectory is not the only possible form of revolutionary time. The French Revolution looked backward to ancient Rome for its historical model; seventeenth-century English rebels appealed to biblical time. Both required what Benjamin referred to as "a tiger's leap into the past" (Walter Benjamin, *Illuminations*, ed. Hannah Arendt, trans. Harry Zohn [New York: Schocken Books, 1969], p. 261).

9. Gorky, cited in Stites, *Revolutionary Dreams*, p. 103.

10. Cited in ibid., p. 42.

11. Stites, *Revolutionary Dreams*, p. 170. (The bomber was developed by Igor Sikorsky, who later emigrated to the United States and become one of its leading aviation engineers.) A veritable aviation mania took hold among workers and peasants after the Bolshevik Revolution, particularly among the young. Voluntary clubs of air enthusiasts were promoted by the Air League (Osoaviakhim), founded in 1923, which had a membership of fifteen million by 1934. The Soviets established a civil air fleet in 1921 (renamed Aeroflot in 1932), contemporaneous with (government-owned) Lufthansa and Air France and (privately owned) Pan American in the United States. The exhortation "Workers, take to the air!" was used in campaigns to raise funds for financing new aircraft, which depended to a surprising degree, if we are to believe the sources, on voluntary contributions. "Some peasants reportedly were so impressed by the gallant fliers of Aeroflot that they contributed part of their crops—rye, oats, wheat, and even suckling pigs—to be converted into cash for flying machines" (Kendall E. Bailes, "Soviet Civil Aviation and Modernization, 1923–1976," in Robin Higham and Jacob W. Kipp, eds., *Soviet Aviation and Air Power: A Historical View* [Boulder: Westview Press, 1977], p. 176).

12. Stites, *Revolutionary Dreams*, p. 30. Bogdanov became head of Proletkult in 1917.

13. From Maxim Gorky, *Confession* (1907), the text that coined the term god-building, cited in Stites, *Revolutionary Dreams*, p. 103. Lenin was (and remained) opposed to god-building, but the idea had Lunacharskii's support. He and Gorky were members of the Capri group of Marxist exiles before the war that also included Bogdanov. Lenin denounced Bogdanov's conception of cultural revolution as the way to socialism in *Materialism and Empirio-criticism* (1909). But he was conciliatory toward Lunacharskii, who rejoined Lenin's good graces and the party just after the Revolution (see Timothy Edward O'Connor, *The Politics of Soviet Culture: Anatolii Lunacharskii* [Ann Arbor: UMI Research Press, 1988], pp. 10–13).

14. According to Fedorov's *Philosophy of the Common Task*, "Death is, one may say, anaesthesia, which is accompanied by the total dismemberment of a corpse, decomposition and dispersal of matter. Collection of the dispersed particles is a question of the cosmotelluric sci-

ence and of art, consequently a task for men, while the putting together of the assembled particles is a question of physiology, histology, the sewing together, so to say, of the bodily tissues of fathers and mothers which is a task for women. . . ." Cited in Ludmila Koehler, *N. F. Fedorov: The Philosophy of Action* (Pittsburgh: Institute for the Human Sciences, 1979), p. 19. Each unique human body decomposed into dust after death, but each could be rebuilt "by matching all the molecules of a similar pattern. Since the molecules would be scattered throughout the universe, man would have to colonize distant planets in order to find their particles. This colonization would also be necessary in order to accommodate all the resurrected as the work progressed." Ayleen Teskey, *Platonov and Fyodorov: The Influence of Christian Philosophy on a Soviet Writer* (Amersham, England: Avebury Publishing Company, 1982), p. 19.

15. The list included Gorky, Bogdanov, Gastev, Maiakovskii, Khlebnikov, and Platonov, all of whom appreciated Fedorov's ideas, though not without criticism. The philosopher's more cultic disciples called themselves "biocosmists," adopting as their slogan "Immortalism and interplanetism." When the young Tsiolkovskii met Fedorov, the latter gave him a copy of Jules Verne's novel *An Air Voyage across Africa* (Koehler, *Fedorov*, p. 81). For Tsiolkovskii's connection to the avant-garde, see Michael Holquist, "Tsiolkovsky as a Moment in the Prehistory of the Avant-Garde," in John E. Bowlt and Olga Matich, eds., *Laboratory of Dreams: The Russian Avant-Garde and Cultural Experiment* (Stanford: Stanford University Press, 1996).

16. "The crowd steps in a new march, their feet have caught the iron tempo. / Hands are burning, they cannot stand idleness. . . . / To the machines! / We are their lever, we are their breathing, their impulse." Aleksei Gastev, "The Factory Whistles" (Gudki), 1913, trans. Kurt Johannson, in *Aleksej Gastev: Proletarian Bard of the Machine Age* (Stockholm: Almqvist & Wiksell International, 1983), p. 76.

17. The aviator is a major figure as well in the futurist opera *Victory over the Sun,* performed in St. Petersburg in December 1913, with libretto by the *zaum* poet Aleksei Kruchenykh and music by Mikhail Matiushin; Malevich designed the lighting, stage sets, and costumes. The opera was rethought in 1920–1921 as an "electromechanical show" by El Lissitzky, who designed its "plastic organization," producing a folio for it that was published in Hannover in 1923. *Victory over the Sun* was restaged with meticulous historical detail in Los Angeles in 1983, a performance that was videorecorded. The opera tells of the capture of the "cheap and pretentious" sun, symbol of rationality and the "old order," by "Futurelandmen" who

then journey to the "10 land," where, despite extreme disorientation, it is "easier to breathe." While there is nothing of realism in the opera, it "seems to have derived from an actual eclipse of the sun that took place in 1913"; see Taylor, *Art and Literature under the Bolsheviks,* vol. 1, pp. 12–13; also El Lissitzky, *Russia: An Architecture for World Revolution,* trans. Eric Dluhosch (Cambridge: MIT Press, 1984), p. 136.

18. The Revolution affected all the arts, visual and literary. But because of the radical change that was claimed to have taken place—and because of the extent of adult illiteracy—it was crucial that the world *look* different. In the social production of meaning, what we today call visual culture was thus of central importance. On the one hand, what there was to see in Russia in 1917–1920 was devastation, the frighteningly brutal effects of famine and civil war. On the other, every banner, placard, store window, and new building was capable of providing a visual expression of the new socialist society, for which, however, an idiom had yet to be established. For the new visual importance of words themselves, where words "take flight, turn somersaults, play leapfrog, crawl and hop over the whole page," see Gerald Janacek, *The Look of Russian Literature: Avant-Garde Visual Experiments, 1900–1930* (Princeton: Princeton University Press, 1984), p. 120.

19. Natalia Goncharova and Mikhail Larionov, *Rayonists and Futurists: A Manifesto* (1913), in John E. Bowlt, ed. and trans., *Russian Art of the Avant-Garde: Theory and Criticism, 1902–1934,* rev. ed. (London: Thames and Hudson, 1988), p. 89. Rayonist is spelled elsewhere rayonnist (Camilla Gray; see below, note 23) and rayist (*The Great Utopia,* and below in this book).

20. Malevich (1916), cited in John Milner, *Kazimir Malevich and the Art of Geometry* (New Haven: Yale University Press, 1996), p. 126.

21. Cited in Anatolii Strigalev, "Nonarchitects in Architecture," in *The Great Utopia,* p. 673.

22. Camilla Gray, *The Russian Experiment in Art 1863–1922,* rev. and enl. by Marian Burleigh-Motley (New York: Thames and Hudson, 1986), p. 180. The term "counterrelief" evoked the analogy of "counterattack" during these war years.

23. Kazimir Malevich, *From Cubism and Futurism to Suprematism* (1915), in Bowlt, ed., *Russian Art of the Avant-Garde,* p. 135.

24. "Malevich considered that, at the sight of his black square 'the sword will fall from the hero's hands and the prayer die on the lips of the saint'" (Boris Groys, "The Birth of Socialist Realism from the Spirit of the Russian

Avant-Garde," in Bowlt and Matich, eds., *Laboratory of Dreams*, p. 202). The *Black Square* was heralded by El Lissitzky in 1920 as the "very source of all creative expression" (cited in Jane A. Sharp, "The Critical Perception of the 0.10 Exhibition: Malevich and Benua," in *The Great Utopia*, p. 39).

25. Malevich was elected as President of the Art Department of the Moscow Council of Soldiers' Deputies in September 1917, that is, before the Bolshevik victory.

26. "On New Systems in Art" (1919), in K. S. Malevich, *Essays on Art 1915–1928*, vol. 1, trans. Xenia Gowacki-Prus and Arnold McMillin, ed. Troels Andersen (Copenhagen: Borgens Forlag, 1968), p. 85.

27. Kazimir Malevich, catalogue of the "Tenth State Exhibition: Non-Objective Creation and Suprematism" (1919), cited in Milner, *Kazimir Malevich and the Art of Geometry*, pp. 171–172; cf. Bowlt, ed., *Russian Art of the Avant-Garde*, p. 145.

28. I am making a distinction between *vanguard* and *avant-garde* temporalities that the artists and political figures did not clearly recognize themselves, as I discuss below. See Peter Osborne, *The Politics of Time: Modernity and Avant-Garde* (London: Verso, 1995), for an insightful philosophical explication of the connection between temporalities and politics generally, and for that of the avant-garde in particular. I am indebted as well to discussions with Osborne for the argument made here.

29. All of these terms were used by members of the avant-garde in Russia at the time of the Revolution; see Bowlt, ed., *Russian Art of the Avant Garde*. "Primitivism" was an anti-urban, anti-industrial stylistic tendency, but the suprematist Ivan Kliun used the term in a different sense, for the beginning of a new era: "We are all primitives of the twentieth century" (cited in Rakitin, "The Artisan and the Prophet," p. 26). In their 1913 manifesto, the rayists recognized no chronology: "We declare that painting is not limited by time" (cited in Gray, *The Russian Experiment in Art*, p. 138).

30. "At no point between 1917 and 1937 did there exist in Soviet Russia a single 'typical' architect or architecture." S. Frederick Starr, *Melnikov: Solo Architect in a Mass Society* (Princeton: Princeton University Press, 1978), p. 9. For the great variety of artistic practice during this period, see Taylor, *Art and Literature under the Bolsheviks*, 2 vols.

31. Korolev designed a statue of Mikhail Bakunin, considerably less radical in style than the proposed statue of Marx, that was in fact erected on Ploshchod Turgeneva in Moscow, 1919. A wooden platform was built to conceal it from the public prior to the unveiling. "But some poor people in the cold winter days carried away the boards for firewood, and one fine morning, to the general consternation, the unveiled monument became visible, and the sight of it caused a real revolt of the populace" (cited in Taylor, *Art and Literature under the Bolsheviks*, vol. 1, p. 60). See also Lodder, "Lenin's Plan," p. 25. Derided as a "scarecrow" by the press, it was demolished before a formal unveiling could take place.

32. Christopher Read, *Culture and Power in Revolutionary Russia: The Intelligentsia and the Transition from Tsarism to Communism* (New York: St. Martin's Press, 1990), p. 94.

33. Proletkult's intellectual and theoretical leader, Aleksandr A. Bogdanov, had a problematic relationship with Lenin that dated back to the prewar years of their exile in Europe. Bogdanov was part of the Vpered (Forward) group and the Capri group during those years, which included Lunacharskii and Gorky (see above, note 14). His Marxist philosophy differed significantly from Lenin's own, specifically in regard to the significance of proletarian culture for the realization of socialism. The slogan of Proletkult was "korgavoe no svoe" (rough and ready but our own). Bogdanov was not a member of the Communist Party. Proletkult, however, did receive Narkompros funding as well as money from independent organizations. Lunacharskii (who rejoined the Bolshevik Party in 1917) was Bogdanov's brother-in-law. See Sheila Fitzpatrick, *The Cultural Front: Power and Culture in Revolutionary Russia* (Ithaca: Cornell University Press, 1992), pp. 20–22.

34. Chagall had trained in Paris before the war; he was back in Russia when the Revolution occurred and stayed, sympathetic to Bolshevism's pledge to promote Jewish artists. He was appointed in 1918 director of the school of art in his native town of Vitebsk, where he continued his primitive-populist style, together with a group of Jewish artists from Vitebsk, Kiev, and Odessa. In 1919 Chagall brought to the school El Lissitzky (also a native of Vitebsk, with whom earlier he had worked on Jewish picture books) to become professor of architecture and head of the Applied Arts department . Lissitzky was under the influence of Malevich, whom Chagall invited to the school in the summer of 1919. Malevich took advantage of Chagall's temporary absence to promote his own program, declaring Chagall's art and methods "old-fashioned" and irrelevant and founding the collective UNOVIS in 1920. Contemporary scholars do not see this move as particularly sinister: "the legendary anecdotes about Malevich's persecution of Chagall prove, upon closer inspection, neither simple nor clearcut" (Aleksandra Shatskikh, "Unovis:

Epicenter of a New World," in *The Great Utopia,* p. 56). In June 1921, Chagall's murals were featured at the twenty-third exhibition of the Central section of IZO Narkompros (see below, note 64), shown in the hall of the State Jewish Kamernyi Theater in Moscow (see Aleksandra Shatskikh, "A Brief History of Obmokhu," in *The Great Utopia,* p. 265n). Despite this sign of appreciation by the new regime, Chagall left Russia shortly thereafter for Berlin and later Paris.

35. See Evgenii Kovtun, "The Third Path to Non-Objectivity," in *The Great Utopia,* pp. 321–328. In 1913 Matiushin wrote the music for the futurist opera *Victory over the Sun* (see above, note 18). After the Revolution he directed the Department of Organic Culture at the Petrograd GINKhUK, where he worked on his system of expanded viewing, or "see-know" (*zorved*), which combined development of physical vision ("circum vision") with that of spiritual intuition. "Referring to optical variables in nature (the housefly has a very wide radius of sight while the dog has a very narrow one), Matiushin maintained that human beings could expand their optical radius. He affirmed that the body contained dormant optical reflexes on the soles of the feet and the back of the neck, and, basing his observations on private experiments, he proceeded to paint what he called landscapes from all points of view." John E. Bowlt, "Body Beautiful," in Bowlt and Matich, eds., *Laboratory of Dreams,* p. 52. The Ender siblings (Mariia, Boris, Kseniia, and Georgii) were all his students.

36. *Pavel Filonov: A Hero and His Fate,* trans. and ed. Nicoletta Misler and John E. Bowlt (Austin, Texas: Silvergirl, 1983), p. 25. Filonov, who immediately gave his support to the October Revolution and was sympathetic to the cultural ideas of Proletkult, "dreamed of organizing an entire network of museums that would display 'low' art forms such as *lubki* [peasant woodcuts] and oleographic prints, and his lifelong desire was to open a museum of his art exclusively for workers" (Nicoletta Misler, "Pavel Filonov, Painter of Metamorphosis," in ibid., p. 25). He was an influential and respected artist in the 1920s, establishing his school of Collective Masters of Analytical Art in Leningrad and publishing his *Declaration of "Universal Flowering."* By the mid-thirties he was in disfavor and summoned repeatedly for questioning. See also below, note 101.

37. Fitzpatrick, *The Cultural Front,* p. 21.

38. This group has been largely overlooked by Western scholars, for whom the Russian revolutionary avant-garde is the seminal moment in art history. During the Cold War period, the AKhRR realist style was lumped together with

Stalinism and dismissed. Yet "AKhRR embraced more artists, produced more art and held more exhibitions than any other group" in the 1920s (Brandon Taylor, "On AKhRR," in Bown and Taylor, eds., *Art of the Soviets,* p. 51). AKhRR was begun in 1922 as an independent organization, financed in part by Narkompros and with particularly close connections to the Red Army. Although it came increasingly under the sway of party members among its ranks, it was not a party platform: "On the one hand it is clear that AKhRR's programme (as well as its style) endeared it to military leaders who had close connections with centers of power within the Party and the government. Yet it is also true that in 1922 there was by no means an enforced 'line' on the arts . . . even though AKhRR's references to 'documentation' and to 'contemporary life' look like reflections of Lenin's preferences for an accessible, popular yet political style" (ibid., p. 55).

39. 1926 was the year of AKhRR's eighth Moscow exhibition, "Life and Being of the Peoples of the USSR," an event displaying over 1,700 works by 298 artists (Taylor, "On AKhRR," p. 61). Still, Taylor cautions against overestimating AKhRR's official endorsement: "By mid-decade, say 1926, it still seems to me far too early to say that AKhRR was *nothing more* than a reflection of official Party policy in the arts" (ibid., p. 68). During the First Five Year Plan, AKhRR published a journal called *Art to the Masses,* which served as "a touchstone for 'official' revolutionary opinion and a guiding light for a whole generation of younger communists" (Taylor, *Art and Literature under the Bolsheviks,* vol. 1, p. 175). At the end of the decade, AKhRR's painting of flattering portraits of Red Army officers (who were often also party members) provoked criticism. AKhRR was dissolved along with all independent cultural organizations in April 1932, but many of its artists continued to thrive during Stalin's years.

40. A younger generation of easel painters, including Iurii Pimenov and Aleksandr Deineka of the OST group, developed individual styles at the end of the decade with qualities that must be considered avant-garde. "Projectionists" (Aleksandr Labas, Kliment Redko, and Aleksandr Tyshler) developed expressionist or surrealist techniques. Easel paintings sometimes expressed social criticism, as in Sergei Luchishkin's *The Balloon Has Gone* of 1926. In it, a child's red balloon has floated away, leaving him deserted in a chillingly bleak suburban landscape. Through an upper story window a hanged man is visible: apparently a suicide" (Taylor, *Art and Literature under the Bolsheviks,* vol. 2, p. 18).

41. *Iskusstvo kommuny* was the official journal of IZO, published in Petrograd from December 1918 to April 1919: "The journal was eclectic and not characterized by

one set of aesthetic ideas" (Christina Lodder, *Russian Constructivism*, [New Haven: Yale University Press, 1983], p. 76). *Lef* has become well known in the West, where its later, influential reception has given distorted impressions of its importance. Its circulation, never more than 5,000, dwindled to 1,500 in the last issue, and it ceased publication in 1925 "through lack of demand" (Taylor, *Art and Literature under the Bolsheviks*, vol. 1, p. 183).

42. See Rakitin, "The Artisan and the Prophet," p. 31. Tatlin was not interested in leading a group. He taught in the State Free Art Studios in Moscow and (after 1919) in Petrograd, where he was active in setting up the Petrograd GINKhUK, and for a short time he directed its Department of Material Culture, which was oriented toward the organization of life and mass production (see Lodder, *Russian Constructivism*, p. 264).

43. Malevich replaced Chagall as head of the Vitebsk art school in November 1919, and founded UNOVIS there the following spring. See Shatskikh, "Unovis."

44. The first head of INKhUK was Vasilii Kandinskii, who resigned in January 1921 when his program of "subjectivism" was rejected. Intense discussions culminated in the founding of the constructivist group that spring.

45. Cited in Shatskikh, "A Brief History of Obmokhu," pp. 260–261. This group, founded in 1919, was funded as an agit-production workshop by Narkompros (beginning in September 1920), and received commissions for literacy posters, street decorations, slogan boards, etc. They worked as a collective, signing their works with the name of the organization (as did UNOVIS). OBMOKhU is most well known for its exhibition in Moscow in May 1921 (the second OBMOKhU exhibition, for long mistakenly presumed to be the third), which, along with numerous literacy posters and other utilitarian works, showed in a separate room the earliest products of the First Working Group of Constructivists of INKhUK (ibid., pp. 257–265).

46. Although constructivists are credited with initiating the move into production in 1921, the Russian avant-garde had similar ideas even before the revolution. In a real sense, constructivism was a continuation of the movement of "art into life" that had begun in Europe and the United States with the arts and crafts movement and had taken an industrial turn with the decorative art produced at the turn of the century. The difference of the movement in postrevolutionary Russia was the absence of commodity logic and the fact that the consumer was here understood as the new collective, the working class. See Susan Buck-Morss, "The City as Dreamworld and Catastrophe," *October* 73 (Summer 1995), pp. 3–26.

47. Theories of production art were developed in the avant-garde journals by Punin, Boris Kushner, and Osip Brik. The differences in understanding among the artists were sometimes very great. Although Tatlin established with Arvatov a "production laboratory" in Petrograd, he claimed that he was never a true productionist: "I want to make the machine with art and not to mechanize art—there is a difference in understanding" (Lodder, *Russian Constructivism*, p. 213). Constructivists claimed that the suprematists' objects were not utilitarian enough; Malevich returned the insult by accusing Tatlin of having planned a Monument to the Third International the structure of which was scientifically unsound and could not be built. In fact, all of the avant-garde can be accused of (or praised for) having what Hubertus Gassner describes as a "utopian supplement" in their work, a theme to which I return below.

48. Nikolai Punin (1918), cited in Gray, *The Russian Experiment in Art*, p. 220.

49. From Maiakovskii's "Order to the Army of Art," in the first issue of *Iskusstvo kommuny* (March 1918). Ivan Puni later reflected that this statement marked the redefinition of futurism, now a "clearly and definitely expressed tendency to go beyond the limits of the work of art enclosed within itself, i.e., the trend toward the liquidation of art as a separate discipline" (cited in Lodder, *Russian Constructivism*, p. 48; Puni's statement is from *Iskusstvo kommuny* no. 19).

50. Shatskikh, "Unovis," p. 57. The neologism "unovistic" entered the Russian language as synonymous with revolutionary style.

51. When Tatlin returned to Moscow in 1927 he taught at the VKhUTEIN (formerly VKhUTEMAS) in the Wood and Metal faculty (Dermetfak) and in the Ceramics faculty, and worked in his Scientific and Experimental Laboratory in the Novodevichii Monastery on his flying machine the Letatlin (discussed in Chapter 3 below). In 1929 he wrote that he viewed his role as an "organizer of everyday life" (Paul Wood, "The Politics of the Avant-Garde," in *The Great Utopia*, p. 11).

52. Rodchenko, cited in Christina Lodder, "The Transition to Constructivism," in *The Great Utopia*, p. 267.

53. Tatlin (1921), cited in Gray, *The Russian Experiment in Art*, p. 219.

54. "If communism which set human labour on the throne and suprematism which raised aloft the square pennant of creativity now march forward together then in the further stages of development it is communism which will have to remain behind because suprematism—which

embraces the totality of life's phenomena—will attract everyone away from the domination of work and from the domination of the intoxicated senses. It will liberate all those engaged in creative activity and make the world into a true model of perfection.... AFTER THE OLD TESTAMENT THERE CAME THE NEW—AFTER THE NEW THE COMMUNIST—AND AFTER THE COMMUNIST THERE FOLLOWS FINALLY THE TESTAMENT OF SUPREMATISM." El Lissitzky, "Suprematism in World Reconstruction" (1920), in Bowlt, ed., *Russian Art of the Avant-Garde*, pp. 154–158. The text of this piece is from a typescript in the Lissitzky archives, reproduced here from Sophie Lissitzky-Küppers, *El Lissitzky: Life, Letters, Texts* (Greenwich, CT: New York Graphic Society, 1968), pp. 327–330.

55. Shatskikh, "Unovis." One of UNOVIS's first projects was to publish (with suprematist graphics) Malevich's theoretical text *On New Systems in Art*, which he described as painting's "declaration of independence' from "objectivity" (i.e., representational art). It was a "new testament" containing commandments for artistic practice, including the obscure mandate to introduce into art a "fifth dimension, or economy" (ibid., p. 40). The sign of this world economy was the sacrosanct black square, sewn by UNOVIS members on their inside cuffs, closest to their palms, while the red square was drawn in their workshops as a sign of the "revolution" in the arts (ibid., pp. 55 and 62). Despite the cultlike practices of UNOVIS, it was democratic in structure: "UNOVIS was a 'party' that accepted all comers: anyone—poet, musician, actor or artisan—who wished to promote the 'augmentation' of the world with new forms could join" (ibid., p. 62).

56. The fact that the struggle was over discourse is politically important. Production art was a rhetoric of revolution, not the actual liquidation of art in favor of factory production. The avant-garde's industrial and commercial designs were experimental and exemplary. They envisioned the new society in terms of socialist *consumption* rather than production. That was the threat to the party. But it also implied meeting the party on its own *time*, a concession with significant implications, as we shall see.

57. Taylor, "On AKhRR," p. 52. In 1917, Proletkult could boast of close to 300 organizations and thirty-four journals (Stites, *Revolutionary Dreams*, p. 71). Lenin's wife Krupskaia, who worked closely with Lunacharskii in Narkompros, complained in April 1918 that Proletkult "was a haven for intellectuals who needed jobs—particularly, she claimed, socialist intellectuals with anti-Bolshevik leanings" (Fitzpatrick, *The Cultural Front*, p. 20). At the October 1920 First All-Russian Congress of the *proletkults*, Lenin sent this message to the party official who

was to speak there: "1. proletarian culture = communism; 2. it is the responsibility of the RKP (Russian Communist Party) 3. the proletarian class = the RKP = Soviet power. Are we all agreed on this?" Matthew Cullerne Bown, *Art under Stalin*, (Oxford: Phaidon Press, 1991), p. 27. Party pressure caused the Congress to vote to relinquish its independence, which Bogdanov had thought so necessary. The art studios of Proletkult collapsed in 1921–1922 under these party attacks; only the Proletkult theater groups (to which for a time Sergei Eisenstein was attached) survived (ibid.).

58. I am not disputing the fact that Lenin's personal taste was opposed to the avant-garde. I am arguing that it was not the reason for the virulence of his attack. Revealing is an account of Lenin's surprise visit in February 1921 to students at VKhUTEMAS. He arrived one night unannounced and spoke with students who innocently expressed their enthusiasm for "Futurist" art: "We will get the literature for you, Vladimir Ilich; we're sure that you too will be a Futurist. It's impossible for you to be on the side of that rotten, old trash." Lenin responded by turning a student's nonrepresentational drawing round and round and asking: "Well, but just how do you connect art with politics?" When students praised Maiakovskii's *Mystery-Bouffe* and Kamenskii's *Engine Mass*, while stating proudly that they never went to the traditional opera, Lenin said, apparently with good humor: "Well, tastes differ" and "I am an old man." Sergei Senkin, cited in Taylor, *Art and Literature under the Bolsheviks*, vol. 1, pp. 93–94.

59. In his notes for a biography of Lenin, Trotsky recalled Lenin's pre-1917 concentrated efforts to speed up the outbreak of revolution by building an ideological base and framework for it "in the shortest time possible." Leon Trotsky, cited in Zenovia A. Sochor, *Revolution and Culture: The Bogdanov-Lenin Controversy* (Ithaca: Cornell University Press, 1988), p. 28.

60. Taylor, *Art and Literature under the Bolsheviks*, vol. 1, p. 184. The article was by Valerian Pletnev, "On the Ideological Front"; it appeared in *Pravda*, 27 September 1922.

61. Cited in Taylor, *Art and Literature under the Bolsheviks*, vol. 1, p. 184.

62. See above, chapter 1, on the left-wing opposition to Lenin; for Bogdanov and Lunacharskii, see O'Connor, *The Politics of Soviet Culture*, pp. 9 and 20, and Fitzpatrick, *The Cultural Front*, p. 22.

63. The Museum of Artistic (later, Painterly) Culture in Moscow was founded in 1919 to exhibit contemporary, "living art." It was directed by the Museum Office of Narkompros, headed by Rodchenko. It was also a source of Western art journals and sponsor of an important series

of lectures, thus functioning as a hub of information and debate. Original members of the board included Tatlin, Malevich, Rodchenko, Stepanova, and Kandinskii; later the board reflected a younger generation: Labas, Tyshler, Nikritin, Kogan, and Viliams. Similar museums were established in provincial towns. The number of purchases for these museums was sizable. In 1919–1920 Rodchenko acquired 1,926 works by 415 artists. Narkompros organized thirty museums in provincial towns, distributing to them 1,211 works (Lodder, *Russian Constructivism,* p. 49).

64. Domestically from 1918 to 1920, IZO (the Department of Fine Arts) in Narkompros organized 28 free state exhibitions without any selecting board to restrict entries. The first of these, held in the Winter Palace in April 1919, exhibited 1,826 works by 299 artists (Lodder, *Russian Constructivism,* p. 49). The artists were eager to participate in the international exhibitions. The younger generation envied older artists who had been in Europe before the Revolution, and international recognition remained a mark of success. Important foreign exhibitions included the "Erste russische Kunstausstellung" in Berlin 1922 and Amsterdam 1923; the "Exhibition of Russian Painting and Sculpture" in New York in 1923; the Soviet Pavilion at the Venice Biennale in 1924, which displayed approximately 600 pieces of art representing a wide range of styles (see Vivian Endicott Barnett, "The Russian Presence in the 1924 Venice Biennale," in *The Great Utopia,* p. 467); and the 1925 Paris Exposition Internationale des Arts Décoratifs et Industriels Modernes, where the Russian Pavilion (designed by Melnikov) included Rodchenko's Workers' Reading Room, a model of Tatlin's Monument to the Third International, and showings of Eisenstein's film *Battleship Potemkin.*

65. When *Lef* was launched during NEP (1923), funding from Gosizdat was secured after Maiakovskii's appeal that "the extreme revolutionary movements in art do not yet have their own journal. . . . We cannot obtain private capital . . . since we are ideologically a communist group" (cited in Taylor, *Art and Literature under the Bolsheviks,* vol. 1, p. 177).

66. Taylor, *Art and Literature under the Bolsheviks,* vol. 1, pp. 92–93.

67. One has the sense that the revolutionary generation, many of whom had shared experiences of persecution under the tsar, European exile, and the insecurities of the Revolution itself, sustained a generational solidarity that made it possible to disagree intensely on an ideological level without this causing persecutory animosities on the personal level. For the younger generation, however, solidarity was imagined more abstractly—as a "class," or as the

Soviet "people"—and brutality against the sanctioned "enemy" tended to be more extreme. Younger artists appear to have led the intolerant attacks against such enemies in the late 1920s, rather than merely going along with the authorities (see below, note 75).

68. Here is an example of the separation of party and state that was discussed in chapter 1. In the 1920s it was not mandatory for artists to join the party, nor was it the rule. A division of labor was accepted between artists or technical experts and the party leadership. The overlap of membership between artists/experts and the party increased during the First Five Year Plan, as the postrevolutionary generation, which had new and different training, came of age.

69. "Art is a powerful means of infecting those around us with ideas, feelings, and moods. Agitation and propaganda acquire particular acuity and effectiveness when they are clothed in the attractive and mighty forms of art" (Lunacharskii, cited in Bowlt, ed., *Russian Art of the Avant-Garde,* pp. 184–185). The revolution needed art, as agitation and propaganda, and art needed the revolution, as a "grand social event" to "provide art with vast material" and "a new artistic soul" (Lunacharskii [1925], cited in ibid., p. 194).

70. Lunacharskii (1920), cited in ibid., p. 185.

71. Lunacharskii (1920), cited in Catherine Cooke, "Socialist Realist Architecture: Theory and Practice," in Bown and Taylor, eds., *Art of the Soviets,* p. 89. "All this work, entirely conscientious and important as it is, has the character of laboratory research. . . . The proletariat and the more cultivated sections of the peasantry did not live through any of the stages of European or Russian art, and they are at an entirely different stage of development" (ibid.).

72. Cited in ibid.

73. In the early 1920s, "Russian modernists abandoned all opposition to the modernization of life effected by industrialization and mass production, and began to assume the functions of oil and engine in the machinery of progress" (Gassner, "The Constructivists," p. 299).

74. Again, I am indebted to Osborne's *Politics of Time* for this argument.

75. Recent scholarship argues that the artists, not the political leaders, most vociferously called for a cessation of cultural autonomy and a unity of cultural line. Charlotte Douglas goes quite far in exonerating everyone but the artists themselves: "Until the mid-1920s, the Party resisted the insistent demand from literary and art groups to endorse a genuine official style. In a decree of June 1925,

however, it finally capitulated, supporting the goal of a culture that was specifically proletarian" (Douglas, "Terms of Transition," in *The Great Utopia*, p. 454). In the context of renewed class warfare in the late 1920s, artists became stridently intolerant of difference, with the journal *Novy Lef* in the lead: "It must be clear that *Novy Lef* was not only sensitive to the new demands for 'class vigilance' in the field of art but that it played a leading role in promulgating that theme—at a time when the Party leadership was by no means committed to that policy" (Taylor, *Art and Literature under the Bolsheviks*, vol. 1, p. 105). My argument is not that it was wrong to consider the class basis of culture, but that it would have been better considered had historical time not been understood as a cosmology of class struggle.

76. As I have worked primarily with English translations of the Russian-language sources, I do not know how carefully (or whether at all) a distinction has been made by the translators between the Russian words *avangard* and *vangard*—or whether the words were used so interchangeably that it does not matter. Bowlt (who has spent much time with the original sources) observes that during World War I, the terms *avant-garde* and *arrière-garde* came into general use in Europe in their original military sense; they were thus part of everyday language (Bowlt and Matich, introduction to *Laboratory of Dreams*, p. 3).

77. Bowlt notes that "avant-garde" was used only intermittently before the Revolution (by Khlebnikov, Malevich, Maiakovskii) and even more rarely by postrevolutionary artists (Filonov and Kakabadze). See Bowlt and Matich, introduction to *Laboratory of Dreams*, pp. 3–5.

78. The term "Russian avant-garde" was applied systematically only after the fact; it was codified by Camilla Gray in her pioneering account, published in 1962, *The Great Experiment: Russian Art 1863–1922* (the later edition, which I cite here, has the title *The Russian Experiment in Art*). This book set the logic of the discourse, connecting Russian artistic modernism to developments in Western Europe. In the 1960s, Soviet artists rediscovered the avant-garde of the twenties, often through Western publications. By the decade of the 1980s, over 100 exhibitions were devoted to "Russian avant-garde art" in Europe, the United States, Russia, and Japan (see Bowlt and Matich, introduction to *Laboratory of Dreams*, p. 5). Because the periodization of the "Russian" avant-garde straddled the political divide of the Bolshevik Revolution, it tended to depoliticize this movement, ignoring the artists' active engagement in revolutionary practice. Because the avant-garde moment was seen to end with the end of the Civil War period and the consolidation of Soviet power, the implica-

tion was that avant-gardism and socialism were incompatible. Renato Poggioli comes to a similar conclusion, equating collectivism with totalitarianism: "Avant-garde art is by its nature incapable of surviving not only the persecution, but even the protection or the official patronage of a totalitarian state and a collective society " (Renato Poggioli, *The Theory of the Avant-Garde*, trans. Gerald Fitzgerald [Cambridge: Harvard University Press, 1968], p. 95). This Cold War presumption has been overturned by revisionist scholarship since the late 1980s, cited in this chapter. My argument should not be seen as a return to the Cold War prejudice, despite the fact that I criticize the cultural avant-garde for submitting to a particular political cosmology. Indeed, I consider the cultural avant-garde in the West to be just as vulnerable to the criticism of presuming historical progress, but here the result has been to reduce avant-garde practice to fashion's repetitive gesture of the "new," as art, like commodities, is endowed with built-in obsolescence. The betrayal of the critical gesture of temporal interruption is arguably greater in the Western case, where political engagement is often not even the intent.

79. Egbert reminds us of this fact, noting that "in the *Communist Manifesto* Marx and Engels had carefully written: 'the Communists do not form a separate party opposed to other working class parties," even if the manifesto clearly positions the proletariat at the "head" of the revolutionary movement that advances history through class warfare. Donald D. Egbert, "The Idea of 'Avant-Garde" in Art and Politics," *American Historical Review* 73, no. 2 (December 1967), p. 354.

80. Lenin uses the term *"avangard"* in quotation marks. He seems to have preferred the Russian word *peredovoe*, which he uses in this text as an adjective to describe the leading "detachment" (*otriad*) or "fighter" (*borets*) of the revolutionary class. The official English translation (authorized by the party) obscures these distinctions by rendering both *avangard* and *peredovoe* as "vanguard." V. I. Lenin, "Chto Delat?," in *Sochineniia* [Works], vol. 5 (Moscow: State Publisher of Political Literature, 1946), pp. 321–494. Compare with V. I. Lenin, *What Is to Be Done?* (New York: International Publishers, 1969).

81. They are in Russian, English, and German, but not in French, Italian, and Spanish, where one term is applied to both culture and politics.

82. See Linda Nochlin, "The Invention of the Avant-Garde: France, 1830–80," in Thomas B. Hess and John Ashbery, eds., *Avant-Garde Art* (London: Collier-Macmillan, 1968), p. 5.

83. When the Germans resumed fighting in the spring of 1918, Lenin retreated seriously from his earlier anti-statist comments, a change in the discourse of the political vanguard that may explain a new intensity in the artists' public criticism of state control—in turn prompting the party to crack down on anarchist intellectual and cultural activity, particularly in the cities. In March 1918, Tatlin published an appeal in the newspaper *Anarkhiia* (Anarchy), urging "all my confederates" to "embark on the path of anarchism" (cited in Gassner, "The Constructivists," p. 302). Malevich wrote in the same newspaper: "Whenever a state is being built, a prison will be erected once the state is there. . . . [The Revolution must] destroy all foundations of the old so that states will not rise from the ashes" (cited in ibid., p. 304; from March to July 1918, Malevich contributed frequently to *Anarkhiia*). Maiakovskii declared in March 1918 that "futurism" was the aesthetic counterpoint of "anarchism," and that only a cultural "revolt of the psyche" would "liberate workers from the constraints of obsolete art" (cited from the first and only issue of *Gazeta futuristov* [Futurists' Newspaper] in ibid., p. 303).

84. Still in Russia the artistic "avant-garde" refers to this particular moment in history and not, as in the West, to the ever-new fashion of artistic radicalism.

85. That this progress was conceived by party theoreticians as "dialectical" does not alter the argument made here. Rather, dialectics became a convenient discourse for maintaining the myth of continuous progress despite apparent setbacks.

86. Trotsky, *Literature and Revolution* (1923), cited in Boris Thomson, *Lot's Wife and the Venus of Milo: Conflicting Attitudes to the Cultural Heritage in Modern Russia* (New York: Cambridge Press, 1978), p. 62. In fairness, Trotsky in this text described the Russian avant-garde as an exception, describing it as a prevision of history's imminent political crisis within the sphere of art. But he believed this visionary power was limited; it would provide "vital sprouts" for future development only when adapted and transformed by a culturally mature working class—in universal, not class terms (a "proletarian art" would "never exist" because the period of proletarian dictatorship was transitory). Trotsky's position after his exile to Mexico (stated in the document written in collaboration with André Breton and Diego Rivera in 1938, "Towards a Free Revolutionary Art") returned to the idea of the artist as a visionary seer, but here it was used to argue unconditionally for the political justification of artistic freedom.

87. See Osborne, *The Politics of Time*. I believe Osborne is correct in describing Walter Benjamin's concept of revolutionary time as "phenomenally lived" rupture, the interruption of daily life, hence fundamentally different from the cosmological temporality that marks the Hegelian-Marxian conception—which was also Lenin's, of course, and that of the vanguard party. But it is problematic to equate, as Osborne does, Benjamin's conception of time with the temporality of the avant-garde—problematic because this theoretical distinction ignores real history. Osborne writes that the Benjaminian experience of the "now" ("now-being" he calls it, in a dubiously Heideggerian move) is "a form of avant-garde experience. For the avant-garde is not that which is historically most advanced in the sense that . . . it has the most history behind it" (ibid., p. 150). But, alas, this is precisely how the avant-garde has understood itself.

88. See Susan Buck-Morss, "Aesthetics and Anaesthetics: Walter Benjamin's Artwork Reconsidered," *October* 62 (Fall 1992), pp. 3–41. See also below, chapter 3.

89. Cf. Bois's distinction between the "Brechtian" Lissitzky, who presents the spectator with a riddle which it is up to him or her to resolve, and the "Stalinist" Lissitzky, who tries to convey "a revolutionary content by means of the cathartic illusionism upon which the traditional [art] was based." Yve-Alain Bois, "El Lissitzky: Radical Reversibility," *Art in America* (April 1988), p. 167.

90. It is thus misleading to speak of an avant-garde "tradition," as if such practices could produce their own historical continuum. I part company here from, e.g., Theodor Adorno and Clement Greenberg, for whom (in Greenberg's words) avant-garde artists, retaining their "personal autonomy" from political parties and their "original talents," work to develop the "inner logic" of their art. For Greenberg, painters "catch up" with the avant-garde artists who are in the lead of a historical continuum that keeps "moving," while the "rear-guard" is occupied by "kitsch," i.e., popular and commercial, "low" art (Tin Pan Alley and Hollywood). These themes are developed in Clement Greenberg, *Art and Culture: Critical Essays* (Boston: Beacon Press, 1961).

91. Cf. Ivan Kudriashev, a pupil of Malevich, who said of his own work in the mid-twenties: "Painting . . . ceases to be an abstract construction of color and form and becomes a realistic expression of our contemporary perception of space" (cited in John E. Bowlt, "Beyond the Horizon," in *Kasimir Malewitsch zum 100. Geburtstag* [Cologne: Galerie Gmurzynska, 1978], p. 248).

92. Anatolii Lunacharskii (1922), cited in Taylor, *Art and Literature under the Bolsheviks*, vol. 1, p. 177.

93. Taylor, *Art and Literature under the Bolsheviks*, vol. 1, p. 124. "Constructivism . . . cannot be said to have fulfilled its programme of transforming the three-dimensional

environment or of influencing to any real extent the production processes of industry" (ibid., p. 133).

94. Malevich, cited in Anatolii Strigalev, "Nonarchitects in Architecture," p. 672. This independence from "naked utilitarianism" made architecture one of the arts: "Thus I understand *all the arts as activity free from all economic and practical ideologies*" (emphasis added). Whereas technical products were "things" the construction of which improved in time—"a cart, a carriage, a locomotive and an airplane are a chain of unconsidered possibilities and tasks"—art "can call its creations *finished works* . . . since their execution is absolute, timeless, and unchanging" (Malevich, cited in ibid., pp. 672–673).

95. *Lef*, no. 1, cited (without date) in Taylor, *Art and Literature under the Bolsheviks*, vol. 1, p. 180.

96. Kazimir Malevich, "Notes on Architecture," cited (without date) in *The Great Utopia*, pp. 672–673.

97. This process of the collectivization of the imagination, aided by illustrated magazines and periodicals, was international and indeed cosmopolitan. Lines of influence (and later friendship) flowed from Le Corbusier's atelier in Paris to the Bauhaus in Weimar to VKhUTEMAS in Moscow, as they did from Malevich to Mondrian and Chaplin to Eisenstein.

98. Gassner, "The Constructivists," p. 299. Gassner describes this supplement in terms of "surplus value."

99. Paradigmatic of this attitude is Lissitzky's letter to Malevich of 1919 describing his architectural models, or Prouns: "Our lives are now being built on a new communist foundation, solid as reinforced concrete, and this is for all the nations on earth. On such a foundation—thanks to the Prouns [his series of drawings of "interchange stations between painting and architecture"]—monolithic communist towns will be built, in which the inhabitants of the world will live." Cited in Lissitzky-Küppers, *El Lissitzky*, p. 21. The fact remains, however, that Lissitzky's Prouns were *not* architectural blueprints but rather drawings meant to *inspire* real construction according to a certain vision, the merits of which, had the future of society remained an open category, might have been debated.

100. See Hans Jürgen Syberberg, *Hitler, a Film from Germany*, trans. Joachim Neugroschel (New York: Farrar, Straus and Giroux, 1982), and Paul Virilio, *War and Cinema: The Logistics of Perception*, trans. Patrick Camiller (London: Verso, 1989).

101. See Boris Groys, *Gesamtkunstwerk Stalin: Die gespaltene Kultur in der Sowjetunion*, trans. from Russian by Gabriele Leupold (Munich: Carl Hanser Verlag, 1988). Groys makes this argument in full acknowledgment of the fact that many of the avant-garde artists were persecuted under Stalin. The toll in lives and careers was high. Maiakovskii (posthumously honored by Stalin) committed suicide in 1930. Filonov was persecuted constantly during the 1930s, and his school of analytical art was crushed. Filonov's student Vasilii Kuptsov was harassed by the state and committed suicide in 1935. Malevich was arrested for a time in 1930 (he died in 1935 just before being notified that his request for a pension had been turned down). Vsevolod Meierkhold was arrested in 1939. Gustav Klutsis was arrested in 1938 and died in a prison camp in Kazakhstan in 1944. Punin was arrested in the war and died in a prison camp in 1953.

102. Note that the argument here concerns art and politics, which are viewed as two forms of cultural production. It does not equate art with what ought properly to be termed "aesthetics," i.e., a form of cognition as "perception through feeling" (see also below, chapter 3).

103. Lenin, *What Is to Be Done?*, p. 167.

104. Stites, *Revolutionary Dreams*, p. 42.

105. See above, chapter 1, HYPERTEXT: FRENCH REVOLUTION.

106. This criticism does not rule out economic planning as socialist policy. It only means that the plan cannot be articulated and executed as tyranny over future *time*. Guidelines, goals, and projections are necessary for any collective endeavor, but, in socialist form, they ought to facilitate democratic participation rather than preventing it and facilitating instead control by the leaders.

107. Walter Benjamin, *Gesammelte Schriften*, vol. 5: *Das Passagen-Werk*, ed. Rolf Tiedemann (Frankfurt: Suhrkamp Verlag, 1982), p. 596.

108. Sigmund Freud, *The Interpretation of Dreams*, trans. and ed. James Strachey (New York: Avon Books, 1965), note p. 84.

109. Nadezhda Krupskaia, cited in Nina Tumarkin, *Lenin Lives! The Lenin Cult in Soviet Russia* (Cambridge: Harvard University Press, 1983), p. 78.

110. Tumarkin, *Lenin Lives!*, p. 162.

111. Forty days is the traditional number on which prayers are said for the dead in the Russian Orthodox church (see ibid., p. 176).

112. Stalin, cited in Vladislav Todorov, *Red Square, Black Square: Organon for Revolutionary Imagination* (Albany: State University of New York Press, 1995), p. 143.

113. Stalin, cited in Nigel Moore, "The Myth of Stalin: The Psychodynamics of Its Utopian Ideals," *Russian History* 11, nos. 2–3 (Summer-Fall 1984), p. 290.

114. Nadezhda Krupskaia, cited in Tumarkin, *Lenin Lives!*, p. 177. Krupskaia never visited the mausoleum.

115. Cited in Tumarkin, *Lenin Lives!*, p. 202.

116. Ibid., p. 204.

117. Cited in Frederick Starr, *Melnikov: Solo Architect in a Mass Society* (Princeton: Princeton University Press, 1978), p. 80, and Gérard Conio, *Le Constructivisme russe*, vol. 2 (Lausanne: L'Âge d'homme, 1987), p. 82.

118. Starr, *Melnikov*, p. 81.

119. Leonid Krasin, cited in Tumarkin, *Lenin Lives!*, pp. 19 and 181.

120. Report of the Funeral Commission, cited in ibid., p. 183.

121. Kazimir Malevich (1924), cited in ibid., p. 190.

122. Tumarkin, *Lenin Lives!*, p. 192.

123. Shchusev, president of the Moscow Architectural Society in 1922, had been involved in plans for the restoration of Moscow, and was chief architect of the 1923 Agricultural and Industrial Exhibition in Moscow (ibid., p. 295n). That neoclassicism became part of revolutionary artistic style has been argued by Katerina Clark in "The Avant-Garde and the Retrospectivists as Players in the Evolution of Stalinist Culture," in John E. Bowlt and Olga Matich, eds., *Laboratory of Dreams: The Russian Avant-Garde and Cultural Experiment* (Stanford: Stanford University Press, 1996), p. 269 and passim. Trotsky in 1923 spoke of (neo-) classicism as a yearning for stable forms following the period of revolutionary newness.

124. Starr, *Melnikov*, p. 83. "When the first glass panels failed to fit, new ones had to be unceremoniously cut from the plate windows of the restaurant 'The Ravine'" (ibid.).

125. Boris Zbarskii, cited in Tumarkin, *Lenin Lives!*, pp. 195–196.

126. Andrei Platonov, *Kotlovan* (1928–1930), cited and trans. in Ayleen Teskey, *Platonov and Fyodorov: The Influence of Christian Philosophy on a Soviet Writer* (Amersham, England: Avebury Publishing Company, 1982), p. 127.

127. Stalin was "the Lenin of today" (Tumarkin, *Lenin Lives!*, p. 253). Future time was collapsed into the present; the socialist utopia was now.

128. Todorov, *Red Square, Black Square*, pp. 14 and 165.

129. Ibid., p. 146. "P.S. In 1990 after extensive demonstrations the mausoleum in Sofia was assaulted . . . [and the Dimitrov mummy] secretly removed through underground passages and solemnly given last honors and buried" (ibid.).

130. See the film by Mark Lewis and Laura Mulvey, *Disgraced Monuments*, 1992.

131. Ilya Zbarski[i] (son of Boris Zbarskii, who worked on the body of Lenin) and Samuel Hutchinson, *A l'ombre du mausolée: une dynastie d'embaumeurs* (Paris: Solin, actes sud, 1997), p. 194.

132. Ibid., pp. 193–199.

133. "New Russia Plumbs Soul in Vain for a Vision," *New York Times* (March 31, 1998), p. A6.

134. Zbarskii and Hutchinson, *A l'hombre du mausolée*, p. 202.

135. Annette Michelson, "Reading Eisenstein Reading *Capital*," part 1, *October* 2 (1976), p. 119.

136. Vance Kepley, Jr., "*Intolerance* and the Soviets: A Historical Investigation," in Richard Taylor and Ian Christie, eds., *Inside the Film Factory: New Approaches to Russian and Soviet Cinema* (New York: Routledge, 1991), p. 56. Rather than censoring the film, the Cinema Committee added their own prologue: "Hear ye, hear ye, O people! . . . Beyond your life in the distant depths of history you will see a broad road that the human race has been following for thousands of years. . . . From the great old mountain that we call life the familiar flows before you and, merging into the rapid change of days, leads unexpectedly to the Soviets. The 'Soviets'—that is our word. What does it mean? In the beautiful valley of life. At the foot of the mountain of history, creating nobody knows what. With passionate faith and the iron strength of conviction. Spread by the magic cauldron of the Revolution—the Soviets! And, looking back across the threshold, remembering the road that mankind has taken, you record in a book and relate to others this last tale of our long enslavement. A tale of basest flattery and the trading of souls. Of the mire and slime and rottenness, from which we emerged with pain and torment towards the radiant Soviets: towards our temples of labour and liberty, through which we shall resurrect everything. The Soviets! The Soviets!—the earth hums. The road of the Soviets—the Soviets are our salvation!!!" Cited in ibid., pp. 58–59.

137. Sergei Eisenstein, cited in Yuri Tsivian, *Early Cinema in Russia and Its Cultural Reception*, trans. Alan Bodger, foreword Tom Gunning, ed. Richard Taylor (New York: Routledge, 1994), p. 62.

138. Mikhail Yampolsky [Iampolskii], "In the Shadow of Monuments," in Nancy Condee, ed., *Soviet Hieroglyphics: Visual Culture in Late Twentieth-Century Russia* (Bloomington: Indiana University Press, 1995), p. 106.

139. James Goodwin, *Eisenstein, Cinema, and History* (Urbana: University of Illinois Press, 1993), p. 84.

140. Yampolsky, "In the Shadow of Monuments," pp. 109–110. Iampolskii has in mind Walter Benjamin's observations on the psycho-social effects of the inflation of German currency during the Weimar Republic, and how it anticipated the advent of fascism. Benjamin wrote in 1926: "Beyond doubt: a secret connection exists between the measure of goods and the measure of life, which is to say, between money and time. When [an inflated] currency is in use, a few million units of which are insignificant, life will have to be counted in seconds, rather than years, if it is to appear a respectable sum. And it will be frittered away like a bundle of bank notes." Walter Benjamin, "One-Way Street," in *Reflections: Essays, Aphorisms, Autobiographical Writings,* ed. and intro. Peter Demetz, trans. Edmund Jephcott (New York: Harcourt Brace Jovanovich, 1979), p. 87.

141. See below, chapter 5.

142. Yampolsky, "In the Shadow of Monuments," p. 101.

143. Ibid. Karl Schlögel notes: "The argument that the water table and ground quality on the banks of the Moscow River could not have 'stood up' to such a building seems to have been thought up retrospectively" (Schlögel, "Shadow of an Imaginary Tower," in *Naum Gabo and the Competition for the Palace of Soviets: Moscow, 1931–1933* [Berlin: Berlinische Galerie, 1992], p. 181).

144. Schlögel, "Shadow of an Imaginary Tower," p. 177.

145. Cited in Igor Golomstock, *Totalitarian Art in the Soviet Union, the Third Reich, Fascist Italy, and the People's Republic of China,* trans. Robert Chandler (London: Collins Harvill, 1990), p. 148.

146. When GINKhUK was closed in 1926, Malevich requested permission for this trip, which included exhibitions of his work. He spent time in Warsaw, Berlin (where he worked on a suprematist film with Hans Richter), and the Bauhaus in Dessau (where he met with Gropius, Moholy-Nagy, and others).

147. Interpretations by art historians are highly charged, as the legitimating coherence of their own disciplinary narrations is at stake in the meaning of Malevich's "great break." I am not competent to judge the controversy—nor even to comment on why the art historians describe Malevich's move as a "great break" (*velikii perelom*), a term coined by Stalin in 1929 to describe the cultural revolution

that he launched in that year, affecting all workers in cultural production, from artists to academicians. I have deferred here to the scholarship of recognized experts on Malevich such as Douglas and Marcadé. Douglas stresses the veiled political protest in these paintings, but comments also that the new peasant pictures "supplied socially and politically acceptable work" which, falsely dated, was "salable to government collections" in the USSR: see Charlotte Douglas, *Kazimir Malevich* (New York: Harry N. Abrams, 1994), pp. 34–35. Valentin Marcadé reads the second series of peasant paintings unequivocally as expressing compassion for the "crucifixion of traditional peasant civilization" caused by mechanization and dekulakization; see his article in Jean-Claude Marcadé, ed., *Cahier Malévich no. 1* (Lausanne: L'Âge d'homme, 1983), p. 12. Douglas notes that Malevich was "a profound believer" (*Malevich,* p. 114), although his spiritualism was metaphysical rather than orthodox. Marcadé reminds us that Malevich never took part in the official rites of the church (*Cahier Malévich no. 1,* p. 14). Several authors note that armless and faceless figures were prevalent in the work of Western European artists at the time: The connection of Malevich to the surrealist de Chirico can be documented; the armless motif appears in Matisse as well (where it has no socially critical meaning).

148. The geometrically drawn figures of the peasant paintings were still recognizably "futurist" and even "suprematist," as Fauc\hereau has emphasized (Serge Fauc\hereau, *Malevich* [New York: Rizzoli, 1992], p. 35). In 1930 Malevich wrote to his friend Kirill Shutko (who was a member of the Communist Party Central Committee): "soon the Brodskys [AKhRR artists] will declare that we [Tatlin, Filonov, himself] are kulaks" (Douglas, *Malevich,* p. 36). Shutko could not protect Malevich from arrest later that year (and was himself arrested in 1938).

149. The show then moved to Kiev, and Malevich traveled with it. In 1928–1930 he went monthly to Kiev to teach art history and published frequently in two Ukrainian reviews, *Nova generatsiia* (New Generation) and *Avangard* (Avant-Garde), which were still receptive to his "futurist" theories.

150. Douglas, *Malevich,* p. 24.

151. Ibid.

152. Ibid., p. 118.

153. Cited in Fauc\hereau, *Malevich,* p. 28.

154. The significance of the beard in Russian orthodoxy was its symbolic meaning, representing the dignity of man created in the image of God (Peter the Great had decreed

shaving off beards as a way of becoming Western). See Marcadé, ed., *Cahier Malévich no. 1,* pp. 10–11.

155. This is Douglas's interpretation (*Malevich,* p. 110). During dekulakization, priests were widely treated as equivalents of kulaks, and religious icons were symbolically taken out and shot (Sheila Fitzpatrick, *Stalin's Peasants: Resistance and Survival in the Russian Village after Collectivization* [New York: Oxford University Press, 1994], p. 61).

156. In a few cases, the inclusion of a railroad track or airplane does connect the peasant figures with modernity broadly understood, but these are background motifs, not directly related to the figures themselves.

157. Not only artists but writers, linguists, and even scientists could be guilty of formalism in a variety of ways, including "abstraction," "positivism," and "mechanism" (see Boris Gasparov, "Development or Rebuilding: Views of Academician T. D. Lysenko in the Context of the Avant-Garde," in Bowlt and Matich, eds., *Laboratory of Dreams,* pp. 133–150).

158. The article is republished in Clement Greenberg, *Art and Culture: Critical Essays* (Boston: Beacon Press, 1961), pp. 3–21; and in *Clement Greenberg: The Collected Essays and Criticism,* ed. John O'Brian, vol. 1 (Chicago: University of Chicago Press, 1986).

159. Serge Guilbaut, *How New York Stole the Idea of Modern Art: Abstract Expressionism, Freedom, and the Cold War,* trans. Arthur Goldhammer (Chicago: University of Chicago Press, 1987), pp. 2 and 11.

160. The beginning of this story has already been told: the fact that Malevich first showed his groundbreaking suprematist painting *Black Square* at "The Last Futurist Exhibition, 0.10," in 1915, calling it the originary point zero of a system of coordinates charting a new cosmic age; the fact that his UNOVIS collective made a bid for suprematism's position as *the* revolutionary art. See above, section 2.1.

161. See Guilbaut, *How New York Stole the Idea of Modern Art,* pp. 158–160 and passim.

162. What Malevich understood as a revolutionary break *out* of time into eternity had become an eternal value within historical time: "Ad Reinhardt . . . with his black square paintings of the late 1950s and their conscious reference to Malevich and Suprematism, arrived at what he termed 'timeless' art" (see the catalogue *American Art in the Twentieth Century: Painting and Sculpture, 1913–1993,* ed. Christos M. Joachimides and Norman Rosenthal [Munich: Prestel, 1993], p. 15).

163. Groys observes that this "success" would have been judged by the early revolutionaries themselves as a failure: "As they understood it, the artists of the Russian avant-garde were producing not objects of aesthetic consumption but projects or models for a total restructuring of the world on new principles, to be implemented by collective actions and social practice in which the difference between consumer and producer, artist and spectator, work of art and object of utility, and so on, disappeared. The fact that these avant-garde projects are hung in present-day museums as traditional works of art, where they are viewed in the traditional light, signals the ultimate defeat of the avant-garde, not its success. The Russian avant-garde lost its historical position: in fact, the true spirit of the Russian avant-garde was more aptly reflected by its place in the locked storerooms of Soviet museums, to which it was consigned as a consequence of its historical defeat, but from which it continued to exercise an influence on the victorious rulers as a hidden menace." Boris Groys, "The Birth of Socialist Realism from the Spirit of the Russian Avant-Garde," in Bowlt and Matich, eds., *Laboratory of Dreams,* p. 195.

164. From Debord's final film, *In girum imus nocte et consumimur igni: A Film,* cited in Thomas F. McDonough, "Rereading Debord, Rereading the Situationists," *October* 79 (Winter 1997), p. 11.

CHAPTER 3
COMMON SENSE

1. Cited in Nina Tumarkin, *Lenin Lives! The Lenin Cult in Soviet Russia* (Cambridge: Harvard University Press, 1983), p. 169.

2. Parts of this chapter draw from my essay "Aesthetics and Anaesthetics: Walter Benjamin's Artwork Essay Reconsidered" (1992), reprinted in *October: The Second Decade* (Cambridge: MIT Press, 1998).

3. Philosophers have quite persistently refused to conflate the brain with the "mind" (alias ego, *âme, Seele,* soul, subject, *Geist*). Descartes gave the soul protection from the "body machine" of the brain-nerves-muscles by locating it in "a certain extremely small gland" suspended in the middle of the brain (see *The Passions of the Soul*). Kant's transcendental consciousness of the self managed to ignore the brain from the start.

4. Contemporary brain research, while impressive in its application of new technologies that allow us to "see" the brain in ever greater detail, has suffered from too little philosophical and theoretical radicalism, while philosophy

risks speaking in a language so archaic, given the new empirical discoveries of neuroscience, that it relegates itself to scholastic irrelevance.

5. If the "center" of this system is not in the brain but, rather, on the body's surface, then subjectivity, far from being bounded within the biological body, plays the role of mediator between inner and outer sensations, the images of perception and those of memory. For this reason, Freud situated consciousness on the surface of the body, decentered from the brain (which he was willing to view as nothing more than large and evolved nerve ganglia).

6. Sergei Luchishkin, *I Love Life Very Much,* cited in Charlotte Douglas, "Terms of Transition: The *First Discussional Exhibition* and the Society of Easel Painters," in *The Great Utopia: The Russian and Soviet Avant-Garde, 1915–1932* (New York: Guggenheim Museum, 1992), pp. 456–457.

7. Terry Eagleton, *The Ideology of the Aesthetic* (Cambridge, Mass.: Basil Blackwell, 1990), p. 13. Eagleton is dealing with the historical birth of aesthetics as a modern discourse (specifically, in the work of the mid-eighteenth-century German philosopher Alexander Baumgarten), and rightly notes the political implications of this anti-Cartesian focus on the "dense, swarming territory" outside of the mind that comprises "nothing less than the whole of our sensate life together," describing it as the "first stirrings of a primitive materialism—of the body's long inarticulate rebellion against the tyranny of the theoretical" (ibid.).

8. Sir Gordon Gordon-Taylor and E. W. Walls, *Sir Charles Bell: His Life and Times* (London: E. & S. Livingstone, 1958), p. 212. In Bell's time, medicine itself was still considered an "art." Moreover, in a time before photography, when the scientific drawing was necessary for recording documentary proof, the artist's work was indispensable for knowledge. During the course of the nineteenth century, medicine was professionalized as a science, whereas art, chased from the field of verisimilitude by technologies of photographic replication, became cordoned off as a separate realm of bourgeois culture and institutionalized within museums. Art that escaped this official space was threatened on the other side with being absorbed into the phantasmagoric field of entertainment, as a part of the commodity world.

9. Cited in ibid., p. 116.

10. Sir Charles Bell, cited in Leo M. Zimmerman and Ilza Veith, *Great Ideas in the History of Surgery,* 2d ed., rev. (New York: Dover, 1967), p. 415.

11. "It was a strange thing to feel my clothes stiff with blood, and my arms powerless with the exertion of using the knife; and more extraordinary still, to find my mind calm amidst such a variety of suffering. But to give one of these objects access to your feelings was to allow yourself to be unmanned [sic] for the performance of a duty. It was less painful to look upon the whole, than to contemplate one." Bell, cited in ibid., p. 414.

12. Later in his life Bell was to endow this resistance with at least a weak theological meaning, as he described his aversion to animal vivisection. See Gordon-Taylor and Walls, *Sir Charles Bell,* p. 111.

13. Walter Benjamin, "The Storyteller" (1936), in *Illuminations,* ed. Hannah Arendt, trans. Harry Zohn (New York: Schocken Books, 1969), p. 84.

14. Walter Benjamin, "One Way Street" (1926), in *Reflections: Essays, Aphorisms, Autobiographical Writings,* ed. Peter Demetz, trans. Edmund Jephcott (New York: Harcourt Brace Jovanovich, 1978), p. 93.

15. Mark Seltzer, *Bodies and Machines* (New York: Routledge, 1992), p. 157.

16. Walter Benjamin, *Charles Baudelaire,* trans. Harry Zohn (London: Verso, 1983), p. 114.

17. Ibid., p. 116.

18. Ibid., p. 133. Benjamin continues (quoting *Capital*): "'Every kind of capitalist production . . . has this in common [. . .] that it is not the workman that employs the instruments of labor, but the instruments of labor that employ the workman. But it is only in the factory system that this inversion for the first time acquires technical and palpable reality.'" (Ibid., p. 132.)

19. Ibid., p. 133.

20. Ibid.

21. Ibid., p. 143.

22. The construction of socialism was defined by Soviet engineers and managers as the "Americanization" of the means of production (Thomas P. Hughes, *American Genesis: A Century of Invention and Technological Enthusiasm, 1870–1970* [New York: Viking, 1989], p. 253). In 1924 Stalin declared "American efficiency" combined with "the Russian revolutionary sweep" to be "the essence of Leninism" (cited in ibid., p. 254).

23. Cf. Lenin's claim in justifying the introduction of "socialist" Taylorism: "The Russian is a bad worker compared with the people in advanced countries . . . [as a result of] the persistence of the hangover from serfdom. . . . The Taylor system, the last word of capitalism in this respect, like all capitalist progress, is a combination of the refined brutality of bourgeois exploitation and a number of the greatest scientific achievements in the field of ana-

lyzing mechanical motions during work, the elimination of superfluous and awkward motions. . . . The possibility of building socialism depends exactly upon our success in combining the Soviet power and the Soviet organization of administration with the up-to-date achievements of capitalism. We must organize in Russia the study and teaching of the Taylor system and systematically try it out and adapt it to our own ends." V. I. Lenin, "The Immediate Tasks of the Soviet Government," in *Selected Works,* 3 vols. (Moscow: Progress Publishers, 1977), vol. 2, pp. 592–593.

24. In the process of U.S. industrialization, the machines themselves were produced by skilled workers, whereas in the USSR the technological-industrial infrastructure was largely imported and the "proletarians," those who ran the machines, were recruited largely from the unskilled, peasant class. At the end of the nineteenth century, skilled industrial workers in the United States felt themselves threatened by the waves of new unskilled immigrants (like their Soviet counterparts, of peasant backgrounds) who were put to work by Taylorist methods on the assembly lines.

25. Taylor published *The Principles of Scientific Management* in 1911, describing the training of workers by means of time-motion studies to perform precise movements so as to produce at scientifically established, optimal speeds and quantities.

26. It was history, not industrialization, that was the alleged cause of mass exhaustion in Russia, due to the physical and psychic shocks of eight years of world war and civil war. Experts spoke of "mass neurasthenia," "mass skizoidisation," and "premature aging" (*iznoshennost*) on the part of the populace, a "great increase in the number of psychically bruised and worn-out people, tending to shrink into themselves, to become apathetic, or to lose the capacity for work." Cited in Toby Clark, "The 'New Man's Body: A Motif in Early Soviet Culture," in Matthew Cullerne Bown and Brandon Taylor, eds., *Art of the Soviets: Painting, Sculpture and Architecture in a One-Party State, 1917–1992* (Manchester: Manchester University Press, 1993), p. 46.

27. "As late as 1924 there were 1,400,000 unemployed, and of these only 24% had any vocational training. (Out of a population of 117 million, 78 million were still illiterate)." Kurt Johansson, *Aleksej Gastev: Proletarian Bard of the Machine Age* (Stockholm: Almqvist & Wiksell International, 1983), p. 106.

28. Taylorism had been introduced into eight Russian factories before World War I. In April 1918 the decision was made, despite the opposition of Russian trade unions,

to set Taylorist organizational goals for Soviet industry. The Central Institute of Labor published educational literature for workers and set up 1,700 outreach stations which trained half a million workers and 20,000 instructors before it was closed in 1938. Gastev called the Central Institute of Labor his last artistic creation. He and members of his family were arrested in Stalin's purges. See Richard Stites, *Revolutionary Dreams: Utopian Vision and Experimental Life in the Russian Revolution* (New York: Oxford University Press, 1989), p. 154 and passim; also Hughes, *American Genesis*, p. 261.

29. The goal of Gastev's institute was the production of the proletariat as new human beings whose mechanically attuned bodies would in turn produce the machines: "We are their lever, we are their breathing, their impulse" (from Gastev, "Poesia rabotsevo udara" [Poetry of the Factory Floor], 1918, cited in Johansson, *Aleksej Gastev,* p. 74). A 1969 film with this title showed rows of workers hammering in unison to the music of Dmitrii Shostakovich (ibid., p. 126).

30. Gastev (1918), cited in ibid., pp. 60, 61.

31. Gastev, cited in ibid., p. 69.

32. Johansson, *Aleksej Gastev,* p. 97. "Machinism is gradually saturating not only the purely industrial aspect of human life; it will fuse enterprises together, it will permeate all areas of everyday life, it will give rise to the mighty edifices which we boldly call machine" (Gastev [1918], cited in ibid., p. 62).

33. Gastev (1923), cited in ibid., p. 68.

34. See Buck-Morss, "Aesthetics and Anaesthetics," for a discussion of this phrase, coined by Walter Benjamin, and of the two meanings, bourgeois and original, of "aesthetics." Gastev's poetry can indeed be compared to that of the Italian futurists, whom Benjamin accused of "aestheticizing" politics in a fascistic sense. The poetry of both glorified the violent power of the new technologies. But whereas the pre-fascist Italian poets wrote ecstatically about the technologies of war, Gastev dreamed of world harmony, while justifying death along the way to this future goal. For Gastev, the path to the revolutionary utopia rides like a locomotive atop a multitude of those sacrificed in the process: "Corpses, dear, warm corpses. . . . / "Be our cross-ties; Hands, make more rails / . . . We shall dash along over you, blessed cross-ties." Aleksei Gastev, "The Bridge" (1918), trans. in Charles Rougle, "'Express': The Future According to Gastev," *Russian History/Histoire Russe* 11, nos. 2–3 (Summer-Fall 1984), p. 267. Those who cannot meet the test of machine precision are destroyed as "human rejects." "Forty thousand—get into a row. / Attention: eyes on the manometer—soldier. / Iron band of

gazes. / Test the line—fire. Shot down the line. Projectile trajectory—ten millimeters from foreheads. / Thirty foreheads licked off—human rejects" (Gastev, "A Packet of Orders" [1921], trans. in ibid., p. 268). Gastev's goal was a workforce with military precision, not a precision army—and even this vision was out of favor by the mid-thirties.

35. For research that rescues this aspect of early Russian cinema, specifically the legacy of the European theorists, see Mikhail Yampolsky [Iampolskii], "Kuleshov's Experiments and the New Anthropology of the Actor," in Richard Taylor and Ian Christie, eds., *Inside the Film Factory: New Approaches to Russian and Soviet Cinema* (New York: Routledge, 1991), pp. 31–50. Delsart had a "mania for the classification of the lexicography of mime . . . [and was] categorical . . . in his insistence on the extreme segmentation of gestures" (ibid., p. 33); D'Undine compared human beings to a dynamo "through which the rhythmic synaesthetic inductive impulses pass. Human emotion is expressed in external movement and . . . that movement can 'inductively' provoke in man the emotion that gave rise to the movement" (ibid., p. 32).

36. Turkin, a member with Kuleshov of the film school group, cited in ibid., p. 42.

37. Ibid., p. 44.

38. Worker at Magnitostroi, cited in Stephen Kotkin, *Magnetic Mountain: Stalinism as a Civilization* (Berkeley: University of California Press, 1995), p. 427n; also p. 94.

39. Although cinema history best remembers Kuleshov's experimentation in montage as "created geography" and "created man" (juxtaposing segments of unconnected space or parts of several human bodies in order to produce the effect of a coherent whole), he himself valued these rhythmic studies, contrasting the body movement of dance with the image movement of cinema ("a dance, filmed from one place—10 meters; a dance, filmed using montage—10 meters"), an exercise that anticipated the work in the 1930s of Hollywood musical director Busby Berkeley (see below, section 4.2, and Yampolsky, "Kuleshov's Experiments," p. 45).

40. See Vance Kepley, Jr., "Mr. Kuleshov in the Land of the Modernists," in Anna Lawton, ed., *The Red Screen: Politics, Society, Art in Soviet Cinema* (New York: Routledge, 1992), p. 143.

41. "In July 1923, a meeting of some 3,500 [Russian] workers was kept waiting for two hours before the speakers arrived to open it. An American journalist present . . . calculated on the spot for Kerzhentsev that the 7,000 man hours lost could have been used to build one or two air-planes. Kerzhentsev was electrified by this revelation. Within a few weeks he . . . founded the League of Time." Stites, *Revolutionary Dreams,* p. 156.

42. Ibid., pp. 156–158. "Even in the country, cows were 'tried' to determine who was responsible for low yields of milk. A virtual craze for efficiency erupted in the economy." The League of Time was dissolved in February 1926, its work declared accomplished (ibid., pp. 158–159).

43. "There were in fact two cults of Ford: an urban cult of 'fordism' among intellectuals and technical personnel that revered a system of efficient production and a rural and lower class cult of Ford himself as a man of magic who could, by means of his 'American' technique, release forces otherwise little understood by the peasant, a mechanical genius and an inventor rather than a master of large scale organization and a manager of space, people, and time." Ibid., p. 49.

44. Ibid., p. 148.

45. This is not to deny the dark side of the picture, the fact that during the period of collectivization and dekulakization the theme of "deliverance from backwardness" became a euphemism for peasant genocide (see Lynne Viola, *Peasant Rebels under Stalin: Collectivization and the Culture of Peasant Resistance* [New York: Oxford University Press, 1996]). Far from belittling this sinister side of the cosmology of backwardness, my point is that its hegemonic power was so great that it could be called upon to justify Stalin's peasant policies, which, in terms of physical suffering ("aesthetics" in the proper sense of the term), could *have* no justification.

46. Stites, *Revolutionary Dreams,* p. 148. "Henry Ford's *My Life* appeared in eight Soviet translated editions, four alone in 1924. . . . Enthusiastic notices and prefaces accompanied these books, and they became required reading for party members, economists, Taylorites, engineers, managers, and technical students. The words *fordizatsiya* and *teilorizatsiya* were common in Soviet towns and universities in the 1920s—both denoting good work habits. To some, Ford's conveyor belt was not only the model for the factory but for society as well." (Ibid.)

47. Ibid., pp. 148–149. Ford shared in the peasant's quasi-religious exaltation of machinery, which he called "the New Messiah" (ibid.).

48. Walter Benjamin, "Moscow," in *Reflections,* p. 124. "If you step through one of the high gateways . . . opening before you, broad and expansive, is a farmyard or a village, the ground is uneven, children ride about in sleighs, sheds for wood and tools fill the corners, trees stand here and

there, wooden staircases give the backs of houses, which look like city buildings from the front, the appearance of Russian farmhouses" (ibid., pp. 124–125).

49. Stites, *Revolutionary Dreams,* p. 163. Against this, Gastev wanted to end the "wildness" in work style and "lyrical disorder" of the people, teaching them to move with precision, like marching troops alert to their terrain (ibid., p. 153).

50. Kotkin, *Magnetic Mountain,* p. 61.

51. Ibid., p. 203.

52. The word *shok* imported from the West was not used.

53. Valentin Kataev, *Time, Forward!,* 1932 novel based on the author's firsthand experience at Magnitogorsk, cited in Stephen E. Hanson, *Time and Revolution: Marxism and the Design of Soviet Institutions* (Chapel Hill: University of North Carolina Press, 1997), p. 157. The novel pits abstract, scientific time against the lived experience of the working day as a collective effort which, if raised at any one point, would raise the tempo of the whole, "bringing the time of socialism closer."

54. Kotkin, *Magnetic Mountain,* p. 204.

55. Ibid., p. 213.

56. Ibid., p. 205.

57. Work was the means to revolutionary health. Bukharin wrote in 1928 that work provided the "armor of proletarian culture" as protection against "alien influences" (cited in Brandon Taylor, *Art and Literature under the Bolsheviks,* vol. 2: *Authority and Revolution, 1924–1932* [London: Pluto Press, 1992], p. 95).

58. The idea of green cities was in accord with the Marxist goal of eliminating the contradictions between country and city, as described by Karl Marx and Friedrich Engels in *The German Ideology* (1845, first published in 1932, by the Marx-Engels Institute in Moscow). This early text by Marx and Engels fueled the urbanist/anti-urbanist debate that began in the late twenties (see below).

59. S. Frederick Starr, *Melnikov: Solo Architect in a Mass Society* (Princeton: Princeton University Press, 1978), p. 171.

60. Starr, *Melnikov,* p. 171. The separate rooms included separate entries: "The relations between wife and husband, between two individuals are voluntary relations. As soon as these relations become a constraint imposed by the conditions of everyday life, they become a form of exploitation. What permits the women and men to be alone or not is the direct link with the outside." Cited in Anatole Kopp, "Housing for the Masses," in *Conference on the Origins of Soviet Culture,* May 1981, Working Paper no. 149

(Washington, D.C.: The Wilson Center, Kennan Institute for Advanced Russian Studies).

61. "He conceived the galleries as being fluid spaces, to be divided up informally by plants, hanging nets, and even portable glass partitions. Through such devices, the individual would gradually become collectivized without being subjected to overt force or to the more subtle coercion of the communal apartments of the day." Starr, *Melnikov,* p. 173.

62. Ibid., p. 176.

63. Ibid., pp. 176–177.

64. Ibid., p. 177.

65. Cited in ibid.

66. Ibid., p. 179. Melnikov spoke of the need to "rationalize the sun" (ibid.).

67. Ibid.

68. Ibid.

69. Ibid., p. 181.

70. Walter Benjamin, *Reflections: Essays, Aphorisms, Autobiographical Writings,* ed. Peter Demetz, trans. Edmund Jephcott (New York: Harcourt Brace Jovanovich, 1978), p. 93.

71. Cited in Richard Stites, *Revolutionary Dreams: Utopian Vision and Experimental Life in the Russian Revolution* (New York: Oxford University Press, 1989), p. 148.

72. See Teresa Brennan's original reading of Marx's theory of value as a theory of (natural) energy (in which "labourpower is precisely energy"), in her book *History after Lacan* (London: Routledge, 1993), chapter 4, particularly pp. 124–127. I am indebted to discussions with Brennan for this section.

73. Karl Marx, "Economic and Philosophical Manuscripts" (1844), in *Early Writings,* intro. Lucio Colletti, trans. Rodney Livingstone and Gregor Benton (New York: Vintage Books, 1975), p. 350. "This communism, as fully developed naturalism, equals humanism, as fully developed humanism equals naturalism; it is the *genuine* resolution of the conflict between man and nature, and between man and man, the true resolution of the conflict between existence and being, between objectification and self-affirmation, between freedom and necessity, between individual and species" (ibid., p. 348).

74. Riazanov was an internationally known Marx scholar who became head of the Marx-Engels Institute (IME) in 1921. He included non-party members on his staff, and was given the funds to create "the largest library in the

world on Marxism. With documents purchased in Western and Central Europe, IME also created a preeminent archive on Marx and the history of socialism. In the ten years of its existence, before the institute was merged with the Lenin Institute upon Riazanov's arrest, it published not only the largest extant scholarly edition of Marx and Engels but Russian editions ranging from the works of Hobbes, Diderot, Hegel, Ricardo, and Kautsky to those of Adam Smith." Michael David-Fox, *Revolution of the Mind: Higher Learning among the Bolsheviks, 1918–1929* (Ithaca: Cornell University Press, 1997), p. 63.

75. For this story see David-Fox, *Revolution of the Mind.*

76. They are seminal to the reception of Marx by the Frankfurt School (Theodor Adorno, Walter Benjamin, Erich Fromm, Max Horkheimer, Leo Löwenthal, Herbert Marcuse, etc.) as well as French existentialism (Alexander Kojève, Henri Lefebvre, Jean Paul Sartre, etc.), to give several particularly influential examples.

77. Georg Lukács, "Preface to the New Edition (1967)," in *History and Class Consciousness: Studies in Marxist Dialectics,* trans. Rodney Livingstone (Cambridge: MIT Press, 1968), p. xxxvi.

78. See above, section 2.1.

79. The metaphor of Kollontai, that sex was no more than a drink of water, shows a lack of utopian investment in this aspect of women's "liberation."

80. See Eric Naiman, *Sex in Public: The Incarnation of Early Soviet Ideology* (Princeton: Princeton University Press, 1997).

81. Alla Efimova, "A Prescription for Life: Sun, Air, and Water in Socialist Realism and Soviet Health Care," manuscript, p. 16.

82. Lunacharskii, referring to Marx's *18th Brumaire,* cited in ibid., p. 13.

83. Even before the Revolution, in the fiction writing of the rocket scientist Konstantin Tsiolkovskii, science is deployed for the overcoming of *stasis* ("death," "gravity") by *movement* ("life," "free space"). See Michael Holquist, "Tsiolkovsky as a Moment in the Prehistory of the Avant-Garde," in John E. Bowlt and Olga Matich, eds., *Laboratory of Dreams: The Russian Avant-Garde and Cultural Experiment* (Stanford: Stanford University Press, 1996), pp. 100–117.

84. Recall El Lissitzky's *Story of Two Squares,* which treats these suprematist geometric forms as human beings (above, section 2.1).

85. The talents of these artists were not always recognized by official culture. Russian animation was founded by Władysław Starewicz, a bookkeeper from Vilna, Poland, who moved his huge collection of butterflies and insects with him to the Moscow studios in 1912 and used it in stop-motion photography to make some of the earliest examples of animated films. Starewicz moved to Paris after the Bolshevik Revolution, where he eeked out a living in his own small studio. Soviet animation, like that in the West, languished (with a few notable successes) until sound film, which brought Vano's *Black and White,* based on a Maiakovskii poem about Cuba, and the work of the Leningrad-based animated filmmaker Tsekhanovskii, who, under studio pressure to reorganize along American lines, refused to compromise by adopting the more "efficient" Disney technologies. Tsekhanovskii collaborated with Dmitrii Shostakovich on a full-length animated cartoon comic opera, based on Pushkin's satirical poem *The Tale of the Priest and His Servant, Blockhead,* but his "opposition to the generally accepted industrialization, plus the increasing suspicion of formalism" on the part of both him and Shostakovich, prevented the film's completion. See Jay Leyda, *Kino: A History of the Russian and Soviet Film* (New York: Collier Books, 1960), pp. 66–67, 119, 274–275, 308–309.

86. Hubertus Gassner, "The Constructivists: Modernism on the Way to Modernization," trans. Jürgen Riehle, in *The Great Utopia: The Russian and Soviet Avant-Garde, 1915–1932* (New York: Guggenheim Museum, 1992), p. 318.

87. Christina Kiaer, "Rodchenko in Paris," *October* 75 (Winter 1996), p. 31. Rodchenko was referring to the objects in his Workers' Club: "Things become comprehending, become friends and comrades of the person, and person learns how to laugh and be happy and converse with things" (Rodchenko, cited in ibid.). Kiaer comments: "Presumably, things can 'converse with' people only through bodily sensations or through fantasy. The club as a Constructivist object cooperates with the body's movements. . . . Expanding and collapsing, encircling and extensive, folded in and disappearing, it is like the human body in its vulnerability. It offers its modern technological forms up to us, inviting us to project our human wishes and fantasies onto it and thus suggesting an alternative definition of the Constructivist object [not as the cold, rationalizing 'modernist nightmare' but] as the 'modernist dream' of the new forms of industrial modernity brought down to human scale." (Ibid., p. 31.)

88. Ibid., p. 8.

89. Ibid., p. 10. Kiaer provides a detailed argument that this disgust was ambivalent in the Freudian sense.

90. Ibid., p. 30n.

91. Rodchenko, cited in ibid., p. 15.

92. Olga Matich, "Remaking the Bed: Utopia in Daily Life," in Bowlt and Matich, eds., *Laboratory of Dreams,* p. 70. "Rodchenko himself designed a variety of beds of this sort" (ibid.) In such an environment, the anthropological type that in the United States today is called the "couch potato" had no place to take root.

93. Christina Lodder, *Russian Constructivism* (New Haven: Yale University Press, 1983), p. 135.

94. Matich, "Remaking the Bed," p. 60. The chest of drawers (*komod*), as the storer of unused things, was a quintessential petit-bourgeois commodity; see Svetlana Boym, *Common Places: Mythologies of Everyday Life in Russia* (Cambridge: Harvard University Press, 1994), pp. 150–157.

95. Matich, "Remaking the Bed," pp. 70–71. Theater sets were a way of propagating a utopian idea of the relationship between material objects and human beings that could not yet be realized, given the lack of capacity to mass-produce these objects.

96. Walter Benjamin, "Moscow" (1927), in *Reflections,* pp. 106–107.

97. Vladimir Papernyi, *Kultura "dva"* (Moscow, 1979; Ann Arbor: Ardis Publishers, 1985). Translations here are extracts from this book published in Vladimir Papernyi, "Movement—Immobility," in Alla Efimova and Lev Manovich, eds. and trans., *Tekstura: Russian Essays on Visual Culture* (Chicago: University of Chicago Press, 1993).

98. Ibid., pp. 56–57.

99. Ibid., p. 61. "Thus the man of Culture Two loses his mobility in geographical space, but as a sort of unusual compensation the culture sets apart special individuals who take upon themselves the heavy burden of travel [the geographic and flight expeditions of the 1930s] while relieving others of this necessity" (ibid.).

100. Ibid., p. 66.

101. "As late as 1933 Le Corbusier still thought that "in Russia everyone was mad about Deurbanism" (ibid., p. 63).

102. Brandon Taylor, *Art and Literature under the Bolsheviks,* vol. 2: *Authority and Revolution, 1924–1932* (London: Pluto Press, 1992), p. 162.

103. Tatlin (1932), cited in ibid., p. 163.

104. The word fuses Tatlin's name with the Russian word "to fly" (*letat'*).

105. "I have made it as an artist. . . . But I count upon my apparatus being able to keep a person in the air, I have taken into account the mathematical side, the resistance of the materials and the surface of the wings. We have to learn to fly with it in the air, just as we learn to swim in the water or ride a bicycle." Tatlin (1932), cited in Lodder, *Russian Constructivism,* p. 215. Although Tatlin gave a paper at the Soviet Ministry of Aviation, "his ideas were received with skepticism" (ibid., p. 300n).

106. Lodder, *Russian Constructivism,* p. 300n. This idea is similar to that of the painter Matiushin, who believed humans could regain their earlier optical capacity in the soles of their feet and back of their neck (see above, chapter 2).

107. Tatlin, cited in Lodder, *Russian Constructivism,* p. 214.

108. Vladimir Tatlin (1933), cited in Taylor, *Art and Literature under the Bolsheviks,* vol. 2, p. 163.

109. Tatlin, cited in Vasilii Rakitin, "The Artisan and the Prophet: Marginal Notes on Two Artistic Careers," in *The Great Utopia,* p. 35.

110. The Interstate Highway Act, passed in the 1950s in the United States, created a system intended for military defense.

111. "Fragen von Karl Eimermacher an Vadim Sidur" (February 1980), in *Vadim Sidur, Skulpturen und Graphiken: 28. August bis 21. September 1980* (Berlin: Kunstamt Charlottenburg, 1980), p. xxxv.

112. Ibid.

113. Ibid., p. xli. It was only in the 1960s that Sidur was exposed to the "Russian avant-garde" as a part of the story of the Western avant-garde.

114. Despite the remilitarization of cultural discourse during the renewed class war of the thirties, despite the regimented army parades before the Kremlin on public holidays, the utopian element of Nazi militarization was lacking. And yet the Soviet Union could be as disrespectful as any Western nation-state of the sovereignty of others, taking advantage of the terms of the Nazi-Soviet Non-Aggression Pact of 1939 to annex previously Russian territories in eastern Poland and the Baltic states. When Finland resisted Stalin's demands, he used force to attain them. Mass conscription for "defense" of the revolution was a basic Soviet institution.

115. Concentration of industry in the western USSR made it vulnerable to Germany's invading army. The focus of Soviet aviation on breaking records—the first landing at the North Pole, the first nonstop flight from Moscow to the United States, by pilots dubbed "Bolshevik knights of culture and progress"—were politically motivated, "aviation stunts that had little relevance to the needs of Soviet

defense and crippled Soviet military aviation unnecessarily in the early years of World War II" (Kendall E. Bailes, *Technology and Society under Lenin and Stalin: Origins of the Soviet Technical Intelligentsia, 1917–1941* [Princeton: Princeton University Press, 1978], pp. 388 and 405). "Moreover, the purges of 1936–37 of top political, economic, and military leaders caused a substantial prewar decline in industrial output" (Susan J. Linz, "Introduction: War and Progress in the USSR," in Linz, ed., *The Impact of World War II on the Soviet Union* [Totowa, N.J.: Rowman and Allanheld, 1985], p. 13).

116. "Although it seems to be true that the prewar structure of the Soviet economy lent itself to rapid conversion to war economy status, the changes in priorities, in demand patterns, and in the extent of labor mobilization indicate unambiguously that the prewar economy was *not* a 'war economy'" (James R. Millar, "Conclusion: Impact and Aftermath of World War II," in Linz, ed., *The Impact of World War II on the Soviet Union*, p. 286).

117. "The economic cost of World War II to the Soviet people . . . was equal to, and possibly even somewhat greater than, the total wealth created during the industrialization drive of the 1930s" (ibid., p. 283). "Unlike other major participants in the war, the Soviet Union lost territory, population and capital stock at the very beginning . . . and was obliged to fight a prolonged war with diminished capacity. Moreover [unlike the Allied powers who were still suffering from the Great Depression], the Soviet economy was fully employed at the outset of war and could not fall back upon excess capacity" (ibid., p. 284).

118. Social effects of the war not often considered are discussed in Linz, ed., *The Impact of World War II on the Soviet Union*, such as: strengthening the population's commitment to the Soviet system by coding it with patriotism (89); transforming the role of religion and creating a new Bible Belt (105); reversing the trend of social democratization within the party by strengthening the position of expert elites (177); causing severe demographic imbalance between the sexes that led to increased interethnic marriages and linguistic russification of the new generation (234).

119. "Soviet official sources report a total of 20 million lives lost in the war, about half of whom were military personnel. Total casualties have never been quoted officially. I have estimated them elsewhere at approximately 30 million—which is about 15 percent of the 1940 population" (Millar, "Conclusion," in Linz, ed., *The Impact of World War II on the Soviet Union*, p. 284).

120. *Vadim Sidur*, p. xxxv.

121. Ibid.

122. Cited in Walter Benjamin, *Gesammelte Schriften*, vol. 5: *Das Passagen-Werk*, ed. Rolf Tiedemann (Frankfurt: Suhrkamp Verlag, 1982), p. 609. Schuhl is referring to the heavy air bombing during the Spanish Civil War in 1936.

CHAPTER 4
CULTURE FOR THE MASSES

1. Natan Altman, "'Futurism' and Proletarian Art" (1918), in John E. Bowlt, ed. and trans., *Russian Art of the Avant-Garde*, rev. and enlarged ed. (London: Thames and Hudson, 1988), pp. 162–163. The artist Vasilii Kuptsov was a student of Filonov; see above, chapter 2, note 101.

2. Maria Gough, "Switched On: Notes on Radio, Automata and the Bright Red Star," in Leah Dickerman ed., *Building the Collective: Soviet Graphic Design, 1917–1937* (New York: Princeton Architectural Press, 1996), p. 45. A 1925 poster by Iulian Shutskii heralded the medium's organizational strategy: "Radio. From the will of millions we will create a single will" (ibid.).

3. Nina Tumarkin, *Lenin Lives! The Lenin Cult in Russia* (Cambridge: Harvard University Press, 1983), p. 68.

4. Electrification was the first centralized state plan for economic development. The slogan "Communism is Soviet power plus the electrification of the whole country" was understood in terms of political gains rather than simple economic rationality, including victory over capitalism at home and abroad. Lenin explained that electrification "will provide a link between town and country, will make it possible to raise the level of culture in the countryside, and to overcome, even in the most remote corners of the land, backwardness, ignorance, poverty, disease, and barbarism." Cited in Jonathan Coopersmith, *The Electrification of Russia, 1880–1926* (Ithaca: Cornell University Press, 1992), p. 154; see also p. 175.

5. Coopersmith, *The Electrification of Russia*, p. 177.

6. Ibid., p. 169.

7. The GOELRO (State Commission for the Electrification of Russia) report of 1920 stated that although energy itself was to be developed as an autarchic national system, "it will be indispensable to resort to technical and material assistance from abroad" (cited in ibid., p. 173).

8. See ibid., pp. 162–167, 178–187. During the Civil War, peat was extensively used as fuel in the cities.

9. In the early years of the First Five Year Plan, as part of what later were termed "hairbrained schemes," there was a serious project to investigate the use of windmills to produce electrical power. It was described in a primer for school children (translated into English in 1931 by members of Teachers College, Columbia University): "In Moscow on Voznesensky Street may be seen a peculiar building. It would not seem so queer except for a tall tower adjoining the building on the right side. This tower is square and almost windowless. On it stands another tower made of glass with a steel frame. And on the very top of the second tower like a weather-cock turns a strange contraption resembling a flying machine of unusual design. This is a department of the Central Aero-Hydraulic Institute where wind motors are invented. And what you see turning on the top of the second tower is a new windmill being tested by the Institute.

"If we should build such windmills throughout the country, we would capture more energy than the whole world requires today. In time, of course, the need will greatly increase. Then, wherever strong winds blow, windmills will be established. The entire country will be covered with a net of electrical wires. And all wind electric stations, as well as others, will work in this net. Windmills will be placed in regular order like figures on a chessboard. They must be placed so that one tower will not interfere with another. For wind, even as light, may cast its shadows. And if one windmill falls into the wind shadow of another, it cannot work. Special stations will be constructed to collect and conserve the energy of the wind in order that it may be used during calm weather.

"But all this is a task of future Five-Year Plans. The present plan sets the following task: to replace the old inefficient village windmills with the windmills of the Central Aero-Hydraulic Institute. And during these five years to raise the strength of all of our wind motors to 500 thousand horsepower." M. Alan [pseudonym of Ilia Iakovlevich Marshak], *New Russia's Primer: The Story of the Five-Year Plan,* trans. George S. Counts and Nucia P. Lodge (New York: Houghton Mifflin Company, 1931), pp. 34–35.

10. "[Abroad] stand opponents, equipped with all the attributes of the strongly developed capitalist economy. It is perfectly clear that in the economic struggle we must be armed in the same areas they are. . . . If we do not work from a base of electrification, our position will be extremely disadvantageous." Gleb Krzhizhanovskii (1920), cited in Coopersmith, *The Electrification of Russia,* p. 176.

11. Ibid., p. 168.

12. Ibid., pp. 162–163. The electrical engineer Gleb Krzhizhanovskii suggested instead "an economic accounting unit based on the amount of manpower needed to pro-

duce a given quantity of wheat, a concept more appropriate to agrarian Russia" (ibid.). But as Coopersmith comments, "Unfortunately for the rural sector, its urban-based brethren defined the road to utopia too narrowly" (ibid., p. 164).

13. Sound film proved effective for the reproduction of the leader's voice as well. Dziga Vertov's 1934 film *Three Songs of Lenin* transposed Lenin's voice from a phonograph recording and improved its clarity. Vertov wrote: "From Lenin's address to members of the Red Army the following words, clearly audible, went into the film: 'Stand firm. . . . Stand united in friendship. . . . Forward, bravely against the enemy. . . . Victory shall be ours. . . . The power of the landowners and capitalists, crushed here in Russia, shall be defeated throughout the entire world!' In this way we found it possible to preserve Lenin's voice on film and to present Vladimir Ilyich speaking from the screen." *Kino-Eye: The Writings of Dziga Vertov,* ed. Annette Michelson, trans. Kevin O'Brien (Berkeley: University of California Press, 1984), pp. 116–117.

14. Cited in Richard Stites, *Revolutionary Dreams: Utopian Vision and Experimental Life in the Russian Revolution* (New York: Oxford University Press, 1989), p. 41.

15. "It began with the playing of Henry Litolphe's *Robespierre Overture.* To the left of the audience was a platform containing dummies of Kerensky and his ministers, with foolishly bobbing heads nodding to the discordant sounds of the French 'Marseillaise' and defended by the Women's Battalion. To the right, across a long catwalk, was the platform of the Red Guards who shouted threats and sang revolutionary songs. From its midst rose the gradually louder cadences of the 'Internationale' engaged in a musical duel with the faltering 'Marseillaise'. . . . As the rival hymn is drowned out, the palace is stormed, the audience joining the attack and melting into the performance." Ibid., p. 96.

16. Natan Altman, cited in Vladimir Tolstoy, Irina Bibikova, and Catherine Cooke, eds., *Street Art of the Revolution: Festivals and Celebrations in Russia, 1918–33* (London: Thames and Hudson, 1990), p. 71.

17. K. N. Derzhaven, 1925, trans. Edward Braun, in *Art in Revolution: Soviet Art and Design since 1917,* catalogue of the exhibit at the Hayward Gallery, London, February 26 to April 18, 1971 (London: Arts Council, 1971), pp. 58–59.

18. Stites, *Revolutionary Dreams,* p. 96.

19. Article in *Vestnik teatra* (Theater Bulletin), November 17, 1919, cited in Brandon Taylor, *Art and Literature under the Bolsheviks,* vol. 1: *The Crisis of Renewal, 1917–1924* (London: Pluto Press, 1991), p. 74. Mass street theater was organized throughout the time of the Civil War. "On 1

May 1919, as Petrograd was suffering the most extreme privations and as Yudenich's [White] armies were on the outskirts of the city, a mass spectacle 'Pageant of the IIIrd International' was performed in the city, apparently well-attended and undisturbed" (ibid.).

20. Cited in Lynn Mally, *Culture of the Future: The Proletkult Movement in Revolutionary Russia* (Berkeley: University of California Press, 1990), p. 125.

21. Lunacharskii, cited in Stites, *Revolutionary Dreams*, p. 98.

22. Lunacharskii (October 1920), cited in Bowlt, ed., *Russian Art of the Avant-Garde*, p. 192.

23. David Mayer, *Sergei M. Eisenstein's Potemkin: A Shot-by-Shot Presentation* (New York: Grossman Publishers, 1972), p. 175.

24. *Eisenstein: Two Films, October and Alexandr Nevsky,* ed. Jay Leyda, trans. Diana Matias (London: Lorrimer Publishing, 1984), p. 47.

25. Interview with N. N. Evreinov, director of *Storming of the Winter Palace,* cited in Tolstoy, Bibikova, and Cooke, eds., *Street Art of the Revolution,* p. 138.

26. This section recycles parts of my article "The Cinema Screen as Prosthesis of Perception," in Nadia Seremetakis, ed., *The Senses Still: Perception and Memory as Material Culture in Modernity* (Chicago: University of Chicago Press, 1997).

27. Valerii Podoroga, "Sergei Eisenstein," presentation at Dubrovnik, October 1990, p. 2.

28. Podoroga, "Sergei Eisenstein," p. 7.

29. *The Crowd,* directed by King Vidor (USA, 1927), thematizes the masses from the very different perspective of one individual who attempts but fails to stand out from the crowd. There is an unforgettable scene criticizing visually the routinized office workplace, as workers leave their individual posts, a room full of identical desks, at the workday's close in a mass-repeated gesture. But the story unfolds for the most part in the domestic space of love, marriage, family, and the individual's struggle for money to survive. Commodities (bought and stolen) become the way the individual tries to avoid being submerged in the crowd.

30. Walter Benjamin, "Potemkinfilm und Tendenzkunst" (1927), in *Gesammelte Schriften,* vol. 2, ed. Rolf Tiedemann and Hermann Schweppenhäuser (Frankfurt am Main: Suhrkamp Verlag, 1977), p. 753. Benjamin had seen the film in a private showing in Moscow in January (ibid., p. 1486).

31. At the time it was made, *October* had its influential supporters, including Lunacharskii and Viktor Shklovskii, but it was criticized in a forum conducted by *Novyi Lef* not only for its distortions of history but also, specifically, for its rendering of "the ceaseless movement of the crowds" which made the movie as a whole "a physiologically intolerable object" (Viktor Portsov, cited in James Goodwin, *Eisenstein, Cinema, and History* [Urbana: University of Illinois Press, 1993], p. 94).

32. The October Revolution changed the status of cinema from its low-culture origins in the prerevolutionary era. Tsivian notes that before the Revolution, the cinema audience was "everyone," represented in literary texts by the prostitute: "The Lumière's first performances [in France] were set up as scientific demonstrations, but in Russia the public was introduced to cinema in rather disreputable circumstances" (Yuri Tsivian, *Early Cinema in Russia and Its Cultural Reception,* ed. Richard Taylor, trans. Alan Bodger, foreword Tom Gunning [New York: Routledge, 1994], pp. 35–36). Tsivian cites Miriam Hansen on the German case as similar: "The cinema, as an art form that thrives at intimate commerce with the urban masses, promising happiness to everyone but faithful to no one, could only be troped as a prostitute" (ibid., p. 37). The cinematic representation of the mass in Soviet cinema can be seen as a means of redeeming the urban masses from morally questionable connotations, transforming them into the antithetical image of the collective hero. Significantly, before the Revolution, it had been the avant-garde that appreciated cinema's democratizing social effect. The symbolist Andrei Bely wrote in 1911: "The cinema is a club. People come together here to undergo a moral experience, to travel to America, to learn about tobacco farming and the stupidity of policemen, to sigh over the *midinette* who has to sell her body. Absolutely everyone comes here to meet their friends: aristocrats and democrats, soldiers, students, workers, schoolgirls, poets and prostitutes" (cited in ibid., p. 35).

33. Jay Leyda, *Kino: A History of the Russian and Soviet Film* (New York: Collier Books, 1973), p. 200.

34. See Lary May, *Screening Out the Past: The Birth of Mass Culture and the Motion Picture Industry* (Chicago: University of Chicago Press, 1980), p. 215.

35. The star's movie character was used directly as an advertising technique to help sell these consumer objects, much as the televised shows of athletic stars are used to sell consumer products today. See Charles Eckert, "The Carole Lombard in Macy's Window," in John Belton, ed., *Movies and Mass Culture* (New Brunswick: Rutgers University Press, 1996).

36. Kotkin, *Magnetic Mountain,* pp. 507–508n.

37. "Images Triumph on the Screen" was the title of one of Malevich's articles. See Annette Michelson, "Reading Eisenstein reading *Capital,*" part 2, *October* 3 (Spring 1976), 82–88.

38. Richter and Malevich planned the film during the latter's trip to Berlin in 1927. See Stephen C. Foster, ed., *Hans Richter: Activism, Modernism, and the Avant-Garde* (Cambridge: MIT Press, 1998), pp. 86–88, 114–116.

39. Cited in Henri Band, "Das Ornament der Masse. Kultur und ideologiekritische Grundmotive im Denken Siegfried Kracauer," in Norbert Krenzlin, ed., *Zwischen Angst-Metapher und Terminus: Theorien der Massenkultur seit Nietzsche* (Berlin: Akademieverlag, 1992), p. 77.

40. The squatters and their families were routed by the police and government cavalry in one of the most controversial acts of President Hoover's administration. During the 1932 Presidential campaign, his Democratic opponent Franklin D. Roosevelt called for "plans like those of 1917 that . . . put their faith once more in the forgotten man at the bottom of the economic pyramid." It became known as his "Forgotten Man" speech. During his inauguration Roosevelt was applauded for saying he would ask Congress for emergency executive powers to "wage war" against the economic depression "as great as the power that would be given to me if we were in fact invaded by a foreign foe" (at a time when the Soviet Union was "waging war" on class enemies, both foreign and domestic, accused of "wrecking" plans to construct socialism). See Martin Rubin, "The Crowd, the Collective, and the Chorus: Busby Berkeley and the New Deal," in Belton, ed., *Movies and Mass Culture,* pp. 72–73.

41. See Denise J. Youngblood, *Movies for the Masses: Popular Cinema and Soviet Society in the 1920s* (New York: Cambridge University Press, 1992), p. 174. Aleksandrov's wife, Liubov Orlova, played Marion Dixon, an unusual role for this Soviet star, who typically portrayed heroines performing male tasks and dressed in male clothing—more tomboy than seductive woman, although what remained traditionally feminine was her schoolgirl subservience to male superiors. See Maria Enzensberger, "'We Were Born to Turn a Fairy Tale into Reality': Grigorii Alexandrov's *The Radiant Path,*" in Richard Taylor and Derek Spring, eds., *Stalinism and Soviet Cinema* (New York: Routledge, 1993), pp. 99–100.

42. "Critiques of Berkeley commonly characterize him as the master of dehumanization, mechanization, and impersonality—a naive abstractionist who reduces human beings to nuts and bolts, mere decorative pieces in a larger formal design. Such interpretations seem incomplete. . . .

The structure of a Berkeley number typically follows this pattern: the individual or couple is established. Then the number opens up, and the individual is absorbed into the mass, woven in and out of it, sometimes lost completely (although only momentarily). Finally, the individual returns, in fact, but somehow redefined by the experience of having dissolved into the group." (Rubin, "The Crowd, the Collective, and the Chorus," p. 78.) Rubin argues that this balance between individual and collective was a general characteristic of American culture in the thirties, true as well of Roosevelt's New Deal, and accounts at least in part for the fact that despite authoritarian trends in U.S. popular culture, a fascist takeover "did not happen here" (ibid., p. 82). I am emphasizing, on the contrary, the antiauthoritarian implications of the *technical* aspects of Berkeley's (and Vertov's) work, the fact that they bring the audience to question how the effects are being produced, and to be aware of the power of the camera to produce a virtual world different from the real one—elements found by Rubin to be "disorienting, dizzying, bedazzling. The mind spins; the world blurs; the line between self and other becomes less distinct" (ibid., p. 80).

43. See Miriam Bratu Hansen, "The Mass Production of the Senses: Classical Cinema as Vernacular Modernism," *MODERNISM/modernity* 6, no. 2 (1999), p. 61. I am indebted to Hansen's extremely original interpretation that changes our whole conception of "classical" cinema.

44. See Vance Kepley, Jr., "Mr. Kuleshov in the Land of the Modernists," in Anna Lawton, ed., *The Red Screen: Politics, Society, Art in Soviet Cinema* (New York: Routledge, 1992), pp. 133–137. On the showing of D. W. Griffith's film *Intolerance* (1916) at the first Congress of the Comintern in Petrograd in 1921, see Vance Kepley, Jr., "*Intolerance* and the Soviets: A Historical Investigation," in Richard Taylor and Ian Christie, eds., *Inside the Film Factory: New Approaches to Russian and Soviet Cinema* (New York: Routledge, 1991), pp. 51–59.

45. Hansen, "The Mass Production of the Senses," p. 61. Hansen argues suggestively that Hollywood movies of the "classical" period provided a form of global vernacular through which "the traumatic effects of modernity were reflected, rejected or disavowed, transmuted or negotiated" (ibid., p. 14).

46. The rocket scientist Konstantin Tsiolkovskii was a consultant for this film and drew designs for its spaceship (Neya Zorkaya, *The Illustrated History of the Soviet Cinema* [New York: Hippocrene Books, 1991], p. 147). *Aelita,* recently reevaluated and praised for its undogmatic celebration of "heterogeneity and topicality," was criticized at the time of its release by Kuleshov and mainstream modernists

at *Lef* and by the Soviet press generally (Ian Christie, "Down to Earth: *Aelita* Relocated," in Taylor and Christie, eds., *Inside the Film Factory*, p. 101). This entertainment film was more popular with Soviet audiences than those of the avant-garde (see Denise J. Youngblood, "The Return of the Native: Jakov Protazanov and Soviet Cinema," in ibid., pp. 103–123).

47. By Sergei Komaraov, 1927. Lunacharskii is rumored to have had the idea. "The plot was quite straightforward. An insignificant cashier at a cinema box office, played by the highly popular Soviet comedian Igor Ilyinsky, is in love. The starstruck object of his attentions promises to return them if he becomes famous. After a number of adventures Ilyinsky becomes an extra in a stunt sequence. He is left suspended in mid-air when Douglas Fairbanks and Mary Pickford visit the studio: the film crew rush out to see them and Ilyinsky falls asleep. Pickford is touched by the scene, Ilyinsky is introduced to her as the 'Soviet Harry Piel', and she plants a kiss on his cheek. The kiss of Mary Pickford makes him famous, and his girlfriend worships him. But after a few days the lipstick wears off and life returns to normal. The fragility of fame and fortune are all too apparent." Richard Taylor, "Ideology and Popular Culture in Soviet Cinema: *The Kiss of Mary Pickford*," in Lawton, ed., *The Red Screen*, pp. 56–57.

48. Youngblood, *Movies for the Masses*, pp. 51–52. Importing the film *The Thief of Baghdad* cost the Soviet government 100,000 U.S. dollars (ibid., p. 64).

49. Vance Kepley, Jr., "Origins of Soviet Cinema," in Taylor and Christie, eds., *Inside the Film Factory*, p. 76. "The figures also reveal that Soviet producers consistently narrowed the gap between revenues generated by their films and those deriving from imports" (ibid.).

50. Ibid., pp. 60–79. Because all foreign trade went through one agency, the film industry could live off other exports. As a result, "good grain harvests bought the film industry its future" (ibid., p. 73). See also Youngblood, *Movies for the Masses*, pp. 50–67.

51. "Recent research has indicated that Stalin's obsession with movies and his dabbling with the minutiae of filmmaking reached bizarre proportions. The dictator loved Western films and made sure they were available to his favorite filmmakers, though not to the public." Youngblood, *Movies for the Masses*, p. 174.

52. There are differences from the Hollywood prototype: the hero is a complex character psychologically, and, as an individual sacrificed for the socialist ideal, he dies at the end. In 1935, at the only Moscow international film festival of the decade, *Chapaev* was screened next to the American film *Viva Villa!* (directed by Jack Conway, 1934). *Viva Villa!* was modeled also after the Western genre but, like *Chapaev* it told the politically radical story of an unschooled, popular peasant leader (Pancho Villa, during the Mexican Revolution of the 1910s) who becomes a commando during civil war, and as a freedom fighter dies as a martyr for the cause of social justice. *Chapaev* was excellent cinema, and it was held up as the model for socialist realism. It won the Grand Prix at the 1937 Paris International Exposition [of the Arts and Technology] as well as the Silver Cup at the Moscow festival of 1935.

53. Medvedkin recalled an example of his social parody in an interview: "Some bricklayers are putting up a new building. They've already put seven floors up and they're putting the eighth up there on the top somewhere. A shoe factory has already moved in downstairs. All this is done in a grotesque circus-like manner. A fantastic machine churns out shoes, but the shoes are useless because you can't put them on. Suddenly there's an enormous crack like lightning through all seven floors. All seven have split open. The shoemaker runs out and shouts, 'Hey, what are you up to?' They reply, 'We've got no time. We're shock-workers.' He protests, 'You mustn't do that!' They go on building, but the edifice has been destroyed. Suddenly from somewhere up above an enormous brick sails down until it hits the shoemaker on the head and crumbles to dust. It's a bad brick. The shoemaker picks up a piece of the brick, rubs it between his fingers and, looking the audience in the eye, says, 'Is this really a brick?'" "Interview with Alexander Medvedkin," in Taylor and Christie, eds., *Inside the Film Factory*, p. 168.

54. After seeing Eisenstein's *Potemkin* in 1926, David O. Selznick, then a young producer for MGM, wrote to an associate praising the film for "a technique entirely new to the screen"; he proposed that the studio study it "in the same way that a group of artists might view and study a Rubens or a Raphael" (cited in Robert Sklar, *Movie-Made America: A Cultural History of American Movies* [New York: Vintage Books, 1976], pp. 155–156). "It is instructive to place the talkie revolution within this context. Hollywood switched to sound at precisely the same period that Soviet silents captured world-wide attention" (p. 156).

55. See Michelson, "Reading Eisenstein Reading *Capital*," part 1, *October* 2 (1976); David Bordwell, *The Cinema of Eisenstein* (Cambridge: Harvard University Press, 1993), pp. 15–21.

56. David Selznick, working for Paramount, called Eisenstein's adaptation "the most moving script I have ever read," but argued against the film as a bad commercial risk (Sklar, *Movie-Made America, p.* 156).

57. Bordwell, *The Cinema of Eisenstein*, pp. 17–20.

58. See Philip Davies and Brian Neve, eds., *Cinema, Politics and Society in America* (New York: St. Martin's Press, 1981). "American political fundamentalism has ever required its bogeymen . . . a conspiratorial and objectively evil alien power whose sole purpose was the overthrow of the government of the United States. In this perennial struggle to root out totemic victims to explain the failure of particular American dreams, no lamb has ever led its populist executioners more willingly to the slaughter than the Communist Party of the USA." (Richard Malthby, "Made for Each Other: The Melodrama of Hollywood and the House Committee on Un-American Activities, 1947," in ibid., p. 80.) But why did Hollywood, the very purveyor of the American dream, provide such an attractive embodiment of the Communist menace? The entertainment industry was the capitalist counterpart of the Communist Party, in that both were guardians of the system's ideological hegemony and both were made scapegoats for the system's failure. It is worth noting that the House of Representatives, the sovereign bastion of U.S. "democracy," was the source of the purging of cultural "enemies"; what made the U.S. case happily different from the USSR's was not Congress but the courts: the "Hollywood Ten" lost their jobs, but they were safe physically, protected by the First Amendment and the legal institutions that backed it.

59. Cited in Richard Taylor, "Ideology as Mass Entertainment: Boris Shumyatsky and Soviet Cinema in the 1930s," in Taylor and Christie, eds., *Inside the Film Factory,* p. 201.

60. Shumiatskii (1935), cited in Peter Kenez, *Cinema and Soviet Society, 1917–1953* (New York: Cambridge University Press, 1992), p. 129.

61. Shumiatskii, cited in Taylor, "Ideology as Mass Entertainment," p. 206. Stalin himself intervened later to enable Eisenstein to make *Aleksandr Nevskii* (Kenez, *Cinema and Soviet Society,* p. 145).

62. Taylor, "Ideology as Mass Entertainment," pp. 196–211.

63. Goodwin, *Eisenstein, Cinema, and History,* p. 149.

64. Taylor, "Ideology as Mass Entertainment," pp. 214–216.

65. One is repeatedly struck by this difference. The erotic allure of the female body is the central emblem of capitalist consumer society, provoking perpetual stimulation without closure, as if to ensure that the act of consumption will never stop. But the erotics of Soviet culture organizes sexual desire in a very different manner. The female body has a worker's physique. The erotics of the body undergoes a displacement; the consumptive power of sexual pleasure is transformed into the productive power of work. In the "boy meets girl meets tractor" genre of Soviet films in the 1930s, sexual romance is submerged within the greater narrative, the social romance of building socialism. Here Rubin is quite right to point out in the U.S. context that "what is most remarkable (and most Berkeleyesque) about the number ["Remember My Forgotten Man"] is its expansion of the political message to a sexual level," an equation of sexual and economic potency. See Rubin, "The Crowd, the Collective, and the Chorus," p. 73.

66. The popularity in the 1930s United States of the gangster film with its ambivalent protagonist, the heroic, antisocial loner who defies the law but is ultimately punished for it, is exemplary. But so is Superman: "Personal power violently employed for social purposes, and which did not necessitate a change in social structure, was extremely attractive. By the end of the 1930s Superman possessed a fundamental strength beyond the normal capabilities of American politicians." (P. H. Melling, "The Mind of the Mob: Hollywood and Popular Culture in the 1930s," in Davies and Neve, eds., *Cinema, Politics and Society in America,* p. 25; see also p. 31.)

67. There is the legendary example of John Ford's 1940 film *The Grapes of Wrath* which, when shown in the Soviet Union, conveyed to audiences the totally unintended message that in the United States during the Great Depression even destitute farmers possessed private automobiles.

68. See Bordwell, *The Cinema of Eisenstein,* pp. 96–110.

69. Margaret Bourke-White, *Eyes on Russia,* preface by Maurice Hindus (New York: Simon and Schuster, 1931), pp. 95–97.

70. *Daesh'* was a publication of the Oktiabr' group of artists, who boasted that of their group "only 6 artists still work in studios, 240 are already out in factories and plants." Cited in Leah Dickerman, "Building the Collective," in Dickerman, ed., *Building the Collective: Soviet Graphic Design, 1917–1937* (New York: Princeton Architectural Press, 1996), p. 32.

71. Report of Albert Kahn Co., Inc. (1939), cited in Anthony C. Sutton, *Western Technology and Soviet Economic Development,* 3 vols. (Stanford: Hoover Institute Press, 1968–1973), vol. 2: *1930–1945* (published 1971), p. 248. Nineteen percent of all architect-designed industrial construction in the United States in the 1930s (totaling $800,000,000) was the work of the Albert Kahn Company (ibid., pp. 250 and 345).

72. Ibid., p. 248. "Gosplan [USSR's State Planning Commission] had decided upon those sectors it wanted developed and their approximate capacities. No foreign influence has been found at the Gosplan level. These plans were then turned over to the Albert Kahn Company for conversion into production units." (Ibid., p. 249.)

73. The First Five Year Plan self-consciously adopted the "American option" of industrial development which put a priority on mining, metallurgy, and machine-building. Again, the reasoning presumed an invariable historical course: "If indeed we hope to catch up with and surpass American industry, we must absorb those technical achievements that exist in America," wrote Sergo Ordzhonikidze, senior party official at Vesenkha (Supreme Council of the National Economy), cited in Kendall E. Bailes, *Technology and Society under Lenin and Stalin: Origins of the Soviet Technical Intelligentsia, 1917–1941* (Princeton: Princeton University Press, 1978), pp. 342–343.

74. "All the structural steel for the plant was purchased in the United States. The speed with which 5700 tons of steel were erected into a framework constitutes a record in Russia, all the more remarkable in view of the fact that the work was done by Russian laborers with little previous experience in this kind of construction." Bourke-White, *Eyes on Russia,* p. 124.

75. Sutton, *Western Technology and Soviet Economic Development,* vol. 2, p. 250.

76. Ibid., p. 434.

77. Cited in ibid., p. 251. Sutton's research, carried out with the support of the politically conservative Hoover Institute, provides evidence for this and other technology transfers from the West to the Soviet Union. Another account records: "Days were given over to an on-the-job training program in actual factory design. In the evening, classes were given by the Kahn staff. By the time the branch office [in Moscow] was dissolved and the staff sent home in March 1932, 521 plants large and small had been designed, and over 4,000 Russian personnel had participated in the training program." (Grant Hildebrand, *Designing for Industry: The Architecture of Albert Kahn* [Cambridge: MIT Press, 1974], p. 129.)

78. Stephen Kotkin, *Magnetic Mountain: Stalinism as a Civilization* (Berkeley: University of California Press, 1995), p. 407.

79. Sutton, *Western Technology and Soviet Economic Development,* vol. 1: *1917–1930* (published 1968), pp. 246–247.

80. In 1929, "Amtorg [the Soviet trade organization in New York] suddenly tripled its orders from American companies.... The stock market collapse of late 1929,

with its bank closings and massive unemployment, meant that from the American point of view, trade with Russia became even more significant. In a depressed market, the Soviet government was a welcome buyer, and competition for Amtorg orders became fierce in the first half of 1930. In many cases Soviet purchases saved American jobs. Soviet-American trade reached a high of $114,399,000 that year." Robert C. Williams, *Russian Art and American Money, 1900–1940* (Cambridge: Harvard University Press, 1980), p. 167. "Most [industrial] goods were produced on credit from American firms. . . . American business . . . pressed for recognition" of the Soviet Union (ibid., p. 16).

81. Sutton, *Western Technology and Soviet Economic Development,* vol. 1, p. 248.

82. Ibid., vol. 1, p. 347; vol. 2, p. 258.

83. Ibid., vol. 1, p. 178.

84. Ibid., p. 254. A Soviet source reported in 1936 that some 6,800 foreign specialists of all types worked in Soviet heavy industry in 1932. Another Soviet source reports that 1,700 American engineers worked in heavy industry (ibid., vol. 2, p. 11). "In 1940 we find individual American engineers in such high regard that the Soviets appealed through diplomatic channels to ensure continuation of their work in the Soviet Union" during the war (ibid., p. 12). John Calder, at one time connected with the River Rouge plant, worked as chief construction engineer at several Soviet industrial sites and was awarded the Order of Lenin; the hero of Nikolai Pogodin's play *Tempo* is known to have been modeled after him (ibid.).

85. Dubbed the "Dream City" by the Soviet press, it was Magnitogorsk that provided the true Soviet counterpart to Hollywood and Los Angeles in the 1930s. Both were the destinations of optimistic youth seeking a new life and success according to hegemonic beliefs in progress. Each was a dreamworld, a "place of miracles" (for constructing socialism and the "new man" with guaranteed employment in one case; for becoming rich and famous as an individual success in the other). In both cases, the reality was a good deal less rosy than the dream. See Kotkin, *Magnetic Mountain,* pp. 73–79.

86. Ibid., p. 402. Kotkin points out the similarity as well in the myth of turning "vacant" territory into an industrial landscape. He cites a contemporary's description of Gary: "Until industry waved its magic wand over the land upon which the vast steel mills of Gary now stand, the place was none other than a bleak, sandy waste, a strip of prairie with virtually no habitation." Of course, both these "empty spaces" contained ecological systems that were perma-

nently devastated by the "miracle" of development (ibid., p. 427n.).

87. Ibid., p. 43. "McKee was to design everything to be as large as possible, allow[ing] for future expansion.... The Soviet authorities gave McKee two *months* to submit complete designs for the largest and most advanced iron and steel plant outside the United States" (ibid., p. 44). "A list of equipment suppliers for Magnitogorsk in an official Soviet publication reads like a 'who's who' of capitalist engineering firms: Otis Elevator, General Electric, Demag, AEG, Krupp, Siemens, Trailer, and so on" (ibid., p. 403n). Freyn Engineering Company, designers and builders of the U.S. Steel plant in Gary, Indiana, had been approached by the Soviets in 1929 but lost the bid, perhaps because Freyn's standard design for blast furnaces was a mere 920–930 cubic meters, whereas McKee's called for 1,200 cubic meters (ibid., p. 402n).

88. At a meeting of Moscow communists, a speaker tied Magnitogorsk to U.S. recognition of the Soviet Union: "The American sirs, convinced of our power and especially of the victories of the first Five-Year Plan, were compelled to recognize us.... Our magnitostrois, our giants of industry, our tremendous growth forced the capitalist countries to take note of us" (cited in ibid., p. 428).

89. Sutton, *Western Technology and Soviet Economic Development,* vol. 2, p. 343.

90. Ibid., p. 329.

91. Williams, *Russian Art and American Money,* p. 12. "Missing manuscripts are usually attributed to a 1931 fire at the Hermitage or to subsequent German devastation; in one case, a Soviet publication of 1950 printed a photograph of Raphael's *Alba Madonna* without noting that for twenty years it had been hanging in the National Gallery of Art in Washington, not in the Hermitage" (ibid., p. 40). Charles Henschel, head of Knoedler, testified in the trial regarding the Mellon purchases: "In the fall of 1928 two friends of mine who were in Europe, in the art business, told me that there was a possibility of getting some of the fine pictures out of the Hermitage in Leningrad, but that in order to do this negotiations would have to be kept absolutely secret, because the Soviet officials did not wish the general public to know that they might dispose of any of their great pictures" (cited in ibid., p. 187).

92. Ibid., p. 41.

93. "During the first three quarters of 1929, prior to the crash of the stock market, the Soviet Union was exporting more than one hundred tons of antiques and jewelry every single month, up sharply from 1928; the total amount of art objects exported during this nine-month

period came to 1,192 tons. A year later in 1930, for the comparable January to September period, the total came to 1,681 tons; of this, 117 tons went directly to the United States." Ibid., p. 168.

94. Ibid. Soon afterward the Soviets "signed a crucial agreement with the German government for millions of marks in desperately wanted industrial credits; Mellon and America were no longer as badly needed" (ibid., p. 175). Other buyers of European masterpieces included the Metropolitan Museum of Art, Philadelphia Art Museum, Rijksmuseum, several German museums (in Cologne, Hannover, Nuremberg), and (the earliest purchaser) the private collector Calouste Gulbenkian who was based in Lisbon (ibid., pp. 182–183).

95. Ibid., p. 153.

96. Ibid., p. 30. The president of Knoedler was Charles Henschel, grandson of the founder. "Henschel's key source of information was Zatzenstein, the head of the Matthiesen Gallery in Berlin, who had his own representative in Moscow, a man named Mansfeld. Zatzenstein had first gotten in touch with Knoedler's through the London dealer Colnaghi's, headed by partners Gutekunst and Gus Meyer. Henschel's contact man with Mellon was Carman Messmore. Thus, a continuous chain of diverse people linked Andrew Mellon in Washington with the Hermitage in Leningrad. Mansfeld in Moscow would inform his boss Zatzenstein in Berlin of an impending sale; Zatzenstein would contact Knoedler's via Colnaghi's in London; Henschel would send Messmore down to see Mellon." (Ibid., pp. 170–171.) Again, the cosmopolitanism of these transactions (and in this case it was an explicitly Jewish cosmopolitan network) is striking. As in the case of the international network of engineers, these individuals were used by Stalin for his own purposes, playing the capitalist competitors against each other. "It is significant that the greatest of all art deals, involving an American buyer and the Soviet government, had to be consummated in Berlin. The United States did not recognize the Soviet government until November 1933 so that the legal risks of any sale on American soil were great. Europe was safer." (Ibid., p. 188.)

97. "Hammer brilliantly perceived in 1931 that the glittering debris of the last Romanovs could be marketed wholesale [through department stores] to wealthy American women who were fascinated with European royalty and aristocracy but doomed to live in a democratic society" (ibid., p. 37). In these cases of public sales, threats of lawsuits from the original owners were always a danger. In May 1931 the entire contents of the Stroganov Palace in Leningrad were auctioned off in Berlin, and the Princess

Stroganov in Paris "claimed the entire collection was her property." The Stroganov family "found little protection from those working for the United States secretary of the treasury, who had just consummated his own private art purchases from the Soviet government" (ibid., p. 178).

98. Ibid., p. 167.

99. "In 1932, the Russian émigré press in Paris and Prague circulated similar reports, adding that these paintings must be considered stolen goods taken from former private collections, but no rumor could pry open the lips of the obdurately silent Mellon or his agents" (ibid., p. 176).

100. Cited in ibid., p. 189.

101. The conflict-of-interest charges were general and wide-ranging, "namely . . . the fact that as treasury secretary Mellon maintained a substantial interest in three hundred corporations with more than $3 billion in capital stock" (ibid., pp. 168–169 and 181). Mellon resigned his office, "demoted" in 1932 to the post of U.S. ambassador to Great Britain—where his passionate art collecting continued.

102. Ibid., p. 184.

103. Ibid., p. 188.

104. Ibid., p. 189.

105. Duveen (1935), cited in ibid., p. 185.

106. See Karl Marx, *Capital*, vol. 1, chap. 1.

107. Cited in Williams, *Russian Art and American Money*, p. 179.

108. Mellon's banking house helped to establish the Union Steel Company on the Monongahela River at the turn of the century, "a complete steel works with two 'monster' blast furnaces and batteries of open hearth furnaces" which later merged with United States Steel. See Harvey O'Connor, *Mellon's Millions: The Biography of a Fortune* (New York: Blue Ribbon Books, 1933), pp. 56–58.

109. Williams, *Russian Art and American Money*, p. 173 (The caption on p. 153 states a different price.)

110. Sutton, *Western Technology and Soviet Economic Development*, vol. 2, p. 402.

111. "By the end of 1938, the Magnitogorsk Works had already produced more than 7.5 million tons of pig iron, 5 million tons of steel, and 3 million tons of rolling stock" (Kotkin, *Magnetic Mountain*, p. 69).

112. "Soviet newspapers gave wide coverage to the problems of unemployment, social unrest, and the difficulties of the New Deal" (ibid., p. 412n).

CHAPTER 5
DREAM AND AWAKENING

1. For a detailed description of the competition, see Karl Schlögel, "The Shadow of an Imaginary Tower," in the exhibition catalog *Naum Gabo and the Competition for the Palace of Soviets, Moscow, 1931–33* (Berlin: Berlinische Galerie, 1992).

2. See above, section 2.2, fragment titled "Reverse Motion."

3. J. H. Matthews, *Surrealism and American Feature Films* (Boston: Twayne Publishers, 1979), p. 62.

4. Schlögel, "The Shadow of an Imaginary Tower," pp. 179–180.

5. In 1931 the competition was announced as finally bringing to fruition the earlier proposal of the First Congress of Soviets (1922) for a building to be erected in Moscow, a "Palace of Labor," that would serve for meetings of the Soviets of the Union. Because this meant building auditoriums for 15,000 and 8,000 people, the scale was necessarily huge. The publicity stated: "Only now, though, with the great successes of socialist construction achieved and the First Five-Year Plan completed in four years . . . are all preconditions fulfilled for realizing the First Congress's decision." Cited in Catherine Cooke, "Mediating Creativity and Politics: Sixty Years of Architectural Competitions in Russia," in *The Great Utopia: The Russian and Soviet Avant-Garde, 1915–1932* (New York: Guggenheim Museum, 1992), p. 707.

6. A model of the Empire State Building was shown in 1931 at the American pavilion at the International Colonial Exhibition in Paris. By the end of the twentieth century it had appeared in approximately ninety movies, of which *King Kong* remained the most famous: "Just as the building was billed as 'The Eighth Wonder of the World,' so was the movie's tragic hero" (John Tauranac, *The Empire State Building: The Making of a Landmark* [New York: Scribner, 1995], pp. 24–25).

7. "Stalin lavished an extraordinary amount of attention on cinema. From the mid-1930s to the end of his days he was the chief censor. He personally viewed and approved every film exhibited in the Soviet Union." Peter Kenez, "Soviet Cinema in the Age of Stalin," in Richard Taylor and Derek Spring, eds., *Stalin and Soviet Cinema* (New York: Routledge, 1993), pp. 62–63. See also above, chapter 4, note 51.

8. A contemporary (1931) Soviet journal, cited in Cooke, "Mediating Creativity and Politics," p. 707. See ibid., p. 698, for sketches of Hamilton's entry for the Palace competition, which resembles Iofan's original contribution

more than it does the final variant, modified by Stalin. The visiting team referred to in the newspaper report must have been the same in which "Roxy" Roth participated, who was impressed by Melnikov's *SONaia SONata* as a model for Radio City Music Hall (see above, section 3.2).

9. See Melnikov's fantastic entry, which, in putting proletarians on top of an inverted pyramid, could be read as a criticism of the growing bureaucracy (S. Frederick Starr, *Melnikov: Solo Architect in a Mass Society* [Princeton: Princeton University Press, 1978], pp. 157–161).

10. Malevich's architectons date to the Leningrad UNOVIS period in the mid-1920s. In the Leningrad exhibition of 1932, Malevich was given a whole room to set up his work, with the help of Suetin. In June 1933 this show opened in Moscow in a changed cultural climate, and the "objectless" artworks of Malevich (along with those of Tatlin, Filonov, Popova, and Altman) were relegated into one crowded room; a reviewer referred to their work as a "serious tragedy": "they elicited such a centrifugal force in their art that it carried them out of art to the beyond, to nowhere, to non-existence" (cited in Charlotte Douglas, *Kazimir Malevich* [New York: Harry N. Abrams, 1994], p. 24).

11. It is possible that this statue was not meant seriously by Malevich but was intended, rather, to mislead the authorities: "An assistant to Malevich, R. Pavlov, recalls that a common plaster figure of Lenin, that had been bought in an ordinary stationery store, was placed on the arkhitekton. When the committee left, the statuette was laughingly taken down and put away until the next unpleasant visit" (Vasilii Rakitin, "The Avant-Garde and Art of the Stalinist Era," in Hans Günther, ed., *The Culture of the Stalin Period* [New York: St. Martin's Press, 1990], p. 184).

12. The 6,200-seat Radio City Music Hall where *King Kong* opened in New York was advertised as "the world's largest picture house"; the *Giant,* the largest theater in Leningrad, built in 1927–1928, seated only 1,000 people.

13. In 1930, for example, Ortega y Gasset described the politically aroused masses as "the primitive in revolt, that is, barbarism" (José Ortega y Gasset, *The Revolt of the Masses,* trans. anonymous [New York: W. W. Norton, 1932], p. 98).

14. When the Chinese cook on board the ship is reprimanded for wanting to join in the struggle—"This is no job for a cook"—the racism takes on a political tone of anti-immigrationism.

15. The discrepancy in their size makes them "a remarkably incongruous bridal couple," but the erotic element is there nonetheless (Matthews, *Surrealism and American Feature Films,* p. 72).

16. "While working on the fight sequences involving Kong and the tyrannosaurs, the movie's chief technician, Willis H. O'Brien, and his first assistant, E. B. Gibson, regularly attended boxing and wrestling matches" (ibid., p. 70).

17. The phrase is from Stuart Ewen and Elizabeth Ewen, *Channels of Desire: Mass Images and the Shaping of American Consciousness* (New York: McGraw-Hill, 1982).

18. Matthews, *Surrealism and American Feature Films,* p. 77.

19. The Supreme Soviet replaced the Congress of Soviets according to the Constitution of 1936, thus changing the palace's name. The site chosen for the palace was that of the Cathedral of Christ the Savior (see above, section 2.2). Built after the victory over Napoleon and a landmark of Moscow's architecture, it was demolished in 1931 with explosive rapidity. Construction on the Palace of the Supreme Soviet began in 1939. Work on the new structure was halted due to the war, still at the level of the foundation pit.

20. Igor Golomstock, *Totalitarian Art in the Soviet Union, the Third Reich, Fascist Italy and the People's Republic of China* (London: Collins Harvik, 1990), p. 275.

21. Mikhail N. Epstein, *After the Future,* trans. Anesa Miller-Pogacar (Amherst: University of Massachusetts Press, 1995), p. 165. This chapter, "Labor of Lust," was first published in 1992.

22. Ibid., pp. 165, 166.

23. Andrei Platonov, *The Foundation Pit/Kotlovan,* bilingual edition, preface by Joseph Brodsky, trans. Thomas P. Whitney (Ann Arbor: Ardis Publishers, 1973). This was the book's first publication. It was not published in the Soviet Union until 1987 (Moscow; an edition was published in Riga in 1988).

24. Presentation at Cornell University, October 1992.

25. Platonov, *The Foundation Pit,* p. 13.

26. Ibid., pp. 3–5.

27. Valerii Podoroga, "The Eunuch of the Soul: Positions of Reading and the World of Platonov," in Thomas Lahusen, ed., *Late Soviet Culture: From Perestroika to Novostroika* (Durham: Duke University Press, 1993), pp. 214–215.

28. The logic of Stakhanovism was similar to that of shock work, which it "came to eclipse (without entirely replacing) . . . as the archetypal form of 'socialist labor.'" Stephen Kotkin, *Magnetic Mountain: Stalinism as a Civilization* (Berkeley: University of California Press, 1995), p. 213.

29. Stalin addressed the first Stakhanovite meeting in November 1935: "[Stakhanovites] are free from the conservatism and inertia of some engineers, technicians, and industrialists. They go boldly forward, breaking outmoded technical norms and creating new and higher ones" (cited in Sheila Fitzpatrick, *The Cultural Front: Power and Culture in Revolutionary Russia* [Ithaca: Cornell University Press, 1992], p. 169).

30. Stalin "emphasized again and again the importance of liberating peasant women from the oppression of the patriarchal family, and made many public appearances with Stakhanovites such as the champion beet grower, Maria Demchenko, and the tractorist, Pasha Angelina" (Sheila Fitzpatrick, *Stalin's Peasants: Resistance and Survival in the Russian Village after Collectivization* [New York: Oxford University Press, 1994], p. 181). "The negative stereotypes such as that of the kulak were all male, while the positive stereotypes such as that of the peasant Stakhanovite tended to be female" (ibid., p. 182). Symbolically, the excelling of peasant women in Stakhanovite values implied the most rapid development (from the most backward stage) of the Soviet "new man."

31. S[ergei] M. Eisenstein, *Selected Works,* ed. Richard Taylor, vol. 1: *Writings 1922–1934* (London: BFI Books, 1988), p. 319.

32. Trans. in James von Geldern and Richard Stites, eds., *Mass Culture in Soviet Russia* (Bloomington: Indiana University Press, 1995), p. 3.

33. Richard Stites, *Revolutionary Dreams: Utopian Vision and Experimental Life in the Russian Revolution* (New York: Oxford University Press, 1989), p. 230.

34. Vasilii Rakitin, "The Artisan and the Prophet: Marginal Notes on Two Artistic Careers," in *The Great Utopia,* p. 35.

35. Cited in Rosalinde Sartori, "Stalinism and Carnival: Organisation and Aesthetics of Political Holidays," in Günther, ed., *The Culture of the Stalin Period,* p. 41.

36. *Pravda* reported his execution for organizing a "military conspiracy" only after the event (see Kotkin, *Magnetic Mountain,* p. 345).

37. Robin Higham and Jacob W. Kipp, eds., *Soviet Aviation and Air Power: A Historical View* (Boulder: Westview Press, 1978), p. 63. The Soviet Union had still not recovered from this decimation of military personnel when Hitler attacked in 1941.

38. Roland Marchand, *Advertising the American Dream: Making Way for Modernity, 1920–1940* (Berkeley: University of California Press, 1985), p. 238.

39. "In 1929 the State Academy of Arts planned to organize an exhibit of petit-bourgeois elements in art and antiaesthetic elements in the workers' everyday life. . . . Mayakovsky decried the effeminate interiors of the new Soviet middle class, with their gramophone records, lace curtains, rubber plants, porcelain elephants, and portraits of Marx in crimson frames." Svetlana Boym, *Common Places: Mythologies of Everyday Life in Russia* (Cambridge: Harvard University Press, 1994), pp. 8–9.

40. *Poshnost'* comes from *poshló,* something that has been and has passed; according to Vladimir Nabokov, it is "unobvious sham . . . not only the obviously trashy but also the falsely important, the falsely beautiful, the falsely clever, the falsely attractive"; in the dictionary of the Soviet Academy of Sciences, it is: "Lacking in spiritual qualities, ordinary, insignificant, worthless, paltry. Not original, worn-out, banal. Indecent, obscene, tasteless, vulgar." Boym summarizes: "This one word encompasses triviality, vulgarity, sexual promiscuity, and lack of spirituality." Ibid., pp. 41–42 and 301n.

41. Ibid., p. 6. Boym is commenting on the criticism made of an ideologically incorrect rubber tree that appears among the new residents' possession depicted in Aleksandr Laktionov's 1952 painting *The New Apartment.* "When I explained *The New Apartment* painting to my American students, they attempted to figure out what specific thing about this plant made it a symbol of bad taste. But no knowledge of horticulture could help. There was no official hostility to exotic flora as such: the sumptuous Moscow subway, one of Stalin's major urban projects, is ornamented with exuberant palm trees and other plants that have never grown in Russia" (ibid., p. 8). The illustrated journal *USSR in Construction* (printed in Moscow in four languages for foreign distribution) provides some clues. Issue no. 5, 1933, has two relevant articles. One is on USSR rubber being extracted from indigenous wild plants, *tau-sagiz, kok-sagiz,* and *Krim-sagiz* (sic). Another is a report on geranium cultivation in Abkhazia for ether oil that used to be imported from Algeria: "For 150 years geraniums grew on Russian window-sills. At the same time in France, Spain and Algeria geranium leaves and stems were made to yield ether oil, which is a valuable product in making perfume and sweetmeats. Now in addition to tobacco and tea, geranium is cultivated in Abkhazia as one of the leading crops. During the current sewing [sic] season geranium will be planted on an area of 800 hectares which will yield about 12,000 kilograms of most valuable ether oil." In other words, the crime of both domestic rubber plants and geraniums was that they were unproductive of use value.

42. Perhaps in the 1930s, rubber plants were not yet markers of bad taste. A 1932 publicity photo of "new men," former peasants Viktor Kalmykov and his wife Emilia Bakke who had become industrial workers, shows Emilia serving up lunchtime soup to newspaper-reading Viktor as sunlight streams in on the white tablecloth and a tree-sized rubber plant thrives behind them. See the photo insert in Stephen Kotkin, *Steeltown, USSR: Soviet Society in the Gorbachev Era* (Berkeley: University of California Press, 1991).

43. Cited in Boym, *Common Places,* p. 35. Maiakovskii's suicide in 1930 was connected to his despair at the return to prerevolutionary consciousness within daily life. In fact domestic symbolism was a contested space in cultural discourse. If coziness was banished in the 1920s by the revolutionary cultural program, the social tastes of the 1930s tended to turn to "middle-class manners and values"— solid, respectable, and pro-family, as distinguished from "bourgeois" luxury, softness, and decadence. Flowers replaced geometric patterns on cloth; new furniture was made in nineteenth-century styles. This conservatism in domestic fashion may have been a compensation for the anxiety produced by the tremendous social and geographic mobility of the thirties. See Gábor T. Rittersporn, "From Working Class to Urban Laboring Mass: On Politics and Social Categories in the Formative Years of the Soviet System," in Lewis H. Siegelbaum and Ronald Grigor Suny, eds., *Making Workers Soviet: Power, Class, and Identity* (Ithaca: Cornell University Press, 1994), p. 270 and passim.

44. Magnitogorsk newspaper, 1930, cited in Stephen Kotkin, *Magnetic Mountain: Stalinism as a Civilization* (Berkeley: University of California Press, 1995), p. 158.

45. Kollontai's position was only the most notorious (and popular among students), not the most widely shared. More commonly, Bolsheviks were ascetics about sexual matters, preferring the sublimated love of comrades and healthy activities of sport to the free love implied in the glass-of-water theory. See "Excerpts from Klara Zetkin: *Reminiscences of Lenin,*" in Rudolf Schlesinger, ed., *The Family in the U.S.S.R.: Documents and Readings* (London: Routledge and Kegan Paul, 1949), pp. 75–79 and passim. It was Lenin who referred to the "trivialities" of private housework as a manifestation of the "backwardness of women" (ibid., p. 78).

46. In January 1921 a law abolished all rents; in July of the same year a monthly charge was reinstated to cover the cost of maintenance and repairs, but the amount remained low.

47. The inadequacies of this conception for feminism (and for socialism) have been argued by Zillah Eisenstein, *The Radical Future of Liberal Feminism* (Boston: Northeastern University Press, 1981), Jean Bethke Elshtain, *Public Man, Private Woman* (Princeton: Princeton University Press, 1981), and Carole Pateman, *The Sexual Contract* (Stanford: Stanford University Press, 1988).

48. Schlesinger, ed., *The Family in the U.S.S.R.,* p. 86.

49. For the most forceful analysis from a radical feminist perspective of why the liberal conception of legal equality is inadequate for achieving real social equality for women, see Zillah Eisenstein, *The Female Body and the Law* (Berkeley: University of California Press, 1989).

50. See Schlesinger, ed., *The Family in the U.S.S.R.,* pp. 81–153, for extensive excerpts from women testifying during the debates in the Soviet parliament over the draft of the revision—amid much "laughter and giggling" from the audience. The concerns were traditional ones, having to do with child support, abandonment, and alimony. The solutions were conceived as providing more "safeguards" for women, which, of course, not only acknowledged the existence of sexual inequality, but codified it (ibid., p. 89).

51. "In one of the barracks I was conversing with a Komsomol. I asked, 'How is it living here?' The young man answered, 'Well, what do you want? Difficulties abound, sometimes quite grave. But we are not depressed. We are bringing a factory into being, then we will live better . . .' How much energy they had. How much enthusiasm! They lived life as builders of Magnitka. Magnitka became their dream, the substance of their lives." Report from the early 1930s, cited in Kotkin, *Magnetic Mountain,* p. 440.

52. "An apprentice . . . kept a diary of his becoming a bona fide steel smelter. . . . Excerpts were published in the factory newspaper telling the tale of his developing relationship with his furnace." Ibid., p. 218.

53. Ibid., pp. 50 and 410n.

54. A 1929 pamphlet, cited in ibid., p. 492n.

55. Magnitogorsk journal, 1931, cited in ibid., p. 73.

56. A 1934 journal article, cited in ibid., p. 437n. Similarly, the Moscow Mining Academy was nicknamed "the nursery of scientists and ministers" (ibid., p. 55).

57. Ibid., p. 218.

58. Cited in ibid.

59. Ibid., p. 66.

60. Ibid., pp. 66–67.

61. See William G. Rosenberg and Lewis H. Siegelbaum, eds., *Social Dimensions of Soviet Industrialization* (Bloomington: Indiana University Press, 1993). A major theme of the

essays in this anthology is that Stalin was father of "the people," not of the working class (p. 372), that people's social identity was based on work rather than class (p. 277), and that "the people," not the working class, were informing on traitors during the purges (p. 317).

62. "And now I'm a citizen of the USSR. Like all citizens, I have the right to a job, to education and to leisure. I can elect and be elected to the soviet." Cited in Kotkin, *Magnetic Mountain,* p. 230.

63. Cited in Kendall E. Bailes, *Technology and Society under Lenin and Stalin: Origins of the Soviet Technical Intelligentsia, 1917–1941* (Princeton: Princeton University Press, 1978), pp. 386–387.

64. Régine Robin, "Stalinism and Popular Culture," in Hans Günther, ed., *The Culture of the Stalin Period* (New York: St. Martin's Press, 1990), p. 24. The 1936 law also made divorces more difficult and expensive.

65. Eric Naiman, *Sex in Public: The Incarnation of Early Soviet Ideology* (Princeton: Princeton University Press, 1997), p. 290.

66. See the descriptions of Moisei Ginzburg's apartments which were to function as "social condensers," and other designs for spacious and modern house-communes, educating their inhabitants in "social justice, equality and progress," in Anatole Kopp, *Town and Revolution: Soviet Architecture and City Planning, 1917–1935,* trans. Thomas E. Burton (New York: George Braziller, 1970), p. 15. (Boym writes: "Paradoxically, the few house-communes that were built in Moscow and Petrograd were never turned into communal apartments but became privileged housing for members of the intellectual elite"; *Common Places,* p. 128.)

67. Boym, *Common Places,* pp. 124–125.

68. "The partition is the central architectural feature of the communal apartment. Most of them are made of plywood and they mark the intersection of public and private spheres within the apartment. After the expropriation of property, the old rooms and hallways were partitioned and subdivided, creating weird angular spaces, with a window opening into a sunless back yard or without any windows. Every tenant exercised her imagination in inventing curtains and screens to delineate their minimum privacy. . . . It let through all the noises, the snoring, the fragments of conversations, the footsteps of the neighbor, and everything else you can think of. The partition served not so much to preserve intimacy as to create an illusion that some intimacy was possible." Ibid., p. 146.

69. Ibid., p. 157. "The artifact is a personal souvenir and a souvenir of privacy itself; it is an object displaced from a common into an individual history" (ibid., p. 159).

70. Cooking remained separate and inhabitants had individual burners. "Because communal life was endlessly bureaucratized according to schedules dictating in detail the use of each oven and sink, the potential for friction was unending" (ibid., p. 147). Crucial documentation of this is Ilya Kabakov's installation *The Communal Apartment,* 1981–1988 (Ronald Feldman Gallery, New York).

71. "Until the 1970s very few apartments had bathrooms (usually separate from the toilet). And where there were bathtubs, they were used for much more important occupations than mere self-indulgent washing. . . . The bathtub became my mother's study, her only private space in the crowded apartment" (Boym, *Common Places,* p. 147). Other uses for the bathtub included doing laundry and storing potatoes (Ilya Kabakov and Boris Groys, *Die Kunst des Fliehens* [Munich: Carl Hanser Verlag, 1991], p. 86).

72. "The toilet was often occupied by some avid reader. The neighbors tried to be discreet, not lining up for the toilet but watching through the half-opened doors of their rooms, planning when to make their strategic move. Sometimes, though, the wait went beyond the limits of their patience and they would bang ferociously on the door. And, of course, the neighbor who did not turn off the lights in the toilet [signaling its vacancy] was considered 'an enemy of the people.'" Boym, *Common Places,* p. 147).

73. Ibid.

74. When it came to drunkenness or boorishness, embarrassment was experienced by witnesses more than by the perpetrators (see ibid., pp. 121–123). Mikhail Bulgakov's play *The Heart of the Dog* tells about a professor's attempt to protect his right to eat "in the dining room and not in the bedroom," by operating to bring "to life a new creature, a new Soviet man with the heart of a dog, to occupy the room that the Housing Committee threatened to expropriate. But this ungrateful Soviet Frankenstein joins up with the Housing Committee to threaten the professor himself." (Ibid., p. 136.)

75. Ibid., p. 102.

76. Apartments were used for exhibitions beginning in the 1960s; in the 1980s this tradition was celebrated by a movement that first called itself MANA (Moscow Archive of New Art), which began to exhibit on a regular basis in Nikita Alekseev's apartment in Moscow and subsequently took on the name "Aptart" (apartment art). This space "gave birth to the most stimulating artistic environment since the avant-garde period." See Margarita Tupitsyn, *Margins of Soviet Art: Socialist Realism to the Present* (Milan: Giancarlo Politi Editore, 1989), p. 113.

77. Susan Strasser, *Never Done: A History of American Housework* (New York: Pantheon Books, 1982), pp. 100, 102–103.

78. This logic had been used by Adam Smith in *The Wealth of Nations.*

79. For the commodity-driven nature of U.S. electrification, see David E. Nye, *Electrifying America: Social Meanings of a New Technology, 1880–1940* (Cambridge: MIT Press, 1990).

80. Marchand, *Advertising the American Dream,* pp. 217–222.

81. Cited in ibid., p. 218.

82. Ibid., pp. 219–220. There was an inverted form of this parable, the "Democracy of Afflictions": halitosis, body odor, dandruff, athlete's foot could strike anyone, and the same remedy was prescribed for all (ibid., p. 218).

83. Cited in ibid., p. 293.

84. Khrushchev still was speaking the discourse of temporal acceleration, however. The Soviet goal was unchanged: to "overtake and surpass the United States," and with their technological help (see his speech to a U.S. audience in Pittsburgh, September 24, 1959, in *Khrushchev in America: Texts and Speeches* [New York: Crosscurrents Press, 1960], p. 164).

85. Roy Medvedev, *Khrushchev: A Biography,* trans. Brian Pearce (Garden City: Anchor Press, 1983), p. 146.

86. A CPSU Central Committee report of spring 1959 indicates that the Soviets were well aware of the U.S. propaganda intent. It noted: "Special attention will be paid to the demonstration of domestic appliances: electric kitchens, vacuum cleaners, refrigerators, air conditioners, etc." Visitors would learn "how American housewives prepare dinner," be "treated to free tastings of the cooked dishes, [as well as] popular movies, color TV (not yet available in the Soviet Union), and souvenirs: lapel pins, model cars, plastic cups, and Pepsi-Cola." (Cited in Walter L. Hixson, *Parting the Curtain: Propaganda, Culture and the Cold War, 1945–1961* [New York: St. Martin's Press, 1996], p. 186.) The U.S. Department of State records indicate that U.S. corporations had persuaded the American Radiator and Standard Sanitary Corporation to provide free of charge 150 toilets, 50 urinals, and 50 wash basins to be installed in a large public rest room for visitors that was "up-to-date, color tiled . . . with all the modern gadgets such as hot hand blowers, ultra-violet sanitation [and] rapid flush toilets" (cited in ibid., p. 189). The Soviet officials "flatly rejected" these plans and installed their own facilities in Sokolniki Park (ibid.).

87. See Zillah Eisenstein, *Hatreds: Racialized and Sexualized Conflicts in the 21st Century* (New York: Routledge, 1996), pp. 148–170. "Neither statism—communist or nationalist—nor capitalist markets, per se, are friends to women" (ibid., p. 153).

88. See Zillah Eisenstein, *The Color of Gender: Reimagining Democracy* (Berkeley: University of California Press, 1994), pp. 15–35.

89. On the psychoanalytics of the "foundational fantasy" embodied in commodities, and of consumer desire as the illusory omnipotence of instant gratification, see Teresa Brennan, *History after Lacan* (New York: Routledge, 1993), pp. 79–117.

90. Walter Benjamin, *Gesammelte Schriften,* vol. 5: *Das Passagen-Werk,* ed. Rolf Tiedemann (Frankfurt: Suhrkamp Verlag, 1982), p. 494.

91. One series from the 1980s consists of portraits of Stalin—looking at himself in a mirror, peeking out the rear window of an automobile, dead on the floor—defying both the obligatory heroic depictions of the Stalinist era and the obligatory erasure of his image after de-Stalinization.

92. Benjamin, *Passagen-Werk,* p. 1048.

CHAPTER 6
LIVED TIME / HISTORICAL TIME

1. The Landau Institute, which my partner, Eric Siggia, was visiting, had long been privileged as a destination for foreign scientists, and was open to domestic talent regardless of party membership.

2. Her father, Vladimir Petrovskii, was Deputy Minister of Foreign Affairs under Gorbachev.

3. When I began a lecture at the Institute by citing Marx, the audience laughed. I had not meant to be funny. What so amused them was my unwitting repetition of the opening rhetorical gesture, a citation from Marx or Lenin, that had been obligatory in every speech delivered there for the past seventy years.

4. Zdenek Mlynar, one of the Czech leaders of the Prague Spring, was a friend of Gorbachev when both were in law school at Moscow State University. See John B. Dunlop, *The Rise of Russia and the Fall of the Soviet Empire* (Princeton: Princeton University Press, 1993), p. 490.

5. This exchange was supported by a grant from the MacArthur Foundation administered through the Peace Studies Program at Cornell.

6. Nancy Ries's skill as an anthropologist allowed us to negotiate our way through the minefield of Soviet gender relations. Our interview with V. V. Mshvenieradze, Deputy Director of the Institute of Philosophy, resulted in official endorsement of our work, as well as a telephone call to V. A. Tishkov, Director of the Institute of Ethnology and Anthropology, who helped make arrangements for Ries's future field work. Tishkov has written a critical and insightful article on the role of the Soviet discourse of anthropology in the construction of ethnic-national identities in the post-Soviet period, "Inventions and Manifestations of Ethno-Nationalism in and after the Soviet Union," in Kumar Rupesinghe et al., eds., *Ethnicity and Conflict in a Post-Communist World: The Soviet Union, Eastern Europe and China* (London: St. Martin's Press, 1992). Ries's dissertation was published by Cornell University Press in 1997, entitled *Russian Talk: Culture and Conversation during Perestroika.*

7. Again, the MacArthur Foundation made that future possible. In 1988–1989 I held a year-long MacArthur Grant for Research and Writing in International Peace and Security.

8. These lectures, in an abbreviated form, provide the core of the argument in chapter 1 (section 1.1) above. They were typeset for publication in *Telos*, but because I would not modify my criticism of Carl Schmitt, they never appeared. The second lecture was published in Russian translation as "Politicheskoe voobrazhaemoe frantsuskoi revolutsii," in W. W. Bibichin, ed., *Filosofiia i revolutsiia: Sravniv s dostignuitim visokii ideal*, part II, an anthology published on the occasion of the bicentennial of the French Revolution (Moscow: Academy of Sciences, 1989), pp. 4–19.

9. The invitation came from Philosophy and Humanities Professor Helena N. Gourko.

10. *Istorikofilosofskii ezhegodnik '90* (Moscow: Nauka, 1991). The complete (wonderfully illustrated) Russian edition of Walter Benjamin's *Moscow Diary* (*Moskovskii dnevnik*), ed. Mikhail Ryklin, trans. S. Romanshko, appeared in 1997 (Moscow: Ad Marginem).

11. Jameson edited an issue of *South Atlantic Quarterly* (Spring 1991) with translations of our Moscow colleagues' work. Tatiana Klimenkova edited and Elena Petrovskaia translated a section of Jameson's book *The Political Unconscious*, to appear in Russian.

12. Important for the change in attitude was the appointment of a new director of the Institute of Philosophy, V. S. Stepin, who gave support to Western contacts in general and Podoroga's group in particular. During my first meeting with him, when I said that it was my third visit to the Institute, he countered with humor: "And each time, you have met with a new director. Perhaps you shouldn't come a fourth time!" Dr. Stepin remained director despite my frequent returns.

13. The conference was planned by Nellie Matroshilova and Mikhail Kuznetsov of the Institute of Philosophy, and by Anatolii Mikhailov of the Institute of World Literature who had translated Lukács's aesthetic theory, as well as texts of Heidegger, into Russian.

14. I attended as an observer, using my influence to add, to the list of Heideggerians invited (the editor of Heidegger's works, Friedrich Wilhelm von Herrman, and a former Heidegger student, W. Anz), the countervoice of Geoffrey Waite, my colleague at Cornell who, along with Habermas-trained Hauke Brunkhorst from Frankfurt and the young Vittorio Hösle from Tübingen, provided an independent and politically critical perspective at the conference. Papers by Richard Rorty, Otto Pöggeler, and Jean-Luc Nancy were read in absentia. The conference proceedings have been published as *Filosofiia Martina Heideggera i sovremennost'*, ed. Mikhail Kuznetzov (Moscow: Academy of Sciences USSR, 1991).

15. My lecture, which I delivered in Russian, focused on a topic with contemporary political relevance: "Derrida, demokratiia i dekonstruktsiia." A gloss on Derrida's essay "Declarations of Independence," it dealt with the authorization of a democratic nation. It was published in *Ezhegodnik: Ad Marginem '93*, the yearbook of the Laboratory of Post-Classical Studies (Moscow: Ad Marginem, 1994).

16. See Jacques Derrida, *Specters of Marx: The State of the Debt, the Work of Mourning, and the New International*, trans. Peggy Kamuf, intro. Bernd Magnus and Stephen Cullenberg (New York: Routledge, 1994).

17. Jacques Derrida, "Back from Moscow, in the USSR," trans. Mary Quaintaire, ed. Peggy Kamuf, in Mark Poster, ed., *Politics, Theory, and Contemporary Culture* (New York: Columbia University Press, 1993), pp. 197–235. Russian trans. in *Jacques Derrida v Moskve: Dekonstruktsiia pyteshestviia* (Moscow: RIK "Kul'tura," 1993). See also Mikhail Ryklin's counterarticle in the latter volume: "Back in Moscow, *sans* the USSR" (English/French title in original).

18. For an account of major events, I have made liberal use of the helpful chronology (1985–1993) appended to the anthology of articles, *Remaking Russia*, ed. Heyward Isham (London: M. E. Sharpe, 1995), pp. 291–305.

19. It is worth reflecting on the fact that the creation of a democratic public sphere *preceded* both market reform and

the abolishment of the one-party system—i.e., markets and parliamentary government were *effects* of democratic practice rather than its precondition. Indeed, if Lewin is correct, the process of creating the new civil society pre-dated Gorbachev's ascendancy by several decades. Lewin argues that once this civil society took shape, the end of the old political and economic order was inevitable. See Moshe Lewin, *The Gorbachev Phenomenon: A Historical Interpretation,* expanded ed. (Berkeley: University of California Press, 1991). Of course, there was nothing inevitable about what kind of order (or disorder) would replace it. The link between "free" elections (parliamentary democracy) and "free" enterprise (capitalist social relations) is ideological rather than factual. History has shown repeatedly that capitalism is able not only to exist but to thrive within authoritarian political regimes.

20. Directed by Vasilii Pichul, *Malenkaia Vera* described the physically and emotionally cramped life of a family in a Soviet industrial city. Judging from letters received by the press, what shocked viewers was less the explicitness of the sex scene than the fact that the woman was on top of the man during it. Nataliia Negoda, who played the leading role in *Little Vera,* later appeared on the cover of the U.S. magazine *Playboy* (May 1989).

21. As First Party Secretary of the Sverdlovsk *obkom,* Yeltsin had swept 90 percent of the votes cast in the March 25 election in the largest and most important electoral district of the country, National Territorial District 1 (Dunlop, *The Rise of Russia,* p. 43).

22. Gorbachev had granted Sakharov the freedom to return from exile in Gorky in 1986.

23. Galina Starovoitova spoke in the terms of this new discourse: "The conflict between Yeltsin and Gorbachev is not simply a dispute between two men who do not like each other. There is an objective historical basis for the conflict: a clash of two opposing tendencies—namely, the striving of Russia to find its sovereignty and the striving of an empire to preserve its former might. The president of the USSR . . . does not have his own territorial domain." Starovoitova, cited in Dunlop, *The Rise of Russia,* p. 24.

24. East German leader Erich Honecker stepped from power on October 18. The Czechoslovakian regime began to feel the threat of mass citizen protest on October 28, although it was not until November 20 that huge demonstrations in Wenceslas Square destabilized the regime, forcing Gustav Husák to resign on December 9. Bulgaria's leader, Todor Zhivkov, resigned apparently voluntarily on November 10. The Romanian leader Nicolae Ceausescu and his wife Elena were executed on Decem-

ber 25, three days after mass demonstrations forced him from office.

25. See, on Eastern Europe, Gale Stokes, *The Walls Came Tumbling Down: The Collapse of Communism in Eastern Europe* (New York: Oxford University Press, 1993); on the USSR, Lewin, *The Gorbachev Phenomenon.*

26. Launched (in collaboration with Eastern European scholars) by Herbert Marcuse and continued by Jürgen Habermas, this course had been meeting since the 1970s. The directors from the West in 1989 were Axel Honneth and Jean Cohen.

27. In March 1990, Podoroga, Petrovskaia, and I met with Jameson at a conference at Duke University, "Soviet Culture Today: Restructuring the Past or Inventing the Future?" Partial proceedings of that conference have been published as *Late Soviet Culture from Perestroika to Novostroika,* ed. Thomas Lahusen with Gene Kuperman (Durham: Duke University Press, 1993). Lahusen, Professor of Slavic Literature at Duke, was the organizer of the conference. Kuperman, along with Jonathan Flatley, both graduate students in comparative literature at Duke, later went to study at Podoroga's Laboratory in Moscow—the first "sparrows," Podoroga called them, migrating after a long and isolating intellectual winter.

28. I met Kozakiewicz at the critical theory course in Dubrovnik in 1989. She invited me to Warsaw early that summer, and was a visitor to Cornell University in November of that year. In June 1990 I attended a conference at her Institute in Warsaw on "The Philosophy of Social Choice."

29. According to Tadek Jarski, the London chairman of Solidarity for Solidarity, the idea came to Gorny and Zazac "when they saw a copy of the 'original' Gary Cooper poster in the lobby of the American Embassy in Warsaw where they were applying for a visa" (Andrew Wornick, *Promotional Culture: Advertising, Ideology and Symbolic Expression* [London: Sage Publications, 1991], p. 151n). Professionals from the United States were imported to Poland to aid in the election campaigns.

30. Jameson was careful to describe postmodernism as a hegemonic norm of late capitalism, a "specific logic of cultural production," opposing the use of the term as "yet another disembodied culture critique or diagnosis of the spirit of the age" (Fredric Jameson, *Postmodernism, or, The Cultural Logic of Late Capitalism* [Durham: Duke University Press, 1992], p. 400).

31. Reading Aijaz Ahmad's book *In Theory: Classes, Nations, Literatures* (New York: Verso, 1992) first made me aware that this was indeed a hegemonic shift, and that it

did not take place in a political and economic vacuum. Ahmad argues compellingly that it is not the idea of postmodernity (or modernity) that is oppressive, but its translation into cultural practices as these terms are disseminated within the postcolonial and global capitalist context. But Ahmad holds onto a classical Marxist scheme (itself an ideological construct) for evaluating this shift more strongly than I think warranted. The transition we are speaking about needs to inform (*trans*form) Marxist theory (questioning, for example, whether any socialism worthy of the name can ever emerge from existing forms of industrialization), at the same time as Marxist theory informs us about the transition.

32. Merab Mamardashvili, "Culture and Philosophy," presentation at Dubrovnik, October 1990. See also his posthumously published *Kak ia ponimaiu filosofiiu* (Moscow: Progress-Kultura, 1992).

33. Elements of this talk, "East/West: Is There a Common Postmodern Culture?" have been incorporated into the constellations in part III of this book.

34. Todorov's work has since been published in English. See his book *Red Square, Black Square: Organon for Revolutionary Imagination* (Albany: State University of New York Press, 1995); also the article "Introduction to the Physiognomy of Ruins," *Yale Journal of Criticism* 6, no. 1 (Spring 1993), pp. 249–257, and his several contributions to *Post-Theory, Games, and Discursive Resistance: The Bulgarian Case*, ed. Alexander Kiossev (Albany: State University of New York Press, 1995).

35. This particular event in which, with gentle charm, Mamardashvili took the authorial and phallic chalk out of my hand as if from a child, was generational as well. Still, there is no doubt that liberation for women in the Soviet Union never included granting equal respect for the power of women as philosophical thinkers (nor does it in the West). Feminist theory did not play a major role at the Dubrovnik meeting. Renata Salecl from Ljubljana was invited but unable to come, so that we missed her contribution on women and ethnic nationalism in Yugoslavia. The presence of the feminist theorist Tatiana Klimenkova, who had been part of our group in Moscow, was also sadly lacking. During my next visit to Moscow in January 1991, we devoted a session to issues of feminism at the Institute of Philosophy. The results were meager, despite the presence of Irina Sandomirskaia, outspoken in her feminism, who worked with Alla Efimova from Rochester, New York, in editing the first issue of *Idioma*, an "International Journal of Post-Totalitarian Cultural Theory" devoted in part to feminist analyses. The situation in Russia has changed over this decade, and feminist artists have taken the lead. One of

them, Anna Alchuk, wife of Mikhail Ryklin, was part of our group.

36. Fredric Jameson, "Conversations on the New World Order," in Robin Blackburn, ed., *After the Fall: The Failure of Communism and the Future of Socialism* (New York: Verso, 1991), p. 260. Although Jameson does not mention the Dubrovnik meeting specifically, it is clearly the experience he has in mind when he speaks of "Yugoslavia, Bulgaria and the Soviet Union" in this essay written in March 1991, five months after our meeting.

37. Ibid., p. 265.

38. Lewis Mumford ("Technology and the Nature of Man," republished in *The New Technocratic Wave in the West* [Moscow, 1986]) was a source for Podoroga's seminal article on Platonov, "The Eunuch of the Soul," first published in *South Atlantic Quarterly* 90, no. 2 (Spring 1991), pp. 358–408; republished in Lahusen, ed., *Late Soviet Culture from Perestroika to Novostroika*. A later presentation, "Machines of Disorder" (1993), credits Gilles Deleuze and Félix Guattari's book *Anti-Oedipus* (Paris, 1972).

39. The term is Michael Holquist's. See his "Prologue" to Mikhail Bakhtin, *Rabelais and His World* (Bloomington: Indiana University Press, 1984), p. xviii.

40. Ryklin's Dubrovnik presentation is incorporated into his article "Bodies of Terror," trans. Molly Williams Wesling and Donald Wesling, preface by Caryl Emerson, *New Literary History* 24, no. 1 (Winter 1993), pp. 45–49.

41. One can say this with more humor and less pathos. In the recent discussion in Russia (initiated by the artists Komar and Melamid in 1991 and called "Monumental Propaganda") on the question of what to do with all the statues of Marx and Lenin and other Communist greats, the art group Medical Hermeneutics diagnosed the situation, suggesting that these statues were understandably tired and should be allowed to go to bed; it was necessary to "give them a rest" (Mikhail Ryklin, "The Fall of the Statues: The Fate of Soviet-Era Monuments," speech at the Society for the Humanities, Cornell University, March 28, 1995).

42. Elena Petrovskaia, "The Path to Gertrude Stein in Contemporary Post-Soviet Culture," *New Literary Review* 27, no. 2 (Spring 1996), p. 333.

43. In an article written in 1974, "The Vanishing Mediator; or, Max Weber as Storyteller," Jameson refers to the role of Protestantism in the transition from feudalism to capitalism as that of a "vanishing mediator": by insisting that the Christian religion (the ideological superstructure of the feudal mode of production) take itself seriously, thus universalizing its relevance in everyday life, it opened the

way for its opposite, the total secularization of daily life. Jameson concludes that Weber's theory of the Protestant ethic is fully compatible with a Marxist theory of the dialectic between substructure and superstructure. See Fredric Jameson, *The Ideologies of Theory: Essays 1971–1986*, vol. 2, *The Syntax of History* (Minneapolis: University of Minnesota Press, 1988), pp. 3–34.

44. This passage from Žižek's Dubrovnik paper was incorporated into a later essay (which I cite here): Slavoj Žižek, "Enjoy Your Nation as Yourself!," in *Tarrying with the Negative: Kant, Hegel, and the Critique of Ideology* (Durham: Duke University Press, 1993), p. 230. Žižek describes the parallels between the role of the present "vanishing mediators" and that of Protestantism in the period of "decadence" at the end of the feudal era: "It could be said that precisely the period of 'decadence' opens up to the ruling ideology the possibility of 'taking itself seriously' and opposing its own social base. . . . In this way, unknowingly, the 'vanishing mediators' unchained the forces of their own final destruction: once their job was done, they were 'overrun by history' (*Neues Forum* scored 3 percent at the elections) and a new 'scoundrel time' sets in, with people in power who were mostly silent during the Communist repression and who nonetheless now indict *Neues Forum* as 'crypto-Communists' " (p. 230).

45. Ibid., p. 228.

46. Ibid., p. 228. Žižek seems to be arguing that this reinstitution of the Big Other, "the fantasy which fills out the void of the vanishing mediators" (p. 232), is inescapable. This leads him to the conclusion that the emergence of ethnic nationalism—or at least something like it—was a historical necessity. Indeed, he sees the fate of Yugoslavia as anticipatory of our future rather than some atavistic residue of the political past: "the first clear taste of the twenty-first century" (p. 223). It appears to lead him to a politics of Hegelian quietism, even though his closing appeal is for "*tarrying with the negative*," that is, sustaining the critical moment earlier articulated by the "vanishing mediators" (p. 237).

47. Ibid., p. 209. See in this context Susan L. Woodward's analysis of how economic pressures from the global capitalist system prefigured the outbreak of war in the former Yugoslavia: *Balkan Tragedy: Chaos and Dissolution after the Cold War* (Washington: Brookings Institution, 1995).

48. Žižek, "Enjoy Your Nation as Yourself!," pp. 210–211.

49. Ibid., p. 220. "In those confused months of the passage of 'really existing socialism' into capitalism, *the fiction of a 'third way' was the only point at which social antagonism was not obliterated*. Herein lies one of the tasks of the 'postmodern' critique of ideology: to designate the elements within

an existing social order which—in the guise of 'fiction,' i.e., of the 'utopian' narratives of possible but failed alternative histories—point toward the system's antagonistic character and thus 'estrange' us from the self-evidence of its established identity." (Ibid., p. 231.)

50. Ibid., p. 231.

51. Ivailo Dichev, "The Post-Communist Condition," presentation at Dubrovnik, October 1990. A different version of this paper, "The Post-Paranoid Condition," is published in Kiossev, ed., *Post-Theory, Games, and Discursive Resistance*, pp. 105–118. Dichev has several articles in this volume.

52. Ivailo Dichev, "The Post-Communist Condition," paper delivered at Dubrovnik, pp. 1–3.

53. See note 27 above.

54. Boris Kagarlitsky, *The Disintegration of the Monolith*, trans. Renfrew Clarke (New York: Verso, 1992), pp. 17–18.

55. See John Miller, *Mikhail Gorbachev and the End of Soviet Power* (New York: St. Martin's Press, 1993), pp. 183–200.

56. Lithuania had never formally given up these claims, although Gorbachev had declared them illegal and invalid. Yeltsin's own conception of the degree of autonomy for groups within Russia was not fully spelled out, but his public statements went quite far. "Most notably, during a three-week trip in August and September 1990 that took him to Tatarstan, Bashkiria, and the Komi Autonomous Republic, he told local elites to 'take all the autonomy you can swallow,' although he added they would be better off sticking with the RSFSR government in opposition to Gorbachev and the old center." Gail W. Lapidus and Edward W. Walker, "Nationalism, Regionalism, and Federalism," in Gail W. Lapidus, ed., *The New Russia: Troubled Transformation* (Boulder: Westview Press, 1995), p. 83.

57. On May 1, 1990, during the traditional May Day parade, thousands of Moscow protesters had jeered Gorbachev and other members of the Soviet leadership standing on top of Lenin's mausoleum. Moscow's mayor was the pro-Yeltsin economist Gavriil Popov. One of the founders of Democratic Russia, he was elected Chairman of the Moscow City Council in March 1990.

58. A revised version has been published, entitled "The Cinema Screen as Prosthesis," in Nadia Seremetakis, ed., *The Senses Still* (Chicago: University of Chicago Press, 1996).

59. In fact, I do not know that they were not. Dunlop notes that in response to the use of force in Lithuania, the European Community (with which the Baltic states had

developed ties in the hopes of joining as independent nations) showed its disapproval by delaying consideration of aid to the USSR (one billion dollars in food and half a billion in technical assistance), and that the U.S. Congress threatened to cut off all aid to the Soviet Union if the repression in Lithuania continued (see Dunlop, *The Rise of Russia*, p. 152). He concludes that "the Western democracies in fact took swift action to punish the USSR for its glaring retreat from democracy and from reform" (ibid.). But this evidence does not rule out the possibility that secretly the Bush administration was having a different sort of exchange with Soviet officials. On November 19, 1990, Bush met privately with Gorbachev at the American Embassy in Paris during an international conference, and tried to secure his "authorization" for the use of U.S. force in the Gulf against Iraq. Gorbachev was resistant. It has been speculated that what he wanted in return was precisely U.S. neutrality in his struggle with the Baltic states, and that Bush at that time complied: "No United States representative turned up at Latvia's National Day celebration in Paris on November 19, nor did Bush make a single reference to Baltic demands for self-determination in his Paris speech about the new world of freedom that he said he was trying to create in Europe. Similarly, a long-scheduled trip by Assistant Treasury Secretary Bruce Bartlett to Vilnius, the capital of Lithuania, to discuss economic matters was abruptly cancelled as 'inappropriate.' " (Jean Edward Smith, *George Bush's War* [New York: Henry Holt and Company, 1992], p. 210.)

60. Bush himself is alleged to have said triumphantly the following morning, "By God, we've kicked the Vietnam Syndrome once and for all!" Cited in James Der Derian, *Antidiplomacy: Spies, Terror, Speed and War* (Cambridge, Mass.: Blackwell, 1992), p. 177.

61. See Mikhail Ryklin, "Metamorphoses of Speech Vision," trans. Clark Troy, in David A. Ross et al., eds., *Between Spring and Summer: Soviet Conceptual Art in the Era of Late Communism* (Cambridge: MIT Press, 1990), pp. 135–145.

62. From October 1990 through April 1991, Gorbachev's policies moved to reflect pro-Soviet interests in what was perceived as a "shift to the right." On February 19, 1991, in a live television interview, Yeltsin expressed the need for Russia to defend its "sovereignty" against "centralized power," and called for Gorbachev's immediate resignation and the transfer of power to a new federation of the republics. On March 10 there were vast demonstrations in support of "Russian sovereignty" throughout the republic. Nonetheless, on March 17, 71 percent of the Russian populace voted in a Soviet-wide referendum in favor of "the preservation of the Union of Soviet Socialist Republics as a renewed federation of equal sovereign republics." Gorbachev claimed the vote as a victory for his position, but the language of the referendum could be interpreted as support for Yeltsin's more decentralized alternative. On March 28, Gorbachev invoked his emergency powers as Soviet president to forbid all rallies in Moscow. The RSFSR parliament voted 532 to 286 to defy this ban. When an estimated 150,000 to 500,000 demonstrators took to the streets, Gorbachev backed down from using force against them. He subsequently agreed to work with Yeltsin and the heads of the other republics for a new version of the union federation that would give the republics greater sovereign power—evidence of a "shift to the left" that, according to the accepted interpretation of events, was a cause of the August coup, staged one day before the new, more decentralized Union treaty was to have been signed (see Dunlop, *The Rise of Russia*, pp. 30–35).

63. See Dunlop for the available data to answer the unsolved "riddles" of the coup: why Gorbachev was so compliant during his "arrest"; why Yeltsin's entourage was allowed to leave his dacha, drive to Moscow, and take up position in the White House (the telephone lines of which were never cut) without being detained or arrested; why the military did not storm the White House on the night of August 19, or the following night (*The Rise of Russia*, pp. 202–217).

64. The power to declare such an emergency is exclusive to sovereign power (see above, chapter 1). The sovereignty that the coup leaders were defending in this case was the "thousand-year-old State"—a term that conflated the histories of the Russian and Soviet empires.

65. According to Gorbachev, foreign radio broadcasts were his only access to what was happening during the coup.

66. Dunlop, *The Rise of Russia*, p. 213. Dunlop believes that "this early judgement" by Western commentators "is one that will likely stand the test of time. . . . Unerringly, [Yeltsin] and his team decided upon a correct strategy" (ibid.).

67. Kagarlitsky, *Disintegration of the Monolith*, p. 136. Kagarlitsky gives the following evidence (in addition to the unsolved "riddles" described by Dunlop; see note 62 above): the television channels controlled by the putschists publicized both Yeltsin's movements and the protest demonstrations; the troops staging the coup were not armed, or were incompletely armed; eyewitnesses claimed there was no blockade around Gorbachev's dacha in the Crimea; there was an epidemic of strange "suicides" of top officials after the putsch's failure; Yeltsin would not have dared risk massive citizen bloodshed had he thought the tanks would really fire on the White House's defenders.

When the leaders of the junta realized that Yeltsin was not going along with the plan, they tried to take real power on 20 August, stating (to Kravchenko, head of All-Union State Radio and Television) that "if they had already been declared traitors and criminals, then they had no other choice than to act accordingly." Yeltsin and his team could have left the White House, but waited until three died in a clash between the army and citizens, thereby according "official legendary status" to "the bloody junta." The putschists fled, "not to Iraq," but to Gorbachev in the Crimea, "where they were successfully arrested": "Yana-yev, Pugo and Kryuchkov's coup had failed; Yeltsin's had succeeded. Gorbachev was delivered to Moscow nominally as the president of a state that no longer existed, but in essence as a hostage to the White House" (*Disintegration of the Monolith*, pp. 133–137).

68. The United States was still a military superpower, if not a financial one: "Unable and/or unwilling to foot the bill for a strategy it devised, the United States insured funding for the military conflict through a global coalition of economic resources assembled under the umbrella of the Gulf War Financial Coordination Committee. Much of the secretary of state's diplomatic activity in the period approaching January 1991 involved soliciting monetary grants from countries around the world—an exercise derisively labelled 'tin-cup diplomacy'; the United States was thus able to secure more than enough contributions (totalling $54.6 billion) to pay for the war." David Campbell, *Politics without Principle: Sovereignty, Ethics, and the Narratives of the Gulf War* (Boulder: Lynne Rienner Publishers, 1993), p. 83.

69. The press picked up Bush's unnuanced comparison of Saddam with Hitler, and World War II was the analogy used for several of the military attacks (see John R. MacArthur, *Second Front: Censorship and Propaganda in the Gulf War* [New York: Hill and Wang, 1992], pp. 71–72). The actual conduct of the United States during the war was marked by "shades of gray," as is documented in chapters 3 and 4 of Campbell, *Politics without Principle*. "Contrary to the videographic image of (in General Colin Powell's word) a 'clean win,' this was a war in which large numbers of people died. It is an obvious point, but the death-free representation of the war (actively cultivated by the Pentagon and implicitly accepted by the media) requires active contestation. This is a task made difficult by the military's aversion to any definitive assessment of Iraqi casualties. Since the military used bulldozers to bury thousands of Iraqui dead in mass graves, in addition to using bulldozers to bury Iraqui troops alive as the ground war began [reported in the New York *Times*, September 15, 1991], it is more than likely that some sort of assessment

has been made. Not to have done so would mean that the United States contravened the Geneva Convention's requirement that belligerents search for the dead, record information that might aid in identification, and establish their cause of death." (*Politics without Principle*, p. 68.)

70. See above, chapter 1. It is significant that Bush acted alone to name the enemy and initiate violence—the quintessential acts of sovereignty—without requesting from the U.S. Congress a declaration of war. Throughout the period of the crisis that began in August 1990, "Bush remained in personal control of American policy. . . . Most important, Bush's original order to General Powell to commence hostilities on January 16 was a singular, unilateral decision made by the president based on his authority as commander in chief. It . . . was not initially revealed to Congress or to the public. A declaration of war was not requested. In fact, the White House sought to mislead the legislators into postponing a debate on American policy in the Gulf until after war had begun." (Smith, *George Bush's War*, pp. 254–255.) Although, in the last days before Bush's ultimatum to Saddam Hussein ran out, Congress did debate, at times eloquently, the wisdom of deploying force in the Gulf, these debates, televised live, were by then academic. Once hostilities began, bipartisan support of the military unquestioningly followed. Bush's solo performance was a clear example of "democratic sovereignty" as a contradiction in terms.

71. Kuwait's status as a "sovereign state" was simply posited as given. Its colonial origins were never examined; its *raison d'être* as a source of Western oil was never discussed. Bush's rhetoric ignored the embarrassing fact that in the Kuwaiti "nation," citizenship was practically never granted to outsiders via naturalization, and that in 1990 more than 60 percent of its total of 2.1 million residents fell into this disenfranchised category. "Kuwaitis comprised only 18 percent of the work force, mostly in the service industries and government. Filipino women cared for Kuwaiti children. Egyptians, Iranians, and Palestinians (the largest foreign contingent at more than 400,000) staffed its banks, offices, and hospitals. Some 10,000 Americans and Britons kept the oil fields running. In 1975, the Kuwaiti government had bought out all foreign interests, but the technical staff of the Kuwait Petroleum Corporation continued to be largely British and American." (Smith, *George Bush's War*, pp. 29–30.)

72. The rhetoric ensured "the reproduction of the myth of the frontier, in which territorial space becomes intertwined with ethical identity such that the fluid boundary and persistent struggle between 'civilization' and 'barbarism' is rendered in terms of geopolitical conflict." Campbell, *Politics without Principle*, p. 22.

73. "When Iraq accepted Kuwait's sovereignty and independence in 1963 (two years after sovereignty had been granted by Britain and first challenged by Iraq), the Agreed Minutes codifying that acceptance referred—in an act of continuous regression to other texts—to correspondence of 1932 between Iraq and Kuwait. Neither the 1932 letters nor the 1963 minutes, however, contained any map . . . to specify clearly the border's location. . . . To try and clarify matters and resolve the dispute between Iraq and Kuwait, the Arab League in 1962 established a Military Patrol Line (MPL) straddled by a buffer zone that was to be free of provocative activities. In contravention of the league's agreement, Kuwait moved drilling rigs into that zone in the 1970s; Iraqi troops then crossed the MPL to drive them back. The ensuing standoff lasted until the early 1980s, when Kuwait moved back in to establish a dozen drilling sites while Iraq was at war with Iran. Establishing a claim to the area, rather than achieving access to the oil per se, motivated the Kuwaitis' actions, because at 12,000 barrels per day, oil from the disputed zone constituted less than one-half of 1 percent of Kuwait's total production." Campbell, *Politics without Principle*, pp. 32–33.

74. The quotation is from Bush's press conference on December 18, 1990, cited in Smith, *George Bush's War*, p. 232.

75. "Greenpeace, which has made the most sustained analysis of casualty figures, estimates that a total of between 177,500 and 243,000 Iraqis were killed during the air war, the ground war, and the aftermath of the war." Campbell, *Politics without Principle*, pp. 68–69.

76. "That the destruction of Iraqi infrastructure was a war aim is evident in the fact that long after Iraqi troops were isolated in the south, targets such as bridges were being hit in the north. Indeed, Baghdad was subject to some of the most intense bombing of the war during the final ground phase. Moreover, many of the sites on the ever expanding target list compiled by U.S. commanders were chosen because of their psychological impact or because the need for foreign assistance in order to rebuild them would generate greater postwar leverage for the allied nations. Whatever the reason, the damage to Iraq's infrastructure—which a United Nations report termed 'near apocalyptic'—is likely to cost more than $30 billion to repair." Campbell, *Politics without Principle*, p. 71.

77. "While President Bush accused Iraq of 'environmental terrorism' for setting off an oil spill in the Gulf, it turned out that about one-third of that spill resulted from allied bombing of oil facilities in southern Iraq and Kuwait." Campbell, *Politics without Principle*, p. 72.

78. The MacArthur and Soros foundations, among others, opened Moscow offices in an attempt to fund Russian citizens directly.

79. Boris Groys implicates the entire avant-garde in the "aestheticization of politics," which for Benjamin is the identifying mark of fascism. He denies the possibility of another function for politically engaged art, which my essay, arguing (through Benjamin) for another meaning of "aesthetics," attempts to redeem. Groys's book has been translated as *Stalin's Total Artwork* (Princeton: Princeton University Press, 1992).

80. Ivailo Dichev wrote in 1990: "The television building was at the center of the Rumanian revolution. In Sofia it has been under siege for months now . . . [but] there is no longer a concrete adversary to be represented, nothing to be broken or burnt and replaced by new symbols. There is simply nothing but television, as all other representations can be televised. . . . Thus the people didn't actually have much to communicate . . . and we saw them in Bucharest, crowding in dozens in front of the camera, pressing into the frame without having much to say. These were revolutions of pure presence: no stratagem, no project for a better world." (Dichev, "The Post-Communist Condition," presentation at Dubrovnik, pp. 11–12; cf. Dichev, "The Post-Paranoid Condition," pp. 115–116.)

81. Der Derian, *Antidiplomacy*, pp. 175 and 191. Simulated realities, even territorial ones, are not new with television. The creation of "new geographies," as the Russian filmmaker Lev Kuleshov called them in the 1920s, was a discovery of early cinema.

82. It was precisely the lack of good photographs due to censorship that characterized the "aesthetics" of the televised coverage of the war. Filling this vacuum became a "design problem" for television. CBS's solution was as follows: "First, there was the opening title animation; second, there were the informational graphics, the fact sheets which we refer to as baseball cards, which depicted the military equipment and the weaponry which was deployed in the Gulf; [third] . . . a map format, which included both animated and still maps; and finally, the graphic depictions of events in the Gulf. Obviously there were no video or battle re-creations or illustrations of the Iraqi defenses or what have you." (Steve Vardy of CBS, cited in MacArthur, *Second Front*, p. 83.)

83. Kagarlitsky points out that Yeltsin's post-coup measures to consolidate control also included media censorship. Yeltsin effectively muzzled his enemies by shutting down the Communist presses and outlawing the party (see Kagarlitsky, *Disintegration of the Monolith*, pp. 137 and 146).

84. The commercial nature of the U.S. media worked effectively to ensure their loyalty. Although network television stations actually lost money in their coverage of the Gulf War, they were competing with each other for audience ratings which, indirectly, translated into advertising accounts. The reasoning was similar when *Newsweek* published an exclusive interview with President Bush which allowed free advertising for the administration line: "It is a business. You want people to buy and read your product. . . . If George Bush is taking *Newsweek* seriously, then readers ought to take it seriously." (Stephen Smith, executive editor of *Newsweek,* cited in MacArthur, *Second Front,* p. 100.)

85. One sympathizes with what one knows, so that the object enters perception as a form of memory. But one empathizes with what is new, entering into the object as a form of discovery. See above, chapter 3.

86. Der Derian writes that televised images "cut both ways": "the video images of the lone Chinese student staring down a column of tanks in Tiananmen Square, the foot of an unknown Lithuanian sticking from under the tread of a Soviet tank in Vilnius, or a group of Los Angeles policemen beating a black motorist"—all of these images have the opposite effect from that produced by the Gulf War's "tightly controlled, abstractly clean images . . . an appealing portrait of military technology solving intractable diplomatic problems" (*Antidiplomacy,* p. 163). Der Derian refers to the controlled images as the "aesthetics" of the Gulf War, whereas I would describe them as *an*aesthetics. His three countercases (images of Tiananmen Square, Vilnius, and Los Angeles), all involving empathic identification with the bodily pain of another *upon whom state-sanctioned violence is being inflicted,* are "aesthetic" experiences in the original sense, as somatic cognition capable of challenging the preconceptions and prejudices of cultural particularity. The fact that it is the ordinary citizen armed with a video camera who so often captures such "live" documentation is significant. The word *democratic* takes on new meaning here.

87. I say cyber*dream,* because the reality may be significantly less utopian (as Todd Gitlin wrote specifically of the 1968 Chicago riots in his book *The Whole World Is Watching*). It needs to be remembered that the "whole world" of a television audience is still a minority of the planet's population. The audience of computer networks is even smaller. Jonathan Crary cautions: "Before supposing 'we' will 'all' soon be in cyberspace, consider an isolated statistic: less than 20 percent of the world's population today have telephones [according to *The Economist,* 23 October 1993]" (Crary, "Critical Reflections," *Artforum,* February 1994, p. 50). But the critical significance of the cyber-

dreamworld is not destroyed by this fact. Even if only one person is watching from the perspective of the "whole world," the positioning of such a virtual audience—whether through television or the Internet—has real and radical political implications.

88. West German television images clearly played a role in undermining the power of Eastern European regimes. Specifically, it was the vision of consumer plenty that had a critical effect, not some ideological defense of capitalist principles. In the case of the Vietnam War, the images that were broadcast fed antiwar sentiments, despite the intent of the U.S. media to provide, as usual, its patriotic support of government policy. The idea of "seeing past the nation" I owe to Zillah Eisenstein. See her book *Hatreds: Racialized and Sexualized Conflicts in the 21st Century* (New York: Routledge, 1996), p. 106 and passim.

89. It was the televisual experience of the Gulf War, and the reconsideration of Walter Benjamin's philosophical anthropology that it provoked, which led to the writing of "Aesthetics and Anaesthetics." At its core is the argument that bodily perception is a form of critical cognition, and therefore a potential source of resistance against oppressive cultural practices.

90. In an essay on Adorno's hermeneutic procedure, Podoroga describes viewing a book of photographs of Auschwitz: As "pure fact," he writes, it "has no power to capture my perception. . . . I cannot penetrate inside . . . [this] catastrophic object . . . *I am the alienated eye deprived of direct ties with my own body.*" The "mechanical distance" of the photograph provides a protection against experiencing Auschwitz as a "metaphysical fact," that is, perceiving, with "the whole of my living body," the "universal cultural catastrophe" of Auschwitz. Reanimation of "the dead space and time of Auschwitz" requires a "double procedure." The first, "not unlike the operation of phenomenological reduction" (*epochē*), rids perception of pregiven cultural or moral meaning through a process—almost childlike—of "immediate immersion" in the object. The second "represents an awakening" from this immersion, which is "*achieved only by means of a physical shock.*" Shock awakens "mimetic forces," producing the "fear of physical pain" which interrupts the transparency of seeing or reading, disturbing its unreflective "communicative function." The "transition" from the viewing or reading position that is merely physical to one that is metaphysical always takes on "the figure of shock." (Valerii Podoroga, "The Phenomenon of Auschwitz and Adorno's Hermeneutical Experience," unpublished manuscript.)

91. The preposition *meta* in ancient Greek means "in the midst of," as well as "above" or "beyond."

92. Ryklin, "Metamorphoses of Speech Vision," p. 137. Ryklin borrows the phrase "thinking through the skin" from Artaud.

93. Ryklin, "Bodies of Terror," pp. 45–49.

94. Podoroga, "The Phenomenon of Auschwitz," p. 4.

95. Ibid.

96. Ibid., p. 6.

97. Cf. Kagarlitsky, *Disintegration of the Monolith,* p. vii (writing in 1992): "The liquidation of the Union has not solved a single national conflict nor has it altered the imperial essence of the state. All of the former Soviet republics proclaiming the foundation of the Commonwealth of Independent States are structurally mini-empires. They contain the same inherent contradictions as the large Union. At the helm stand local leaders, who as a rule have come to power through semi-free elections and the manipulation of public opinion. Not one of the former Soviet republics constituting the Commonwealth possess normally functioning democratic institutions. The law is frequently disregarded and the rulers treat the state as if it were their own property."

98. The workshop (funded by Cornell, and again by the MacArthur Foundation) was organized by Hal Foster, who had just joined the faculty in art history, Geoffrey Waite of Cornell, and myself, working together with Alla Efimova, Russian born, who was writing her dissertation on Stalinist art. Planning was coordinated with Annette Michelson of New York Univeristy, who joined us with her colleagues Richard Allen, Mikhail Iampolskii, and Michael Taussig. Also present were our friends Vladislav Todorov from Bulgaria, who was studying as a Fulbright scholar at the University of Pennsylvania, and Helena Kozakiewicz from Poland, who was in residence at Cornell with an ACLS research grant. Ernesto Laclau and Chantal Mouffe joined us for part of the time, as did David Bathrick, who addressed the comparative case of East Germany. In the final session, Laura Mulvey showed rushes of her new documentary, *Disgraced* Monuments, that traced the fate of monumental art after the breakup of the Soviet Union.

99. When Todorov argued that the working class was "created by Stalin" as an "effect" of the cultural discourse, Mulvey was quick to retort that this "effect" had been "decomposed by Thatcher." Michael Taussig argued that the constructed nature of culture did not disprove materialism, as "the real is really made up." Podoroga challenged Western definitions of totalitarianism by stressing the accidental nature of daily existence under the Soviet "Plan." Opposing Western optimism concerning *glasnost'*, Ivanov

described *perestroika*'s pathos: the repair shops themselves were in need of repair. Foster rightly understood what was at stake, foreseeing the need to rewrite all the narratives of the artistic avant-garde given the fresh experiences of the present, a task he described in terms of Freud's concept of "deferred action."

100. Derrida, "Back from Moscow, in the USSR," p. 202.

101. The eugenics and race studies at Harvard produced knowledge used by the Dillon Commission established by the U.S. Congress to study the "immigration problem" (1907–1911).

102. Charles S. Maier, "The Collapse of Communism: Approaches for a Future History," *History Workshop* 31 (Spring 1991), p. 39. Maier notes that "socialist economies have not always failed so clamorously" (p. 35): "Through the 1950s and 1960s, Eastern and Western European societies enjoyed roughly comparable rates of growth. Socialism and capitalism alike responded to the opportunities and demands of recovery from the ravages of the war. To be sure, the West remained ahead of the East, but it had started from a more advanced position. It also benefited from the impulse provided by the undamaged United States economy" (p. 39). "On the basis of their overall performance into the 1960s, serious-minded economists could still argue that central planning might serve developing countries better as a model than western capitalism. Socialism—in the stringent sense of national planning, state ownership of key sectors, and firm control of the national accumulation process—beckoned to intellectuals in India, Egypt and the developing world for two decades after the war. Even when reformers in eastern Europe argued for liberalization after the enforced centralization of the 1950s, they proposed decentralized management, not privatization" (pp. 40–41).

103. "As recently as the late 1970s the West European policy makers remained sensitive about abandoning the Depression-bred idea that double-digit unemployment was a scandal. Econometric studies have suggested that the reluctance to sack workers in Western Europe in the 1970s had made their adjustment to the oil crisis more cumbersome than in the United States where the right to lay off workers was hardly contested. But by the early 1980s in Western Europe the ideological barriers to unemployment had been breached. Not many officials embraced the monetarist idea that being out of work was a quasi-voluntary choice or reflected a finicky attitude toward the jobs being offered. But they did come to accept that having a tenth of one's national labor force out of work for a period of several years was a condition of industrial modernization. . . . The new wisdom thus provided a theodicy

of unemployment, justifying the economy's way to man. . . . The distress effectively ended the support for social democratic political leadership in West Germany, the United States, and Great Britain. It forced the governing Socialists in France and Spain to become as orthodox as their conservative (or neo-liberal) opposition. Emerging from the 1970s, some of the Western industrial cities might be industrial wastelands, but offices were computerized, and services had expanded. Therapists, travel agents and insurance clerks replaced printers and puddlers. But this painful decade of restructuring was hardly attempted in most of Eastern Europe [where high levels of unemployment remained politically unacceptable]." Maier, "The Collapse of Communism," p. 49.

104. It is interesting that Stokes, who set out to write a *political* history of the fall of Eastern European socialist regimes, was led to tell the economic story of how loans from international banks entangled these regimes within the world market. During the Reagan decade of the 1980s, U.S. government loans (as well as permission for admission into the IMF) were used in directly political ways—rewarding certain actions and punishing others—in order to undermine socialist regimes. See Stokes, *The Walls Came Tumbling Down*, pp. 18–19, 42 (on Poland), 58 (on Romania), and passim. By the time of its fall, East Germany, the supposed economic leader of the Warsaw Pact, was indebted to West Germany by $40 billion, a figure that astonished Gorbachev and could not be paid back. See Philip Zelikow and Condoleezza Rice, *Germany Unified and Europe Transformed* (Cambridge: Harvard University Press, 1995).

105. This was the result of a conscious decision by the USSR to end its economic autarchy, as well as that of Eastern Europe. Joint ventures with Western firms also date from this period. See Christopher Chase-Dunn, *Global Formation: Structures of the World-Economy* (Cambridge, Mass.: Blackwell, 1991), p. 85 and passim.

106. "Why could not socialism have continued, it might be asked, to remain an enclave of heavy industry [and] Fordist assembly lines, a continuing living monument to the economic technology of the 1950s? The problem was that the Communist world could no longer remain an enclave. It had set its ideological validation on the competition with the West, and it was falling further behind. There were too many connections for the East to be a closed system." (Maier, "The Collapse of Communism," pp. 49–50.) On the integration of socialist economies into the "periphery" of the capitalist world system, see the prescient article by Valerie Bunce, "The Empire Strikes Back: The Evolution of the Eastern Bloc from a Soviet Asset to a So-

viet Liability," *International Organization* 39, no. 1 (Winter 1985), pp. 1–46.

107. Cosponsored with the *Ekonomicheskaia Gazeta* and USSR Chamber of Commerce and Industry, it was entitled "The Soviet Union in the 1990s: Perestroika and Global Opportunities for East-West Economic Cooperation."

108. See Michael Mandelbaum, introduction to Shafiqul Islam and Michael Mandelbaum, eds., *Making Markets: Economic Transformation in Eastern Europe and the Post-Soviet States* (New York: Council on Foreign Relations Press, 1993), p. 3.

109. Jeffrey D. Sachs, "Accelerating Privatization in Eastern Europe: The Case of Poland," Wider Working Papers 92, September 1991 (Helsinki: Wider Publications, 1991), pp. 5 and 8.

110. Jeffrey Sachs, "Western Financial Assistance and Russia's Reforms," in Islam and Mandelbaum, eds., *Making Markets*, p. 143.

111. Sachs, "Accelerating Privatization," p. 9. There was barely "still time to accomplish a massive privatization of industry before the political and social resistance dangerously slows the process" (ibid., p. 27).

112. Sachs, "Accelerating Privatization," p. 1. The urgency of the need to privatize is ultimately ideological: Private property is the bedrock of capitalism, not economic recovery. It is possible to work toward the latter, and to encourage entrepreneurial activity, without privatization. See the distinction made between property rights (ownership) and property use (entitlement), and the argument that these two aspects should be "unbundled," allowing private profits to be gained from the use of state property—whereas privatization does not similarly guarantee productive use of property assets—in Maciej Perczyński et al., eds., *After the Market Shock: Central and East-European Economies in Transition* (Aldershot: Dartmouth, 1994), esp. pp. 300–302.

113. One critic notes that "odd arguments" were being "advanced in international banking circles," one of which (from a World Bank document of 1993) suggested "that very deep collapse might enhance the attractiveness of transforming economies for foreign capital" (Jo'zef Pajestka, "Systemic Transformation in the Light of Global Change," in Perczyński et al., eds., *After the Market Shock*, p. 18).

114. Pekka Sutela, "The Economic Transition in Russia," in Timo Piirainen, ed., *Change and Continuity in Eastern Europe* (Aldershot: Dartmoth, 1994), pp. 63 and 67.

115. Michael Mandelbaum, introduction to *Making Markets,* p. 15. What exactly would it mean to make the judgment that free markets *had* "worked"? For whom? To what end? To say that a nation's "economy" is "healthy" is not to say that the benefits of that health are evenly or justly distributed. In fact a growing disparity between rich and poor has been the result generally of 1980s global economic restructuring. Against the argument that was particularly popular in Poland that decline is inevitable in transition, "it is simply not true that all countries engaged in [market] transformation have experienced similar breakdowns. The outstanding example is that of China" (Pajestka, "Systemic Transformation in the Light of Global Change," p. 18).

116. Mandelbaum, introduction to *Making Markets,* p. 15.

117. Ibid., p. 11.

118. For the metaphor of "sunlight" in Stalinist discourse, and of "shock" as the way to economic utopia, see above, chapter 3. The Russian word "acceleration" (*uskorenie*), which is a key term in Sachs's discourse (see "Accelerating Privatization," p. 1), was a root metaphor for economic transformation during the entire Soviet period (as noted above, chapter 1).

119. One critic writes: "Whatever the merits of the restructuring argument, one has to wonder how it can explain and justify the *depth* of the actual decline. I cannot visualize any quantitative vindication of very prolonged and deep collapse. I have in mind, of course, not pure theoretical deliberations but arguments strong enough to convince society. The restructuring argument is reminiscent of the argument for the necessity of sacrifices in the interests of socialist industrialization which was in use during the 1950s. There may, however, be one difference. Sacrifices for industrialization in conditions of economic backwardness seem more convincing than sacrifices for the restoration of capitalism." Pajestka, "Systemic Transformation in the Light of Global Change," p. 18).

120. All quotations are from *Making Markets,* written by economists, the majority of whom have Harvard credentials.

121. This group adheres to another, more widespread language peculiarity, characteristic of social scientists in general, the marked preference for alliteration in the titles of books and articles, and in the statements of major premises. For example, the conclusion of *Making Markets* speaks of the paradox that the state needs actively to *plan* market liberalization through the four policy wheels of "sequencing, stress, speed, and sectoralism" (p. 199). I am at a loss to interpret this phenomenon, although I have observed it for years among my colleagues. Perhaps the

poetic device of alliteration provides the illusion of logical coherence, covering over what are in fact gerrymandered analytical divisions of the empirical world.

122. Sutela, "The Economic Transition in Russia," p. 62.

123. Cf. Jameson's version of Benjamin's sixth thesis on the philosophy of history: "Today cultural imperialism lies in the export of the experts: not even national tradition is safe from them if they win; but can we still imagine their losing?" (Jameson, *After the Fall,* p. 268).

124. Shafiqul Islam, "Conclusion: Problems of Planning a Market Economy," in Islam and Mandelbaum, eds., *Making Markets,* p. 182. Such aid was meager and self-interested. Kagarlitsky wrote in 1992: "The West has supposedly decided to grant generous aid to Yeltsin. . . . Yet somehow even the modest amount agreed, no more than $24 billion, is to be paid over a period of years. It is to be used to support the currency and to maintain service payments on debts to Western institutions" (Kagarlitsky, *Disintegration of the Monolith,* p. ix). Two years later, Alexander Dallin wrote: "It took no great skill to discover, sitting in Moscow, that American assistance had been far more meager than advertised, that it served in large measure to benefit American corporations or security interests and did little for the Russian economy at large" (Dallin, "Where Have All the Flowers Gone?," in Gail W. Lapidus, ed., *The New Russia: Troubled Transformation* [Boulder: Westview Press, 1995], p. 254).

125. Islam, conclusion to *Making Markets,* p. 199.

126. Polish minister of industry, cited in Pajestka, "Systemic Transformation in the Light of Global Change," p. 25.

127. Ideologically, these two "freedoms" were strongly linked in the West's interpretation of the fall of socialism. Of course, empirically they had not been. South Korea and Argentina became powerful "free-market" economies under dictatorial rule, just as mainland China is doing today. Advocates for political democracy as the precondition for market reform were strongest among the radical Communists during the last years of the old regimes—those "vanishing mediators" who also tended to be democratic in their own political practice. More recently, Western scholars have argued that the sequence should be reversed: capitalism must come first as the precondition for democracy.

128. Perhaps "no longer" is not quite accurate. Kagarlitsky claims that in Russia, "Westernizers . . . have always relied on the old Byzantine principle according to which power in society must be concentrated in the hands of the possessors of 'knowledge,' or as it has been put in more recent times, the 'enlightened classes'"; this elitism is

presently particularly intense: "Westernizing ideology in its pure form has never before enjoyed such influence in Russia. And it has never been as anti-democratic, as dangerous, as now in the 1990s" (*Disintegration of the Monolith,* pp. 42–43). Boris Groys describes Westernization in Russian history as operating according to the principle of inoculation: Western ideas are injected into elites in small doses in order to immunize the country against a general infection of the masses (conversation with the author, Moscow, November 1993).

129. As early as 1990, in the last year of Gorbachev's rule, a widely discussed interview appeared in the *Literaturnaia Gazeta* in which two intellectuals, I. Kliamkin and A. Migranian, speculated that a dictatorship might indeed be necessary if a market economy was ever to be established in the country. The interview "became the main cultural event of 1990, since it signalled the collapse of the last myths which the intelligentsia tried to foster about itself . . . [that it stood for the] 'good of the people' " (Kagarlitsky, *Disintegration of the Monolith,* p. 39). In August 1990 an article by the Russian economist Gavriil Popov appeared in the *New York Review of Books* which discussed the dangers of democracy if economic reforms were to be implemented. At that time, the "Westerners" who favored a capitalist transformation of society were elitists in their political philosophy; it was the nationalists and communists— the "conservatives"—who championed the interests of the "people" against precipitous economic reform.

130. In fact, throughout 1993, the constitutionality of Yeltsin's actions was challenged by both parliament and the Supreme Soviet. On March 28, he narrowly escaped a vote of impeachment.

131. Two years later the exchange rate was 5,000 rubles to the dollar; in the crisis of September 1998 it fell to 1 dollar to 20,000 (old) rubles (in new rubles, 1 to 20).

132. "Through a network of financial organizations acting as intermediaries, the nomenklatura is selling, often at 'dumping prices,' raw materials, oil, and competitive Russian manufactured products on the Western market. They have deposited part of the proceeds from these sales in Western bank accounts but have spent most of their profits on Western-made goods, which they subsequently resell at a profit in Russia. Thus, the process of state property privatization initially took the form of a privatization of foreign trade." Victor Zaslavsky, "From Redistribution to Marketization: Social and Attitudinal Change in Post-Soviet Russia," in Lapidus, ed., *The New Russia,* pp. 124–125.

133. "According to Russian estimates, the incomes in these groups could have been hundreds of times higher than the country's average wages" (Zaslavsky, "From Redistribution to Marketization," p. 119).

134. Ibid., p. 125. "The nomenklatura as a whole has been remarkably successful in making use of its enormous 'head start' in the process of privatization. Already during the Gorbachev period, those who were charged with administering the redistributive machinery of state had begun to commercialize it. . . . Many, particularly younger members of the nomenklatura moved into the organs of state administration and seized the opportunity to legally exploit state enterprises. Striking deals with newly created private firms, they often became co-owners, underwriting operations with their investment. Making extensive use of personal contact, they began to market information, services, and official licensing. Playing the role of essential middlemen, they began to capitalize on an extremely ill-developed and lopsided market characterized by a near total absence of freely accessible information and business 'networking' contacts between wholesalers and retailers." (Ibid., p. 124.)

135. Jan Kregel et al., "The Post-Shock Agenda," in Perczyński et al., eds., *After the Market Shock,* p. 293. Critics of IMF orthodoxy have made a compelling case for the fallibility of its basic tenets, both logically and in terms of empirical results. The real successes of Asian "tigers" Taiwan and Korea have been based on those import substitution policies that "liberalization" orthodoxy dismissed as "reinventing the wheel" (see Kurt Bayer, "Strategic Planning for Industrial Restructuring," in ibid., pp. 72–75); "privatization" has been minimal on mainland China during a period when markets have been thriving (see Pajestka, "Systemic Transformation in Light of Global Change," pp. 18–19); the goal of zero inflation as a means of achieving economic stabilization has had harmful effects in several South American countries (see Jonathan Kirshner, "Disinflation, Structural Change, and Distribution," *Revew of Radical Political Economics* 30, no. 1 [1998], pp. 53–89).

136. When Jeffrey Sachs resigned as economic advisor to Yeltsin, he blamed the IMF for the economic *and* political failure in Russia, claiming that the IMF made adherence to the guidelines of orthodoxy the precondition for loans, rather than seeing loans as the precondition for adherence to the guidelines. See Sachs, "The Reformers' Tragedy," op-ed article in the *New York Times,* January 23, 1994, p. E17.

137. Isham, ed., *Remaking Russia,* p. 305.

138. My essay "Envisioning Capital: Political Economy on Display," *Critical Inquiry* 21 (Winter, 1995), is drawn from the material of these lectures.

139. Brochure, "Russian State University for the Humanities" (Moscow 1993), p. 3. The intention was "to restructure the entire system of humanities education, and to establish not yet another university but a university of a new type, both in form and in content" (ibid.). The university's rector, the historian Iurii Afanasev, had championed the tradition of the Paris Annales School even before *glasnost'*, and served as a deputy in the Congress of People's Deputies of May-June 1989, when he was part of the original Yeltsin-Sakharov opposition group.

140. Not only were the Russian students critical and challenging intellectually, but I benefited from the attendance of two U.S. graduate students who were in Moscow doing research for their dissertations: Alla Efimova from the University of Rochester, who had worked with us at the Cornell conference in 1992, and Christina Kiaer from Berkeley's Department of Art History, whose work on the early Bolshevik theory of the commodity was especially relevant to the course. I have learned much from these two young women. See their dissertations: Alla Efimova, "The Art of Seduction: Aesthetics of the Soviet Era" (Ph.D. dissertation, University of Rochester, 1996), and Christina Kiaer, "The Russian Constructivist 'Object' and the Revolutionizing of Everyday Life, 1921-1929" (Ph.D. dissertation, University of California, Berkeley, 1995). See also Christina Kiaer and Eric Naiman, eds., *Subjects in Formation in Early Soviet Culture* (Ithaca: Cornell University Press, 1999).

141. The French government has taken the greatest initiative in this regard, establishing a French College within the Moscow State University (which imports French professors to hold lectures), supporting joint publishing ventures, and subsidizing translations of French texts. The implications of this are profound, ensuring that contemporary French theory has the greatest influence on the post-*glasnost'* generation of Russian intellectuals.

142. Again, given the waning interest in things Russian, foreign funding had become difficult to obtain. A very modest proposal that I drafted jointly with philosophy professors Valerii Gubin and Valodii Filatov to fund a "Humanities Center" at the university, which might support visits from U.S. professors and the purchase of U.S. books and periodicals, failed to find a funding source. My thanks to colleagues in the United States who gave their support by agreeing to serve on a board to administer this proposed program: Seyla Benhabib, Hal Foster, Miriam Hansen, Fredric Jameson, Martin Jay, Annette Michelson, and Wolfgang Natter. Academic travelers to Russia might contact Gubin and Filatov at Department of Philosophy, Russian State University for the Humanities, 6, Miusskaia Sq., Moscow, 125267; telephone (095) 250-5109.

143. The director is Aleksandr Ivanov. The address is: Ad Marginem Press, 5/7 1st Novokuznetskii Per., 113184 Moscow; telephone (095) 951-9360; email ad-marg@rinet.ru.

144. Valerii Podoroga's recent publications include *Fenomenologiia tela* (Moscow: Ad Marginem, 1995); *Vyrazhenie i smysl* (Moscow: Ad Marginem, 1995); and *Metafizika landshafta: Kommunikativnye strategii v filosofskoi kulture XIX-XX vv.* (Moscow: Nauka, 1993). Elena Petrovskaia's new book is *Glaznye zabavy* (Moscow: Ad Marginem, 1997); Mikhail Ryklin's is *Iskustvo kak prepriatstvie* (Moscow: Ad Marginem, 1997).

145. This building at 14 Volkhonka Street, a classic example of eighteenth-century architecture located behind the Pushkin museum, now houses the IREX and Soros offices as well. The telephone in this building for the Laboratory for the Study of Post-Classical Studies is (095) 200-3250.

146. Braudel describes clearly the distinction between capitalism and markets: "Galbraith talks about 'the two parts of the economy,' the world of the 'thousands of small and traditional proprietors' (the market system) and that of the 'few hundred . . . highly organized corporations' (the industrial system). Lenin wrote in very similar terms about the coexistence of what he called 'imperialism' (or the new monopoly capitalism of the early twentieth century) and ordinary capitalism, based on competition, which had, he thought, its uses. I agree with both Galbraith and Lenin on this. . . . [Above the layer of the market economy] comes the zone of the anti-market, where the great predators roam and the law of the jungle operates. This—today as in the past, before and after the industrial revolution—is the real home of capitalism." (Ferdinand Braudel, *Civilization and Capitalism, 15th-18th Century,* vol. 2: *The Wheels of Commerce,* trans. Sian Reynolds [Berkeley: University of California Press, 1992], pp. 229-230.) A "free" market economy would be, in contrast, one in which there were "no loaded dice" (Braudel, *Civilization and Capitalism,* vol. 3, p. 628).

147. For a "multiple worlds" theory relevant to this development, see Antonio González-Walker, "The Fifth World(s): Discourse and the Politics of Cultural Transformation in the Virtual Age" (Ph.D. dissertation, Cornell University, 1996).

148. "I don't know how radical you are or how radical I am. I am certainly not radical enough; that is, one must always try to be as radical as reality itself." V. I. Lenin, cited in Alexander Cockburn, "Radical as Reality," in Blackburn, ed., *After the Fall,* p. 167.

BIBLIOGRAPHY

Ahmad, Aijaz. *In Theory: Classes, Nations, Literatures.* New York: Verso, 1992.

Arendt, Hannah. *Imperialism: Part Two of The Origins of Totalitarianism.* New York: Harcourt Brace Jovanovich, 1968.

Art in Revolution: Soviet Art and Design since 1917. Exh. cat., Hayward Gallery, 26 February–18 April 1971. London: Arts Council, 1971.

Baczko, Bronislaw. *Comment sortir de la Terreur? Thermidor et la Révolution.* Paris: Gallimard, 1989.

Bailes, Kendall E. *Technology and Society under Lenin and Stalin: Origins of the Soviet Technical Intelligentsia, 1917–1941.* Princeton: Princeton University Press, 1978.

Bakhtin, Mikhail. *Rabelais and His World.* Preface by Michael Holquist. Bloomington: Indiana University Press, 1984.

Balibar, Etienne. "Le Racisme: Encore un universalisme." *Mots* 18 (March 1989), pp. 7–19.

Belton, John, ed. *Movies and Mass Culture.* New Brunswick: Rutgers University Press, 1996.

Benjamin, Walter. *Charles Baudelaire.* Trans. Harry Zohn. London: Verso, 1983.

Benjamin, Walter. *Gesammelte Schriften.* 6 vols. Ed. Rolf Tiedeman and Hermann Schweppenhäuser. Frankfurt am Main: Suhrkamp Verlag, 1974–1984.

Benjamin, Walter. *Illuminations.* Ed. Hannah Arendt. Trans. Harry Zohn. New York: Schocken Books, 1969.

Benjamin, Walter. *Moskovskii dnevnik.* Ed. Mikhail Ryklin. Trans. S. Romanshko. Moscow: Ad Marginem, 1997.

Benjamin, Walter. *Reflections: Essays, Aphorisms, Autobiographical Writings.* Ed. Peter Demetz. Trans. Edmund Jephcott. New York: Harcourt Brace Jovanovich, 1978.

Benjamin, Walter, et al. *Istorikofilosofskii ezhegodnik '90.* Moscow: Nauka, 1991.

Benningsen, Alexandre A., and S. Enders Wimbush. *Muslim National Communism in the Soviet Union: A Revolutionary Strategy for the Colonial World.* Chicago: University of Chicago Press, 1980.

Bibichen, W. W., ed. *Filosofiia i revolutsiia: Sravniv s dostignuitim visokii ideal.* Moscow: Academy of Sciences, 1989.

Blackburn, Robin, ed. *After the Fall: The Failure of Communism and the Future of Socialism.* New York: Verso, 1991.

Bois, Yve-Alain. "El Lissitzky: Radical Reversibility." *Art in America* (April 1988), pp. 162–178.

Bordwell, David. *The Cinema of Eisenstein.* Cambridge: Harvard University Press, 1993.

Bottomore, Tom, ed. *A Dictionary of Marxist Thought.* Cambridge: Harvard University Press, 1983.

Bourke-White, Margaret. *Eyes on Russia.* Preface by Maurice Hindus. New York: Simon and Schuster, 1931.

Bowlt, John E., ed. and trans. *Russian Art of the Avant-Garde: Theory and Criticism, 1902–1934.* Rev. ed. London: Thames and Hudson, 1988.

Bowlt, John E., and Olga Matich, eds. *Laboratory of Dreams: The Russian Avant-Garde and Cultural Experiment.* Stanford: Stanford University Press, 1996.

Bown, Matthew Cullerne. *Art under Stalin.* Oxford: Phaidon Press, 1991.

Bown, Matthew Cullerne, and Brandon Taylor, eds. *Art of the Soviets: Painting, Sculpture and Architecture in a One-Party State, 1917–1992.* Manchester: Manchester University Press, 1993.

Boym, Svetlana. *Common Places: Mythologies of Everyday Life in Russia.* Cambridge: Harvard University Press, 1994.

Braudel, Fernand. *Civilization and Capitalism, 15th–18th Century.* Vol. 2, *The Wheels of Commerce.* Trans. Sian Reynolds. Berkeley: University of California Press, 1992.

Brennan, Teresa. *History after Lacan.* New York: Routledge 1993.

Buck-Morss, Susan. "Aesthetics and Anaesthetics: Walter Benjamin's Artwork Essay Reconsidered." In *October: The Second Decade.* Cambridge: MIT Press, 1998.

Buck-Morss, Susan. "The Cinema Screen as Prosthesis of Perception." In Nadia Seremetakis, ed., *The Senses Still: Perception and Memory as Material Culture in Modernity.* Chicago: University of Chicago Press, 1997.

Buck-Morss, Susan. "The City as Dreamworld and Catastrophe." *October* 73 (Summer 1995), pp. 3–26.

Buck-Morss, Susan. "Derrida, demokratiia i dekonstruktsiia." In *Ezhegodnik: Ad Marginem '93.* Moscow: Ad Marginem, 1994.

Buck-Morss, Susan. "Envisioning Capital: Political Economy on Display." *Critical Inquiry* 21 (Winter 1995), pp. 434–467.

Bunce, Valerie. "The Empire Strikes Back: The Evolution of the Eastern Bloc from a Soviet Asset to a Soviet Liability." *International Organization* 39, no. 1 (Winter 1985), pp. 1–46.

Campbell, David. *Politics without Principle: Sovereignty, Ethics, and the Narratives of the Gulf War.* Boulder: Lynne Rienner Publishers, 1993.

Carr, Edward Hallett. *The Soviet Impact on the Western World.* New York: Macmillan, 1954.

Castoriades, Cornelius. *L'Institution imaginaire de la société.* Paris: Editions du Seuil, 1975.

Chase-Dunn, Christopher. *Global Formation: Structures of the World-Economy.* Cambridge, Mass.: Blackwell, 1991.

Clark, Katerina. *The Soviet Novel: History as Ritual.* Chicago: University of Chicago Press, 1981.

Cohen, Stephen. *Bukharin and the Russian Revolution: A Political Biography.* New York: Alfred A. Knopf, 1973.

Condee, Nancy. *Soviet Hieroglyphics: Visual Culture in Late Twentieth-Century Russia.* Bloomington: Indiana University Press, 1995.

Conquest, Robert. *The Harvest of Sorrow: Soviet Collectivization and the Terror-Famine.* New York: Oxford University Press, 1986.

Coopersmith, Jonathan. *The Electrification of Russia, 1880–1926.* Ithaca: Cornell University Press, 1992.

Crary, Jonathan. "Critical Reflections." *Artforum* (February 1994), pp. 48–51.

Curran, Thomas J. *Xenophobia and Immigration, 1820–1930.* Boston: Twayne Publishers, 1975.

David-Fox, Michael. *Revolution of the Mind: Higher Learning among the Bolsheviks, 1918–1929.* Ithaca: Cornell University Press, 1997.

Davies, Philip, and Brian Neve, eds. *Cinema, Politics and Society in America.* New York: St. Martin's Press, 1981.

Der Derian, James. *Antidiplomacy: Spies, Terror, Speed and War.* Cambridge, Mass.: Blackwell, 1992.

Derrida, Jacques. "Back from Moscow, in the USSR." Trans. Mary Quaintaire. Ed. Peggy Kamuf. In Mark Poster, ed., *Politics, Theory, and Contemporary Culture.* New York: Columbia University Press, 1993.

Derrida, Jacques. *Specters of Marx: The State of the Debt, the Work of Mourning, and the New International.* Trans. Peggy Kamuf. Intro. Bernd Magnus and Stephen Cullenberg. New York: Routledge, 1994.

Dichev, Ivailo. "The Post-Communist Condition." Presentation at Dubrovnik, October 1990.

Dickerman, Leah, ed. *Building the Collective: Soviet Graphic Design 1917–1937.* New York: Princeton Architectural Press, 1996.

Douglas, Charlotte. *Kazimir Malevich.* New York: Harry N. Abrams, 1994.

Dunlop, John B. *The Rise of Russia and the Fall of the Soviet Empire.* Princeton: Princeton University Press, 1993.

Eagleton, Terry. *The Ideology of the Aesthetic.* Cambridge, Mass.: Blackwell, 1990.

Efimova, Alla. "A Prescription for Life: Sun, Air, and Water in Socialist Realism and Soviet Health Care." Unpublished ms.

Efimova, Alla, and Lev Manovich, eds. and trans. *Tekstura: Russian Essays on Visual Culture.* Chicago: University of Chicago Press, 1993.

Egbert, Donald D. "The Idea of 'Avant-Garde' in Art and Politics." *American Historical Review* 73, no. 2 (December 1967), pp. 339–366.

Eisenstein, S[ergei] M. *Selected Works.* 2 vols. Ed. Richard Taylor. London: BFI Books, 1988.

Eisenstein, Zillah. *The Color of Gender: Reimagining Democracy.* Berkeley: University of California Press, 1994.

Eisenstein, Zillah. *The Female Body and the Law.* Berkeley: University of California Press, 1989.

Eisenstein, Zillah. *Hatreds: Racialized and Sexualized Conflicts in the 21st Century.* New York: Routledge, 1996.

Elshtain, Jean Bethke. *Public Man, Private Woman.* Princeton: Princeton University Press, 1981.

Epstein, Mikhail N. *After the Future.* Trans. Anesa Miller-Pogacar. Amherst: University of Massachusetts Press, 1995.

Ewen, Stuart, and Elizabeth Ewen. *Channels of Desire: Mass Images and the Shaping of American Consciousness.* New York: McGraw-Hill, 1982.

Faucherau, Serge. *Malevich.* New York: Rizzoli, 1992.

Faure, Christine, ed. *Les Déclarations des droits de l'homme de 1789: Textes réunis et présentés par Christine Faure.* Paris: Editions Payot, 1988.

Filonov, Pavel. *Pavel Filonov: A Hero and His Fate: Collected Writings on Art and Revolution, 1910–1940.* Trans. and ed. Nicoletta Misler and John E. Bowlt. Austin, Texas: Silvergirl, 1983.

Fitzpatrick, Sheila. *The Cultural Front: Power and Culture in Revolutionary Russia.* Ithaca: Cornell University Press, 1992.

Fitzpatrick, Sheila. *The Cultural Revolution in Russia, 1928–1931.* Bloomington: Indiana University Press, 1978.

Fitzpatrick, Sheila. "The Foreign Threat during the First Five-Year Plan." *Soviet Union / Union soviétique* 5 (1978), pt. 1.

Fitzpatrick, Sheila. *The Russian Revolution.* New York: Oxford University Press, 1982.

Fitzpatrick, Sheila. *Stalin's Peasants: Resistance and Survival in the Russian Village after Collectivization.* New York: Oxford University Press, 1994.

Fitzpatrick, Sheila, et al., eds. *Russia in the Era of NEP: Explorations in Soviet Society and Culture.* Bloomington: Indiana University Press, 1991.

Furet, François. *Interpreting the French Revolution.* Trans. Elborg Forster. New York: Cambridge University Press, 1989.

Getty, J. Arch. *Origins of the Great Purges: The Soviet Communist Party Reconsidered, 1933–1938.* New York: Cambridge University Press, 1985.

Getzler, Israel. *Kronstadt, 1917–1921: The Fate of a Soviet Democracy.* New York: Cambridge University Press, 1983.

Gleason, Abbot, Peter Kenez, and Richard Stites, eds. *Bolshevik Culture: Experiment and Order in the Russian Revolution.* Bloomington: Indiana University Press, 1985.

Golomstock, Igor. *Totalitarian Art in the Soviet Union, the Third Reich, Fascist Italy and the People's Republic of China.* London: Collins Harvik, 1990.

González-Walker, Antonio. "The Fifth World(s): Discourse and the Politics of Cultural Transformation in the Virtual Age." Ph.D. diss., Cornell University, 1996.

Goodwin, James. *Eisenstein, Cinema, and History.* Urbana: University of Illinois Press, 1993.

Gordon-Taylor, Sir Gordon, and E. W. Walls. *Sir Charles Bell: His Life and Times.* London: E. & S. Livingstone, 1958.

Gray, Camilla. *The Russian Experiment in Art, 1863–1922.* Rev. and enl. Marian Burleigh-Motley. New York: Thames and Hudson, 1986.

The Great Utopia: The Russian and Soviet Avant-Garde, 1915–1932. New York: Guggenheim Museum, 1992.

Greenberg, Clement. *Art and Culture: Critical Essays.* Boston: Beacon Press, 1961.

Groys, Boris. *Gesamtkunstwerk Stalin: Die gespaltene Kultur in der Sowjetunion.* Trans. (from Russian) Gabriele Leupold. Munich: Carl Hanser Verlag, 1988.

Guilbaut, Serge. *How New York Stole the Idea of Modern Art: Abstract Expressionism, Freedom, and the Cold War.* Trans. Arthur Goldhammer. Chicago: University of Chicago Press, 1987.

Günther, Hans, ed. *The Culture of the Stalin Period.* New York: St. Martin's Press, 1990.

Hansen, Miriam Bratu. "The Mass Production of the Senses: Classical Cinema as Vernacular Modernism." *MODERNISM/modernity* 6, no. 2 (1999), pp. 59–77.

Hanson, Stephen E. *Time and Revolution: Marxism and the Design of Soviet Institutions.* Chapel Hill: University of North Carolina Press, 1997.

Harding, Neil, ed. *The State in Socialist Society.* Albany: State University of New York Press, 1984.

Heller, Mikhail. *La Machine et les rouages: La formation de l'homme soviétique.* Trans. Anne Coldefy-Faucard. Paris: Callmann-Lévy, 1985.

Heller, Mikhail, and Aleksandr Nekrich. *Utopia in Power: The History of the Soviet Union from 1917 to the Present.* Trans. Phyllis B. Carlos. New York: Summit Books, 1985.

Hess, Thomas B., and John Ashbery, eds. *Avant-Garde Art.* London: Collier-Macmillan, 1968.

Higham, Robin, and Jacob W. Kipp, eds. *Soviet Aviation and Air Power: A Historical View.* Boulder: Westview Press, 1977.

Hildebrand, Grant. *Designing for Industry: The Architecture of Albert Kahn.* Cambridge: MIT Press, 1974.

Hixson, Walter L. *Parting the Curtain: Propaganda, Culture and the Cold War, 1945–1961.* New York: St. Martin's Press, 1996.

Holquist, Peter. "State and Violence as Technique: The Logic of Violence in Soviet Totalitarianism." In Amir Weiner, ed., *Modernity and Population Management.* Stanford: Stanford University Press, in press.

Huggins, Martha K., ed. *Vigilantism and the State in Modern Latin America: Essays on Extralegal Violence.* New York: Praeger, 1991.

Hughes, Thomas P. *American Genesis: A Century of Invention and Technological Enthusiasm, 1870–1970.* New York: Viking, 1989.

Isham, Heyward, ed. *Remaking Russia.* London: M. E. Sharpe, 1995.

Islam, Shafiqul, and Michael Mandelbaum, eds. *Making Markets: Economic Transformation in Eastern Europe and the Post-Soviet States.* New York: Council on Foreign Relations Press, 1993.

Jameson, Fredric. *The Ideologies of Theory: Essays 1971–1986.* Vol. 2, *The Syntax of History.* Minneapolis: University of Minnesota Press, 1988.

Jameson, Fredric. *Postmodernism, or, The Cultural Logic of Late Capitalism.* Durham: Duke University Press, 1992.

Janacek, Gerald. *The Look of Russian Literature: Avant-Garde Visual Experiments, 1900–1930.* Princeton: Princeton University Press, 1984.

Joachimides, Christos M., and Norman Rosenthal. *American Art in the Twentieth Century: Painting and Sculpture, 1913–1993.* Munich: Prestel, 1993.

Johannson, Kurt. *Aleksej Gastev: Proletarian Bard of the Machine Age.* Stockholm: Almqvist & Wiksell International, 1983.

Jones, Robert A. *The Soviet Concept of "Limited Sovereignty" from Lenin to Gorbachev: The Brezhnev Doctrine.* London: Macmillan, 1990.

Kabakov, Ilya, and Boris Groys. *Die Kunst des Fliehens.* Munich: Carl Hanser Verlag, 1991.

Kagarlitsky, Boris. *The Disintegration of the Monolith.* Trans. Renfrew Clarke. New York: Verso, 1992.

Kasimir Malewitsch zum 100. Geburtstag. Cologne: Galerie Gmurzynska, 1978.

Kenez, Peter. *Cinema and Soviet Society, 1917–1953.* New York: Cambridge University Press, 1992.

Kenworthy, Eldon. *America/Américas: Myth in the Making of U.S. Policy toward Latin America.* University Park: Pennsylvania State University Press, 1995.

Khrushchev, Nikita. *Khrushchev in America: Texts and Speeches.* New York: Crosscurrents Press, 1960.

Kiaer, Christina. "Rodchenko in Paris." *October* 75 (Winter 1996), pp. 3–35.

Kiaer, Christina. "The Russian Constructivist 'Object' and the Revolutionizing of Everyday Life, 1921–1929." Ph.D. diss., University of California, Berkeley, 1995.

Kiaer, Christina, and Eric Naiman, eds. *Subjects in Formation in Early Soviet Culture.* Ithaca: Cornell University Press, 1999.

Kiossev, Alexander, ed. *Post-Theory, Games and Discursive Resistance: The Bulgarian Case.* Albany: State University of New York Press, 1995.

Kirshner, Jonathan. "Disinflation, Structural Change, and Distribution." *Review of Radical Political Economics* 30, no. 1 (1998), pp. 53–89.

Koehler, Ludmila. *N. F. Fedorov: The Philosophy of Action.* Pittsburgh: Institute for the Human Sciences, 1979.

Koenker, Diane P., et al., eds. *Party, State, and Society in the Russian Civil War: Explorations in Social History.* Bloomington: Indiana University Press, 1989.

Kopp, Anatole. "Housing for the Masses." In *Conference on the Origins of Soviet Culture,* May 1981. Working Paper no. 149. Washington, D.C.: The Wilson Center, Kennan Institute for Advanced Russian Studies.

Kopp, Anatole. *Town and Revolution: Soviet Architecture and City Planning, 1917–1935.* Trans. Thomas E. Burton. New York: George Braziller, 1970.

Kotkin, Stephen. *Magnetic Mountain: Stalinism as a Civilization.* Berkeley: University of California Press, 1995.

Kotkin, Stephen. *Steeltown, USSR: Soviet Society in the Gorbachev Era.* Berkeley: University of California Press, 1991.

Krenzlin, Norbert, ed. *Zwischen Angst-Metapher und Terminus: Theorien der Massenkultur seit Nietzsche.* Berlin: Akademieverlag, 1992.

Kryzanek, Michael J. *U.S.-Latin American Relations.* New York: Praeger, 1985.

Kuznetzov, Mikhail, ed. *Filosofiia Martina Heideggera i sovremennost'.* Moscow: Academy of Sciences USSR, 1991.

Laclau, Ernesto, and Chantal Mouffe. *Hegemony and Social Strategy: Towards a Radical Democratic Politics.* New York: Verso, 1985.

Lahusen, Thomas, and Gene Kuperman, eds. *Late Soviet Culture: From Perestroika to Novostroika.* Durham: Duke University Press, 1993.

Langley, Lester D. *American and the Americas: The United States in the Western Hemisphere.* Athens: University of Georgia Press, 1989.

Lapidus, Gail W., ed. *The New Russia: Troubled Transformation.* Boulder: Westview Press, 1995.

Lawton, Anna, ed. *The Red Screen: Politics, Society, Art in Soviet Cinema.* New York: Routledge, 1992.

Lenin, V. I. "Chto delat?" In *Sochineniia,* vol. 5. Moscow: State Publishers of Political Literature, 1946.

Lenin, V. I. *Selected Works.* 3 vols. Moscow: Progress Publishers, 1977.

Lenin, V. I. *State and Revolution.* New York: International Publishers, 1969.

Lenin, V. I. *What Is to Be Done?* New York: International Publishers, 1969.

Lewin, Moshe. *The Gorbachev Phenomenon: A Historical Interpretation.* Expanded ed. Berkeley: University of California Press, 1991.

Lewin, Moshe. *The Making of the Soviet System: Essays in the Social History of Interwar Russia.* New York: Pantheon Books, 1985.

Leyda, Jay, ed. *Eisenstein: Two Films, October and Alexandr Nevsky.* Trans. Diana Matias. London: Lorrimer Publishing, 1984.

Leyda, Jay. *Kino: A History of the Russian and Soviet Film.* New York: Collier Books, 1973.

Linz, Susan J., ed. *The Impact of World War II on the Soviet Union.* Totowa, N.J.: Rowman and Allanheld, 1985.

Lissitzky, El. *Russia: An Architecture for World Revolution.* Trans. Eric Dluhosch. Cambridge: MIT Press, 1984.

Lissitzky-Küppers, Sophie, ed. *El Lissitzky: Life, Letters, Texts.* Greenwich, Conn.: New York Graphic Society, 1968.

Lodder, Christina. *Russian Constructivism.* New Haven: Yale University Press, 1983.

Lukács, Georg. *History and Class Consciousness: Studies in Marxist Dialectics.* Trans. Rodney Livingstone. Cambridge: MIT Press, 1968.

MacArthur, John R. *Second Front: Censorship and Propaganda in the Gulf War.* New York: Hill and Wang, 1992.

Maier, Charles S. "The Collapse of Communism: Approaches for a Future History." *History Workshop* 31 (Spring 1991), pp. 35–50.

Malevich, K[azimir] S. *Essays on Art 1915–1928,* vol. 1. Ed. Troels Andersen. Trans. Xenia Gowacki-Prus and Arnold McMillin. Copenhagen: Borgens Forlag, 1968.

Mally, Lynn. *Culture of the Future: The Proletkult Movement in Revolutionary Russia.* Berkeley: University of California Press, 1990.

Mamardashvili, Merab. *Kak ia ponimaiu filosofiiu.* Moscow: Isd. gruppa "Progress": "Kultura", 1993.

Marcadé, Jean-Claude, ed. *Cahier Malévich no. 1.* Lausanne: L'Âge d'Homme, 1983.

Marchand, Roland. *Advertising the American Dream: Making Way for Modernity, 1920–1940.* Berkeley: University of California Press, 1985.

Marshak, Ilia Iakovlevich [pseudonym M. Alan]. *New Russia's Primer: The Story of the Five-Year Plan.* Trans. George S. Counts and Nucia P. Lodge. New York: Houghton Mifflin, 1931.

Marx, Karl. *Early Writings.* Intro. Lucio Colletti. Trans. Rodney Livingstone and Gregor Benton. New York: Vintage Books, 1975.

Marx, Karl, and Friedrich Engels. *The German Ideology.* Moscow: Progress Publishers, 1976.

Massell, Gregory J. *The Surrogate Proletariat: Moslem Women and Revolutionary Strategies in Soviet Central Asia.* Princeton: University of Princeton Press, 1974.

Matthews, J. H. *Surrealism and American Feature Films.* Boston: Twayne Publishers, 1979.

May, Lary. *Screening Out the Past: The Birth of Mass Culture and the Motion Picture Industry.* Chicago: University of Chicago Press, 1980.

Mayer, Arno J. *Political Origins of the New Diplomacy, 1917–18.* New Haven: Yale University Press, 1959.

Mayer, David. *Sergei M. Eisenstein's Potemkin: A Shot-by-Shot Presentation.* New York: Grossman Publishers, 1972.

McDonough, Thomas F. "Rereading Debord, Rereading the Situationists." *October* 79 (Winter 1997), pp. 3ff.

Medvedev, Roy. *Khrushchev: A Biography.* Trans. Brian Pearce. Garden City: Anchor Press, 1983.

Medvedev, Roy. *Let History Judge: The Origins and Consequences of Stalinism.* Trans. George Schriver. New York: Columbia University Press, 1989.

Michelson, Annette. "Reading Eisenstein Reading Capital." Part 1, *October* 2 (Summer 1976), pp. 27–38; part 2, *October* 3 (Spring 1977), pp. 82–88.

Miller, John. *Mikhail Gorbachev and the End of Soviet Power.* New York: St. Martin's Press, 1993.

Milner, John. *Kazimir Malevich and the Art of Geometry.* New Haven: Yale University Press, 1996.

Motyl, Alexander J. *Will the Non-Russians Rebel? State, Ethnicity, and Stability in the USSR.* Ithaca: Cornell University Press, 1987.

Mujal-León, Eusebio, ed. *The USSR and Latin America: A Developing Relationship.* Boston: Unwin Hyman, 1989.

Naiman, Eric. *Sex in Public: The Incarnation of Early Soviet Ideology.* Princeton: Princeton University Press, 1997.

Naum Gabo and the Competition for the Palace of Soviets, Moscow, 1931–33. Berlin: Berlinische Galerie, 1992.

Nye, David E. *Electrifying America: Social Meanings of a New Technology, 1880–1940.* Cambridge: MIT Press, 1990.

O'Connor, Edward. *The Politics of Soviet Culture: Anatolii Lunacharskii.* Ann Arbor: UMI Research Press, 1988.

O'Connor, Harvey. *Mellon's Millions: The Biography of a Fortune.* New York: Blue Ribbon Books, 1933.

Ortega y Gasset, José. *The Revolt of the Masses.* New York: W. W. Norton, 1932.

Osborne, Peter. *The Politics of Time: Modernity and Avant-Garde.* London: Verso, 1995.

Palij, Michael. *The Anarchism of Nestor Makhno, 1918–1921: An Aspect of the Ukrainian Revolution.* Seattle: University of Washington Press, 1976.

Pateman, Carole. *The Sexual Contract.* Stanford: Stanford University Press, 1988.

Perczyn'ski, Maciej et al., eds. *After the Market Shock: Central and East-European Economies in Transition.* Aldershot: Dartmouth, 1994.

Petrovskaia, Elena. *Chast' sveta.* Moscow: Ad Marginem, 1995.

Petrovskaia, Elena. *Glaznye zabavy.* Moscow: Ad Marginem, 1997.

Petrovskaia, Elena. "The Path to Gertrude Stein in Contemporary Post-Soviet Culture." *New Literary Review* 27, no. 2 (Spring 1996), pp. 329–336.

Piirainen, Timo, ed. *Change and Continuity in Eastern Europe.* Aldershot: Dartmouth, 1994.

Platonov, Andrei. *The Foundation Pit/Kotlovan* [bilingual edition]. Preface Joseph Brodsky. Trans. Thomas P. Whitney. Ann Arbor: Ardis Publishers, 1973.

Pocock, J. G. A. *The Machiavellian Moment: Florentine Political Thought and the Atlantic Republican Tradition.* Princeton: Princeton University Press, 1975.

Podoroga, Valerii. "Eunuch of the Soul: Positions of Reading and the World of Platonov." *South Atlantic Quarterly* 90, no. 2 (Spring 1991), pp. 358–408.

Podoroga, Valerii. *Fenomenologiia tela.* Moscow: Ad Marginem, 1995.

Podoroga, Valerii. *Metafizika landshafta kommunikativnye strategii v filosofskoi kulture XIX–XXVI.* Moscow: Nauka, 1993.

Podoroga, Valerii. "The Phenomenon of Auschwitz and Adorno's Hermeneutical Experience." Unpublished ms.

Podoroga, Valerii. "Sergei Eisenstein." Presentation at Dubrovnik, October 1990.

Podoroga, Valerii. *Vyrazhenie i smysl.* Moscow: Ad Marginem, 1995.

Poggioli, Renato. *The Theory of the Avant-Garde.* Trans. Gerald Fitzgerald. Cambridge: Harvard University Press, 1968.

Read, Christopher. *Culture and Power in Revolutionary Russia: The Intelligentsia and the Transition from Tsarism to Communism.* New York: St. Martin's Press, 1990.

Ries, Nancy. *Russian Talk: Culture and Conversation during Perestroika.* Ithaca: Cornell University Press, 1997.

Rosenberg, William G., and Lewis H. Siegelbaum, eds. *Social Dimensions of Soviet Industrialization.* Bloomington: Indiana University Press, 1993.

Ross, David A., et al., eds. *Between Spring and Summer: Soviet Conceptual Art in the Era of Late Communism.* Cambridge: MIT Press, 1990.

Rougle, Charles. "'Express': The Future According to Gastev." *Russian History/Histoire russe* 11, nos. 2–3 (Summer-Fall 1984), pp. 258–268.

Rupesinghe, Kumar, et al., eds. *Ethnicity and Conflict in a Post-Communist World: The Soviet Union, Eastern Europe and China.* London: St. Martin's Press, 1992.

Rush, Myron, ed. *The International Situation and Soviet Foreign Policy: Key Reports by Soviet Leaders from the Revolution to the Present.* Columbus: Merrill Publishing Co., 1970.

Ryklin, Mikhail. "Bodies of Terror." Trans. Molly Williams Wesling and Donald Wesling. Preface by Caryl Emerson. *New Literary History* 24, no. 1 (Winter 1993), pp. 45–49.

Ryklin, Mikhail. "The Fall of the Statues: The Fate of Soviet Era Monuments." Speech at Cornell University, March 1995.

Ryklin, Mikhail. *Iskustvo kak prepriatstvie.* Moscow: Ad Marginem, 1997.

Ryklin, Mikhail, ed. *Jacques Derrida v Moskve: Dekonstruktsiia pyteshestviia.* Moscow: RIK "Kul'tura," 1993.

Sachs, Jeffrey D. "Accelerating Privatization in Eastern Europe: The Case of Poland." Wider Working Papers 92, September 1991. Helsinki: Wider Publications, 1991.

Sachs, Jeffrey D. "The Reformers' Tragedy." *New York Times,* January 23, 1994, p. E12.

Schlesinger, Rudolf, ed. *The Family in the U.S.S.R.: Documents and Readings.* London: Routledge and Kegan Paul, 1949.

Schmitt, Carl. *Der Begriff des Politischen.* Berlin: Duncker & Humblot, 1932. Trans. as *The Concept of the Political.* Trans. George Schwab, intro. Leo Strauss. New Brunswick: Rutgers University Press, 1976.

Schmitt, Carl. *Der Nomos der Erde im Völkerrecht des Jus Publicum Europaeum.* 2d ed. Berlin: Duncker & Humblot, 1972.

Seller, Maxine. *To Seek America: A History of Ethnic Life in the United States.* New York: Jerome S. Ozer, 1977.

Seltzer, Mark. *Bodies and Machines.* New York: Routledge, 1992.

Siegelbaum, Lewis H., and Ronald Grigor Suny, eds. *Making Workers Soviet: Power, Class, and Identity.* Ithaca: Cornell University Press, 1994.

Sklar, Robert. *Movie-Made America: A Cultural History of American Movies.* New York: Vintage, 1976.

Slezkine, Yuri. *Arctic Mirrors: Russia and the Small Peoples of the North.* Ithaca: Cornell University Press, 1994.

Smith, Jean Edward. *George Bush's War.* New York: Henry Holt and Company, 1992.

Sochor, Zenovia A. *Revolution and Culture: The Bogdanov-Lenin Controversy.* Ithaca: Cornell University Press, 1988.

Starr, S. Frederick. *Melnikov: Solo Architect in a Mass Society.* Princeton: Princeton University Press, 1978.

Stites, Richard. *Revolutionary Dreams: Utopian Vision and Experimental Life in the Russian Revolution.* New York: Oxford University Press, 1989.

Stokes, Gale. *The Walls Came Tumbling Down: The Collapse of Communism in Eastern Europe.* New York: Oxford University Press, 1993.

Strasser, Susan. *Never Done: A History of American Housework.* New York: Pantheon Books, 1982.

Sutton, Anthony C. *Western Technology and Soviet Economic Development.* 3 vols. Stanford: Hoover Institute Press, 1968–1973.

Syberberg, Hans Jürgen. *Hitler, a Film from Germany.* Trans Joachim Neugroschel. New York: Farrar, Straus and Giroux, 1982.

Szporluk, Roman. *Communism and Nationalism: Karl Marx versus Friedrich List.* New York: Oxford University Press, 1988.

Tauranac, John. *The Empire State Building: The Making of a Landmark.* New York: Scribner, 1995.

Taylor, Brandon. *Art and Literature under the Bolsheviks.* Vol. 1, *The Crisis of Renewal, 1917–1924.* London: Pluto Press, 1991. Vol. 2, *Authority and Revolution, 1924–1932.* London: Pluto Press, 1992.

Taylor, Richard, and Ian Christie, eds. *Inside the Film Factory: New Approaches to Russian and Soviet Cinema.* New York: Routledge, 1991.

Taylor, Richard, and Derek Spring, eds. *Stalinism and Soviet Cinema.* New York: Routledge, 1993.

Teskey, Ayleen. *Platonov and Fjordorov: The Influence of Christian Philosophy on a Soviet Writer.* Amersham, England: Avebury Publishing Company, 1982.

Thompson, John M. *Russia, Bolshevism, and the Versailles Peace.* Princeton: Princeton University Press, 1966.

Thompson, Kenneth. *Interpreters and Critics of the Cold War.* Baton Rouge: Louisiana State University Press, 1981.

Thomson, Boris. *Lot's Wife and the Venus of Milo: Conflicting Attitudes to the Cultural Heritage in Modern Russia.* New York: Cambridge Press, 1978.

Tilly, Charles, ed. *The Formation of Nation-States in Western Europe.* Princeton: Princeton University Press, 1975.

Todorov, Vladislav. "Introduction to the Physiognomy of Ruins." *Yale Journal of Criticism* 6, no. 1 (Spring 1993), pp. 249–257.

Todorov, Vladislav. *Red Square, Black Square: Organon for Revolutionary Imagination.* Albany: State University of New York Press, 1995.

Tolstoy, Vladimir, Irina Bibikova, and Catherine Cooke, eds. *Street Art of the Revolution: Festivals and Celebrations in Russia, 1918–1933.* New York: Vendome Press, 1990.

Tsivian, Yuri. *Early Cinema in Russia and Its Cultural Reception.* Ed. Richard Taylor. Trans. Alan Bodger. Foreword Tom Gunning. New York: Routledge, 1994.

Tumarkin, Nina. *Lenin Lives! The Lenin Cult in Soviet Russia.* Cambridge: Harvard University Press, 1983.

Tupitsyn, Margarita. *Margins of Soviet Art: Socialist Realism to the Present.* Milan: Giancarlo Politi Editore, 1989.

Ulmen, G. L. "American Imperialism and International Law: Carl Schmitt on the US in World Affairs." *Telos* 72 (Summer 1987).

USSR in Construction (Moscow). Issue no. 5, 1933.

Vadim Sidur, Skulpturen und Graphiken: 28. August bis 21. September 1980. Berlin: Kunstamt Charlottenburg, 1980.

Vertov, Dziga. *Kino-Eye: The Writings of Dziga Vertov.* Ed. Annette Michelson. Trans. Kevin O'Brien. Berkeley: University of California Press, 1984.

Viola, Lynne. *Peasant Rebels under Stalin: Collectivization and the Culture of Peasant Resistance.* New York: Oxford University Press, 1996.

Virilio, Paul. *War and Cinema: The Logistics of Perception.* Trans. Patrick Camiller. London: Verson, 1989.

Volger, Carolyn M. *The Nation State: The Neglected Dimension of Class.* Hants, England: Gower Publishing Company, 1985.

Von Geldern, James, and Richard Stites, eds. *Mass Culture in Soviet Russia*. Bloomington: Indiana University Press, 1995.

Von Hagen, Mark. *Soldiers in the Proletarian Dictatorship: The Red Army and the Soviet Socialist State, 1917–1930*. Ithaca: Cornell University Press, 1990.

Weber, Max. *From Max Weber: Essays in Sociology*. Ed. and trans. H. H. Gerth and C. Wright Mills. New York: Oxford University Press, 1958.

Williams, Robert C. *Russian Art and American Money, 1900–1940*. Cambridge: Harvard University Press, 1980.

Winchakul, Tongchai. *Siam Mapped: A History of the Geo-Body of a Nation*. Honolulu: University of Hawaii Press, 1994.

Wohlforth, William Curti. *The Elusive Balance: Power and Perceptions during the Cold War*. Ithaca: Cornell University Press, 1993.

Woodward, Susan L. *Balkan Tragedy: Chaos and Dissolution after the Cold War*. Washington: Brookings Institution, 1995.

Wornick, Andrew. *Promotional Culture: Advertising, Ideology and Symbolic Expression*. London: Sage Publications, 1991.

Youngblood, Denise J. *Movies for the Masses: Popular Cinema and Soviet Society in the 1920s*. New York: Cambridge University Press, 1992.

Zbarski, Ilya, and Samuel Hutchinson. *A l'ombre du mausolée: Une dynastie d'embaumeurs*. Paris: Solin, Actes Sud, 1997.

Zelikow, Philip, and Condoleezza Rice. *Germany Unified and Europe Transformed*. Cambridge: Harvard University Press, 1995.

Zimmerman, Leo M., and Ilza Veith. *Great Ideas in the History of Surgery*. 2d ed. New York: Dover, 1967.

Žižek, Slavoj. *Tarrying with the Negative: Kant, Hegel, and the Critique of Ideology*. Durham: Duke University Press, 1993.

Zorkaya, Neya. *The Illustrated History of the Soviet Cinema*. New York: Hippocrene Books, 1991.

ILLUSTRATION CREDITS

All Russian Museum of Decorative and Folk Art, Moscow: fig. 5.15

Associated Press: fig. 6.4

Merrill C. Berman Collection: figs. 2.14, 2.17, 2.37 (color plate 8)

BFI National Library: figs. 5.5, 5.10

Margaret Bourke-White Estate: figs. 4.30, 4.35, 5.11

Grisha Brushkin: fig. 6.1

Susan Buck-Morss: figs. 2.59 (color plate 12), 6.8

Ronald Feldman Fine Arts, New York: figs. 2.58, 3.22 (color plate 9), 5.9, 5.26 (color plate 7); photos by D. James Dee except fig. 2.58

John Goto: figs. 2.50, 2.51

Ilya and Emila Kabakov: figs. 3.4, 3.26 (color plate 3), 5.21, 5.23

David King Collection: figs. 2.43, 4.34, 5.16, 5.30

Komar and Melamid: figs. 2.58, 3.22 (color plate 9), 5.9, 5.26 (color plate 7), 6.9

Maria Konstantinova: fig. 2.60

Aleksandr Kosolapov: figs. 2.29 (color plate 1), 2.30, 5.27 (color plate 13)

Mark Lewis: fig. 2.45

El Lissitzky: figs. 2.15, 2.26, 5.19 (color plate 6)

Magnum Photos: fig. 5.25

Igor Makarevich: fig. 6.2

Marlborough Gallery, London: fig. 6.10

Konstantin Melnikov: figs. 2.33, 2.34, 3.19, 3.20, 3.21

Mosfilms: figs. 4.22, 4.26

Museum of Modern Art, New York: figs. 2.5, 2.57

Museum of Modern Art, Oxford: fig. 2.18

Irina Nakhova: fig. 3.3

National Gallery of Art, Washington: fig. 4.36

Pertsy Group: fig. 2.46

Dmitrii Prigov: fig. 5.32 (color plate 11)

Reuters/Str/Archive Photos: fig. 2.38

Rizzoli: fig. 5.29 (color plate 4)

Aleksandr Rodchenko: figs. 3.24, 4.6, 4.7, 5.31 (color plate 10)

Russian State Archive of Kino-Photo-Documentary, Moscow: figs. 3.15, 3.16, 4.2, 4.3, 5.17

Mikhail Ryklin: fig. 6.3

Vadim Sidur Museum, Moscow: figs. 3.33, 3.34, 3.37, 3.38, 3.39

Leonid Sokov: fig. 4.17 (color plate 5)

State Historical Museum, Moscow: fig. 2.19

State Russian Museum, St. Petersburg: figs. 2.6, 2.10,
2.13, 2.52, 2.55, 2.56, 3.9

State Shchusev Museum, Moscow: figs. 2.23, 2.27, 3.18,
6.7

Syrkina Collection, Moscow: fig. 5.14

Tretiakov Gallery: figs. 2.3 (color plate 2), 2.9, 2.12, 2.27,
3.18, 4.13, 5.8

Universal Studios: fig. 4.27

Warner Brothers: fig. 4.21

World Wide Photos: fig. 5.24

INDEX

Page numbers in italics refer to images.